Lecture Notes in Computer Science 10771

Commenced Publication in 1973
Founding and Former Series Editors:
Gerhard Goos, Juris Hartmanis, and Jan van Leeuwen

Editorial Board

More information about this series at http://www.springer.com/series/7411

Robert Beverly · Georgios Smaragdakis
Anja Feldmann (Eds.)

Passive and Active Measurement

19th International Conference, PAM 2018
Berlin, Germany, March 26–27, 2018
Proceedings

 Springer

Editors
Robert Beverly
Naval Postgraduate School
Monterey, CA
USA

Anja Feldmann
Max Planck Institute for Informatics
Saarbrücken
Germany

Georgios Smaragdakis
Technical University of Berlin
Berlin
Germany

ISSN 0302-9743   ISSN 1611-3349   (electronic)
Lecture Notes in Computer Science
ISBN 978-3-319-76480-1   ISBN 978-3-319-76481-8   (eBook)
https://doi.org/10.1007/978-3-319-76481-8

Library of Congress Control Number: 2018934350

LNCS Sublibrary: SL5 – Computer Communication Networks and Telecommunications

Printed on acid-free paper

This Springer imprint is published by the registered company Springer International Publishing AG
part of Springer Nature
The registered company address is: Gewerbestrasse 11, 6330 Cham, Switzerland

Preface

We are excited to present the proceedings of the 19th annual Passive and Active Measurement (PAM) conference. This year, PAM was held in Berlin, Germany, during March 26–27. After almost two decades, PAM continues to provide an important venue for emerging and early-stage research in network measurement – work that seeks to better understand complex, real-world networked systems in the wild and to provide critical empirical foundations and support to network research.

This year's proceedings demonstrate the import and extent to which measurements pervade systems – from protocols to performance to security. In total, we received 50 submissions from authors representing 62 unique institutions (17 countries), of which the Technical Program Committee (TPC) selected 20 for publication. Particular attention this year was paid to ensuring that the TPC was as broadly representative as possible, including both junior and senior researchers. We are indebted to this hard-working TPC that ensured that each paper received at least four reviews, and carried out a lively (and, in several cases spirited) on-line discussion to arrive at the final program. TPC members were asked to provide constructive feedback, bearing in mind PAM's focus and goals that recognize promising early work. As chairs, we valued interesting and ambitious submissions that generated discussion and/or dissent over submissions that received consistently mediocre reviews. To ensure the quality of the program and equanimity of the presented results, each paper was assigned a shepherd from the TPC who reviewed the paper. We are delighted with the final set of 20 papers and hope the readers find them as valuable and provocative as we do.

We would be remiss not to thank the Steering Committee for help and guidance while organizing the conference, Hamed Haddadi for publicity, Florian Streibelt for managing the review system and conference website, and Birgit Hohmeier-Toure for truly outstanding local support. Last, we thank all of the researchers who make PAM such an interesting and important conference year after year.

March 2018

Robert Beverly
Georgios Smaragdakis

Organization

General Chair

Anja Feldmann   TU Berlin, Germany

Program Co-chairs

Georgios Smaragdakis   TU Berlin and MIT, Germany/USA
Robert Beverly   Naval Postgraduate School, USA

Publicity Chair

Hamed Haddadi   Imperial College London, UK

Local Arrangements Chair

Birgit Hohmeier-Toure   TU Berlin, Germany

Steering Committee

Fabio Ricciato   University of Salento, Italy
George Riley   Georgia Institute of Technology, USA
Ian Graham   Endace, New Zealand
Neil Spring   University of Maryland, USA
Nevil Brownlee   The University of Auckland, New Zealand
Nina Taft   Google, USA
Matthew Roughan   University of Adelaide, Australia
Rocky K. C. Chang   The Hong Kong Polytechnic University, SAR China
Yong Liu   New York University, USA
Xenofontas Dimitropoulos   University of Crete, Greece
Mohamed Ali (Dali) Kaafar   Data61-CSIRO, Australia

Program Committee

Steven Bauer   MIT, USA
Fabian Bustamante   Northwestern University, USA
Matt Calder   Microsoft/USC, USA
Ignacio Castro   Queen Mary – University of London, UK
Rocky Chang   Hong Kong Polytechnic University, SAR China
kc Claffy   CAIDA/UCSD, USA
Italo Cunha   Universidade Federal de Minas Gerais, Brazil
Alberto Dainotti   CAIDA/UCSD, USA

Sponsors

Contents

DNS

Certificates

Interdomain Routing

Analyzing Protocols

Models and Inference

Detecting ICMP Rate Limiting
in the Internet

Hang Guo$^{(\boxtimes)}$ and John Heidemann$^{(\boxtimes)}$

Computer Science Department and Information Sciences Institute,
USC, Los Angeles, USA
hangguo@usc.edu, johnh@isi.edu

Abstract. ICMP active probing is the center of many network measurements. Rate limiting to ICMP traffic, if undetected, could distort measurements and create false conclusions. To settle this concern, we look systematically for ICMP rate limiting in the Internet. We create *FADER*, a new algorithm that can identify rate limiting from user-side traces with minimal new measurement traffic. We validate the accuracy of FADER with many different network configurations in testbed experiments and show that it almost always detects rate limiting. With this confidence, we apply our algorithm to a random sample of the whole Internet, showing that *rate limiting exists* but that *for slow probing rates, rate-limiting is very rare*. For our random sample of 40,493 /24 blocks (about 2% of the responsive space), we confirm 6 blocks (0.02%!) see rate limiting at 0.39 packets/s per block. We look at higher rates in public datasets and suggest that fall-off in responses as rates approach 1 packet/s per /24 block is consistent with rate limiting. We also show that even very slow probing (0.0001 packet/s) can encounter rate limiting of NACKs that are concentrated at a single router near the prober.

1 Introduction

Active probing with pings and traceroutes (both often using ICMP echo requests) are often the first tool network operators turn to assess problems and are widely used tools in network research. Studies of Internet address usage [4,10], path performance [13], outages [15,19], carrier-grade NAT deployment [18], DHCP churn [14] and topology [3,12] all depend on ICMP.

An ongoing concern about active probing is that network administrators rate limit ICMP. Administrators may do *traffic policing*, limiting inbound ICMP, and routers often *rate-limit generation of ICMP error messages* (ICMP types 3 and 11, called here ICMP NACKs). However recent work has emphasized probing as quickly as possible. For IPv4 scanning, ISI Internet Censuses (2008) send 1.5k probe/s [10], IRLscanner (2010) sends 22.1k probe/s [11], Trinocular (2013) sends 20k probes/s [15], ZMap (2013) sends 1.44M probes/s [5], or 14M probes/s in their latest revision [2], and Yarrp (2016) sends 100k probes/s or more [3]. Interest in faster probing makes rate limit detection a necessary part of measurement, since undetected rate limiting can silently distort results.

© Springer International Publishing AG, part of Springer Nature 2018
R. Beverly et al. (Eds.): PAM 2018, LNCS 10771, pp. 3–17, 2018.
https://doi.org/10.1007/978-3-319-76481-8_1

Although rate limiting is a concern to active probing, we know only two prior studies that explicitly look for rate limiting in the general Internet [6,17]. Both of their mechanisms are expensive (requiring hundreds of vantage points or server-side traffic of Google's CDN) and neither of them look at rate limiting to ICMP echo requests in forward path (Sect. 6). Unlike this prior work, we want to study forward-path ICMP rate limiting in global scale without intensive traffic probing or extensive sever-side data.

Our first contribution is to provide FADER (Frequent Alternation Availability Difference ratE limit detector), a new lightweight algorithm to detect and estimate forward-path ICMP rate limit across the Internet. Our approach works from a single vantage point, and requires two scans at different rates, detecting rate limits that take any value between those rates.

Our second contribution is to re-examine two existing public datasets for signs of ICMP rate limiting in the whole Internet. First, we use random samples of about 40k /24 blocks to show that *ICMP Rate limiting is very rare in the general Internet* for rates up to 0.39 packets/s per /24: only about 1 in 10,000 /24 blocks are rate limited. Second, we look at higher rate scans (up to 0.97 packets/s per /24) and show the response fall-off in higher rates is consistent with rate limiting from 0.28 to 0.97 packets/s per /24 in parts of the Internet.

Finally, although low-rate scans do not usually trigger rate limiting, we show that rate limiting explains results for error replies when Internet censuses cover non-routed address space.

2   Modeling Rate Limited Blocks

Our detection algorithm uses models of rate limiting in commercial routers.

2.1   Rate Limit Implementations in Commercial Routers

We examined Cisco and Juniper router manuals and two router models (Cisco ME3600-A and Cisco 7204VXR); most routers implement ICMP rate limiting with some variation on a token bucket.

With a token bucket, tokens accumulate in a "bucket" of size B tokens at a rate of L tokens/s. When a packet arrives, it consumes one token and is forwarded, or the packet is discarded if the token bucket is empty (assuming 1 token per packet). Ideally (assuming smooth traffic), for incoming traffic of P packets/s, if $P < L$, the traffic is below rate limit and will be passed without loss. When $P > L$, initially all packets will be passed as the bucket drains, then packet loss and transmission will alternate as packets and tokens arrive and are consumed. In the long run, when $P > L$, egress traffic exits at rate L packets/s.

We only model steady-state behavior of the token bucket because our active probing (Sect. 4) lasts long enough (2 weeks, 1800 iterations) to avoid disturbance from transient conditions.

2.2 Modeling Availability

We first model *availability* of a rate limited block—the fraction of IPs that respond positively to probing. We consider both the *true* availability (A), ignoring rate limiting, and also the *observed* availability ($\hat{A}$) affected by rate limiting.

Two observations help model availability. From Sect. 2.1, recall that L packet/s pass when P packet/s enter token bucket. Therefore L/P is the proportion of probes that pass. Second, if N IPs in target block are responsive, a non-rate-limited ping hits a responsive IP with probability N/n_B (n_B represent number of IP in a /24 block: 256). Combining above two observations gives us Eq. 1.

$$A = \frac{N}{n_B} \text{ and } \quad \hat{A} = \begin{cases} A(L/P), & \text{if } P > L \\ A, & \text{otherwise} \end{cases} \tag{1}$$

$$R = \frac{N}{n_B} P \quad \text{and} \quad \hat{R} = \begin{cases} R(L/P), & \text{if } P > L \\ R, & \text{otherwise} \end{cases} \tag{2}$$

2.3 Modeling Response Rate

Response rate is the positive responses we receive from target block per second. In our model (Eq. 2), we consider both the *true* value (R), ignoring rate limit, and the *observed* value ($\hat{R}$), affected by rate limit.

2.4 Modeling Alternation Count

Response Alternation is defined as the transition of an address from responsive to non-responsive or the other way around. Rate limits cause *frequent alternation* between periods of packet response and drops as the token bucket fills and drains. Frequent alternation helps distinguish rate limiting from other sources of packet loss such as networks outages (since outages are long-lived). Frequent alternation is, however, less effective in distinguishing rate limiting from transient network congestion because congestion losses are randomized and create frequent alternation. An additional round of probing ensures the detection results are robust against transient network congestion.

We model the count of observed response alternations, $\hat{C}$, both accurately and approximately. The accurate model (in our technical report [9] due to space) fits measured values precisely but are not computable because our data has $r = 1800$ iterations and the number of states scales as 2^r. The approximate model (Eq. 3) provides single expression covering all r but fits only when $P \gg L$ (so that consecutive packets from same sender are never passed by token bucket). We use it in our evaluation since it is feasible to solve when $r = 1800$.

$$\hat{C} = 2(L/P)Nr, \quad \text{when } P \gg L \tag{3}$$

$$\hat{L} = \frac{n_B \hat{A}_H P_H}{\hat{N}_L} \tag{4}$$

3 Detecting Rate Limited Blocks

The models (Sect. 2) assist our detection algorithm.

3.1 Input for Detection

Our detection algorithm requires *low-* and *high-rate* measurements as input.

Low-rate measurements must be slower than any rate limit that are detected. Fortunately the routers we study have minimal values for rates, and we believe our low-rate, at 0.0001 pings/s per block, is below that in most cases (Sect. 4.4 describes one exception). Low-rate captures the true availability (A) of target blocks.

High-rate measurements must exceed the target rate limit. It sets the upper bound for FADER's detection range. In addition, high-rate measurements must be repeated to use our alternation detection algorithm (Algorithm 3.1). Validation in Sect. 5.1 shows that 6 repetitions is sufficient but our data include 1800 repetitions.

Both low- and high-rate measurements need to last a multiple of 24 h to account for regular diurnal variations in address usage [16].

Algorithm 1. Frequent Alternation Test

Input:
  $\hat{C}$: observed response alternation count in fast scan
  r: number of probing rounds in fast scan
  $\hat{N_L}$: responsive IP count observed in slow scan
  $\hat{N_H}$: responsive IP count observed in each round of fast scan (where responsive IPs observed at ith round is $\hat{N_{H_i}}$)

Output:
  O_{fat}: results of frequent alternation test

1: **if** $\hat{C} > (2\hat{N_L}r)/T_{rej}$ **and** NotDirTmpDn($\hat{N_H}, \hat{N_L}, r$) **then**
2: | $O_{fat} \leftarrow$ Passed // has freq alternations
3: **else**
4: | $O_{fat} \leftarrow$ Failed // no freq alternations
5: **end if**

6: **function** NotDirTmpDn($\hat{N_H}, \hat{N_L}, r$)
7: | **for** $i = 1$ **to** r **do**
8: | | **if** $\hat{N_{H_i}} \geq \hat{N_L}$ **then**
9: | | | **return** $false$
10: | | **end if**
11: | **end for**
12: | **return** $true$
13: **end function**

Algorithm 2. FADER

Input:
  $\hat{A_L}/\hat{A_H}$: measured block availability in slow/fast scan
  $\hat{N_L}$: responsive IP count in slow scan
  T_{rej}: lower bound of RL-Rej phase
  O_{fat}: result of frequent alternation test

Output:
  O_{fader}: detection result of FADER

1: **if** $\hat{A_L} = 0$ **or** $\hat{A_H} = 0$ **or** $\hat{N_L} < 10$ **then**// blk down
2: | $O_{fader} \leftarrow$ Can-Not-Tell
3: **else if** $(\hat{A_L} - \hat{A_H})/\hat{A_L} > 0.1$ **then**// significant $\hat{A}$ drop in faster probing
4: | **if** $\hat{A_H}/\hat{A_L} < 1/T_{rej}$ **then** // in RL-Rej
5: | | $O_{fader} \leftarrow$ Can-Not-Tell
6: | **else**
7: | | **if** $O_{fat} =$ Passed **then**
8: | | | $O_{fader} \leftarrow$ Rate-Limited
9: | | **else** // no freq alternations
10: | | | $O_{fader} \leftarrow$ Can-Not-Tell
11: | | **end if**
12: | **end if**
13: **else**// no significant $\hat{A}$ drop in faster probing
14: | $O_{fader} \leftarrow$ Not-Rate-Limited
15: **end if**

3.2 Four Phases of ICMP Rate Limiting

The models from Sect. 2 allow us to classify the effects of ICMP rate limiting into four phases (Fig. 1). These phases guide our detection algorithm:

1. Non-RL ($P < L$): before rate limiting takes effect,
2. RL-Tran ($L < P < 1.1L$): rate limiting begins to reduce $\hat{A}$ with alternating responses.

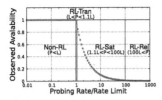
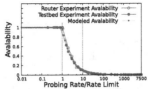
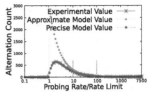

Fig. 1. Four phases of ICMP rate limiting

Fig. 2. Availability model validation results (Color figure online)

Fig. 3. Alternation count model validation results

3. RL-Sat ($1.1L < P < 100L$): significant $\hat{A}$ drop and frequent alternation.
4. RL-Rej ($P > T_{rej}L$, $T_{rej} = 100$): most packets are dropped ($\hat{A} < 0.01N/n_B$) and response alternations are rare.

These phases also identify regions where no algorithm can work: rate limits right at the probing rate (RL-Tran phase, due to not enough change in response), or far above it (RL-Rej phase, because the block appears completely non-responsive, giving little information). We use empirical thresholds $1.1L$ and $100L$ to define these two cases.

In Sect. 5.2 we show that our algorithm is correct in the remaining large regions (Non-RL and RL-Sat), provided $P < 60L$.

3.3 Detecting Rate Limited Blocks

FADER is inspired by observations that the RL-Tran phase is narrow, but we can can easily tell the difference between the Non-RL and RL-Sat phases. Instead of trying to probe at many rates, we probe at a slow and fast rate, with the hope that the slow probes observe the Non-RL phase and the high-rate brackets the RL-Tran phase. If the target block shows much higher availability in slow probing, we consider the block a rate limit *candidate* and check its traffic pattern for signs of rate limiting: consistent and randomized packet dropping and passing.

We first introduce *Frequent Alternation Test* (Algorithm 3.1). This subroutine identifies the consistent and randomized packet dropping caused by rate limiting (by looking for large number of responses alternations).

Threshold $(2\hat{N}_L r)/T_{rej}$ is derived from our approximate alternation count model (Eq. 3). As low-rate measurement is assumed non-rate-limited, we have $\hat{N}_L$ (responsive IPs count in low-rate measurement) $= N$ (responsive IP count when non-rate-limited). Recall we give up detection in RL-Rej phase (Sect. 3.2), we have $P < T_{rej}L$. Substituting both into alternation count model, for a rate limited block, there must be at least $(2\hat{N}_L r)/T_{rej}$ response alternations.

Function NotDirTmpDn filters out diurnal and temporarily down blocks, which otherwise may become false positives because their addresses also alternate between responsive and non-responsive. NotDirTmpDn checks if any round of the high-rate measurement looks like the daytime (active period) of diurnal block or the up-time of temporarily down blocks, satisfying $\hat{N}_{H_i} \geq \hat{N}_L$.

Next, we describe our detection algorithm FADER (Algorithm 3.1). FADER detects if target block is rate-limited, producing "cannot tell" for blocks that are non-responsive or respond too little. No active measurement system can judge the status of non-responsive blocks; mark such block as cannot-tell rather than misclassifying them as rate limited or not.

In our experiments we see cannot-tell rates of 65% when $P = 100L$ and in average only 2.56 IPs respond in each target block (Sect. 5.2); these rates reflect the fundamental limit of any active probing algorithm rather than a limit specific to our algorithm.

Threshold $\hat{N}_L < 10$ used in line 1 is empirical, but chosen because very sparse blocks provide too little information. Test $(\hat{A}_L - \hat{A}_H)/\hat{A}_L > 0.1$ (line 3) is derived by substituting $P > 1.1L$, the lower bound of RL-Sat phase (where we start to detect rate limit), into availability model (Eq. 1). Test $\hat{A}_H/\hat{A}_L < 1/T_{rej}$ (line 4) is derived by substituting $P > T_{rej}L$ (RL-Rej phase, where we give up detection), into availability model (Eq. 1).

Once a target block is detected as rate limited, we estimate its rate limit ($\hat{L}$) by Eq. 4 which is derived by inverting our availability model (Sect. 2.2). (We estimates the effective rate limit at each target/24 block, or the aggregate rate limit of intermediate routers across their covered space. We do not try to differentiate between individual hosts in a /24 block because two scans provide too few information about host).

4   Results: Rate Limiting in the Wild

We next apply FADER to existing public Internet scan datasets to learn about ICMP rate limiting in the Internet. (We validate the algorithm later in Sect. 5.)

4.1   How Many Blocks Are Rate Limited in the Internet?

We first apply FADER to find rate limited blocks in the Internet, confirming what we find with additional probing.

Input data: We use existing Internet censuses and surveys as test data [10]. Reusing existing data places less stress on other networks and allows us to confirm our results at different times (Sect. 4.2). Table 1 lists the public datasets we use [8].

Table 1. Datasets used in this paper

Start date (duration)	Size (/24 blocks)	Alias	Full name
2016-08-03 (32 days)	14,460,160	it71w census	internet_address_census_it71w-20160803
2016-08-03 (14 days)	40,493	it71w survey	internet_address_survey_reprobing_it71w-20160803
2016-06-02 (32 days)	14,476,544	it70w census	internet_address_census_it70w-20160602
2016-06-02 (14 days)	40,493	it70w survey	internet_address_survey_reprobing_it70w-20160602

Table 2. it71w detection results

Blocks studied	40,493	(100%)	
Not-rate limited	24,414	(60%)	
Cannot tell	15,941	(39%)	
Rate limited	111	(0.27%)	*(100%)*
False positives	105	(0.25%)	*(95%)*
True positives	6	(0.015%)	*(5%)*

Table 3. Effects of each FADER step

Test name	Number of blocks (ratio)		
	Input	Passed	Filtered
Availability diff	40,403	2,088 (5.2%)	38,315 (94.8%)
Freq alternation	2,088	111 (5.3%)	1,977 (94.7%)
Re-probing	111	5 (4.5%)	106 (95.5%)

Censuses (0.0001 pings/s per block) and surveys (0.39 pings/s per block) define the low- and high-rates that bound rate limits detected by our algorithm. We could re-run FADER with higher rates to test other upper bounds; we report on existing higher rate scans in Sect. 4.3.

Surveys probe about 40k blocks about 1800 times over two weeks, supporting frequent alternation detection. Censuses cover almost the entire unicast IPv4 Internet, but we use only the part that overlaps the survey. With a 2% of the responsive IPv4 address space, randomly chosen, our data provides a representative of the Internet.

Initial Results: Here we apply FADER to it71w, the latest census and survey datasets, in Table 2. We find that *most blocks are not rate limited* (60%), while a good number (39%) are "cannot tell", usually because they are barely responsive and provide little information for detection (without additional information, no one could tell if these blocks are rate limited or not). However, *our algorithm classifies a few blocks* (111 blocks, 0.27%) as apparently rate limited.

Validation with additional probing: To confirm our results, we next re-examine these likely rate-limited blocks, We re-probe each block, varying probing rates from 0.01 to 20 ping/s per block to confirm the actual rate limiting. Our additional probing is relatively soon (one month) after our overall scan.

Figure 4 shows this confirmation process for one example block. Others are similar. In this graph, red squares show modeled availability assuming the block is rate limited (given the rate limit estimation from FADER in Table 4). The green line with diamonds shows the availability if the block is not rate limited. As Fig. 4 shows, this block's measured availability (blue dots) tightly matches the modeled value with rate limiting while diverging from values without rate limiting. We also apply similar confirmation process to this block's measured response rate (omitted, but details in our technical report [9]). These data show that this block, 182.237.200.0/24, is rate limited.

Although this example shows a positive confirmation, we find that most of the 111 blocks are false positives (their availabilities and response rates in re-probing do not match rate limit models). Only the 6 blocks listed in Table 4 are indeed rate limited. We design our algorithm to favor false positives for two reasons. First, favoring false positives (by using necessary conditions as detection signals) avoids missing rate-limited blocks (false negatives). Second, this trade-off (favoring false positives over false negatives) is required to confirm the near-absence of rate limiting we observe. We rule out the possibility that

Table 4. True rate limited blocks in it71w census and survey.

/24 Block	Response rate (measured, pkts/s)	Availability rate limit (ping/s per blk)		
		($\hat{A}_L$, %)	(measured)	(estimated)
124.46.219.0	0.009	9.77	0.09	0.09
124.46.239.0	0.08	53.13	0.15	0.12
182.237.200.0	0.06	58.98	0.10	0.12
182.237.212.0	0.04	27.34	0.15	0.10
182.237.217.0	0.06	49.61	0.12	0.13
202.120.61.0	0.35	17.58	1.99	0.32

these false positives are caused by concurrent high-rate ICMP activities at our target blocks by observing over long duration and at different times (Sect. 4.2).

We use additional verification to confirm true positives. Among the 6 rate limited blocks, 5 belong to the same ISP: Keumgang Cable Network in South Korea, while the last block is from Shanghai Jiaotong University in China. We have contacted both ISPs to confirm our findings, but they did not reply.

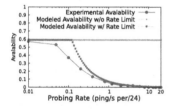

Fig. 4. Confirming block 182.237.200/24 is rate limited with additional probing. (Color figure online)

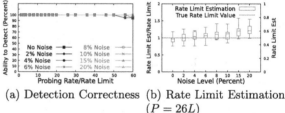

(a) Detection Correctness (b) Rate Limit Estimation ($P = 26L$)

Fig. 5. FADER validation: with packet loss

Our first conclusion from this result is *there are ICMP rate-limited blocks, but they are very rare*. We find only 6 blocks in 40k, less than 0.02%. Thus it is almost always safe to probe in this range (up to 0.39 packets/s per block).

Second, we see that each of FADER's steps rule out about 95% of all the blocks entering that rule (as in Table 3). However, even after two phases of filtering, there is still a fairly high false positive rate in the remaining blocks, since only 6 of 111 (5.4%) are finally confirmed as rate limited.

Finally, we show that *when* we detect rate limiting, our *estimate of the rate limit* are correct in general. Table 4 shows this accuracy: five out of six rate limits observed in re-probing (which is estimated by measuring $\hat{R}$, $\hat{A}_L$ and inverting our response-rate model Eq. 2) closely match FADER's estimates.

However our rate limit estimation (0.32 ping/s per block) for block 202.120.61/24 is 5 times smaller than the rate limit (1.99 pings/s per block) observed in re-probing. When we review the raw data, we believe the rate limit for this block *changed* between our measurements.

4.2 Verifying Results Hold over Time

To verify our approach works on other datasets, we also apply FADER to it70w census and survey data. This data is taken two months before it71w and sharing 76% of the same target blocks. Detection results of it70w data agrees with our previous conclusion, resulting in about the same number of blocks identified as rate limited (0.3%, 138 of 40,493), and the same fraction as actually limited (0.012%, 5). Of blocks that we confirm as rate limited after re-probing, four also are detected and confirmed in it71w. The fifth, 213.103.246.0/24, is from ISP Swipnet of Republic of Lithuania and is not probed in it71w.

We observe inconsistencies between it70w and it71w for two blocks: 124.46.219.0/24 and 202.120.61.0/24 (detected as rate-limited in it71w, but as Can-Not-Tell and Not-Rate-Limited respectively in it70w) We believe the former block is hard to measure: with only 25 (9.8%) responsive addresses, and the latter actually changed its use between the measurements (supporting details in our technical report [9]).

4.3 Is Faster Probing Rate Limited?

Having shown that rate-limited blocks are very rare up to 0.39 packets/s, we next evaluate if *faster* probing shows signs of rate limiting, as advocated by ZMap [2] and Yarrp [3].

We study Zippier ZMap's 50-s TCP-SYN probing datasets (private dataset obtained from the authors [1], the public ZMap datasets are lower rates), from 0.1M to 14M packet/s, which we estimate as 0.007 to 0.97 packets/s per /24 block. We show rate limiting could explain the response drop-off at higher rates. Although both our models and FADER are originally designed for ICMP rate limiting, they also detect TCP-SYN rate limiting because they detect the actions of the underlying token bucket.

ZMap performs a series of 50-s experiments from 0.1M to 14M packets/s [2]. Each experiment targets a different random sample of a 3.7 billion IP pool. Their results show overall availability (the fraction of positive responses of all hosts that are probed) is roughly stable up to 4M packets/s. However, when probing rates exceed 4M packets/s, the availability starts to decline linearly (the blue dots in Fig. 6, from their paper [2]). They state that they do not know the exact reason for this decline.

We believe rate limiting explains this drop—once rate limits are exceeded, as the packet rate increases, availability drops. We also believe that there are roughly the same amount of rate limiting at each packet rate between 4M and 14M packets/s in the Internet, causing the overall availability drop to be linear.

We would like to apply FADER directly to Zippier ZMap's 50-s probing results. Unfortunately we cannot because the target IPs are not known for each run (they do not preserve the seed, so we do not know addresses that do not respond), and they do not repeat addresses, so we cannot test response alternation. (We chose not to collect new, high-rate ZMap data to avoid stressing target networks.) However, we can statistically estimate how many addresses do no not respond, allowing us to evaluate rate-limiting for high-rate scans (up to 14M packets/s).

We create a model of their measurement process and show rate limiting can explain their drops in response rate. Full details of this model are in our technical report [9]. We show availability of many ZMap target blocks matches our expectation of rate limiting by statistically estimating the number of IPs probed in each target block.

Potential Limiting at High Probe Rates: Figure 6 compares our model of ZMap measurement process (the red squares) against reported Zippier ZMap experiments (blue circles). Observing that rate limits are consistent with the drops in response of ZMap at high speeds, we next apply FADER (without the frequent alternation test) to ZMap data, looking for blocks that appear to be rate limited.

We statistically estimate the number of IPs probed in each block. Recall each 50-s scan send pseudo-random probes into the same 3.7 billion IPv4 pool, assuming uniform sampling, about same number of IP will be sampled from each /16 block in the pool. (Here we look at /16 blocks instead of /24 blocks because larger blocks decrease the statistical variance.) As a consequence, for a 50-s ZMap scan of P packets/s, approximately $50P/(3.7 \times 10^9) \times 2^{16}$ IPs are probed in each /16 block, given $50P/(3.7 \times 10^9)$ as the fraction of addresses probed in 50s, against a target 2^{16} addresses in size. We then estimate availability of each /16 block as the fraction of target IPs that respond positively to probes.

We next apply FADER to detect rate limiting (assuming all blocks pass Frequent Alternation Tests). For each ZMap target block, we use slowest 50-s scan (0.1M packets/s) as the low-rate measurement and test each of the other 15 faster scans as high-rate measurement. This gives us 15 test results (each at a different high rate), for each target block. We consider a block as potentially rate limited if it is detected as rate limited in at least one test. We do not consider the other blocks (cannot tell or not-rate limited) further.

Table 6 shows detection results. Most ZMap target blocks (53,149 blocks, 93.99%) are cannot tell in all 15 FADER tests (43,067 of them due to target block went dark during low-rate measurement and provide no information for detection). A good number of them (3,090 blocks, 5.46%) are classified as rate-limited in at least one FADER test and are considered potentially rate-limited. It is worth noting that most (69.68%) of these potentially rate-limited blocks are consistently classified as rate-limited in most FADER tests (at least 13 out of 16 tests), supporting our claim that those blocks are potentially rate-limited.

Since we omit Frequent Alternation Tests and our algorithm is optimized to avoid false negatives, we know many of these potential rate limited blocks

Table 5. 2 ZMap blocks showing multiple rate limits

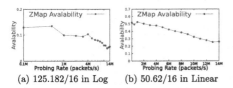

(a) 125.182/16 in Log   (b) 50.62/16 in Linear

Table 6. Applying 15 FADER tests to ZMap /16 blocks

blocks studied	56,550	(100%)	
0 rate limited	53,460	(94.54%)	
≥ 1 rate limited	3,090	(5.46%)	*(100%)*
≥ 13 rate limited	2,153	(3.81%)	*(69.68%)*
< 13 rate limited	937	(1.66%)	*(30.32%)*

may be false positives. To further filter out false detection, we manually check a 565 (1%) random sample of 56,500 ZMap target blocks. Of these sample blocks, 31 are detected as rate-limited in at least one FADER test and are considered potentially rate-limited.

We find the other 534 blocks (cannot tell or not-rate limited) to be true negative. They either have almost zero $\hat{A}_L$ or $\hat{A}_H$ (providing no information for detection) or become more available at higher probing rate (opposing our expectation of reduced availability at faster scan)

All 31 potential rate-limited blocks show reduced availability at higher probing rates (regardless of jitters caused by probing noises and distortions introduced by our statistical estimation), matching our expectation of rate limited blocks. We also find 7 of them appear to have more than one rate limits. For example, block 125.182/16 in Table 5a looks like a superposition of $\hat{A}$ curves of two rate limits: one at 0.5M packets/s, the other at 4M packets/s (recall the ideal $\hat{A}$ curve of rate limited block in Fig. 1). Block 50.62/16 in Table 5b, on the other hand, show nearly linear drops in availability as probing rates get higher, suggesting it consists of multiple rate limits (reasons are similar as in our modeling of ZMap experiments). We manually check each /24 blocks in those two /16 blocks, and it appears that those /24 blocks indeed have multiple rate limits. This observation supports our claim that different parts of the /16 have different rate limits.

4.4   Rate Limiting of Response Errors at Nearby Routers

Having shown that probing rates up to 0.39 pings/s trigger rate limits on almost no *target* blocks, we also observe a case where even slow probing (0.0001 ping/s per block) can trigger rate limits in reverse path because *traffic to many targets is aggregated at a nearby router*. Our technical report gives details of this case [9].

5   Validation

We validate our model against real-world routers and our testbed, and our algorithm with testbed experiments. (We also tried to contact two ISPs about ground truth, but we got no response Sect. 4.1)

5.1 Does the Model Match Real-World Implementations?

We next validate our models for availability, response alternation, and response rate of rate-limited blocks. We show they match the ICMP rate limiting implementations in two carrier-grade, commercial routers and our testbed.

Our experiments use two commercial routers (Cisco ME3600-A and Cisco 7204VXR) and one Linux box loaded with Linux filter iptables as rate limiters. Our measurement target is a fully responsive /16 block, simulated by one Linux box loaded with our customized Linux kernel [7]. In each experiment, we run a 6-round active ICMP probing, with the rate changing from below the limit to at most 7500× the rate limit (while fixing rate limit).

We begin with validating our *availability model* from Eq. 1. Figure 2 shows model predicted availability (red line with squares) closely matches router experiments (blue line with circles) and testbed experiments (blue line with dots) from below to above the rate limit.

We validate our *response rate model* from Eq. 2. We omit this data due to space limitations, but our response rate model is accurate from a response rate of 0.01 to 90× the rate limit.

We next validate our models of alternation counts (Eq. 3) with testbed experiments. Figure 3 shows our precise model (red square) fits perfectly from below the rate limit up to 7500× the rate limit while our approximate model (green diamond) fits when $P \gg L$ (in our case when $P > 10L$).

We are unable to validate alternation count model with commercial routers; the routers are only available for a limited time. But we believe testbed validations shows the correctness of our alternation counts models since we have already shown rate limiting in testbed matches that of two commercial routers.

5.2 Correctness in Noise-Free Testbed

We next test the correctness of FADER in a testbed without noise (supporting graphs in our technical reports [9]). For noise-free experiment, we run high-rate probing from $1.6L$ to $240L$ stressing FADER beyond its designed detecting range $P < 60L$. FADER detection is perfect for $P < 60L$. However, as we exceed FADER's design limit ($60L$), it starts marking blocks as can-not-tell. The fraction of can-not-tell rises as P grows from $60L$ to $144L$ (when $P = 100L$, 65% blocks are marked as can-not-tell). Fortunately, even when the design limit is exceeded, FADER is *never incorrect* (it never gives a false positive or false negative), it just refuses to answer (returning can-not-tell).

In addition to detecting rate limiting, FADER gives an estimate of what that rate limit is. Varying P from L to $144L$, FADER's rate limit estimate is within 7% (from -4.2% to $+6.9\%$) when $P < 60L$, and it drops gradually as the design limit is exceed.

5.3 Correctness in the Face of Packet Loss

We next consider FADER with packet loss which could be confused with loss due to rate limiting. We vary the amount of random packet loss from 0 to 60%.

Figure 5a shows FADER's detection as packet loss increases. There is almost no misdetection until probe rates become very high. At the design limit of $P = 60L$, we see only about 4% of trials are reported as cannot tell.

While ability to detect is insensitive to noise, our estimate of the rate limit is somewhat less robust. Figure 5b shows that packet loss affects our estimate of the value of the rate limit (here we fix $P = 26L$, but we see similar results for other probe rates). Error in our rate limit is about equal to the dropping rate (at 20% loss rates, the median estimate of rate limit is 20.72% high).

5.4   Correctness with Partially Responsive Blocks

We next consider what happens when blocks are only partially responsive. Partially responsive blocks are more difficult for FADER because probes sent to non-responsive addresses are dropped, reducing the signal induced by rate limiting. Here we vary probe rate for different density blocks. (We hold other parameters fixed and so do not add packet loss.)

In Fig. 7a we vary the relative probing rate and plot separate lines for each level of block responsiveness. In general, the number of can-not-tell increase as block responsiveness falls, but only when the probe rate is also much greater than the rate limit. In the worst case, with only 10% of IPs responding at a probe rate 60× the rate limit, 35% of tries report can-not-tell and no wrong answer is given.

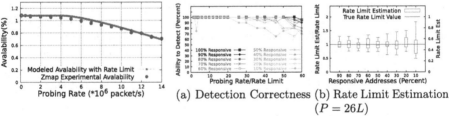

(a) Detection Correctness (b) Rate Limit Estimation $(P = 26L)$

Fig. 6. Modeled availability (Red) matches ZMap probing results (Blue) (Color figure online)

Fig. 7. FADER validation: with partially responsive target blocks

Figure 7b shows the rate limit output by FADER as the block density changes. We show median and quartiles with box plots, and minimum and maximum with whiskers. The median stays at the true value, but the variance increases, as shown by generally wider boxes and whiskers. Here $P = 26L$; we see similar results at other probing rates.

6   Related Work

Two other groups have studied detecting rate limits in the Internet.

Work from Universite Nice Sophia Antipolis studies rate limiting for tracer-outes [17]. Specifically, they study ICMP, Type 11, Time exceeded replies on reverse paths. They detect rate limits by sending TTL-limited ICMP echo requests from 180 vantage points, varying the probing rate from 1 to 4000 ping/s and looking for constant response rates as a sign of rate limits. They studied 850 routers and found 60% to do rate limiting. Our work has several important differences. The overall result is quite different: they find 60% of reverse paths are rate limited in 850 routers, measured up to 4000 ping/s, while we find only 0.02% of forward paths are rate limited in 40k /24 blocks, measured up to 0.39 pings/s per /24.

We believe that both their results and ours are correct. Many routers have reverse-path rate limiting on by default, consistent with their results. Our app-roach provides much broader coverage and generates less additional traffic by reusing existing data. Our work uses different signals (availability difference and frequent alternation) for detection. Finally, we focus on forward path, so our results apply to address allocation information, while they focus on reverse path, with results that apply to fast traceroutes.

Google recently examined traffic policing, particularly in video traffic [6]. Their analysis uses sampled measurement from hundreds of Google CDNs to millions of users of YouTube. They provide a thorough analysis on the prevalence of policing and the interaction between policing and TCP. They also provide suggestions to both ISP and content providers on how to mitigate negative effect of traffic policing on user experience. Their focus on TCP differs from ours on ICMP rate-limiting. Their coverage is far greater than ours, although that coverage is only possible because Google is a major content provider. They find fairly widespread rate limiting of TCP traffic, but their subject (TCP video) is much faster than ours (ICMP) that such differences in results are not surprising.

7   Conclusion

Undetected rate limiting can silently distort network measurement and bias research results. We have developed FADER, a new, light-weight method to detect ICMP rate limiting. We validated FADER against commercial routers and through sensitivity experiments in a testbed, showing it is very accurate at detecting rate limits when probe traffic is between 1 and 60× the rate limit.

We applied FADER to a large sample of the Internet (40k blocks) on two separate dates. We find that only a tiny fraction (0.02%) of Internet blocks are ICMP rate limited up to 0.39 pings/s per /24. We also examined public high-rate datasets (up to 1 ping/s per /24) and showed their probing results are consistent with rate limitings. We only see significant rate limiting on reverse path when routers near the prober see a large amount of traffic. We conclude that low-rate ICMP measurement (up to 0.39 ping/s per block) are unlikely to be distorted while high-rate measurement (up to 1 ping/s per block) risks being rate limited.

References

1. Adrian, D., Durumeric, Z., Singh, G., Halderman, J.A.: 50-second scans dataset in paper "Zippier ZMap: Internet-Wide Scanning at 10 Gbps", obtained from David Adrian by request (2014)
2. Adrian, D., Durumeric, Z., Singh, G., Halderman, J.A.: Zippier ZMap: internet-wide scanning at 10 Gbps. In: USENIX Workshop on Offensive Technologies (2014)
3. Beverly, R.: Yarrp'ing the internet: randomized high-speed active topology discovery. In: ACM Internet Measurement Conference. ACM, November 2016
4. Dainotti, A., Benson, K., King, A., Claffy, K.C., Kallitsis, M., Glatz, E.: Estimating internet address space usage through passive measurements. ACM Computer Communication Review (2014)
5. Durumeric, Z., Wustrow, E., Halderman, J.A.: ZMap: fast internet-wide scanning and its security applications. In: USENIX Security Symposium (2013)
6. Flach, T., Papageorge, P., Terzis, A., Pedrosa, L., Cheng, Y., Karim, T., Katz-Bassett, E., Govindan, R.: An internet-wide analysis of traffic policing. In: ACM SIGCOMM (2016)
7. Guo, H.: rejwreply: a Linux kernel patch that adds echo-reply to feedback type of iptable REJECT rule. https://ant.isi.edu/software/rejwreply/index.html
8. Guo, H., Heidemann, J.: Datasets in this Paper. https://ant.isi.edu/datasets/icmp/
9. Guo, H., Heidemann, J.: Detecting ICMP rate limiting in the Internet. Technical report ISI-TR-717, USC/Information Sciences Institute, May 2017
10. Heidemann, J., Pradkin, Y., Govindan, R., Papadopoulos, C., Bartlett, G., Bannister, J.: Census and survey of the visible internet. In: ACM Internet Measurement Conference (2008)
11. Leonard, D., Loguinov, D.: Demystifying service discovery: implementing an internet-wide scanner. In: ACM Internet Measurement Conference, November 2010
12. Luckie, M., Dhamdhere, A., Huffaker, B., Clark, D., Claffy, K.: bdrmap: inference of borders between IP networks. In: ACM Internet Measurement Conference (2016)
13. Madhyastha, H.V., Isdal, T., Piatek, M., Dixon, C., Anderson, T., Krishnamurthy, A., Venkataramani, A.: iPlane: an information plane for distributed services. In: 7th USENIX Symposium on Operating Systems Design and Implementation (2006)
14. Moura, G.C.M., Gañán, C., Lone, Q., Poursaied, P., Asghari, H.: How dynamic is the ISPs address space? Towards Internet-wide DHCP churn estimation. In: IFIP Networking Conference (2015)
15. Quan, L., Heidemann, J., Pradkin, Y.: Trinocular: understanding internet reliability through adaptive probing. In: ACM SIGCOMM (2013)
16. Quan, L., Heidemann, J., Pradkin, Y.: When the internet sleeps: correlating diurnal networks with external factors. In: ACM Internet Measurement Conference (2014)
17. Ravaioli, R., Urvoy-Keller, G., Barakat, C.: Characterizing ICMP rate limitation on routers. In: IEEE International Conference on Communications (2015)
18. Richter, P., Wohlfart, F., Vallina-Rodriguez, N., Allman, M., Bush, R., Feldmann, A., Kreibich, C., Weaver, N., Paxson, V.: A multi-perspective analysis of carrier-grade NAT deployment. In: ACM Internet Measurement Conference (2016)
19. Schulman, A., Spring, N.: Pingin' in the rain. In: ACM Internet Measurement Conference (2011)

On the Characteristics of Language Tags
on the Web

Joel Sommers[(✉)]

Colgate University, Hamilton, NY, USA
jsommers@colgate.edu

Abstract. The Internet is a global phenomenon. To support broad use
of Internet applications such as the World Wide Web, character encodings have been developed for many scripts of the world's languages and
there are standard mechanisms for indicating that content is in a particular language and/or tailored to a particular region. In this paper
we study the empirical characteristics of *language tags* used in HTTP
transactions and in web pages to indicate the language of the content
and possibly the script, region, and other information. To support our
analysis, we develop a new algorithm to infer the value of a missing language tag for elements used to link to alternative language content. We
analyze the top-level page for websites in the Alexa Top 1 Million, from
six geographic perspectives. We find that one third of all pages do not
include any language tags, that half of the remaining sites are tagged
with English (en), and that about 10 K sites have malformed tags. We
observe that 80 K sites are multilingual, and that there are hundreds
of sites that offer content in the tens of languages. Besides malformed
tags, we find numerous instances of correctly formed but likely erroneous
language tags by using a Naïve Bayes-based language detection library
and comparing its output with a given page's language tag(s). Lastly,
we comment on differences in language tags observed for the same site
but from different geographic vantage points or by using different client
language preferences via the HTTP `Accept-Language` header.

1 Introduction

The Internet and World-Wide Web were originally designed by a relatively homogeneous, English-speaking group of engineers and scientists with no explicit technical concern for supporting languages other than English [3]. Although early
web designs used ASCII character encoding and lacked any provision for indicating the language of the text within an HTML page, both HTTP and HTML
have evolved to support character encodings for many scripts of the world's languages, and to support multiple ways for indicating the language of a page or
elements within a page [2,4]. The culmination of these capabilities is that today,
web browsers routinely inform web servers about a user's language preferences
through the HTTP `Accept-Language` header [4], servers can use the expressed
preferences to deliver desired content, if it is available, and browsers can display
text in the native script of a user's preferred language.

© Springer International Publishing AG, part of Springer Nature 2018
R. Beverly et al. (Eds.): PAM 2018, LNCS 10771, pp. 18–30, 2018.
https://doi.org/10.1007/978-3-319-76481-8_2

Language tags are used to indicate the language(s) preferred by a client, or the language of text or elements within content delivered by a server[1]. Language tags provide important context for web content and there are a number of reasons why it is critical that they be constructed correctly and used in ways to enhance the semantics of web pages and elements within pages. First, browsers may use language tags for rendering content, *e.g.*, right-to-left rendering for some languages, or highlighting/translating content in a user's preferred language. Second, appropriate language tags on internationalized and localized pages can help search engines respond to queries with appropriate content and thus increase site traffic and ad revenue[2]. Third, screen readers for the visually impaired may use language tags for determining whether to read content within a page or whether to ignore content. Fourth, language tag attributes on hyperlinks (*e.g.*, `hreflang` tag within `<a> elements`) can be used to indicate the availability of alternative language content; browsers may use such attributes to help users find preferred content. Lastly, including appropriate language tags can help speakers of underserved (so-called "minority") languages to find and better utilize content. Understanding the nature of how language tags are used across the web may provide a useful perspective on how to improve access to desired content and to bridge the global digital divide.

In this paper we analyze the empirical characteristics of language tags found in HTTP response headers and within HTML pages. We gather data from the Alexa Top 1 Million sites from six geographic vantage points by using a commercial VPN service. We focus on the top-level document (URI path /) for each site, recognizing that this may not give a comprehensive view of a site's language offerings. We perform two types of requests: one in which the `Accept-Language` (A-L) header is set to * to accept *any* language and one in which the `Accept-Language` header is set to a list of (*de jure* or *de facto*) official languages or commonly-used languages within the same region from which we launch our requests. We refer to the data collected using `Accept-Language: *` as our *default* language data and to the data collected using a region-specific A-L header as *langpref* data. We collect both HTTP response headers and the content of the top-level document; we do not access any linked resources (*e.g.*, JavaScript, iframes, images, etc.) nor do we execute any JavaScript code. In total, we performed 12 million web requests (not including retries due to transient errors), collecting a total of about 500 GB of compressed HTTP headers and content for analysis.

For each A-L variant (default and langpref) and for each VPN location, we extract language tags that indicate the *primary* language of content on the page, and we also extract language tags from every element within the page in order to gain a perspective on the breadth of languages in which content is offered for a given site. Specifically for hyperlink elements, we describe an algorithm for inferring the value of a missing language tag for links that are used to lead

---

[1] The structure and valid values of language tags are specified in IETF BCP 47 [9] and the IANA language subtag registry [1], respectively, as discussed below.

[2] https://searchenginewatch.com/sew/howto/238631/localization-for-international-search-engine-optimization.

to alternative language content on the same site. We find that, overall, one third of all pages do not include any language tags, and that another third of pages are tagged with English as the primary language. We find that our inference algorithm contributes to 1–3% of language tags found, which varies depending on VPN vantage point and the default and langpref A-L header. We observe that 80 K sites out of the Alexa Top 1 Million are multilingual, and that about 30 K of those sites offer content in two languages with some of the remaining sites offering many tens of languages. We find that nearly 1% (about 10 K sites) of all language tags are malformed, and we find additional instances of correctly formed but likely erroneous language tags by using an off-the-shelf Naïve Bayes-based language detection library and comparing its output with a page's primary language tag. Lastly, we comment on region, script, and private-use subtags observed within language tags, and differences observed across VPN vantage points. We note that the code used to perform our study is publicly available[3] and our data will be made publicly available.

2   Background and Related Work

The structure and content of language tags used by Internet protocols and applications is described in IETF BCP 47 [9]. Language tags are formed from one or more *subtags*, which may refer to a language, script, region, or some other identifying category. The simplest language tag can include just a language subtag (*e.g.*, en (English), de (German), cy (Welsh)), but BCP 47 permits script subtags (*e.g.*, Cyrl (Cyrillic)), region subtags (*e.g.*, AR (Argentina)), and private-use subtags, among other features [7]. In practice, it is common for language tags to include between one and three subtags, *e.g.*, es (Spanish, not specific to any region), pt-BR (Brazilian Portuguese), zh-Hant-CN (Chinese, Traditional script, in China). Valid subtags within the categories defined in BCP 47 are detailed in the IANA language subtag registry [1], which serves as a kind of meta-registry of tags defined by other standards organizations.

The choice of a language tag to use in relation to web content may not be simple, and the W3C offers guidance on forming a language tag (keep it as short as possible) and how to correctly use tags in HTML documents [7,10]. The latest guidance regarding HTML is that the language tag for a page should be specified in the lang attribute of the top-level <html> element. If any divisions within a page are targeted at speakers of different languages, each of those divisions should similarly include an appropriate lang attribute. For links on a page that lead to alternative language content, the hreflang attribute can include an appropriate language tag [8], or <link rel=alternate> tags can include a URI to an alternative representation (*e.g.*, different language content)[4].

Unfortunately, previous versions of HTML and XHTML have used different mechanisms for indicating the language of a page and of elements within a

---

[3] https://github.com/jsommers/weblingo.
[4] https://searchenginewatch.com/sew/how-to/2232347/a-simple-guide-to-using-rel-alternate-hreflang-x.

page. For example, XHTML defines an attribute `xml:lang` which plays a similar role as the `lang` attribute in HTML5 [8]. Moreover, the HTTP response header `Content-language` has also been defined to indicate the intended language audience of a response, and particular `<meta http-equiv=content-language>` tags have been used to convey the same information. When multiple language indications are present on a page, the guidance provided by W3C from a *browser* perspective to determine the primary language of a server response is to first prefer the `lang` or `xml:lang` attributes if they are present, followed by the `<meta>` header if present, followed by the HTTP `Content-Language` header if present.

Web browsers may also inform servers of a user's language preferences through the HTTP `Accept-Language` header [4,5]. The value supplied in this header can be one or more language tags, with optional *quality* values indicating an order of preference. Quality values range from 1 (most preferred) to 0 (not wanted). For example, `cy;q=0.9`, `en;q=0.5`, `*;q=0.3` indicates that Welsh (`cy`) is most preferred, following by English, followed by anything else. The process of a server matching content preferences indicated by HTTP `Accept`-headers and available resources is known as *content negotiation* [5]. Although it can be unclear from a client's perspective how a server has decided to return a specific version of a resource, HTTP servers *should* include a `Vary` header indicating the parts of a request that influenced a server's decision.

There has been little prior work on studying language tags within HTML pages and in HTTP transactions. One recent work is [11], in which the authors report on the top 10 most common language tags found in `A-L` headers from clients that were making a request for a JavaScript instrumentation library. Besides that paper, the most closely related efforts are works that have sought to survey the number of documents available in various languages on the web. In [6] and references therein, the authors state that as of 1997, English was the language of 82.3% of pages, "followed by German (4.0%), Japanese (3.1%), French (1.8%) and Spanish (1.1%)". The dominance of English was also observed in [12] in 2002 (68% of pages), with increases in Japanese and Chinese content. We are not aware of studies that have focused specifically on evaluating language tags available in HTML pages and in HTTP transactions.

3   Methodology

To drive our empirical analysis of language tags we developed a web crawler in Python, leveraging the widely-used `requests` module, along with the `certifi` module to enable better TLS certificate verification[5]. We set the `User-Agent` string to a value equivalent to a recent version of the Google Chrome browser, and configured `requests` to allow up to 30 redirects before declaring failure. We also set connection and response timeouts to conservative values of 60 seconds each. We configured our crawler host to use the Google public DNS servers (8.8.8.8 and 8.8.4.4) and parallelized our crawler to speed the measurement process.

---

[5] http://docs.python-requests.org/en/master/.

We used the Alexa Top 1 million sites as the basis for our study[6]. Although this list of websites is crafted from the point of view of one (albeit very large) cloud provider, we argue that it is adequate for gaining a broad view of today's web. In our future work we are considering how to expand the scope of the websites under study in order to measure a larger portion of the web and to improve coverage of sites that serve content for less dominant languages. For each web site, we made a request for the top-level resource (URI path /). Although accessing one document on each site may not give a comprehensive picture of a site's possible multilingual offerings, we argue that since it is anecdotally commonplace for a provider to link to different versions of a site from the top-level URI, it should still give a reasonably complete view.

It is also common for different sites to geolocate clients in an attempt to deliver appropriate content. To account for this, we used a commercial VPN service and launched requests through six different geographic locations. Moreover, for each site, we made two requests using two different versions of the HTTP `Accept-Language` header. In the first, we set the header to accept any language (*), and in the second we set the header to include a prioritized set of languages based on the *de jure* or *de facto* official languages of the VPN location used; we use the curated GeoNames.org list of country codes and languages for this purpose[7]. Table 1 lists the specific country codes and language preferences for the six VPN locations we used. For each of these language preferences, we explicitly set English to be least preferred given its traditional dominance in web content.

For each request and response exchange, we store the full HTTP request and response headers, along with the full (compressed) response content and metadata such as the time a request started and ended and the original hostname used in the request. We retried any errored requests up to three times, storing error information in our logs, as well as any information about redirects. No additional requests were made for directly linked content, such as JavaScript,

Table 1. Accept-Language headers used for langpref (non-default language) experiments. The region code refers to the country from which HTTP requests are launched.

Region	`Accept-Language` value in HTTP requests
AR	`es-AR;q=1.0, es-419;q=0.9, es;q=0.7, it;q=0.6, de;q=0.4, fr;q=0.3, gn;q=0.1`
GB	`cy-GB;q=1.0, cy;q=0.8, gd;q=0.6, en-GB;q=0.4, en;q=0.2`
JP	`ja;q=1.0`
KE	`sw-KE;q=1.0, sw;q=0.8, en-KE;q=0.5, en;q=0.2`
TH	`th;q=1.0`
US	`es-US;q=1.0, es;q=0.8, haw;q=0.7, fr;q=0.5, en-US;q=0.3, us;q=0.2`

---

[6] http://s3.amazonaws.com/alexa-static/top-1m.csv.zip.
[7] http://download.geonames.org/export/dump/countryInfo.txt.

CSS, image files, or iframes. We did not execute any embedded JavaScript. We note that anecdotally, some sites use JavaScript to dynamically add widgets to allow a user to select a preferred language. Due to our measurement methodology, we missed any of these instances that would have included explicit or inferable language tags. In our future work we intend to quantify the number of sites that use such techniques.

Overall, we made 12 million web requests, not including retries because of transient errors (1 million sites, 6 VPN locations, 2 A-L header values), resulting in approximately 500 GB of request and response data. For each instance of VPN location and A-L header value, there were approximately 70 K requests that resulted in unrecoverable errors. The most common error was DNS failure ($\approx$50 K) followed by connection failures and timeouts ($\approx$19 K). We also observed TLS errors ($\approx$200), content decompression errors ($\approx$ 500), and a handful of internationalized domain name errors ($\approx$15).

We used the Python BeautifulSoup4 module[8] with the lxml[9] parser to analyze content and extract language tags. There was no existing Python module to rigorously validate language tags for structure and content, so we created one as part of our work[10]. Our module conforms to BCP 47 and enables validation and extraction of subtags within a language tag. We also used the langcodes module for analyzing text on pages (used in our inference algorithm, described below)[11]. While this module can also parse language tags, we found it to accept tags that would not be considered valid by BCP 47. Lastly, we used a Python port of the Compact Language Detector (pycld2[12]) to detect the language within text on pages. Internally, this module uses a Naïve Bayes classifier to detect the language. It is widely used and includes support for 165 languages.

We observed in our initial analysis that there were many sites that did not include lang or hreflang attributes (or any other metadata) to indicate that a hyperlink leads to alternative language content. As a result, we developed an algorithm for analyzing hyperlink (<a>) tags to determine whether a language tag should be *inferred*. The basic approach of our algorithm is to extract several components from a link tag: (1) the domain (if any) in the href attribute, (2) the URI path in the href attribute, (3) any query parameters in the URI, (4) keys and values for other attributes within the tag, and (5) the text. We analyze each of these components for "language indicators":

- For the domain, we match the left-most domain (most specific) with language and/or country subtags. For example, https://es.wikipedia.org contains Spanish-language content.
- For the URI path, it is not uncommon for web sites to include the language tag (and possibly region subtag) in the first one or two components. For example, http://www.ikea.com/us/en/ provides English content for US-based users.

---

[8] https://www.crummy.com/software/BeautifulSoup/.

[9] http://lxml.de.

[10] https://github.com/jsommers/langtags.

[11] https://github.com/LuminosoInsight/langcodes.

[12] https://github.com/aboSamoor/pycld2.

- For some sites, query parameters are used to indicate the language. For example, Google uses the query key `hl` (for "human language") to indicate the language, such as https://www.google.com/?hl=cy.
- Other sites use non-standard attributes (*i.e.*, not `lang` or `hreflang`) to indicate the language of the linked content. We've observed sites to use `data-lang=de` as an attribute to refer to German content, for example.
- Lastly, the clickable text is often either a language subtag or the name of a language, *in the language of the page content*. We use the `langcodes` module to map language names to subtags.

The algorithm seeks to match the inferred language tag from at least two indicators, and requires that the original text harvested from two indicators be *different*. This requirement is to avoid false inferences in situations such as when the subdomain matches a valid language tag (*e.g.*, ru) and the link text *includes* the word Russia, but also includes other words (*e.g.*, "News from Russia"). Table 2 shows examples of what our algorithm would infer for three (real) example links. Through extensive manual inspection of links and inferences, we found that our algorithm is conservative in the sense that it does not make inferences on *all* links that lead to alternative language content, but the inferences it makes are sound. In other words, in our manual inspections we observed some false negatives, but no false positives. In future work we plan to examine how our algorithm can be improved. Overall, we found that our inference method contributed about 1–3% of all language tags found. Of all the tags found through the inference algorithm, approximately 5% were tags that had not been previously observed, *i.e.*, the number of total language tags observed was expanded via our inference method.

Table 2. Examples of hyperlinks links from which the language tag can be inferred.

Markup	Language inferred
`<a href="#"rel="lt">litvn</a>`	Lithuanian (lt) (Hungarian site)
`<a class="site-topbar__link" href="/en/personal"tabindex="0"><span class="site-topbar__langs__text"> English</span></a>`	English (en) (Swedish site)
`<a href="javascript:setLang('ar');"> Arabic</a>`	Arabic (ar) (English site)

4   Results

In this section we describe the results of our analysis. We begin by discussing the prevalence of malformed language tags and sites that do not include any language tags. As noted above, various types of errors prevented data collection for approximately 70 K of the 1M sites. For the remaining sites, about

330 K do not include any language tags at all; this number varies between 329 K and 335K depending on A-L setting and VPN location. Of sites that include language tags, we observed about 4 K sites to use malformed *primary* language tags (across all language tags, not just primary, about 10 K were malformed). To extract the primary language tag for a page, we first consider the lang (or xml:lang) attribute, followed by any <meta> header, followed by any HTTP Content-Language header, in that order. Table 3 summarizes the most common types of errors we found. Other malformed tags included HTML fragments, apparent Boolean values (*e.g.*, False), apparent "codes", and other garbage. Considering all the malformed tags, it is clear that they fall into one of two categories: semantic errors (*e.g.*, including a region subtag instead of a language tag) or programmer/developer errors (*e.g.*, uninterpolated language variables).

Table 3. Most common malformed tag types.

Type of problem	Example	% of total
Country/region code used as language code	cn	32%
Language name	Deutsch	17%
Character encoding instead of language tag	UTF-8	5%
Non-interpolated placeholder	{{ currentLanguage }}	4%
Other malformed tags		42%

Next, we examine the collection of valid primary language tags found for each site from various geographic perspectives. Figure 1 shows a bargraph for the top 30 most frequent language tags found, from each VPN vantage point. Data are shown for the default A-L header. We note that the data shown comprise about 85% of all valid primary language tags and that the tail is long: there are around 180 distinct primary language tags discovered. As for *how* the primary language tags were found, on average about 94% come from the <html> tag's lang attribute, another 2% come from the xml:lang attribute, 1.5% come from the <meta http-equiv ...> header, and 2.5% come from the HTTP Content-language header.

We observe in the figure some apparent effects that IP geolocation has on the language tag presented in the response. For example, with the TH vantage point we observe an increase in occurrences of the th language code. There are similar increases for es in AR and ja in JP (which are relatively smaller due to the log scale) and for sw in KE (not shown in the plot).

We observe two clear apparent anomalies in the plot: the dip in ko for GB, and the dip in fa for JP. Regarding the Korean language tag, we observe similar patterns for the ko language tag for other vantage points with a non-default A-L header (shown below). It appears that there are a large number of Korean sites that erroneously include the ko subtag but for non-Korean language content. It is unclear presently which set of parameters causes a change in these sites'

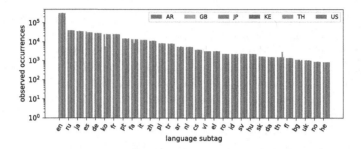

Fig. 1. Primary language observed for all vantage points for top 30 most frequently observed languages, with default `Accept-Language` header. Note the log scale.

behaviors, but it may be that a commonly used library or service within Korea is at the root of the issue. For the `fa` dip observable from the JP vantage point, we are not yet able to speculate on the cause. Interestingly, we also observe a slight rise in `uk` (Ukrainian) for GB, which is likely due to misusing a region tag (which should be `GB` in any case).

We also examined differences in the primary language tags observed between the default `A-L` and langpref `A-L` for each vantage point. For the TH vantage point (not shown due to space constraints), we observe an increase in occurrences of `th` as the primary language when the `A-L` header is set to strongly prefer Thai language content. Beyond that, however, the impact of content negotiation due to the non-default (langpref) `A-L` header is unclear. Specifically, we observe increases in non-Thai language subtags (*e.g.* in `bg` (Bulgarian)!), and similar phenomena are observed in data collected from other vantage points. In particular, compared with accepting a default language, the specific `A-L` header causes an *increase* in the occurrences of primary language tags for languages that are not even included in the preference list. Further, we note that the HTTP specification states that servers *should* include a `Vary` header indicating which client preferences went into determining the content delivered [5]. However, we observe a mere 40 sites that include an indication of `Accept-Language` in the `Vary` header response, which is far below the number of (fairly significant) differences we observe. Clearly, content negotiation plays a larger role than is indicated by the `Vary` header, which we intend to investigate as part of our future work.

In Fig. 2 we show the distribution of the total number of language subtags observed across all sites. From this figure we see that about 330 K contain zero language subtags (far left bar), and that about 520 K sites are apparently unilingual (*i.e.*, we observe a single language subtag). On about 80 K sites, we observe more than one language subtag. From this, we infer that about 80 K sites of the Alexa 1M are multilingual; of those, about 30 K are bilingual. At maximum, we observe 376 distinct language subtags on one site (not shown in the figure) and at least 45 sites offer some content in 100 languages or more. From our analysis, it is not clear *how much* content is offered in any given language, although

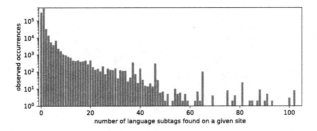

Fig. 2. Number of languages observed to be offered per site. Note the log scale.

we believe that the fact that *any* content is offered multiple languages to be of interest for the purpose of our study.

Next, we aggregate the counts of all language subtags discovered across all sites and show the distribution in Fig. 3, showing the top 50. We cannot view this distribution as giving an accurate sense for the prevalence of various languages across the web, but we believe that the figure nonetheless provides an interesting view of language diversity on the web. Of note in the figure are the large number of occurrences the private language tag x-default, which the W3C recommends to avoid whenever possible [10] (although we note that very few of these appear as the primary language tag). Also, we observe the presence of two languages that are on the UNESCO endangered languages list[13] (each with a status of Vulnerable): Belarussian (be) and Basque (eu). Lastly, we note that our ranking of most prevalent languages observed on the web differs from those published in prior work [6,12]. In particular, Russian and Japanese appear much more frequently than when those prior studies were done.

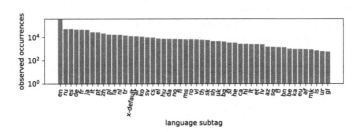

Fig. 3. Frequency of language tags seen across all sites. Note the log scale.

Next, we consider additional components in language tags, such as the region subtag. In Fig. 4, we show the distribution of region subtags observed in primary language tags from the KE vantage point (langpref A-L setting). First, we note that a total of 284 K sites included a region subtag (which is a fairly consistent figure across all vantage points and A-L settings), and we observed a total of

---

[13] http://www.unesco.org/languages-atlas/.

28   J. Sommers

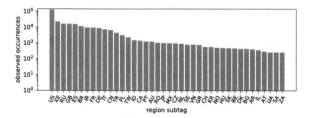

Fig. 4. Frequency of observed region subtags in primary language tags observed in data collected from the KE vantage point. Note the log scale.

227 distinct region subtags. For some vantage points, we observe many fewer distinct region subtags (as few as 160). Interestingly, we observe that the KE region subtag is the second most common. We infer from this (and results from other vantage points) that many sites geolocate client IP addresses and blindly include a region code based on client location. We note also that the inclusion of the region subtag runs counter to W3C advice [10], which is to only include the region subtag when it provides distinct information about site localization.

Lastly, we compare primary language subtags with the result of using the `pycld2` language detection library on the content. For this analysis, we only consider sites/pages for which a primary language tag is included and valid since we wish to understand whether a given language tag is likely to be accurate. Figure 5 shows results for the default A-L setting for the AR vantage point. The top 40 most frequently occuring primary language subtags are shown. We observe in the figure that in many cases, the primary language subtag is close-to-correct. Interestingly, it appears that there are a number of pages in Hindi (`hi`) that are mis-tagged (though it may also be that `pycld2` is incorrect for some of these cases). Information from this analysis could be used to inform sites of misconfigurations, or suggestions to improve the localization of their site by including the appropriate language tag(s).

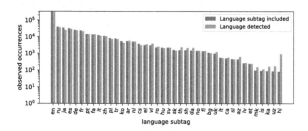

Fig. 5. Primary language tag versus language detected using a Naïve Bayes language detection library, for the AR vantage point. Note the log scale.

5   Summary and Conclusions

In this paper we study the empirical characteristics of language tags observed on web pages and in HTTP transactions. We examine the sites in the Alexa top 1 million, gathering data from six geographic vantage points and using two different settings for the HTTP `Accept-Language` header. We find that about 1/3 of all sites do not include a primary language tag, and that English (`en`) is the most commonly occurring language subtag. We find many occurrences of malformed tags and that about 8% of sites are multilingual. We analyze the prevalence of different language subtags across all sites and vantage points, and comment on various anomalies observed in the data.

In our ongoing work, we are considering a number of directions. First, we plan to examine how HTTP content negotiation affects language tag inclusion, and how it may impact users who are trying to find content in their preferred language. We are also examining ways to broaden our language subtag inference algorithm to consider other elements (*e.g.*, form entries) that indicate the availability of alternative language content on a site. Lastly, we are looking at ways to expand our study beyond the Alexa top 1 million list in order to gain a more comprehensive view of human language on the web.

Acknowledgments. We thank Alex Nie '20 and Ryan Rios '20, who contributed to earlier stages of this work for their summer research. We also thank Ram Durairajan for insightful comments on this work, as well as the anonymous reviewers. Lastly, we thank the Colgate Research Council, which provided partial support for this research.

References

1. IANA Language Subtag Registry. https://www.iana.org/assignments/language-subtag-registry/language-subtag-registry
2. World Wide Web Consortium. Internationalization techniques: Authoring HTML and CSS, January 2016. https://www.w3.org/International/techniques/authoring-html
3. Abbate, J.: Inventing the Internet. MIT Press, Cambridge (2000)
4. Fielding, R., Reschke, J.: RFC 7230: Hypertext Transfer Protocol (HTTP/1.1): Message Syntax and Routing, June 2014. https://tools.ietf.org/html/rfc7230
5. Fielding, R., Reschke, J.: RFC 7231: Hypertext Transfer Protocol (HTTP/1.1): Semantics and Content, June 2014. https://tools.ietf.org/html/rfc7231
6. Grefenstette, G., Nioche, J.: Estimation of English and non-English language use on the WWW. In: Content-Based Multimedia Information Access, vol. 1, pp. 237–246 (2000)
7. Ishida, R.: Language tags in HTML and XML. https://www.w3.org/International/articles/language-tags/
8. Ishida, R.: Declaring language in HTML (2014). https://www.w3.org/International/questions/qa-html-language-declarations
9. Phillips, A., Davis, M.: Tags for Identifying Language, September 2009. https://www.rfc-editor.org/rfc/bcp/bcp47.txt

10. Ishida, R.: Choosing a Language Tag (2016). https://www.w3.org/International/questions/qa-choosing-language-tags
11. Thomas, C., Kline, J., Barford, P.: IntegraTag: a framework for high-fidelity web client measurement. In: 2016 28th International Teletraffic Congress (ITC 28), vol. 1, pp. 278–285 (2016)
12. Xu, F.: Multilingual WWW. Knowledge-based information retrieval and filtering from the web **746**, 165 (2003)

Narrowing the Gap Between QoS Metrics and Web QoE Using Above-the-fold Metrics

Diego Neves da Hora[1]([✉])[iD], Alemnew Sheferaw Asrese[3],
Vassilis Christophides[2], Renata Teixeira[2], and Dario Rossi[1]

[1] Telecom Paristech, Paris, France
{diego.nevesdahora,dario.rossi}@telecom-paristech.fr
[2] Inria, Paris, France
{vassilis.christophides,renata.teixeira}@inria.fr
[3] Aalto University, Espo, Finland
alemnew.asrese@aalto.fi

Abstract. Page load time (PLT) is still the most common application Quality of Service (QoS) metric to estimate the Quality of Experience (QoE) of Web users . Yet, recent literature abounds with proposals for alternative metrics (e.g., Above The Fold, SpeedIndex and their variants) that aim at better estimating user QoE. The main purpose of this work is thus to thoroughly investigate a mapping between established and recently proposed objective metrics and user QoE. We obtain ground truth QoE via user experiments where we collect and analyze 3,400 Web accesses annotated with QoS metrics and explicit user ratings in a scale of 1 to 5, which we make available to the community. In particular, we contrast domain expert models (such as ITU-T and IQX) fed with a single QoS metric, to models trained using our ground-truth dataset over multiple QoS metrics as features. Results of our experiments show that, albeit very simple, expert models have a comparable accuracy to machine learning approaches. Furthermore, the model accuracy improves considerably when building per-page QoE models, which may raise scalability concerns as we discuss.

1 Introduction

The Web remains one of the dominant applications in the Internet. Originally designed to deliver static contents such as text and images, it evolved to serve very dynamic and complex content: it is not uncommon for modern pages to include hundreds of objects and dozens of scripts, placed at different servers hosted in different domains [11]. Given this complexity, the Web architecture and protocol landscape evolved as well, aiming at more efficient operation and to enhance the end user QoE: the introduction of Content Delivery Network (CDN) and different protocols such as HTTP2 [7], SPDY [16], QUIC [19] are some of the efforts in this regard.

© Springer International Publishing AG, part of Springer Nature 2018
R. Beverly et al. (Eds.): PAM 2018, LNCS 10771, pp. 31–43, 2018.
https://doi.org/10.1007/978-3-319-76481-8_3

Measuring the impact of different network and Web browsing configurations on Web browsing performance is essential to enhance user satisfaction. The metric most commonly used to measure the performance of Web browsing has been the Page Load Time (PLT), which holds true for both research [13,21,25–27] and industry [1,2,4]. Recent studies [3,8,10,15,18,24], however, started to question the relevance of using PLT to measure quality of user experience. The main skepticism is that whereas PLT measures the precise time at which the page finishes loading, the experience of the user depends on the whole process up to that time and the rendering time at the browser. As such, a number of alternative metrics, which we review in Sect. 2.1, such as the Above-the-Fold (ATF) time [10], SpeedIndex [3], Object/ByteIndex [8] and PerceptualSpeedIndex [15] have been proposed to bridge this gap.

The approach adopted by the measurement community for computing metrics like ATF time and SpeedIndex requires taking a series of screenshots of the Webpage loading progress and post-processing the captured frames. Unfortunately, this approach is computationally intensive, which makes these metrics complex to measure [15]. Our first contribution (presented in Sect. 3) is to propose a **tractable method to estimate the ATF metric, and offer an open-source implementation as a Chrome extension** [5].

Still, to date the relationship between this class of objective metrics and the user subjective feedback (e.g., via explicit ratings summarized with Mean Opinion Score (MOS)) remains to be elucidated. Indeed, while models mapping PLT to an estimated MOS do exist [14,17] (see Sect. 2.2), to the best of our knowledge, extensions of these models to leverage these new metrics are still lacking. Recently, Gao et al. [15] evaluated machine learning models that use these new metrics as features to forecast A/B test results, where users are asked to compare two Webpages loading side-by-side and identify which one loads faster. Although Gao et al.'s work [15] represents an important step in the right direction, A/B tests are a special case: i.e., we still miss an answer to the more general question of how to estimate QoE of a single page a given user visits.

In this paper, we thoroughly investigate a mapping $f(\cdot)$ between user QoE, expressed in terms of subjective MOS, and some QoS factor x that represents objective measured properties of the browsing activity. In particular, we are interested in cases where x can be any combination of the above objective metrics and where the mapping $f(\cdot)$ is either defined by a domain expert (e.g., according to popular models like ITU-T [17] or IQX [14]) or data-driven models learned using classic machine learning algorithms (e.g., SVR regression, CART trees).

The other main contribution of this paper (presented in Sect. 4) is to **perform a thorough assessment of expert models (ITU-T [17], IQX [14], etc.) and contrast them to models learned from the data using different machine learning algorithms**, which our investigation finds to have surprisingly comparable accuracy performance. Our analysis relies on a dataset with 3,400 Web browsing sessions where users explicitly rated the quality of the session. This dataset extends our previous effort [9] and we make available to the community [28]. We conclude that expert models for Web QoE can easily accommodate new time-related metrics beyond PLT, and that their accuracy is comparable to that of data-driven models. Still, we gather that there is room for improvement, as a single expert model is hardly accurate for the wide variety of Web pages. At the same time, while we find that per-page models have superior forecast performance, the approach is clearly not scalable, which opens new interesting research questions for the community to address, which we discuss in Sect. 4.4. We conclude in Sect. 5.

2   Background and Related Work

This section first discusses the existing metrics that aim to capture Web QoS, which we build on to define a practical method to infer the ATF time in Sect. 3. Then, it presents the existing models to estimate Web QoE from these QoS metrics, which we evaluate in Sect. 4.

2.1   Web QoS Metrics

The Web browsing process is complex with the request, download, and rendering of all objects making up a Webpage. Hence, measuring when the page has finished loading from the user's perspective is challenging. The literature introduces two classes of objective QoS metrics, which we exemplify with the help of Fig. 1.

Time Instants. The time to load a Web page has a number of components, such as the time at which the first byte is received (TTFB), the time at which the first object is painted (TTFP) by the browser, the parsing of the Document Object Model (DOM), to the complete download (PLT, that we measure using the onLoad browser event) or the rendering of the full page (VisualComplete). We notice that whereas network-related time-instant metrics (e.g. TTFB, DOM, PLT) are easy to measure, rendering-related metrics (e.g. TTFP, VisualComplete) are harder to define across browsers [20]. An interesting metric proposed by Google in this class is represented by the ATF time [10], defined as the time at which the content shown in the visible part of the Webpage is completely rendered. Albeit interesting, the ATF metric is neither available in Webpagetest[1],

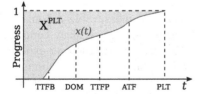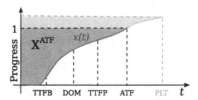

Fig. 1. Illustration of time-instant (x-axis labels) and time-integral metrics (shaded surface). The time horizon of the time-integral metrics can be limited to, e.g., (a) PLT or (b) Above-the-Fold time instants.

---

[1] https://www.webpagetest.org/.

nor defined in W3C's navigation timing specifications.[2] This omission is possibly due to the fact that the ATF time is significantly more complex to measure, as it requires taking screenshots during the rendering process and a post-processing stage of the captured frames. One of our contributions is to propose a practical way to approximate the ATF time, as well as provide an open source implementation.

Time Integrals. Another class of metrics recognizes that a single time instant hardly captures all the complexity of interactions between the user and the rendering process of the page. Instead, this class integrates the loading time over all events of a given type throughout the evolution of a page progress. Following Google's original SpeedIndex (SI) [3] definition, a number of generalizations have been proposed in the literature [8,15]. Metrics in this class fit the general form:

$$X^{end} = \int_0^{t_{end}} (1 - x(t))dt \tag{1}$$

where X^{end} is the value of the metric, t_{end} indicates an event considered as time horizon and $x(t) \in [0,1]$ is the completion rate at time t. In particular, SpeedIndex (SI) [3] measures $x(t)$ as the visual progress using mean pixel histogram difference computed until the VisualComplete time. ObjectIndex (OI) and ByteIndex (BI) [8] use the percentage of objects (and bytes) downloaded until the PLT. Finally, PerceptualSpeedIndex (PSI) [15] uses Structural Similarity to measure the visual progress $x(t)$ and cut the time horizon at either the PLT, or at an arbitrary time earlier than PLT.

One interesting question is how to select t_{end}. A previous A/B study [15] showed two pages rendering processes side by side, and asked users to click on the page that completed faster: the best predictor uses the Time to Click as t_{end}, which considerably improves PSI accuracy in estimating user QoE [15]. Our experiments show that setting t_{end} with the ATF time is a good option, and our method to compute the ATF time enables measuring it during normal user browsing (i.e., without requiring user intervention).

2.2   Web QoE Models

The metrics introduced in the previous section are measurable automatically from the browser (even though those involving rendering are fairly complex to compute). These metrics, however, may not directly capture the user experience (or QoE), which is often measured explicitly by an opinion score and summarized with the MOS. There are two main approaches for mapping of QoS metrics into MOS: *expert models*, where domain experts specify a closed form function and use MOS data to fit model parameters, or *machine learning models*, where MOS data is used to train the model.

---

[2] https://www.w3.org/TR/navigation-timing/.

Expert Models. Two well established [22], models of Web QoE are the ITU-T recommendation model [17] and the IQX [14] hypothesis. The ITU-T model follows the Weber-Fechner Law and assumes that the user QoE has a logarithmic relationship with the underlying QoS metric. The model is in the form:

$$QoE(x) = \alpha \log(x) + \gamma, \tag{2}$$

where x is the QoS metric (typically, PLT) and with α, γ parameters. The ITU-T models are derived for three different contexts (fast, medium, and slow networks) with a different minimum and maximum session time for the different contexts so that QoE $\in [1, 5]$.

Alternatively, the model based on the IQX hypothesis [14] postulates an exponential interdependency between QoE and QoS metrics. The idea of the model is that if the QoE is high, a small variation in the underlying QoS metric will strongly affect the QoE. Instead, a degradation in QoS metric will not lower QoE as much if the overall QoE is already bad. Under IQX, for a given change in QoS metric the change of QoE depends on the current level of QoE as:

$$QoE(x) = \alpha e^{-\beta x} + \gamma \tag{3}$$

where x is a QoS metric and with α, β, γ parameters. We evaluate both logarithmic and exponential models in Sect. 4.

Machine Learning. While machine learning algorithms have been used to model QoE for VoIP [12], video streaming [6] or Skype [23], its application to Web browsing is still lacking. One marked exception is the work by Gao et al. [15], where authors formulate a ternary classification task (i.e., A is faster, B is faster, none is faster) and employ Random Forest and Gradient Boosting ML techniques with QoS metrics such as those described in Sect. 2.1 as input features. In this paper, we focus on a more difficult task, formulated as a regression problem in the support $MOS \in [1, 5] \subset \mathbb{R}$, and additionally contrast ML results to those achievable by state of the art expert models.

3   Approximating the ATF time

One way to calculate the ATF time is to monitor the page rendering process and identify when the pixels on the visible part of the page, also known as the *above-the-fold* part, stop changing. This can be done by monitoring the individually rendered pixels (or histograms of the rendering) and detecting when they stabilize. This approach, however, is processing intensive and difficult to apply in the wild, as the overhead may impair user experience. Webpages also contain visual jitter due to, for example, layout instabilities or carousel elements [15], making it harder to detect the ATF time using pixel comparison methods.

Methodology. We propose a method to approximate the ATF time from the browser itself without requiring image processing. We leverage the browser's ability to determine the position of objects inside a fully rendered page and the recorded loading times of HTTP requests. Our method works as follows. First, we detect all the elements of the Webpage and the browser window size. Then, we trace loading time and resource type for all HTTP requests, and determine which objects are rendered above-the-fold. To do so, we use simple heuristics to classify resource types between images, JavaScripts (JS), CSS, HTML, etc. For objects that are directly rendered (e.g., of the image class), the coordinates make it obvious whether they are, at least partly, above-the-fold. For objects for which we have no direct indication whether they are used for rendering (e.g., styles that are defined through CSS; visual changes generated by JS), we conservatively assume they are required for rendering above-the-fold content. More formally, denoting with T_o the loading time of object o, and letting $\mathcal{I}$ be the set of all images, $\mathcal{I}_{ATF}$ the subset of images whose coordinates are at least partially above-the-fold, $\mathcal{J}$ the set of all JavaScript HTTP requests and $\mathcal{C}$ the set of all CSS requests, we calculate the Approximate ATF (AATF) time as:

$$AATF = \max_{o}\{T_o | o \in \mathcal{J} \cup \mathcal{C} \cup \mathcal{I}_{ATF}\} \qquad (4)$$

We stress that AATF should not be considered as a replacement metric for ATF: to that extent, it would be necessary to comprehensively validate AATF against pixel-based measurements of ATF, which we leave for future work. At the same time, our experiments indicate that AATF has a good discriminative power as it helps ameliorate forecasts of user MOS, and as such has value on its own.

Implementation. We implemented the method to approximate the ATF time as an open-source Chrome extension [5]. The script executes after the `onLoad` event triggers. We use jQuery to detect visible DOM objects. For each object, we detect its position and dimensions on the page. We use this information alongside the dimension of the browser window, which we obtain using JavaScript, to determine which DOM objects are visible and above-the-fold. We use the `Window.performance` API to obtain the name, type, and timing information about the resources loaded in the page. We compare the `src` field of DOM object to the url of HTTP request to match HTML objects to its corresponding timing information. Finally, we calculate the AATF time using (4). Figure 2 shows and comments an example of the results from the extension applied when browsing the Amazon Webpage. It can be seen that only 8 of the 154 images are located above-the-fold (circled in blue in Fig. 2), with a significant difference between PLT, ATF and derived metrics.

Approximations and Limitations. As in any real-world deployment, we find a number of technicalities which complicates the process of detecting the resources located above the fold. For instance, some Webpages contain sliding images which keep rotating in the above-the-fold area. Additionally, there are

Fig. 2. Extension example: *Time-instant* metrics show that whereas DOM loads at 2.62 s, all objects above the fold are rendered on or before AATF=5.37 s and then the page finishes loading at PLT=16.11 s. By definition, *Time-integral* metrics are even shorter $BI^{AATF} < BI^{PLT} < AATF$, hinting that PLT may be significantly off with respect to timescales relevant to the user perception. (Color figure online)

cases where images happen to be above-the-fold but also overlap, so that some of them are not actually visible. For the sake of simplicity, we assume that all the images are visible for the AATF time calculation, which makes a conservative approximation. Also, in our current implementation, we consider images but do not take into account other multimedia object types (e.g., Flash) that may be relevant and that we leave for future work.

In some cases, we find image HTTP requests that do not match to any known HTML object. This issue happens, for example, when the background image of buttons is put into place using CSS (circled in red in Fig. 2). Although we cannot reliably detect if these "unmatched" images are above or below the fold, we can still calculate the AATF time either considering that those images are always "above" (i.e., which upper bounds the AATF time) or "below" the fold (i.e., a lower bound). Our investigation reveals that whereas the PLT vs AATF difference is significant, these low-level details have no noticeable impact on the AATF time computation (not reported here for lack of space).

4   Modeling WebQoE

In this section, we thoroughly explore how Web QoS metrics relate to user QoE. We detail the dataset used in this analysis, explore how well expert models can predict QoE, and to what extent machine learning approaches present an advantage in comparison to expert models.

4.1   Dataset

To assess the impact of application QoS on QoE, we extend our previous experiment on measuring Web user experience [9]. We gather 8,689 Web browsing sessions from 241 volunteers, that we make available at [28]. During each Web browsing session, a script guides the user to select one Webpage from a list, open the page on the browser, and provide QoE feedback using the Absolute Category Rating (ACR) (from 1-Bad to 5-Excellent). For lack of space, we refer readers to [9] for a detailed presentation of our experimental setup.

In this work, we focus on 12 non-landing Webpages from the Alexa top 100 popular pages in France, with diverse page size (0.43–2.88 MB), number of objects (24–212), and loading times varying by over one order of magnitude. Since we rely on volunteers to obtain user opinion scores, we employ basic dataset sanitization techniques. First, we remove from the dataset all samples with no user rating or where the page failed to load completely. Then, we remove users who failed to complete at least 10 reviews. We keep 224 out of the original 241 users, and 8,568 out of 8,689 reviews. Finally, we restrict our analysis to only 12 out of the 25 original Webpages comprising a significant number of reviews and experimental conditions, which leaves us with 3,400 user ratings.

We obtain MOS values by averaging the opinion score of a Webpage for specific user groups. These groups are defined based on the distributional characteristics of the input QoS metric x, whose impact on MOS we are interested to assess. We grouped the user ratings of each page in 6 bins, specifically at every 20th percentile of metric x until the 80th percentile, and further break the tail in two bins each representing 10% of the population. All volunteers used identical devices during the experiments. The models we obtain implicitly assume the experimental conditions observed in this dataset such as the screen size, performance expectation, and device capabilities.

4.2   Expert Models

Application Metrics. To assess how well a function $f(\cdot)$ applied to a QoS metric x correlates with MOS, we consider the following time-instants: (i) the time to load the DOM, (ii) the time to load the last visible image or other multimedia object AATF and (iii) the time to trigger the onLoad event PLT. We additionally include time-integral metrics with either an AATF time or PLT time-horizon: specifically, we consider (iv) two ByteIndex $\text{BI}^{AATF} < \text{BI}^{PLT}$ metrics, where $x(t)$ express the percentage of bytes downloaded at time t, and (v) two ObjectIndex $\text{OI}^{AATF} < \text{BI}^{PLT}$ metrics, where $x(t)$ counts the percentage of objects downloaded at time t. Finally, we define (vi) two ImageIndex $\text{II}^{AATF} < \text{II}^{PLT}$ metrics, where $x(t)$ only considers the size of objects of the image class, to purposely exacerbate the prominent role of images in the visual rendering of a page.

Figure 3(a) assesses the impact of the nine selected QoS metrics on QoE, using the IQX model. We observe that, apart from DOM, all metrics show a strong (> 0.8) Pearson correlation with MOS. Specifically, we see that counting bytes (BI) and especially image bytes (II) is more valuable than counting objects (OI). Additionally, results confirm the importance of evaluating time-integrals by narrowing their time-horizon before the PLT (as suggested by Gao et al. [15]), confirming the importance of estimating the ATF time (as proposed in this paper). Overall, the metric with best correlation to MOS is II^{AATF} (0.85), with

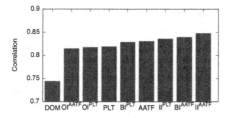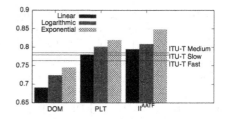

Fig. 3. Expert models: Impact of (a) explanatory QoS metric x for the $f(\cdot)$ =IQX hypothesis and (b) combined impact of metric x and mapping function $f(\cdot)$

PLT ranking seventh (0.81). These results confirm the soundness of using the AATF time as proxy of user-perceived page loading time [24].

Mapping Functions. We use three functions to map QoS metrics to user QoE: specifically, a linear $\mathbf{1}(\cdot)$ function, a logarithm function of the form of (2), and an exponential function of the form of (3). While the rationale behind (2) and (3) come from the Weber-Fetchner law and the IQX hypothesis, we stress that many works still *directly* compare PLT statistics, which is analogous to a simplistic linear mapping. We carefully calibrate the model parameters using the non-linear least squares Marquardt-Levenberg algorithm. In Fig. 3(b) we contrast how these different mappings correlate to QoE for a relevant subset of the QoS metrics: specifically, we select the most widely used metric (PLT) as well as those metrics exhibiting the worst (DOM) and the best (II^{AATF}) correlation with user QoE. We also compare results with the reference obtained by default ITU-T models for slow/medium/fast network conditions using the PLT metric.

Among the default ITU-T models, the model for medium networking conditions shows the stronger correlation to QoE in our dataset. This can be explained by users' expectation of network performance, since the experimental network conditions mirror that of Internet Web access. It is worth noting that the uncalibrated ITU-T medium model is still better than a linear mapping of PLT to QoE. We observe across all metrics in our dataset that the exponential mapping is superior to logarithmic, which is in turn superior to simply using a linear mapping to estimate QoE. It is easy to observe that our proposed metrics based on the AATF time (particularly, II^{AATF}) consistently yields the strongest correlation with MOS, across all functions.

4.3 Machine Learning

We evaluate different machine learning techniques to learn regression models that predict user QoE. Note that the learned function $f(\cdot)$ maps a vector $\underline{x}$ to MOS, compared to the expert models where x is a scalar metric. We evaluate the performance of three state-of-the-art machine learning algorithms: Support Vector Regression (SVR), Classification And Regression Tree (CART), and AdaBoost with CART (BOOST) implemented using the sci-kit learn Python module.

Parameter Tuning. We tune the hyper-parameters of the ML algorithms using grid optimization. Namely, we select the best combination of parameters $\epsilon \in [10^{-2}, 1]$, $\gamma \in [10^{-3}, 10]$ and $C \in [1, 10^4]$ for SVR, minimum number of samples per leaf $\in [1, 10]$ and tree depth $\in [1, 10]$ for CART and BOOST, and number of boosted trees $\in [10, 10^3]$ for BOOST. Grid optimization outputs $\epsilon = 0.3$, $\gamma = 10^{-3}$, and $C = 10^4$ for SVR, and suggests 4 samples per leaf and tree depth of 2 for both CART and BOOST, and 10^2 trees for BOOST.

Feature Selection. We employ three strategies for building predictors using different sets of features from our dataset. The first baseline strategy considers as features the 9 *raw* metrics defined in Sect. 4.2. The second strategy feeds the ML model with the output of the 3 expert models computed on the 9 raw metrics, for an *extended set* of 27 features (notice that since one mapping function is linear, there are 18 additional features beyond the raw ones). Finally, as performance upper bound, we perform an *exhaustive search* of feature subsets from the extended set, to select the combination that minimizes the Root Mean Squared Error (RMSE) of the predictor. The selected combinations include few features (3–5 out of 9) that vary across ML algorithms, although the sets consistently include II^{PLT} (all algorithms) AATF and II^{AATF} (all but one).

Results. We evaluate ML predictors using leave-one-out cross-validation. Figure 4 shows the (a) correlation and (b) RMSE between MOS and the ML model, for the full set of algorithms and feature selection strategies. We also report, as a reference, the performance of the best expert model (exponential, II^{AATF}), a traditional model (logarithmic, PLT), and the worst expert model (linear, DOM). Similar considerations hold for both correlation (the higher the better) or RMSE (the lower the better): BOOST presents a small advantage over CART trees, although SVR outperforms them both. Yet, the picture clearly shows that SVR results are on par with the best expert model, with a small advantage arising in the optimistic case of an exhaustive search for feature selection.

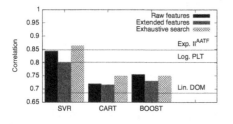 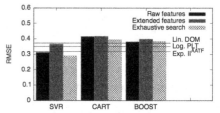

Fig. 4. Comparison of ML algorithm using different feature sets against reference expert models, for correlation and RMSE metrics

4.4   Discussion

We believe that there is further room for improvement. Notably, we argue that, due to the variety of Webpages, the attempt to build a one-size-fit-all model is doomed to fail. To show this, we report in Fig. 5 an extreme example, where (a) we build a model per Webpage and (b) contrast the RMSE results in the per-page vs. all-pages model cases: it is immediate to see that RMSE drastically decreases under fine grained models – the gap is comparably larger than what could be reasonably achieved by further refining the metrics definition, or by the use of more complex expert (or learned) models. Clearly, given the sheer number of Webpages, it would be highly unrealistic to attempt to systematically build such fine-grained models. At the same time, we believe that due to the high skew of Web content, it would be scalable to (i) build per-page models for only very popular pages (e.g. the top-1000 Alexa) and (ii) build per-class models for the rest of pages, by clustering together pages with similar characteristics. Whereas our dataset currently includes few pages to perform a full-blown study, we believe that crowdsourcing efforts such as Gao et al. [15] and systematic share of dataset can collectively assist the community to achieve this goal.

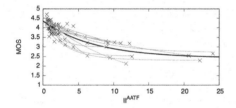 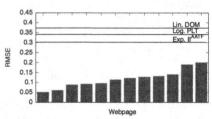

(a) Black: one model for all pages, Gray: one model per page

(b) Lines: one model for all pages, Bars: one model per page

Fig. 5. Discussion: one model for all pages vs. one model per page

5   Conclusions

This paper narrows the gap between QoS and QoE for Web applications. Our contributions are, first, to motivate, define and implement a simple yet effective method to compute an Approximated ATF time (AATF) [5], which is also useful to narrow the time-horizon of time-integral metrics [15]. Second, we carry on a large campaign to collect a dataset of nearly 9,000 user subjective feedback, which we use for our analysis and make available to the community [28]. Finally, we systematically compare expert vs. data-driven models based on a set of QoS metrics, which include the ATF time approximation and variants. In a nutshell, our results suggest that whereas considering PLT metric with linear mapping should be considered a discouraged practice. Using (i) an exponential IQX mapping, (ii) over time-integral metrics considering ByteIndex progress of image-content only, and (iii) narrowing the time-horizon to the AATF time, provides a sizeable improvement of Web QoE estimation. Finally, we found that (iv) calibrated expert models can provide estimations on par with state-of-the-art ML algorithms.

Acknowledgments. We are grateful to our shepherd Mike Wittie and to the anonymous reviewers, whose useful comments helped us improving our work. This work has been carried out at LINCS (http://www.lincs.fr) and benefited from support of NewNet@Paris, Ciscos Chair "Networks for the Future" at Telecom ParisTech and the EU Marie curie ITN program METRICS (grant no. 607728).

References

1. https://googlewebmastercentral.blogspot.fr/2010/04/using-site-speed-in-web-search-ranking.html
2. http://googleresearch.blogspot.fr/2009/06/speed-matters.html
3. https://sites.google.com/a/webpagetest.org/docs/using-webpagetest/metrics/speed-index
4. Alexa Internet Inc. http://www.alexa.com
5. Approximate ATF chrome extension. https://github.com/TeamRossi/ATF
6. Bampis, C.G., Bovik, A.C.: Learning to predict streaming video QoE: distortions, rebuffering and memory. CoRR, abs/1703.00633 (2017)
7. Belshe, M., Peon, R., et al.: Hypertext Transfer Protocol Version 2 (HTTP/2). RFC 7540 (2015)
8. Bocchi, E., De Cicco, L., et al.: Measuring the quality of experience of web users. In: ACM SIGCOMM CCR (2016)
9. Bocchi, E., De Cicco, L., Mellia, M., Rossi, D.: The web, the users, and the MOS: influence of HTTP/2 on user experience. In: Kaafar, M.A., Uhlig, S., Amann, J. (eds.) PAM 2017. LNCS, vol. 10176, pp. 47–59. Springer, Cham (2017). https://doi.org/10.1007/978-3-319-54328-4_4
10. Brutlag, J., Abrams, Z., et al.: Above the fold time: Measuring web page performance visually (2011)
11. Butkiewicz, M., Madhyastha, H.V., et al.: Characterizing web page complexity and its impact. IEEE/ACM Trans. Netw. **22**(3), 943 (2014)
12. Charonyktakis, P., Plakia, M., et al.: On user-centric modular QoE prediction for VoIP based on machine-learning algorithms. IEEE Trans. Mob. Comput. **15**, 1443–1456 (2016)
13. Erman, J., Gopalakrishnan, V., et al.: Towards a SPDY'ier mobile web? In: ACM CoNEXT, pp. 303–314 (2013)
14. Fiedler, M., Hoßfeld, T., et al.: A generic quantitative relationship between quality of experience and quality of service. IEEE Netw. **24**(2), 36 (2010)
15. Gao, Q., Dey, P., et al.: Perceived performance of top retail webpages in the wild: insights from large-scale crowdsourcing of above-the-fold QoE. In: Proceedings of ACM Internet-QoE Workshop (2017)
16. Google: SPDY, an experimental protocol for a faster web. https://www.chromium.org/spdy/spdy-whitepaper
17. ITU-T: Estimating end-to-end performance in IP networks for data application (2014)

18. Kelton, C., Ryoo, J., et al.: Improving user perceived page load time using gaze. In: Proceedings of USENIX NSDI (2017)
19. Langley, A., Riddoch, A., et al.: The QUIC transport protocol: design and internet-scale deployment. In: Proceedings of ACM SIGCOMM (2017)
20. Minutes of TPAC Web Performance WG meeting. https://www.w3.org/2016/09/23-webperf-minutes.html
21. Qian, F., Gopalakrishnan, V., et al.: TM3: flexible transport-layer multi-pipe multiplexing middlebox without head-of-line blocking. In: ACM CoNEXT (2015)
22. Schatz, R., Hoßfeld, T., Janowski, L., Egger, S.: From packets to people: quality of experience as a new measurement challenge. In: Biersack, E., Callegari, C., Matijasevic, M. (eds.) Data Traffic Monitoring and Analysis. LNCS, vol. 7754, pp. 219–263. Springer, Heidelberg (2013). https://doi.org/10.1007/978-3-642-36784-7_10
23. Spetebroot, T., Afra, S., et al.: From network-level measurements to expected quality of experience: the Skype use case. In: M & N Workshop (2015)
24. Varvello, M., Blackburn, J., et al.: EYEORG: a platform for crowdsourcing web quality of experience measurements. In: Proceedings of ACM CoNEXT (2016)
25. Varvello, M., Schomp, K., et al.: Is The Web HTTP/2 Yet?. In: Proceedings of PAM (2016)
26. Wang, X.S., Balasubramanian, A., et al.: How speedy is SPDY? In: USENIX NSDI, pp. 387–399. USENIX Association, Seattle (2014)
27. Wang, X.S., Krishnamurthy, A., et al.: Speeding up web page loads with Shandian. In: USENIX NSDI (2016)
28. Web QoE dataset. https://newnet.telecom-paristech.fr/index.php/webqoe/

Security and Privacy

Internet Protocol Cameras with No Password Protection: An Empirical Investigation

Haitao Xu[1], Fengyuan Xu[2](✉), and Bo Chen[3]

[1] Northwestern University, Evanston, IL 60201, USA
hxu@northwestern.edu
[2] National Key Laboratory for Novel Software Technology, Nanjing University, Nanjing, China
fengyuan.xu@nju.edu.cn
[3] Michigan Technological University, Houghton, MI 49931, USA
bchen@mtu.edu

Abstract. Internet Protocol (IP) cameras have become virtually omnipresent for organizations, businesses, and personal users across the world, for the purposes of providing physical security, increasing safety, and preventing crime. However, recent studies suggest that IP cameras contain less than ideal security and could be easily exploited by miscreants to infringe user privacy and cause even bigger threats. In this study, we focus on the IP cameras without any password protection. We conduct a large-scale empirical investigation of such IP cameras based on *insecam.org*, an online directory of IP cameras, which claims to be the largest one in the world. To this end, we have monitored the site and studied its dynamics with daily data collection over a continuous period of 18 days. We compute daily number of active IP cameras and new cameras on the site, and infer people's usage habit of IP cameras. In addition, we perform a comprehensive characteristic analysis of IP cameras in terms of the most used TCP/UDP ports, manufactures, installation location, ISPs, and countries. Furthermore, we explore other possibly existing security issues with those cameras in addition to no password protection. We utilize an IP scanning tool to discover the hidden hosts and services on the internal network where a vulnerable IP camera is located, and then perform a vulnerability analysis. We believe our findings can provide valuable knowledge of the threat landscape that IP cameras are exposed to.

Keywords: IP camera · IoT security · Vulnerability analysis

1 Introduction

An Internet Protocol (IP) camera refers to a video camera which is attached to a small web server and allows the access to it via Internet protocols. Along with

© Springer International Publishing AG, part of Springer Nature 2018
R. Beverly et al. (Eds.): PAM 2018, LNCS 10771, pp. 47–59, 2018.
https://doi.org/10.1007/978-3-319-76481-8_4

the growing security needs and the development of IoT technologies, IP cameras are being widely used to monitor areas such as offices, houses, and public spaces. However, recent reports [8, 10, 11] and studies [12, 16] have shown that IP cameras contain less than ideal security, and could be exploited and fully controlled by miscreants to infringe user privacy and even launch large-scale DDoS attacks [4, 9, 14].

Username and password is the most widely used form of authentication in practice to prevent unauthorized access. However, an incredible number of IP cameras are found to have no password protection (or more exactly, with password of null or empty) and are having their live video feeds streamed on *insecam.org*, a popular website with hundreds of thousands of visitors daily.

Most previous works mainly focus on summarizing various vulnerabilities of IP cameras and making suggestions on potential mitigation solutions. In this paper, based on the data provided by the site *insecam* about its listed IP cameras, we conduct an in-depth, large-scale quantitative evaluation of vulnerable IP cameras with no password protection. Specifically, we performed daily collection on *insecam* over a continuous period of 18 days. As a result, we observed 28,386 unique IP cameras, from 31 timezones[1], 136 countries, and 25 manufacturers, streaming their live video feeds on *insecam* without awareness of IP camera owners. In addition to those currently active IP cameras, we managed to exhaust and collect all the history records of IP cameras ever streaming on *insecam*, with a total number of 290,344. We then performed a comprehensively characteristic analysis of those IP cameras and also conducted vulnerability analysis of the internal networks where those IP cameras reside with an attempt to identify more vulnerabilities.

Our work is the first measurement study on IP cameras using *insecam.org* as a data source. Based on the assumption that all the information posted on *insecam* about the IP cameras is correct, we highlight the following findings: (1) there are about 20,000 to 25,000 active cameras shown on insecam each day and 215 new cameras are added daily on average; (2) 87.4% IP cameras on insecam are from the three geographic regions - Europe, East Asia, and North America, while United States alone contributes 22.5% of those cameras; (3) monitoring the on/off state of IP cameras could reveal usage habit of IP cameras; (4) more than a half of cameras are from the two manufacturers, Defeway and Axis; (5) a third of IP cameras use the port 80 to communicate to their administrative interface; (6) about a quarter of hosts where an IP camera resides have remote access ports 22 (SSH) and 23 (Telnet) open, which make them more vulnerable to attackers; (7) nearly all those cameras were running extremely old and vulnerable web server software, most of which are found to bear tens of CVE (Common Vulnerabilities and Exposures) vulnerabilities. We believe our findings can provide valuable knowledge of the threat landscape that IP cameras are facing.

---

[1] There are 39 different timezones currently in use in the world [6].

2   Background

In this section, we briefly introduce IP cameras and the site *insecam.org*.

IP cameras. An IP camera contains a CPU and memory, runs software, and has a network interface that allows it to communicate to other devices and be remotely controlled by users. Different from CCTV cameras (closed-circuit television cameras), IP cameras have the remote access features for administration and video monitoring. However, the remote accessibility can be exploited by a hacker, especially when users adopt default settings and credentials for the web administrative interface.

insecam.org. This site is reported to have existed since September 2014. It is claimed to be the world largest directory of network live IP video cameras. The first time the site attracted media attention was in November 2014 [8,10,11], when journalists reported that the site provided a directory for countless private IP cameras which streamed privacy-sensitive live video feeds. Since then, the site administrator seems to have enforced strict policies that only filtered IP cameras can be added to the directory. However, there are still hundreds of thousands of IP cameras listed on the site without their owners' awareness. In addition, all IP cameras on *insecam* are accessible without any authentication (i.e., no password protection) and the live video stream can be directly viewed by any visitors across the world.

3   Measurement Methodology and Dataset

insecam.org collects a large set of currently active IP cameras that have no password protection. And those cameras seem not to be remotely controlled or interfered by *insecam*. According to the policy described on the homepage of *insecam* [7], anyone could request the site administrators to add an IP camera to the directory by providing the IP and port of the camera. For each active IP camera, *insecam* streams its live video feeds on the site for visitors to watch and also provides relevant metadata information including the camera IP, port, manufacturer, geolocation information (country, city, and timezone), and a tag describing the subject of the video feed (e.g., animal, street) if available. An IP camera turnéd off by its owner cannot be accessed on *insecam*, and thus the total number of active cameras shown on *insecam* is always changing. In addition, each IP camera is assigned a unique ID by *insecam* and the ID of an IP camera could usually lead to a webpage displaying the IP camera metadata information.

Our general goal is to evaluate the seriousness of security issues with vulnerable IP cameras through the study on *insecam*. Our measurement methodology is driven by three specific goals. First, we wish to examine the dynamics of *insecam* in terms of daily number of active IP cameras and new cameras on the site. Second, we want to characterize those IP cameras without password protection in terms of their manufacturers, installation location, ISPs, and countries. Third, we want to explore the possibility that a vulnerable camera could be leveraged as a pivot point onto the internal network.

We built a Python crawler that allows us to automatically collect the information about the IP cameras posted on *insecam*. Considering the always changing number of active cameras due to turning on or off, we ran the crawler at least four times each day at six-hour time interval. The collected information suffices for our purposes of examining *insecam* dynamics and characterizing IP cameras, except the information about what ISPs are hosting those vulnerable IP cameras. We then queried the IP addresses of *insecam* cameras in an online IP geolocation database [5] to obtain the corresponding ISP information.

In addition, based on the observation that the camera IDs on *insecam* are all integers and the camera IDs in our collected dataset have many missing values, we assume that *insecam* assigns *sequential* IDs to its cameras, and conjecture that those missing camera IDs correspond to the IP cameras which were ever collected on *insecam* but are currently not accessible due to either no longer working or password setup. We ran the crawler to request the corresponding web pages for the camera metadata information. In this way, we believe we are able to exhaust or at least very close to collect all the history records of IP cameras ever appearing on *insecam*.

We also utilized an IP scanning tool [1] to discover the hidden hosts and services which co-reside with the vulnerable IP cameras in the same internal network. We paid special attention to the services (e.g., `SSH` and `Telnet`) which are often probed by attackers as the starting point for further attacks. We then performed vulnerability analysis based on the collected co-residing information.

Dataset. Through daily data collection over a continuous period of 18 days, from September 25, 2017 to October 12, 2017, we have observed 28,386 unique, active IP cameras listed on *insecam*, which are from 31 timezones, 136 countries, and 25 manufacturers. For each of them, we collected its metadata information displayed on *insecam*, and probed it several times a day in the following days to determine its on/off state at that time. In addition, based on the observation that the minimum and maximum values of the IDs assigned by *insecam* for still active IP cameras are 1 and 560,293, respectively, we queried all camera IDs falling within $[1, 570, 000]$ one by one in *insecam*, and finally were able to collect the metadata information for 290,344 IP cameras (28,386 active ones included), for each of which *insecam* still maintains a webpage. We conjecture that *insecam* at least has posted 560,293 unique, vulnerable IP cameras in the past three years since the website was created; currently 290,344 (51.8%) of them still left "crumbs" for us able to track, and the reason why the information about the rest 48.2% cameras is totally missing on *insecam* is still an open question; the currently active IP cameras only occupy at most 5.1% (28,386 out of 560,293) of all IP cameras ever disclosed by *insecam*.

Ethical Consideration. In our study, we collect data from *insecam*, a publicly available website, for 18 days. During our data collection, we did not receive any concerns or get warnings from *insecam*. In addition, we anonymized the collected metadata information before using it for study. We strictly abide by the copyright licenses if present. Therefore, our work will not introduce any additional risk to *insecam* or the owners of the IP cameras listed on *insecam*.

4   Dynamics of *insecam*

We examined the dynamics of *insecam* based on collected data and present the findings as follows.

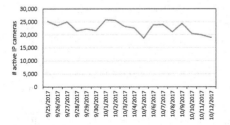

Fig. 1. Daily active IP cameras with dates.

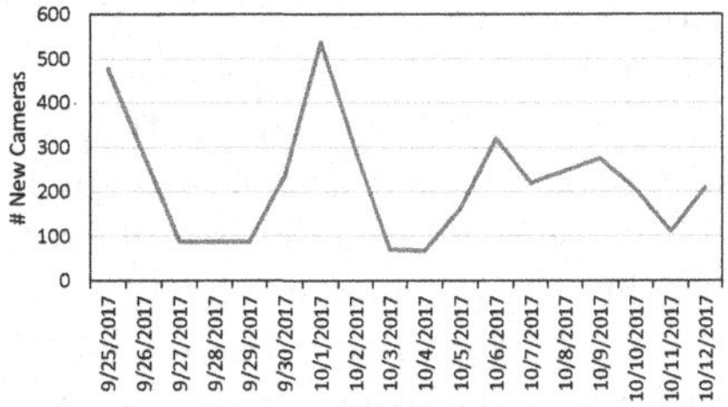

Fig. 2. Daily new IP cameras with dates.

4.1   Daily Active IP Cameras Listed on *Insecam*

Figure 1 shows the number of daily active IP cameras in the time period during which we ran our crawler. We can see that there are about 20,000 to 25,000 active cameras shown on *insecam* each day. Those cameras only represent the tip of the iceberg, since the site administrator claimed to have filtered out all cameras which may invade people's private life. Furthermore, any visitors to *insecam* have direct access to the live video feeds of those cameras from across the world, which suggests a very serious privacy issue caused by IP cameras with no password protection.

4.2   Daily New Cameras Added on *Insecam*

The number of daily new cameras reflects the popularity of *insecam*, to some extent. We also examine how many new cameras are added to *insecam* daily. By new cameras, we mean the cameras which IP addresses are not seen before in our current dataset. It is possible that an IP camera could have a different IP address if DHCP is enabled. Considering the claim made by *insecam* that all IP cameras are manually added, we assume that the use of DHCP would not cause the same IP camera to be given a new camera ID. We reached out to the site admin to confirm but received no response.

Figure 2 shows the number of daily new cameras on *insecam* in the time window we monitored. The daily new camera number varies greatly with date, with the maximum of 537, the minimum of 67, and the average number of 215. Thus, *insecam* seems to have developed quite well since November 2014, at the time *insecam* was rebuked by many medias [8,10,11].

4.3   Top Timezone with Most Cameras Collected on *Insecam*

IP cameras on *insecam* are well organized by timezone. We would like to know which geographic areas contribute most cameras to *insecam*. We confirmed that the geolocation information provided by *insecam* is correct by comparing the geolocation information shown on *insecam* with the information returned by Maxmind for the same IP. Figure 3(a) depicts top 10 timezones with the most IP cameras disclosed on *insecam*. The timezone UTC+01:00, mainly representing Western Europe, contributes the most cameras and has 5,186 active cameras listed on average at a time, occupying 23.1% of all active cameras worldwide. The timezone UTC+02:00, mainly referring to Eastern Europe, comes second, with the average number of 4,522 cameras. The third and fourth timezones are UTC+09:00 (Northeast Asia) and UTC-05:00 (Eastern America), with 2,414 and 2,186 active cameras on average, respectively. In summary, the three geographic regions - Europe, East Asia, and North America - contribute the most IP cameras on *insecam*, 87.4% in total.

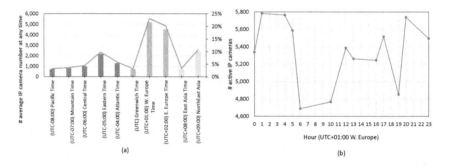

Fig. 3. (a) Top timezones with the most cameras posted on *insecam*. (b) The average number of active IP cameras in the hour of a day in UTC+01:00, West Europe.

4.4   Usage Habit of IP Cameras Within a Day

During our several times of polling of an IP camera within a day, we always observed that a proportion of IP cameras become inaccessible within some time period. We conjecture that the IP camera owners may often turn off their cameras during some time period in a day. Thus, we would like to examine the diurnal pattern of usage of IP cameras within a day.

We analyze the change in the average number of active IP cameras per hour within a single day throughout the 18 days for the timezone UTC+01:00, the one with the most IP cameras on *insecam*, and illustrate the results in Fig. 3(b). It clearly shows that the number of active IP cameras[2] does change with the hour of the day. Specifically, there are more IP cameras to be on during the nighttime

---

[2] Active IP cameras refer to the IP cameras whose video feeds are accessible online.

period from 17:00 in the afternoon to 5:00 in the next early morning, except the time 19:00, probably an outlier. And the active IP camera number peaks at 1:00 am. In contrast, there are fewer IP cameras on in the daytime, from 6:00 to 16:00 in the figure. The finding seems reasonable given that the main purpose of IP cameras is to increase safety and prevent crime.

5   Characterization of *Insecam* IP Cameras

In this section, we examine various characteristics of the IP cameras listed on *insecam*. We want to answer the following questions: (1) what countries are having the most vulnerable IP cameras without password protection, (2) what organizations are hosting those cameras, (3) where are they being installed, (4) what are the manufacturers of those cameras, and (5) what TCP/UDP ports are used by IP cameras for communication to its administrative interface.

5.1   Top Countries and ISPs Contributing *Insecam* IP Cameras

As mentioned before, the currently active IP cameras on *insecam* are from up to 136 countries, that is, 209 IP cameras on average per country. Figure 4(a) shows the top 10 countries which contribute 61.2% IP cameras on *insecam*. United States tops the list and has more than 4,500 IP cameras listed on *insecam*, 22.5% out of all *insecam* cameras. Turkey and Japan come second and third, with 1,604 and 1,303 IP cameras, respectively. It seems that all the top 10 countries are either developed countries or countries with large populations.

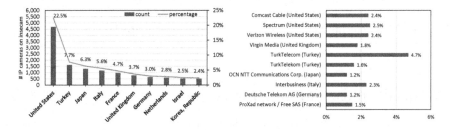

Fig. 4. (a) Top 10 countries contributing the most IP cameras on *insecam*. (b) Top 10 ISP responsible for the IP addresses of *insecam* cameras.

By querying the IP addresses of *insecam* cameras in an online IP geolocation database [5], we obtain the corresponding ISP information. There are 4,094 unique ISPs responsible for the IP addresses of *insecam* cameras. Figure 4(b) provides the top 10 ISPs and their origin countries. Reasonably, the top ISPs belong to the top 10 countries in Fig. 4(a). Specifically, three out of the top 10 ISPs are from United States, which are Comcast, Spectrum, and Verizon. In addition, up to 296 (7.2%) ISPs could be identified to be universities and colleges, from 26 countries.

5.2   Installation Locations of *Insecam* IP Cameras

insecam assigns a tag describing the subject or installation location of the video feed (e.g., animal, street). We verified the correctness of the installation location information provided on *insecam* by manually viewing tens of camera live feeds. Based on the tag information associated with 7,602 IP cameras, we present the distribution of *insecam* IP cameras by installation location in Fig. 5(a). It shows that most IP cameras are being installed in public places such as street, city, beach, mountain, and parking lots, and only a small proportion are deployed in private areas such as pool, office, and house. However, the results do not reflect the whole picture of vulnerable IP cameras in the world, given that *insecam* was almost shut down by authorities in 2014 due to too many private IP cameras being streamed on the site at that time [8,10,11] and that the site administrator claims in the home page that only filtered cameras are available on the site and the site does not stream private or unethical cameras. Nevertheless, the video feeds of a significant proportion of current active *insecam* cameras still contain privacy-sensitive content.

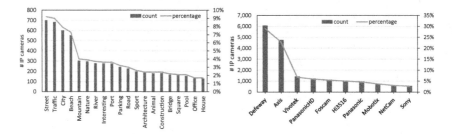

Fig. 5. (a) Top 20 installation places of the *insecam* cameras. (b) Top 10 manufacturers of those *insecam* cameras.

5.3   Manufacturers of *Insecam* Cameras

The complicated manufacturing and distribution chain in the IP camera market has resulted in too many vendors selling IP cameras. We are not sure about how *insecam* gets the manufacturer information of an IP camera or whether such information is correct. But we observe that the access URL to video feeds of an IP camera could be used for fingerprinting the manufacturer information. For instance, axis-cgi/mjpg/video.cgi, the substring of such a URL, indicates that a camera is manufactured by Axis. We manually inspected several pieces of manufacturer information provided by *insecam* and verified that they appear correct. We provide the distribution of those *insecam* IP cameras by manufactures in Fig. 5(b). Among the 20,923 IP cameras with the manufacturer metadata information, the two manufacturers Defeway and Axis dominate the cameras, occupying 29% and 22.7%, respectively. Most other manufacturers occupy no more than 5% each.

5.4   TCP/UDP Ports Used by *Insecam* Cameras

We also examined on which port an *insecam* IP camera is working. Figure 6(a) provides the top 10 most used ports. The top 10 ports are 80-84, 8000, 8080-8082, and 60001. Port 80 (HTTP) is the most used port by IP cameras to communicate to their administrative interface, occupying 32.8%. The uncommon port 60001 comes second, occupying about 15%. Further examination reveals that 96.5% of *insecam* cameras using port 60001 are `Defeway` cameras, which is interesting since the port seems to have the power of fingerprinting the manufacturer of an IP camera and thus could be exploited by miscreants.

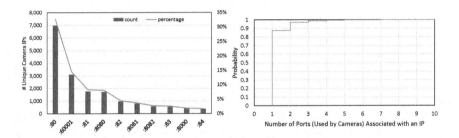

Fig. 6. (a) Top 10 ports used by *insecam* cameras. (b) CDF of the number of ports per IP address of *insecam* cameras.

One IP address could be associated with multiple IP cameras, with each one using a different port. Figure 6(b) gives the cumulative distribution function (CDF) of the number of ports used by IP cameras (i.e., the number of *insecam* IP cameras) associate with one IP address. It shows that 87.5% IP addresses are connected with only one IP camera, about 10% IP addresses are associated with two IP cameras, and 3% IP addresses are with three or more IP cameras. Note that the results represent a lower bound of the number of IP cameras associated with an IP address, since it is probable that an IP address is indeed connected with multiple cameras but only one IP camera gets posted on *insecam*.

5.5   Exhaust Historical IP Cameras Ever Posted on *Insecam*

In addition to the currently available and active IP cameras on *insecam*, we manage to exhaust or at least very close to collect all the history records of IP cameras ever appearing on *insecam*. We were able to collect the metadata information for 290,344 IP cameras (28,386 active ones included), and present the distribution of those cameras by country in Fig. 7(a).

The figure shows the top 10 countries which have the most IP cameras ever disclosed on *insecam* since the creation of *insecam* in September 2014. We can see that 9 out of the 10 countries have had more than 10,000 vulnerable IP cameras posted by *insecam*. `United States` still tops the list, with more than 45,000 IP cameras ever posted. `China` comes second, with more than 25,000 IP cameras

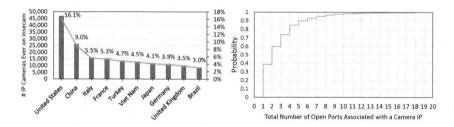

Fig. 7. (a) Top 10 countries ever contributing the most IP cameras on *insecam*. (b) CDF of the number of ports per IP address of *insecam* cameras.

ever listed on the site, which is quite strange given our current observation that only 188 *insecam* IP cameras on average at any specific time are from China. It is still unknown why there is a huge decrease in the number of IP cameras from China on *insecam*. One clue is that the *insecam* administrator points out two ways out for an IP camera, which are either contacting him to remove IP cameras from *insecam* or simply setting the password of the camera. Compared with the current top 10 countries shown in Fig. 4(a), Viet Nam and Brazil also appear in the top 10 countries which contribute the most vulnerable cameras on *insecam* in the past several years.

6   Vulnerability Analysis of Internal Network of IP Cameras

In addition to the vulnerability of no password protection, we would like to explore other possible vulnerabilities of those *insecam* IP cameras from the perspective of an attacker. To this end, we first utilized an IP scanning tool [1] with an attempt to discover the hidden hosts and services co-residing in the same internal network as the vulnerable IP cameras. Specifically, the tool sends probes to an IP address and returns information including (1) whether the host is up, (2) responding TCP and UDP port numbers, (3) services and their versions behind open ports, and so on. We may run the tool on an IP address multiple times to make sure that the host is not down and we can gather the relevant information.

6.1   Open Ports

Number of Open Ports per IP Address. We first examine the open ports associated returned for an IP address. Figure 4(a) depicts the CDF of the number of open ports associate with the IP address of an IP camera. We can see that an IP camera often has several other open ports. Specifically, 38.5% IP addresses seems to be exclusively used for IP cameras; more than 60% IP addresses have at least two open ports; about 40% IP addresses have three or more open ports; about 10% IP addresses have at least 6 open ports. On average, an IP address has 3 open ports. 31 IP addresses have more than 100 open ports, and 14 IP addresses have more than 200 open ports.

Remote Access Ports. In addition, we paid special attention to the services (mainly SSH and TELNET) which tend to be exploited by attackers for malicious activities such as DDoS attacks. Mirai, the IoT-based botnet that took the Internet by storm in late 2016, was found to harvest bots by sending probes on TCP ports 22 (SSH) and 23 (TELNET) [14]. In our test, 22.4% of alive hosts (i.e., responding to pings) have ports 22 and/or 23 open. These remote access ports make those IP cameras vulnerable to the Mirai-like attacks.

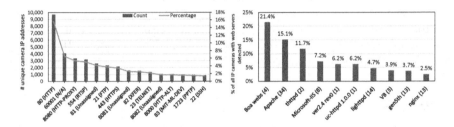

Fig. 8. (a) Top 15 most common open ports on the host of an *insecam* camera. Words in parentheses denote the corresponding protocols or services running on the ports. (b) Top 10 most popular web servers of *insecam* IP cameras. Numbers in parentheses denote the number of web server versions.

Most Common Open Ports. Figure 8(a) shows the top 15 most common open ports on the host of an *insecam* IP camera. Compared to Fig. 6(a), there are many more kinds of port numbers (services) commonly accessible on the host, such as 21 (FTP), 22 (SSH), 23 (TELNET), 443 (HTTPS), 554 (RTSP), and 1723 (PPTP). Some services are directly related to IP cameras, including HTTPS, RTSP, and PPTP, while some could be easily exploited by attackers as a pivot point to the internal network, such as FTP, SSH, and TELNET, especially when the co-residing IP cameras could be directly accessed due to no password protection.

6.2 Web Servers

With the help of the IP scanning tool, we are able to detect a total of 300 different versions of web servers use by 2,564 IP cameras. The different versions of web servers were then aggregated to the web server software. Figure 8(b) shows the top 10 web server software used by IP cameras. Numbers in parentheses denote the number of web server versions used. Specifically, four different versions of Boa web server software are used most, about 21.4%. Apache HTTP server is also prevalent, and up to 34 versions were used by 15.1% IP cameras. The thttpd web server software comes third, with 11.7% rate.

Furthermore, we studied the release dates of the popular versions of web servers as well as the number of known CVE (Common Vulnerabilities and Exposures) vulnerabilities contained in them. We found that nearly all those cameras were running extremely old and vulnerable web server software. For example, the most popular web server software, Boa, has been discontinued since 2005 [3]. Most popular web servers have been found to bear a significant number of CVE vulnerabilities. Specifically, all 34 versions of Apache HTTP server have 3 to 49 vulnerabilities, and 19 vulnerabilities on average [2]. All the two thttpd web server versions contain 2 to 3 vulnerabilities. All 8 Microsoft IIS versions contain 1 to 9 vulnerabilities, and 5 on average. 84.6% (11 out of 13) nginx web server versions used have 1 to 3 known vulnerabilities. Such vulnerabilities could include authentication bypass vulnerability, cross-site scripting (XSS) vulnerability, buffer overflow, directory traversal, and many other vulnerability types. They allow attackers to gain administrator access and execute arbitrarily malicious code on IP cameras and other internal network devices.

7   Related Work

Previous studies on IP cameras are the most related works. Stanislav et al. [19] conducted a case study on baby monitor exposures and vulnerabilities. They found that most vulnerabilities and exposures are trivial to exploit by a competent attacker and can only be effectively mitigated by disabling the device and applying a firmware update. Albrecht et al. [12] presented a real-world hacking incident that the baby monitor was hacked and then turned on the owners, and provided precautions to reduce the chance of getting hacked. Campbell [16] focused on the vulnerability analysis of the authentication mechanisms of IP cameras, discussed potential attacks, and presented mitigation solutions. Costin [17] reviewed the threats and attacks against video surveillance systems at different levels and provided a set of recommendations to increase the security of those systems. Nearly all above works aim to provide a good summary of existing attacks and possible mitigation solutions, but none of them conduct a deep, large-scale quantitative analysis of vulnerable IP cameras as we do.

Many other works studied security issues in general IoT systems or in other IoT devices. Amokrane [13] reviewed security challenges and attack surface in IoT. The author showcased the accessibility of IoT attack surface with several real-world cases on exploitation and attacking IoT devices. Apthorpe et al. [15] investigated the privacy vulnerability of encrypted IoT traffic and found that the network traffic rate of IoT devices can reveal user activities even when the traffic is encrypted. Rotenberg et al. [18] performed an evaluation of authentication bypass vulnerabilities in SOHO (Small Office/Home Office) routers and found that a significant number of routers could be potentially taken control over by attackers due to misconfiguration issues. Our work focuses on estimating the size of vulnerable IP cameras and characterizing them.

8   Conclusion

IP cameras have come prevalent in our everyday lives. The need for comprehending and solving various security and privacy issues surrounding IP cameras has become pressing. Our work represents one of such efforts. In this paper, we conducted a large-scale comprehensive measurement study of IP cameras without password protection. We collected data from *insecam*, the world biggest directory of live IP cameras without password protection. We first studied the dynamics of the site, then performed a detailed characteristic analysis on those IP cameras, and finally conducted vulnerability analysis of the internal networks where IP cameras reside. Our work produces a serials of interesting findings, which are expected to provide valuable knowledge of the current threat landscape that IP cameras are facing.

Acknowledgement. We would like to thank our shepherd Mark Gondree and anonymous reviewers for their insightful and detailed comments. This work was partially supported by Microsoft Research Asia, CCF-NSFOCUS Kunpeng Research Fund, and Alipay Research Fund. Any opinions, findings, and conclusions or recommendations expressed in this material are those of the authors and do not necessarily reflect the views of the funding agencies. The co-author F. Xu is the contact author.

References

1. Angry IP Scanner. http://angryip.org/
2. Apache web server CVE vulnerabilities. https://goo.gl/FaWh8y
3. Boa (web server): https://goo.gl/6d251V
4. Breaking Down Mirai: An IoT DDoS Botnet Analysis. https://goo.gl/7VcfMh
5. DB-IP: IP Geolocation and Network Intelligence. https://db-ip.com/
6. How Many Time Zones Are There? https://goo.gl/fWwFxQ
7. Insecam - World biggest online cameras directory. http://www.insecam.org/
8. Insecam Displays Unsecured Webcams Worldwide. https://goo.gl/hBqpni
9. The Botnet That Broke the Internet Isn't Going Away. https://goo.gl/VqFi7f
10. Webcam 'creepshot' pictures shared on Reddit. https://goo.gl/ffKtTK
11. Website spies on thousands of people. https://goo.gl/SdbVcc
12. Albrecht, K., Mcintyre, L.: Privacy nightmare: when baby monitors go bad [opinion]. IEEE Technol. Soc. Mag. **34**(3), 14–19 (2015)
13. Amokrane, A.: Internet of things: security issues, challenges and directions. In: C&ESAR 2016, p. 70 (2016)
14. Antonakakis, M., et al.: Understanding the mirai botnet. In: USENIX Security 2017 (2017)
15. Apthorpe, N., Reisman, D., Feamster, N.: A smart home is no castle: privacy vulnerabilities of encrypted IoT traffic. arXiv preprint arXiv:1705.06805 (2017)
16. Campbell, W.: Security of internet protocol cameras-a case example (2013)
17. Costin, A.: Security of CCTV and video surveillance systems: threats, vulnerabilities, attacks, and mitigations. In: TrustED, pp. 45–54. ACM (2016)
18. Rotenberg, N., Shulman, H., Waidner, M., Zeltser, B.: Authentication-bypass vulnerabilities in SOHO routers. In: SIGCOMM Posters and Demos (2017)
19. Stanislav, M., Beardsley, T.: Hacking IoT: a case study on baby monitor exposures and vulnerabilities. Rapid 7 (2015)

RARE: A Systematic Augmented Router Emulation for Malware Analysis

Ahmad Darki$^{(\boxtimes)}$, Chun-Yu Chuang$^{(\boxtimes)}$, Michalis Faloutsos$^{(\boxtimes)}$,
Zhiyun Qian$^{(\boxtimes)}$, and Heng Yin$^{(\boxtimes)}$

University of California, Riverside, CA, USA
{adark001,cchua010}@ucr.edu, {michalis,zhiyunq,heng}@cs.ucr.edu

Abstract. How can we analyze and profile the behavior of a router malware? This is the motivating question behind our work focusing on router. Router-specific malware has emerged as a new vector for hackers, but has received relatively little attention compared to malware on other devices. A key challenge in analyzing router malware is getting it to activate, which is hampered by the diversity of firmware of various vendors and a plethora of different platforms. We propose, RARE, a systematic approach to analyze router malware and profile its behavior focusing on home-office routers. The key novelty is the intelligent augmented operation of our emulation that manages to fool malware binaries to activate irrespective of their target platform. This is achieved by leveraging two key capabilities: (a) a static level analysis that informs the dynamic execution, and (b) an iterative feedback loop across a series of dynamic executions, whose output informs the subsequent executions. From a practical point of view, RARE has the ability to: (a) instantiate an emulated router with or without malware, (b) replay arbitrary network traffic, (c) monitor and interact with the malware in a semi-automated way. We evaluate our approach using 221 router-specific malware binaries. First, we show that our method works: we get 94% of the binaries to activate, including obfuscated ones, which is a nine-fold increase compared to the 10% success ratio of the baseline method. Second, we show that our method can extract useful information towards understanding and profiling the botnet behavior: (a) we identify 203 unique IP addresses of C&C servers, and (b) we observe an initial spike and an overall 50% increase in the number of system calls on infected routers.

1 Introduction

Compromising routers is emerging as a new type of threat with potentially devastating effects [24]. For example, on October 2016, in Mirai botnet attack there has been a series of DDoS attacks on *Dyn, Inc.* servers using IoT devices including routers [2]. The lack of mature protection technologies makes this a fertile ground for attacks. We argue that a compromised router provides significant new capabilities to an attacker, beyond those of a compromised end-device. By compromising a router, the attacker can: (a) access or block the network packets

© Springer International Publishing AG, part of Springer Nature 2018
R. Beverly et al. (Eds.): PAM 2018, LNCS 10771, pp. 60–72, 2018.
https://doi.org/10.1007/978-3-319-76481-8_5

going through it, (b) steal cookies and session IDs [25] to impersonate the user or compromise her privacy, and (c) hijack and redirect communication via a DNS redirection to rogue DNS server.

Attacking and protecting routers is significantly different compared to laptops and desktops, therefore new methods and tools are needed. First, routers have limited resources in terms of CPU, and memory. Therefore, malware developers have less resources in their disposition. However, the same challenges apply to the security solutions as well. Second, routers have variable device configurations [16] that decreases the applicability of both malware, and system analysis tools. The former is a challenge for malware authors, while the latter is a challenge for any emulation capability, which needs to pretend to be many different configurations in order to get firmware and malware to run. Finally, many, if not most, router firmware are proprietary, and thus difficult to emulate [6].

Our goal in this paper is to fully understand router malware binaries and their operation focusing on off-the-self home-office routers. The desired output of this work is two-fold. First, we want to analyze the malware in order to create an environment that will "fool" it to activate and reveal its behavior. Second, we want to profile and distinguish the behavior of an infected router from that of a benign one. The overarching challenge is the plethora of proprietary firmware and hardware router configurations, as we mentioned above. In addition, there is a scarcity of tools for static analysis for MIPS and ARM architectures, which are the most common platforms for routers. Such tools could have helped inform the emulation environment. As we will see below, a straightforward emulation attempt could have a very low success rate in fooling the malware to activate.

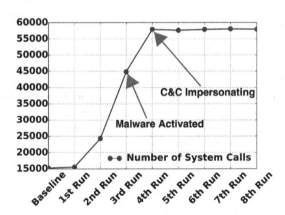

Fig. 1. RARE gets the router malware to activate and communicate with the C&C server in the 3rd run of its iterative operation. We plot the number of system calls for each 1300 s of a run. The baseline approach is shown first. The 1st run of RARE is an emulation informed by the static analysis only. Each subsequent run is informed by the previous run.

Router malware has received relatively little attention compared to malware on other devices. We can distinguish the following areas of research: (a) developing emulator capabilities [4,13,17,27], (b) vulnerability analysis for embedded devices, [6,10,11,14], and (c) malware analysis focusing on PC and smartphone based malware [9,20–22]. We discuss related work in Sect. 4.

We propose, RARE (Riverside's Augmented Router Emulator), a systematic approach to analyze router malware and understand its behavior in depth. The key novelty is the augmented operation of our approach, which fools malware binaries to activate irrespective of their preferred target platform. In other words, instead of trying to guess the right router platform for each malware, we start with a generic one and we carefully and iteratively "adapt" it to fool the malware. This is achieved by leveraging two key capabilities: (a) a static level analysis that informs the dynamic execution, and (b) an iterative feedback loop across a series of dynamic runs, the output of which informs the subsequent run. We provide an overview of our approach in Fig. 2.

From a practical point of view, RARE has the ability to run the malware on an emulated router and consists of the following modules, whose goal is to: (a) extract information for malware execution by analyzing the binary statically, (b) create an emulated router enhanced with the appropriate configurations that a malware needs for its execution, (c) inject malware into the router and fool it to activate, (d) replay pre-recorded network traffic with crafted C&C responses to malware requests, (e) enhance the emulation using information derived from the previous runs. This process works in an iterative fashion to enhance the emulation using information from previous runs in order to have the malware to activate itself.

We evaluate our approach using 221 router-specific malware binaries from a community-based project, which requested to be anonymous. Our results can be summarized in the following points.

a. Achieving 94% malware activation success ratio, and 88.8% for obfuscated malware. We show that our system is successful in fooling malware to activate, as **94%** of our binaries become active. We say that a malware binary activates, when the malware attempts to communicate with the C&C server. By contrast, an emulation without any of our augmented functions, which we refer to as **baseline**, can activate only 10% of the binaries. Furthermore, our approach manages to activate 88.8% of our obfuscated binaries, which are the types of binaries that are especially crafted to outplay static analysis techniques. We show the iterative operation of our approach in Fig. 1, where we plot the number of system calls for each run. Note that the malware is activated within a sandboxed environment and thus does not pose any threat to real devices.

b. Extracting useful information: IP addresses, and domains. Having this powerful capability, we are able to extract useful information for the malware. We find **203 malicious IP addresses and domains**, and we naturally consider these addresses to be malicious, since they are or have been used for botnet communications. Note that using just static analysis, we find less than 25% of these C&C communication addresses and domain names.

c. Developing infected router profiles. We identify features for detecting infected routers. Specifically, we observe an initial spike and a 50% increase in the number of system calls in infected routers. We also observe an initial large spike and a subsequent slight increase in the number of active processes.

Our emulation capability is a powerful building block towards understanding router malware. As a preview of the capabilities provided by RARE, we discuss how we assumed the botmaster role for two malware binaries at the end of Sect. 3. Finally, we intend to make our tool, the malware binaries, and the data traces available upon request to researchers.

2   System Design and Implementation

We present an overview and highlight the novel capabilities of our approach.

Philosophy. We adopt the following approach: we start with a general purpose platform and learn what the malware needs to activate through a sequence of executions.

A visual depiction of RARE is shown in Fig. 2. The key capabilities of the system are listed below: (a) it can perform static analysis on the malware to extract information for its execution, (b) it can instantiate an emulated router with hints on what configurations the malware wants to "see", (c) it can replay arbitrary network traffic and response to malware requests, and (d) it can monitor the malware and provide information to subsequent runs of the same malware. If the malware fails to activate, we repeat the process, and the last step provides information that guides the new execution.

Defining success: malware activation. We set as our goal for the emulation the activation of malware: we want the malware to feel "comfortable" within the emulator, so as to attempt to contact its bot-master. After reaching this point,

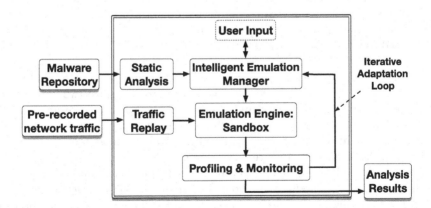

Fig. 2. Overview of the key components of our approach. A key novelty is the feedback loop that enables previous runs of the malware to inform the subsequent run in order to fool the malware to activate.

we enter a new stage: if the C&C server responds, the malware will enter a stand by mode waiting for C&C commands. We define this stage as "activated" stage of the malware. A subsequent goal is to turn one's self into the bot-master, by reverse engineering the communication protocol with the bot, which we achieve for some of our binaries (see the discussion in Sect. 3).

We present the key functionality, novelty and challenges of each module.

a. Static Analysis Module. The first step is to analyze a given malware binary statically to extract as much information as possible. The purpose is dual: (a) we want to inform the dynamic execution, and (b) we want to understand as much about the malware, which could have independent interest. Specifically, this module provides the following information to the dynamic execution: (a) IP addresses and domains that malware will possibly contact, and (b) files and resources that the malware will attempt to access. This information is collected by the Intelligent Execution module and is provided to the Emulation Engine module. In more detail, we currently use IDA-Pro [18] for the static analysis, but one could envision using other tools with similar capabilities. In addition, we developed an initial capability to extract the high level structure of the code by lifting the binaries to Intermediate Representation [26], which could provide data dependencies. The IDA-Pro tool is an excellent foundation, but so some of the desired functionality was missing. Therefore, we developed several non-trivial plug-ins, specifically for MIPS and ARM architectures, such as extensions to extract communication tokens, and control flow information which are the main components that assists this module. Naturally, we will make our plugins available to the community.

b. Emulation Engine Module. This module provides the basic capabilities for emulating the router with the provided augmenting information and records execution traces. This module can: (a) instantiate an emulated router, (b) inject malware into the router, (c) replay pre-recorded network traffic or crafted C&C responses for the malware requests, (d) receive commands and information from the Intelligent Emulation malware in order to convince the malware to activate. The emulation is hosted in an Ubuntu server and QEMU [5] (an open source and widely used tool) is used to emulate the router hardware of interest, which here is ARM and MIPS.

We have made significant extensions and engineering in order to enable all the functionality. For example, we modify QEMU to recognize two subnets to represent the enterprise network and the rest of the Internet. We also added the ability to interact with the router through the network interfaces connecting to subnets, which is further discussed in the Traffic Replay module. For the firmware of the instantiated router, we use OpenWrt [1], which is fairly widely used codebase and it is considered as a reference firmware for routers. OpenWrt has the essential basic modules of a home router such as DHCP server, packet forwarding and routing, and a web interface. We added the monitoring capabilities to the instantiated router to collect execution traces for the router for further behavioral analysis, which we discuss in the Profiling and Monitoring module.

c. Intelligent Emulation Manager. The key novelty of RARE is represented by the Intelligent Emulation Manager module. This module drives the emulation in a way that achieves malware activation. First, it uses information from static and dynamic analysis in the previous two modules. The intelligence of the emulation is based on a feedback loop that gets execution information from each run. Every run is a clean start of the router augmented with information about the malwares requirement to fully execute itself. This loop represents the learning process of our approach. Second, the module facilitates the manual interaction with the malware, such as crafting C&C responses.

d. Traffic Replay Module. To observe a router in its natural element, we developed the Traffic Replay module, for replaying arbitrary network traffic to the router. Our module can get a real trace of two directions, incoming and outgoing, and replay it through the emulated router. This module is built on top of `tcpreplay` [3], but significantly we added new functionality. For example, the concept of incoming and outgoing traffic needed significant engineering, as it was not fully provided by tcpreplay. We also needed to take care of implementation issues, such as timing the replay traffic through the router. The network traffic we use is real traffic data from project *MAWI* [7], ensuring that we capture the beginning of each TCP flow across different days and different hours. Another key feature in this module is its ability to inject traffic at the command of the Intelligent Emulation Manager. This allows us to impersonate the C&C server by providing server responses and commands. In other words, our approach combines the knowledge of who the malware attempts to talk to, and what the malware expects to hear, through the deep profiling in the Static Analysis and Profiling and Monitoring modules, and we expect to be able to fully explore the intention and capability of the malware.

e. Profiling and Monitoring Module. This module synthesizes information from the static analysis and dynamic executions with the following goals. We want to: (a) understand the malware in order to create an environment that will make it to activate, and (b) profile the behavior of the infected router in order to distinguish it from that of a benign one. We list the types of data that this module collects and analyzes.

– Network Traffic: The module collects the network traces for both router interfaces (think incoming and outgoing) and analyzes them. The goal is to observe packets and flows generated by the malware, so that we can respond to them as if we are the C&C server. We can determine if a packet is generated by the malware by comparing the log files of the execution with and without the malware.
– OS System Calls: The module also collects the system calls at the operating system level. The goal is to extract information for augmenting the next iteration of the emulation. For example, the malware usually checks for existence of different files in the system as a means to infer which platform it is operating on. Another family of malware uses the */proc/sysinfo* file to infer the CPU architecture, while in another family they use `banner` file.

– System Processes: The module also monitors the processes in the router, which provides a complementary view on the behavior and intentions of the malware. For example, several malware binaries kill: (a) processes in the router in order to free up resources for themselves, (b) security processes, such as the `iptable` firewall process, and (c) user access processes, such as the `http server` process.

This module initiates the feedback-loop by providing the information to the Intelligent Emulation Manager to ensure that it can "fool" the malware to reveal itself and even believe that it is communicating with its C&C server.

Finally, this high-level description of our approach can be seen as a blueprint for a router malware analysis tool. Although in RARE, we have made specific implementation decisions for each module, functions and methodologies can be modified and replaced easily due to its modular design.

3   Evaluation

We evaluate our method to assess the effectiveness of RARE in activating the malware and profiling the behavior of malware.

The malware binaries. In our evaluation, we use malware binaries that were collected from a community-based project, that requested to stay anonymous. These sources use honeypot and manual effort to collect these malware binaries. We have a total of 221 unique malware binaries targeting MIPS Big Endian (BE), MIPS Little Endian (LE), and ARM architectures. We focus on these architectures given that they are the most common ones in routers.

Network traffic. A key feature of our emulation is that we can do experiments using arbitrary network traffic. We report results with real network traffic from `MAWI` [8] with a duration of 1300 s. Note that we have experimented with other data traces, and also observed the router with no traffic at all. We obtained qualitative similar results, which we do not report here due to space limitations.

The baseline approach. We define the baseline approach, as an emulation using the RARE infrastructure (OpenWrt over QEMU) but without any of the intelligence of our approach. We inject the malware in such an instance of an emulated router, and we monitor its behavior as the traffic passes through.

Evaluation. For each malware and data trace, we compare the following approaches in executions with and without the malware: (a) Baseline run: which is the approach described above. (b) RARE run: The emulation gets augmented with the information extracted from the malware in each run. We define each execution as k^{th} run, being 1st emulation informed by *Static Analysis* module and later runs informed by the behavior observed in the previous run.

Defining failure: no malware activation by the 6th run. Setting a high standard for our approach, we require that we achieve malware activation by the sixth run. If this does not happen, we consider this a failure.

A. Evaluating RARE: 94% malware activation success. Using our tool we have been able to reach activation for 208 malware binaries out of 221. Table 1 details this success by comparing RARE with baseline approach. We report the average number of runs that RARE needed in order to reach activation for the binaries in that group that reach activation. We see that RARE requires a relatively low number of repetitions on average, namely three. We also separate the malware based on the target architecture: ARM, MIPS BE, and MIPS LE.

Table 1. The success ratio of our solution RARE compared to a baseline method.

	Binaries	Baseline		RARE		
		Raw No.	Percentage	Raw No.	Percentage	Avg. Runs
All	221	**23**	**10.4%**	**208**	**94.1%**	3
Obfuscated	45	**5**	**11.1%**	**40**	**88.8%**	3
ARM	101	11	10.9%	91	90.1%	3
MIPS BE	77	6	7.8%	75	97.4%	2
MIPS LE	43	6	14%	42	97.6%	3

RARE exhibits great performance even for obfuscated malware. We compare the two approaches on 45 obfuscated malware binaries, as, for these binaries, static analysis cannot be used. Although there is a drop, our approach maintains a success ratio of 88.8%.

What does the malware need to activate? We observe an interesting and systematic progression in the types of requests that the malware generates. In the first few runs, the malware binaries typically attempt to change or check the existence of files, such as configuration files such as /etc/ISP_name or web interface files from *Linksys* and TP-Link routers, which are found specifically in home routers routers or specific brands of routers. Subsequently, some binaries attempt to tamper with different routing services, such as libnss and DNS, or change the routing table to subvert traffic. Typically, in the last run before the activation stage, the malware tries to resolve the hostname to locate its C&C server. In response, we inject DNS lookup responses using our Traffic Replay module. Note that, in our system, we retrieve the request that led to the failure using the Profiling and Monitoring module, we prepare for the subsequent run accordingly. As an example, when running one of the binaries an HTTP request to userRpm/SoftwareUpgradeRpm.htm (part of the TP-Link web interface) is observed which tampers with the installed firmware on the router. Failure to respond to this request will interrupt malware's execution. Using the Intelligent Emulation Manager module the appropriate web interface is installed for the next clean run of the router emulation.

Why do some malware fail to activate? This is an open question, which we will continue to investigate in our future work. In many of the malware requests listed above, we are able to provide a fake answer or a fake file. In most of the

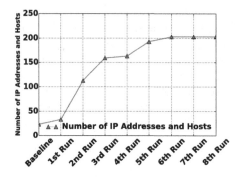
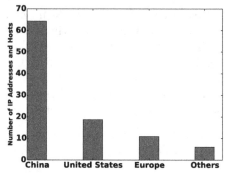

Fig. 3. The number of extracted IP addresses and hosts rises with every run.

Fig. 4. Distribution of the geolocation of the detected IP addresses.

cases where we fail to do so, the malware tries to dynamically link to a custom library, which are not publicly available. Furthermore, these malware binaries are usually obfuscated, so faking the libraries is not straightforward.

B. Extracting useful information: 203 botnet IP addresses/hosts. We highlight initial elements of the information that we can extract with our approach. Overall, we find that RARE finds 203 malicious entities, IP addresses and host names, which are used used by the malware for botnet communications.

Static analysis: 48 addresses and hosts. Using static analysis, we traversed the CFG for all the paths from binary's *Entry Point* to system call `connect` and traced the input arguments values. We were able to extract 22 unique IP addresses and 26 host names.

RARE dynamic analysis: 155 addresses and hosts. Using RARE's consecutive runs, we extracted an additional 155 IP addresses and hosts. As shown in Fig. 3 with every run the number of extracted IP addresses and hosts rises until the 6th run after which no new IP or hosts are detected.

The dynamic analysis finds 75% of the malicious entities. The corollary of the observations above is that the dynamic analysis is essential in detecting malicious entities of botnet communication. Using just static analysis, we find less than 25% of these C&C communication addresses and domain names. The issue is that the malware often obfuscates the addresses and the domain names, by using hexadecimal numbers and using number transformation and encryption techniques. For example, one binary has the following address generation approach: a hardcoded hexadecimal base value, and a function that adds decimals values to this base to obtain a series of IP addresses.

What is the geographical distribution of these malicious Internet entities? In Fig. 4, we do a reverse look up to identify the geolocation of the IP addresses, and we observe that China (64.3%) and United States (18.7%) are the top destinations for hosting C&C servers. Many times these botnet entities could be compromised machines. In Fig. 3, we plot the number of malicious IP addresses extracted at each run of RARE. Initially, more information is extracted with each run, but this stops by the sixth or seventh execution for most binaries. In future work we intend to study the uniqueness and timeliness of the IP addresses that we find compare to well known blacklists.

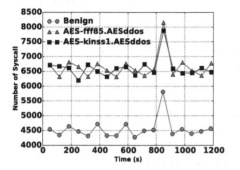

Fig. 5. The number of system calls of a benign and two infected routers for the last 1200 s of the execution. The infected routers have consistently 1.5 times more system calls.

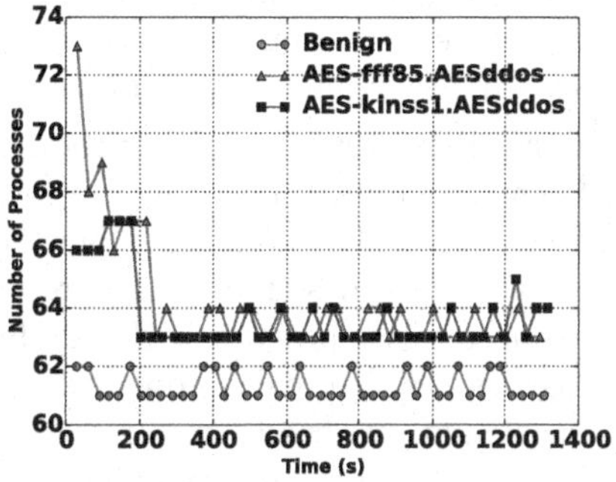

Fig. 6. The number of active processes of a benign and two infected routers for our 1300 s experiment. Initially, the malware spawns child processes to make itself persistent.

C. Profiling infected router behavior. Our approach gives us the ability to compare the behavior of non-infected and infected router with a rich set of information at both the network and OS layers.

In all malware, we observe an increase in the number of system calls of almost 50% or more in an infected router compared to a benign one. Figure 1 shows a comparison of the number of system calls between infected router using the baseline, and the different RARE executions (numbers 1 to 8). This particular malware binary, reaches the activation stage at the third run. On the fourth run, we impersonate the C&C and we start issuing commands to the malware.

To better understand the malware, we show the number of system calls over time for two infected routers compared to a benign one in Fig. 5. For visual clarity, we show only 1200 s of the execution to avoid the huge initial spike, which corresponds typically to the reconnaissance of each malware. However, we do show the initial spike in the number of processes of an infected router in Fig. 6: the malware makes itself persistent by spawning child processes.

Discussion: Becoming the botmaster. Using RARE we identify the functions available on two of the malware binaries from MIPS LE and MIPS BE. This was achieved by combining the static analysis and profiling information after the execution. We were able to convince the malware that we are the botmaster, and we were able to have it do: (1) HTTP flooding, (2) reverse shell, and (3) kill processes based on their process ID.

4   Related Work

We briefly review related work due to space limitations.

Emulation techniques: Several emulation techniques and tools exist, but they mostly focus on PC and Android platforms: `Anubis` [4], `PANDA` [12], `DECAF` [17]. The approach is to simulate the target platform and apply monitoring tools to record the execution traces of the malware. PC and Android platforms and malware differ significantly from router-specific ones, which is our focus here.

Vulnerability detection in embedded systems: Several recent studies focus on detecting vulnerabilities in the firmware of embedded devices [6,10]. Chen et al. [6] argue that emulating platforms for specific firmware is not a trivial task since it includes emulating hardware components designed by vendors who do not necessarily practice a global Hardware/Software design standard. Other approaches [28] use real hardware to overcome this difficulty, but introduce the high cost and overhead. In our case, with thousands of router configurations, this approach would be very expensive and time consuming.

PC and smartphone malware studies: Many studies propose malware analysis tools using static or dynamic analysis. In static analysis, several studies focus on Control Flow Graphs characteristics [9,19]. Static analysis on binary code requires platform specific tools, so PC-based or smartphone bases tools do not work for ARM and MIPs platforms. A limitation of the static analysis is that it does not work for obfuscated malware [23]. Several studies use dynamic analysis to classify and distinguish between different families of malware by studying the operation at the OS level [15,20,22]. In the PC and smartphone space, getting the malware to activate is an easier task given the more limited diversity in these platforms.

5   Conclusion

We propose, RARE, a comprehensive approach to analyze router malware. The key novelty is the augmented operation of our approach: instead of trying to guess the right router platform for each malware, we start with a generic one and we iteratively "adapt" it to fool the malware.

Our system provide the following key capabilities: (a) perform static analysis on the malware, (b) instantiate an emulated router, (c) inject malware into the router and fool it to activate, (d) replay arbitrary network traffic, and (e) profile the malware behavior. Using real router malware, we are able to show that: (a) our system works effectively and manages to activate 94% of all our binaries, and (b) we can extract useful and insightful information from the execution of the malware. First, we find that we can identify malicious IP addresses and domain names, which subsequently could be investigated and blocked in firewall filters. Second, we identify tell-tale signs of an infected router operation, such as 50% increase of the system calls.

Our approach is a solid first step towards developing a key capability for an under-served segment of devices. Although the results are already promising, we plan on expanding the capabilities significantly in two different dimensions. First, we will develop a more extensive static analysis capability, where we could infer the structure and key operations of the malware code. Second, we will further explore how to fully interact, and ultimately control both a bot, but ultimately a C&C server.

References

1. Openwrt embedded devices linux. https://openwrt.org/. Accessed 22 Sep 2017
2. Antonakakis, M., et al.: Understanding the Mirai botnet. In: 26th USENIX Security Symposium (USENIX Security 2017) (2017)
3. Appneta: Tcpreplay (2016). http://tcpreplay.appneta.com/
4. Bayer, U., et al.: Dynamic analysis of malicious code. J. Comput. Virol. **2**(1), 67–77 (2006)
5. Bellard, F.: QEMU, a fast and portable dynamic translator. In: USENIX, FREENIX Track (2005)
6. Chen, D.D., Woo, M., Brumley, D., Egele, M.: Towards automated dynamic analysis for linux-based embedded firmware. In: NDSS (2016)
7. Cho, K., Mitsuya, K., Kato, A.: Traffic data repository maintained by the MAWI working group of the wide project (2005). http://mawi.wide.ad.jp/mawi
8. Cho, K., et al.: Traffic data repository at the wide project. In: USENIX, ATEC (2000)
9. Christodorescu, M., Jha, S.: Static analysis of executables to detect malicious patterns. Technical report, Wisconsin Univ-Madison Department of Computer Sciences (2006)
10. Costin, A., et al.: Automated dynamic firmware analysis at scale: a case study on embedded web interfaces. In: Asia CCS (2016)
11. Costin, A., Zaddach, J., Francillon, A., Balzarotti, D., Antipolis, S.: A large-scale analysis of the security of embedded firmwares. In: USENIX Security (2014)
12. Dolan-Gavitt, B., et al.: Tappan zee (north) bridge: mining memory accesses for introspection. In: ACM SIGSAC CCS. ACM (2013)
13. Enck, W., et al.: Taintdroid: an information-flow tracking system for realtime privacy monitoring on smartphones. ACM TOCS **32**, 5 (2014)
14. Feng, Q., et al.: Scalable graph-based bug search for firmware images. In: ACM SIGSAC CCS (2016)
15. Gasparis, I., Qian, Z., Song, C., Krishnamurthy, S.V.: Detecting android root exploits by learning from root providers. In: USENIX Security (2017)
16. Hampton, N., et al.: A survey and method for analysing soho router firmware currency. In: Australian Information Security Management Conference (2015)
17. Henderson, A., et al.: Make it work, make it right, make it fast: building a platform-neutral whole-system dynamic binary analysis platform. In: ACM STA (2014)
18. Hex-Rays: IDA pro disassembler (2008)
19. Kinable, J., Kostakis, O.: Malware classification based on call graph clustering. J. Comput. Virol. **7**, 233–245 (2011)
20. Kolbitsch, C., et al.: Effective and efficient malware detection at the end host. In: USENIX Security Symposium (2009)
21. Kolbitsch, C., Holz, T., Kruegel, C., Kirda, E.: Inspector gadget: automated extraction of proprietary gadgets from malware binaries. In: IEEE S&P (2010)

22. Lanzi, A., et al.: Accessminer: using system-centric models for malware protection. In: ACM CCS (2010)
23. Moser, A., et al.: Limits of static analysis for malware detection. In: IEEE ACSAC (2007)
24. Papp, D., et al.: Embedded systems security: threats, vulnerabilities, and attack taxonomy. In: IEEE PST (2015)
25. Paquet-Clouston, M., et al.: Can we trust social media data?: Social network manipulation by an IoT botnet. In: ACM Conference on Social Media & Society (2017)
26. Song, D., Brumley, D., Yin, H., Caballero, J., Jager, I., Kang, M.G., Liang, Z., Newsome, J., Poosankam, P., Saxena, P.: BitBlaze: a new approach to computer security via binary analysis. In: Sekar, R., Pujari, A.K. (eds.) ICISS 2008. LNCS, vol. 5352, pp. 1–25. Springer, Heidelberg (2008). https://doi.org/10.1007/978-3-540-89862-7_1
27. Tam, K., et al.: Copperdroid: automatic reconstruction of android malware behaviors. In: NDSS (2015)
28. Zaddach, J., Bruno, L., Francillon, A., Balzarotti, D.: Avatar: a framework to support dynamic security analysis of embedded systems' firmwares. In: NDSS (2014)

Revisiting the Privacy Implications of Two-Way Internet Latency Data

Brian Trammell$^{(\boxtimes)}$ and Mirja Kühlewind

Networked Systems Group, ETH Zurich, Zurich, Switzerland
`trammell@tik.ee.ethz.ch`

Abstract. The Internet measurement community is increasingly sensitive to the privacy implications of both active and passive measurement. Research into the drawbacks of network data anonymization has led the community to investigate data sharing techniques, as well as to focus on active measurements and active measurement datasets. A key metric in these datasets is round-trip-time (RTT) as measured e.g. by `ping` or `traceroute`. This paper examines the assumption that the analysis of Internet RTT data is safe for open research by posing the question: what potentually-private inferences can be made about a remote target given periodic latency measurements from known vantage points under one's control? We explore the risks to end-user privacy both through a review of diverse literature touching on the subject as well as on the analysis of RTT data from fixed and mobile Internet measurement infrastruture. While we find that the common assumption of safety generally holds, we explore caveats and give recommendations for mitigation in those cases where it may not.

1 Introduction

The Internet measurement research community has long been concerned with the privacy impact of its measurements on the end users of the Internet. The personally-identifiable nature of IP addresses, for example, as it is linkable to end-user activity, is well-understood, and even a subject of current regulation[1], with a body of literature on anonymization techniques [1] and the effectiveness thereof [2] to protect this information. However, other information that can be gleaned from passive observation of traffic at multiple layers [3] can be used to track end users as well. Encryption of application-layer payload does not necessarily provide protection from tracking [4]. As the inferences that we make as Internet measurement researchers are inextricably related to the inferences necessary to perform user tracking, ethical standards are necessary to minimize end-user harm [5].

There is, however, a common understanding that certain types of data are safer than others. Simple round-trip time or two-way delay information between

---

[1] e.g. the European General Data Protection Regulation (GDPR); see http://www.eugdpr.org.

© Springer International Publishing AG, part of Springer Nature 2018
R. Beverly et al. (Eds.): PAM 2018, LNCS 10771, pp. 73–84, 2018.
https://doi.org/10.1007/978-3-319-76481-8_6

two infrastructure addresses, for example as widely used in diagnostics and operations using `ping` or `traceroute`, and as publicly available at scale via active measurement platforms such as RIPE Atlas[2], is taken to be unthreatening. Even a latency time series gleaned from user traffic says more about the dynamics of the network paths that traffic took than anything about the user's behavior.

In this paper, we examine that assumption by considering the components of end-to-end round trip time, defining possible threat models for RTT privacy and evaluating the utility of latency data for the defined attackers. There are two broad concerns here. First, since RTT is related to distance, RTT measurements from a set of distributed vantage points could be used to determine the location of an endpoint and its associated end-user. Second, since RTT has a component of far-end delay, RTT measurements over a period of time could be used to glean information about the relative level of activity on some remote endpoint. Depending on the resolution of this information, different inferences could be made. Even low-resolution information from a home network could be used to guess whether someone is at home during a given time period, for example. We examine both of these concerns in this work.

We conclude that RTT information is generally safe to use, but should be treated as sensitive in specific circumstances, and provide guidance to mitigate privacy risk when handling this data in Sect. 5.

This paper is, in part, an answer to a related question raised in the IETF QUIC working group. As QUIC's transport layer headers are encrypted, passive RTT measurement as available with TCP [6] is not available in QUIC. A proposal to add explicit RTT measurement to QUIC's wire image in the spirit of IPIM [7] was met with concern that passive RTT measurement might pose a privacy risk. Though this paper is more concerned with active RTT measurement, its insights are applicable to passive measurement as well, with the caveat that an entity in position to perform passive traffic measurement is in a position to gain more information about a given target than a random endpoint in the Internet armed only with `ping`.

This paper is designed to be easily reproducible: the Jupyter notebooks used in the analyses in this paper are available online[3], including code and/or instructions for the retrieval of the source data we used.

2   Components of End-to-End Latency

We begin with an examination of the components of end-to-end latency as can be observed at either endpoint of a transport-layer connection, the sender of an ICMP Echo Request, or the observer of a TCP flow with full information about sequence and acknowledgment numbers and timestamps in both directions of a flow. This observable RTT RTT_{obs} is given by Eq. 1, for f hops in one direction and r hops in the opposite direction, where D_{prop} is propagation delay on a link, D_{queue} is queueing delay at a forwarding node, D_{proc} is processing delay at a

---

[2] https://atlas.ripe.net.
[3] https://github.com/mami-project/rtt-privacy-paper.

forwarding node, D_{stack} is stack delay at the remote endpoint (the time it takes for a packet to make it from the network interface to the application and back, including acknowledgment delay [8] when traffic is unidirectional), and D_{app} is application delay at that endpoint.

$$RTT_{obs} = \sum_{n=0}^{f}(D_{prop_{n \to n+1}} + D_{queue_n} + D_{proc_n})+$$
$$\sum_{m=0}^{r}(D_{prop_{m \to m+1}} + D_{queue_m} + D_{proc_m})+ \tag{1}$$
$$D_{stack} + D_{app}$$

This equation illustrates the confounding effect of end-to-end RTT measurement, which we will explore in more detail later. Each potential threat to privacy uses only one component of delay measured in the observable RTT, but all components are mixed together in a given RTT sample. The challenge in exploiting this information is then to reduce the irrelevant components to a known constant. For example, in the geolocation case, the desired RTT would be (a) perfectly symmetric and (b) made up of only propagation delay (c) in a straight line between endpoints, which would allow a distance measurement as in Eq. 2, where $c_{internet}$ is the speed of light in the Internet, assuming a known and constant factor for refraction in optical fiber and/or propagation in other physical media. $dist$ is an inequality because even in an ideal case (c) does not hold: the light path following the great circle between two points and the light path actually followed by physical Internet infrastructure differ.

$$dist < \frac{\sum_{n=0}^{f} D_{prop_{n \to n+1}} + \sum_{m=0}^{r} D_{prop_{m \to m+1}}}{2} \times c_{internet} \tag{2}$$

On the flip side, if light distance could be known, and processing and queueing delay were zero, these terms could be subtracted out from yielding only stack and application delay, turning RTT observations into "load" observations as in Eq. 3.

$$load \propto D_{stack} + D_{app} \tag{3}$$

The utility of RTT measurements to various geolocation and activity fingerprinting tasks, then, is directly related to the separability of these terms. This is the question we address in the rest of this work.

3   Latency and Geoprivacy

We first examine the geoprivacy question. The threat model here is one of an attacker armed with RTT measurements between a target with unknown location and distributed vantage points with known location, who wants to know the location of the target with arbitrary accuracy.

There is a wide array of recent literature related to this subject. Much of this focuses on "exclusion" based approaches, which uses assumptions about $c_{internet}$ to successively determine where a node or endpoint with unknown location *cannot* be. For example, Cicalese et al. [9] used active RTT measurement to discover and heuristically geolocate anycast infrastructure in the Internet: IP adresses whose RTT-derived circles of exclusion from known vantage points do not overlap must be anycasted.

In any case, much of the literature focuses explicitly on improving the accuracy of latency-based geolocation techniques; i.e., on the attacker's side of the question we pose. Indeed, this underpins the provision of location-based services. Latency has been used to improve IP geolocation accuracy [10–12], and uncover potential fraud [13].

A common theme here is that the vantage points must be optimally selected, since unwanted error terms in RTT_{obs} increase with distance, so accuracy depends highly on the distance of the vantage points to the targets. In the case of passive or opportunistic RTT measurement, one must instead be lucky to be able to observe low-latency paths to the target. Katz-Bassett et al. [14] showed that accuracy under 100 km was possible by augmenting delay measurements with known topology information, and Gueye et al. [15] extended this approach with the use of multilateration, bringing the median error distance down to 25 km for the region of Western Europe.

These proposals are based on previously proposed techniques: IDMaps [16], a multicast-based service for geolocating, and IP2Geo [17] that is based in the first step on the location information of the closest DNS resolver. Model-based approaches for predicting the distance between measured network nodes [18] further refine this, and have achieved a median errors on the order of 30 km [19, 20].

More recently a method to utilize crowd-sourcing has been proposed to use smart-phones as landmarks and leveraging their GPS and WiFi-based location information [21]. Their measurement shows an median error of several hundred kilometers, reflecting both the use of a mobile dataset (where D_{proc} is generally higher) and the variability of real-world data, as compared to the testbed-based measurements of earlier works. Unsurprisingly, this work also confirms that the accuracy highly depends of the distance of the selected landmark to the measurement target.

Other work in location-based services [22–25] focuses on locating nodes in a virtual coordinate system (VCS), as opposed to physical space, following the argument of Ratnasamy et al. [26] that such high accuracy location in physical space is unnecessary for common location-aware services such as content server selection. These approaches are ideal for providing selection of distributed services without necessarily enabling geolocation of endpoints.

Our work is also related to location attacks against low-latency anonymity networks such as TOR. Ries et al. [27] investigate how virtual network coordinate systems can be utilized for timing attacks and exploitation of timing information and also conclude that small changes in latency can have a high influence on the accuracy. The availability of large numbers of latency samples has been shown to increase the success of such attacks as well [28,29], and these become even more powerful if timestamp information is available and samples can be correlated based on clock skew [30]. However, given their architectural peculiarity, observations about these networks do not translate well to the impact on privacy in the non-anonymized Internet. Therefore, we do not address the case of anonymity networks in this work.

3.1   Measurements with Atlas and MONROE

We revisit the question by examining latency measurements taken with the RIPE Atlas and MONROE [31] measurement platforms. Both provide us with latency measurements between vantage points with known location toward targets with known location: Atlas through its anchoring measurements, and MONROE via periodic pings toward the MONROE collection infrastructure.

Exclusion. We start by using Atlas anchoring measurements to attempt geolocation by exclusion, exploiting the inequality for *dist*, the observation that the RTT between two endpoints cannot be less than the speed of light in the medium of the Internet multiplied by twice the distance between those endpoints. We looked at all anchoring ICMP traceroute measurements on Monday 2 October 2017 to a set of 39 anchors, and filter out any measurements from probe-anchor pairs with reported locations less than 500 m from each other[4]. We assume that each of our RIPE Atlas Anchor targets is unicasted. This yields a total of 9.61 million individual measurements over 22,072 probe-anchor pairs. We then took the minimum end-to-end RTT measurement for each probe-anchor pair, taking this to be the best measurement for exclusion purposes.

We then draw exclusion circles corresponding to each probe's minimum RTT at that probe's location, and examine the intersection of these circles. We note

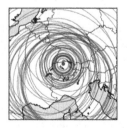 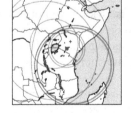 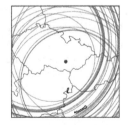

(a) Glattbrugg, Switzerland   (b) Nairobi, Kenya   (c) Brno, Czechia

Fig. 1. Exclusion circles around selected anchors (red dot) and associated MaxMind Geolite City geolocation result (green cross) (Color figure online)

---

[4] Here, the reasoning is that such pairs are either colocated in the same rack, or possible connected to the same local- or metropolitan-area network, and as such do not accurately reflect Internet RTT measurement.

that for 35 of the 39 anchors, intersection gives no additional information; i.e. the closest probe's exclusion circle is completely covered by that of the next closest probe. RTT location via exclusion is therefore largely a matter of luck of the location of the known vantage point. An illustration of this most common case is shown in Fig. 1(a). In the other cases, either the refinement to the exclusion area is insignificant, or the location estimate covers a large region with or without intersection. Figure 1(b) shows an example of this case; note here that the both the location estimate and IP geolocation yield national-scale results.

Though sometimes comparatively remote probes can refine each others' exclusion circles, in no case did we find such a refinement resulting in a reasonably accurate location estimate: the uncertainty in RTT simply grows too quickly with distance. Figure 1(c) illustrates this. Here, estimates from Prague and Vienna yield an area roughly the size of Czechia, but do exclude Prague.

When the IP address of the target is known, IP address geolocation can also be used to estimate its location. We therefore attempt to geolocate each anchor based on its IPv4 address in the freely-available MaxMind GeoLite City database[5], which we take as a worst-case IP geolocation result, noting that better IP geolocation databases will yield better results [32]. We compare the error between the geolocation result and the anchor's declared location with the uncertainty circle for each probe. Here we find that only 140 of 22079 of our anchor-probe pairs have less uncertainty than IP geolocation error, and only 14 of the 39 anchors, generally in areas with a very high probe density, have a measurement from at least one such probe. This further underscores the role of luck in vantage point selection.

We take the RIPE Atlas anchoring measurement dataset to be representative of Internet RTT measurements. Given that opportunities for location area reduction by intersection are not significant in this dataset, we now make a simplifying assumption that the best estimate for the location of an anchor is the center of the uncertainty circle of the probe with the lowest minimum RTT, and therefore that the error in the best estimate is simply the distance from that probe to the anchor. Median error in the Atlas dataset is 39 km while the median IP geolocation error is 16 km. We note that even though our methodology is far simpler than those described in the literature, it achieves comparable accuracy, underscoring the finding that skill (or luck) in vantage point placement is the dominant factor in accuracy in geolocation by exclusion using RTT measurements.

Atlas measurements are largely from residential or infrastructure networks toward infrastructure networks. Recent work by Bajpai et al. [33] shows our findings also to be applicable to the location of residential subscribers. This analysis of Atlas and SamKnows measurements of last-mile latency finds latency to depend on provider, technology, and point of presence, with median (two-way) latencies per provider between 5 and 20ms. Last-mile latency is therefore responsible, on its own, for an exclusion radius between about 500 km and 2000 km.

---

[5] As retrieved from https://stat.ripe.net on 10 October 2017.

We therefore take the location of residential endpoints to be more challenging than location by exclusion of Atlas anchors.

Note that while landmark selection is a challenge for active measurement, when RTT information is observed passively, e.g. during a transport or application-layer handshake, or using passive TCP measurement [6], the increased flatness of the Internet topology [34] implies that there is a decent chance to observe active communications between a client and a nearby content server.

Linear Distance Modeling. We also attempted trilateration through the creation of a linear model relating RTT to distance; i.e. $dist_{est} = f(RTT_{obs})$, based both on Atlas and MONROE measurements. The linear models we derived from our measurements (Atlas: $RTT = 0.0190 \times dist + 22.317$ with $r = 0.86$; MONROE[6]: $RTT = 0.0154 \times dist + 37.0735$ with $r = 0.78$, for RTT in milliseconds and distance in kilometers) are too imprecise to use as a basis for trilateration, with variance and last-mile latency making distance estimation even less feasible on mobile networks.

However, in examining the absolute (Fig. 2(a)) and relative (Fig. 2(b)) error in these models, a guideline for using RTT measurement for location estimation emerges. Restricting RTT data in ways that are possible using only simple inference or measurement can lead to better models with less error. Figure 2 also shows error results for models based on subsets of the Atlas RTT data, considering only pairs with a minimum RTT less than 50 ms, or considering only short paths (with less than 6 hops).

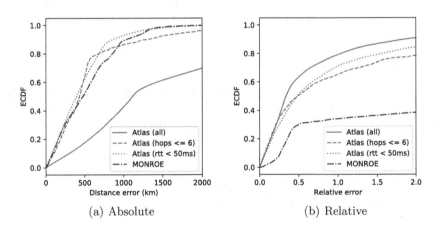

(a) Absolute   (b) Relative

Fig. 2. Distance error for linear models

---

[6] MONROE nodes provide GPS metadata for mobile nodes for location ground truth. We split MONROE data from 1 September 2017 into 5 min bins (300 pings) and associated the geographic average GPS location with the minimum RTT in each bin to yield 3,863 samples from 45 nodes.

4 Load Telemetry

RTT measurement is of interest to in-network operations precisely because it can be used to gain insight into the functioning and malfunctioning of network devices. An unusual D_{queue_n} or D_{proc_n} is often indicative of a fault to be corrected. This is the basic insight behind the measurement of in-network buffering performed by Netalyzr [35] and other measurement platforms, and has been used more recently in the inference of congestion at network interconnects [36]. Load on the endpoint can also be visible in RTT measurements, as shown by Holterbach et al. [37], who showed in a study of the load dependent accuracy of the Atlas platform that several milliseconds of RTT error could be induced and measured by varying the load on RIPE Atlas probes.

This utility, however, has a flipside, as it necessarily exposes information about D_{queue_n} or D_{proc_n} to any device on path which can use active or passive measurement of RTT. More precisely, we now consider a threat model where the attacker knows an IP address associated with a given target, and wants to estimate activity on that target's network. Here, the attacker can leverage four assumptions about common characteristics of residential access networks to successfully determine activity on a residential customer's network:

- The access link is usually the bottleneck link for residential access, so latency variation is due to D_{queue} on the two directions of this link.
- Residential access links are frequently "bufferbloated" [35,38]; i.e., modems have overdimensioned buffers that lead to high D_{queue} under load.
- In many markets, a single customer has a single public IP address at a single point in time, so an ICMP ping to a given address will traverse the access link. Note that this assumption does not hold when carrier-grade NAT is used to conserve IP addresses [39].
- ICMP packets, if not blocked, will generally share a queue with other packets, and can therefore be used to measure D_{queue} induced by other traffic.

In other words, remote buffer measurement is possible, and can be used to infer activity on residential networks. We ran a simple proof-of-concept activity inference attack against one of the authors' home networks to illustrate this point.

We pinged an author's public IP address in Zurich ten times a second from vantage points in Amsterdam and Singapore, while subjecting the inbound network link to varying load through TCP downloads using `curl` at various rate limits. The results are shown in Fig. 3. Idle and active periods are clearly visible due to RTT change from baseline from both the near and far vantage point, even down to a 300 kB/s downstream rate limit, one tenth of the capacity of the link. This author's home access network is also home to a RIPE Atlas probe. Indeed, examining the 5-minute RTT series from second-hop latency measurements from this probe on a different day show clear diurnal peaks in maximum RTT measured during morning and evening weekday network activity, indicating that load telemetry is even possible with very limited RTT data.

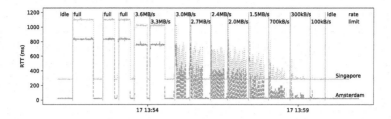

Fig. 3. RTT time series from Amsterdam and Singapore toward a typical residential cable access network in Zürich with a 30 Mbit download link, during downloads from that network with various rate limits.

The success of load telemetry via RTT data is dependent on each of these assumptions holding. Indeed, in a similar test against a virtualized endpoint in a datacenter, where the bufferbloat assumption does not hold, we saw no significant difference in RTT regardless of generated load.

We have made an automated version of this load telemetry measurement available as an online tool[7]. Initial analysis of data collected duing beta testing of this tool from 26 access networks shows that remote load telemetry is possible on a minority of examined networks: 13 (50%) on which ICMP ping is always blocked, 9 (35%) which are pingable but on which there is no apparent correlation between RTT and load, and 4 (15%) on which RTT is correlated with load.

The ability to perform load telemetry of a remote network using RTT data illustrates the well-known utility of RTT data to queue delay measurements. However, variance in queueing delay is often indicative of other kinds of activity, indicating that RTT data may be privacy-sensitive in limited circumstances.

5   Conclusions and Recommendations

We have confirmed the network operations rule of thumb that 1ms of RTT is 100 km of distance, and the findings of previous studies that RTT measurement can provide location accuracy on the order of 30 km to 100 km. That a very basic exclusion-based methodology can perform as well as techniques with higher complexity using publicly available datasets shows that luck in vantage point selection is the dominant factor in accuracy. The sensitivity of RTT measurements for geoprivacy is therefore related to the minimum RTT represented by those measurements. However, RTT measurement is less accurate than IP geolocation using even the most basic, free databases. We therefore recommend care in dissemination of RTT measurement datasets in those cases where the datasets themselves are dominated by samples on the order of less than 10ms, and/or where one (but not both) IP addresses are anonymized.

As for load telemetry, the ability for RTT measurements to provide insight into network queueing delay can be used to infer human activity on networks

---

[7] https://pingme.pto.mami-project.eu.

where certain assumptions hold. While the ongoing reduction of bufferbloat in residential access networks will mitigate the utility of RTT measurements for the inference of residential activity long equipment replacement cycles in these networks mean that bufferbloat will be with us for some time to come. In any case, high-resolution, long-duration RTT datasets collected from networks where bufferbloat is likely should be treated with care.

Acknowledgments. Many thanks to RIPE for making Atlas available to the research community, and to the MONROE project for access to the mobile dataset used in this work. Thanks to the anonymous reviewers and our shepherd, Ramakrishna Padmanabhan, for comments improving the organization and focus of this paper. Thanks also to the members of the IETF QUIC Working Group RTT Design Team for the discussions leading to this paper. This project has received funding from the European Union's Horizon 2020 research and innovation programme under grant agreement No. 688421, and was supported by the Swiss State Secretariat for Education, Research and Innovation (SERI) under contract number 15.0268. The opinions expressed and arguments employed reflect only the authors' views, and not those of the European Commission or the Swiss Government.

References

1. Moore, D., Claffy, K.C: Summary of anonymization best practice techniques, December 2008. https://www.caida.org/projects/predict/anonymization/
2. Burkhart, M., Schatzmann, D., Trammell, B., Boschi, E., Plattner, B.: The role of network trace anonymization under attack. SIGCOMM Comput. Commun. Rev. **40**(1), 5–11 (2010)
3. Coull, S., Wright, C., Monrose, F., Collins, M., Reiter, M.: Playing devil's advocate: inferring sensitive information from anonymized network traces. In: Proceedings of the 14th Annual Network and Distributed Systems Security Symposium, San Diego, CA, USA (2007)
4. Barnes, R., Schneier, B., Jennings, C., Hardie, T., Trammell, B., Huitema, C., Borkmann, D.: Confidentiality in the face of pervasive surveillance: a threat model and problem statement. RFC 7624, RFC Editor, August 2015
5. Partridge, C., Allman, M.: Ethical considerations in network measurement papers. Commun. ACM **59**(10), 58–64 (2016)
6. Strowes, S.D.: Passively measuring TCP round-trip times. Commun. ACM **56**(10), 57–64 (2013)
7. Allman, M., Beverly, R., Trammell, B.: Principles for measurability in protocol design. SIGCOMM Comput. Commun. Rev. **47**(2), 2–12 (2017)
8. Ding, H., Rabinovich, M.: TCP stretch acknowledgements and timestamps: findings and implications for passive RTT measurement. SIGCOMM Comput. Commun. Rev. **45**(3), 20–27 (2015)
9. Cicalese, D., Joumblatt, D.Z., Rossi, D., Buob, M.O., Augé, J., Friedman, T.: Latency-based anycast geolocation: algorithms, software, and data sets. IEEE J. Sel. Areas Commun. **34**(6), 1889–1903 (2016)
10. Grey, M., Schatz, D., Rossberg, M., Schaefer, G.: Towards distributed geolocation by employing a delay-based optimization scheme. In: 2014 IEEE Symposium on Computers and Communications (ISCC), pp. 1–7, June 2014

11. Hillmann, P., Stiemert, L., Rodosek, G.D., Rose, O.: Dragoon: advanced modelling of IP geolocation by use of latency measurements. In: 2015 10th International Conference for Internet Technology and Secured Transactions (ICITST), pp. 438–445, December 2015

12. Wang, Z., Mark, B.L.: Robust statistical geolocation of Internet hosts. In: 2015 IEEE Globecom Workshops (GC Wkshps), pp. 1–6, December 2015

13. Abdou, A., Matrawy, A., van Oorschot, P.C.: CPV: delay-based location verification for the internet. IEEE Trans. Dependable Secure Comput. 14(2), 130–144 (2017)

14. Katz-Bassett, E., John, J.P., Krishnamurthy, A., Wetherall, D., Anderson, T., Chawathe, Y.: Towards IP geolocation using delay and topology measurements. In: Proceedings of the 6th ACM SIGCOMM Conference on Internet Measurement, IMC 2006, pp. 71–84. ACM, New York (2006)

15. Gueye, B., Ziviani, A., Crovella, M., Fdida, S.: Constraint-based geolocation of internet hosts. IEEE/ACM Trans. Networking 14(6), 1219–1232 (2006)

16. Francis, P., Jamin, S., Jin, C., Jin, Y., Paxson, V., Raz, D., Shavitt, Y., Zhang, L.: IDMaps: a global Internet host distance estimation service. In: Proceedings of IEEE INFOCOM, pp. 210–217 (2000)

17. Padmanabhan, V.N., Subramanian, L.: An investigation of geographic mapping techniques for internet hosts. SIGCOMM Comput. Commun. Rev. 31(4), 173–185 (2001)

18. Laki, S., Mátray, P., Hága, P., Csabai, I., Vattay, G.: A model based approach for improving router geolocation. Comput. Netw. 54(9), 1490–1501 (2010)

19. Wong, B., Stoyanov, I., Sirer, E.G.: Geolocalization on the internet through constraint satisfaction. In: Proceedings of the 3rd Conference on USENIX Workshop on Real, Large Distributed Systems, WORLDS 2006, vol. 3, p. 1. USENIX Association, Berkeley,(2006)

20. Dong, Z., Perera, R.D., Chandramouli, R., Subbalakshmi, K.: Network measurement based modeling and optimization for IP geolocation. Comput. Netw. 56(1), 85–98 (2012)

21. Ciavarrini, G., Luconi, V., Vecchio, A.: Smartphone-based geolocation of internet hosts. Comput. Netw. 116(Supplement C), 22–32 (2017)

22. Ng, T.S.E., Zhang, H.: Global network positioning: a new approach to network distance prediction. SIGCOMM Comput. Commun. Rev. 32(1), 73–73 (2002)

23. Dabek, F., Cox, R., Kaashoek, F., Morris, R.: Vivaldi: a decentralized network coordinate system. SIGCOMM Comput. Commun. Rev. 34(4), 15–26 (2004)

24. Chen, Y., Xiong, Y., Shi, X., Deng, B., Li, X.: Pharos: a decentralized and hierarchical network coordinate system for Internet distance prediction. In: IEEE GLOBECOM 2007 - IEEE Global Telecommunications Conference, pp. 421–426, November 2007

25. Lim, H., Hou, J.C., Choi, C.H.: Constructing internet coordinate system based on delay measurement. IEEE/ACM Trans. Networking 13(3), 513–525 (2005)

26. Ratnasamy, S., Handley, M., Karp, R., Shenker, S.: Topologically-aware overlay construction and server selection. In: Proceedings, Twenty-First Annual Joint Conference of the IEEE Computer and Communications Societies, vol. 3, pp. 1190–1199 (2002)

27. Ries, T., State, R., Engel, T.: Measuring anonymity using network coordinate systems. In: 2011 11th International Symposium on Communications Information Technologies (ISCIT), pp. 366–371, October 2011

28. Hopper, N., Vasserman, E.Y., Chan-Tin, E.: How much anonymity does network latency leak? ACM Trans. Inf. Syst. Secur. 13(2), 13:1–13:28 (2010)

29. Serjantov, A., Sewell, P.: Passive attack analysis for connection-based anonymity systems. In: Snekkenes, E., Gollmann, D. (eds.) ESORICS 2003. LNCS, vol. 2808, pp. 116–131. Springer, Heidelberg (2003). https://doi.org/10.1007/978-3-540-39650-5_7

30. Murdoch, S.J.: Hot or not: revealing hidden services by their clock skew. In: Proceedings of the 13th ACM Conference on Computer and Communications Security, CCS 2006, pp. 27–36. ACM, New York (2006)

31. Alay, O., Lutu, A., Garcia, R., Peon-Quiros, M., Mancuso, V., Hirsch, T., Dely, T., Werme, J., Evensen, K., Hansen, A., Alfredsson, S., Karlsson, J., Brunstrom, A., Khatouni, A.S., Mellia, M., Marsan, M.A., Monno, R., Lonsethagen, H.: Measuring and assessing mobile broadband networks with MONROE. In: 2016 IEEE 17th International Symposium on A World of Wireless, Mobile and Multimedia Networks (WoWMoM), pp. 1–3, June 2016

32. Gharaibeh, M., Shah, A., Huffaker, B., Zhang, H., Ensafi, R., Papadopoulos, C.: A look at router geolocation in public and commercial databases. In: Internet Measurement Conference (IMC), November 2017

33. Bajpai, V., Eravuchira, S.J., Schönwälder, J.: Dissecting last-mile latency characteristics. SIGCOMM Comput. Commun. Rev. **47**(5), 25–34 (2017)

34. Ager, B., Chatzis, N., Feldmann, A., Sarrar, N., Uhlig, S., Willinger, W.: Anatomy of a large European IXP. In: Proceedings of the ACM SIGCOMM 2012 Conference on Applications, Technologies, Architectures, and Protocols for Computer Communication. SIGCOMM 2012, pp. 163–174. ACM, Helsinki (2012)

35. Kreibich, C., Weaver, N., Nechaev, B., Paxson, V.: Netalyzr: illuminating the edge network. In: Proceedings of the 10th ACM SIGCOMM Conference on Internet Measurement, IMC 2010, Melbourne, Australia, pp. 246–259 (2010)

36. Luckie, M., Dhamdhere, A., Clark, D., Huffaker, B., claffy, k.: Challenges in inferring Internet interdomain congestion. In: Proceedings of the 2014 Conference on Internet Measurement Conference, IMC 2014, Vancouver, BC, Canada, pp. 15–22 (2014)

37. Holterbach, T., Pelsser, C., Bush, R., Vanbever, L.: Quantifying interference between measurements on the RIPE Atlas platform. In: Proceedings of the 2015 Internet Measurement Conference, IMC 2015, Tokyo, Japan, pp. 437–443. ACM (2015)

38. Gettys, J., Nichols, K.: Bufferbloat: dark buffers in the internet. Queue **9**(11), 40:40–40:54 (2011)

39. Lutu, A., Bagnulo, M., Dhamdhere, A., Claffy, K.C.: NAT revelio: detecting NAT444 in the ISP. In: Karagiannis, T., Dimitropoulos, X. (eds.) PAM 2016. LNCS, vol. 9631, pp. 149–161. Springer, Cham (2016). https://doi.org/10.1007/978-3-319-30505-9_12

CDNs

Fury Route: Leveraging CDNs to Remotely Measure Network Distance

Marcel Flores[✉], Alexander Wenzel, Kevin Chen, and Aleksandar Kuzmanovic

Northwestern University, Evanston, USA
marcelflores2007@u.northwestern.edu

Abstract. Estimating network distance between arbitrary Internet endpoints is an essential primitive in applications ranging from performance optimization to network debugging and auditing. Enabling such a primitive without deploying new infrastructure was demonstrated via DNS. However, the proliferation of DNS hosting has made DNS-based measurement techniques far less dependable. In this paper, we show that the heterogeneous infrastructure of different CDNs, combined with the proliferation of the EDNS0 client-subnet extension (ECS), enables novel infrastructureless measurement. We design Fury Route, a system that estimates network distance by utilizing ECS to construct a virtual path between endpoints via intermediate CDN replicas.

Fury Route requires no additional infrastructure to be deployed. The measured endpoints do not need to participate by sending or responding to probes. Fury Route further generates no load on endpoints. It only queries DNS, whose infrastructure is designed for large loads. We extensively evaluate Fury Route and demonstrate that (*i*) the key to Fury Route's ability to construct virtual paths lies in the heterogeneity of the underlying CDNs, (*ii*) Fury Route is effective in revealing relative network distance, needed in many real-world scenarios, (*iii*) caching can dramatically reduce Fury Route's DNS overhead, making it a useful system in practice.

1 Introduction

The ability to estimate network distance between arbitrary endpoints on the Internet is fundamentally necessary in numerous scenarios [16]. Such estimates have been shown to heavily correlate with actual end-to-end performance (in terms of throughput and delay) between the two endpoints [23,30].

With King [16], Gummadi *et al.* showed that DNS infrastructure could be effectively utilized to measure network distance without access to any of the endpoints. By using open recursive DNS resolvers and by relying on the proximity of clients and servers to their authoritative DNS servers, they manage to approximate the distance between the endpoints. Nonetheless, 15 years later, the Internet has become a much different place. On one hand, the number of open recursive DNS resolvers is rapidly decreasing [17]. On the other hand, DNS hosting (*i.e.*, outsourcing DNS services to the cloud [1–3,5–8]), is fundamentally

© Springer International Publishing AG, part of Springer Nature 2018
R. Beverly et al. (Eds.): PAM 2018, LNCS 10771, pp. 87–99, 2018.
https://doi.org/10.1007/978-3-319-76481-8_7

blurring the assumption of co-location of endpoints (both clients and servers) and authoritative DNS servers.

We present Fury Route, a system that aims to estimate the network distance between arbitrary Internet endpoints. Fury Route relies on (*i*) the existence of different Content Distribution Networks (CDNs) and their heterogeneous deployment (*ii*) CDNs' common desire to direct clients to nearby CDN replicas, and (*iii*) the proliferation of EDNS0 client-subnet extension (ECS) [12], a mechanism by which a host issuing DNS requests can indicate the origin of the request *Fury Route constructs a virtual path between source and destination, consisting of CDN replicas from different providers, by issuing ECS requests on behalf of endpoints and intermediate CDN replicas.* We show that the length of such a constructed path correlates with the latency between the two endpoints.

Fury Route requires no additional infrastructure to be deployed. The measured endpoints do not need to cooperate by sending or responding to probes. Fury Route generates no load on the parties involved: It only queries DNS, whose infrastructure is designed to handle large loads. While Fury Route utilizes the DNS infrastructure, it is in no way impacted by availability of recursive DNS resolvers, nor is it affected by DNS hosting. Fury Route utilizes the mapping work done by CDNs, and it effectively extracts this information via DNS.

We evaluate Fury Route using ground truth obtained from PlanetLab and RIPE Atlas platforms, testing from around 9000 nodes well distributed across countries and networks. We find that in the median case, Fury Route is able to construct chains between more than 80% of origin and destination pairs. This significantly outperforms other evaluated systems, *i.e.*, King [16] and iPlane [19], which have the convergence rate of 4% and 56% on the same data set, respectively. We further demonstrate that despite its infrastructureless properties, Fury Route shows accuracy comparable to iPlane, which conducts large-scale Internet measurements for this purpose. In particular, Fury Route is able to correctly order up to 83% of destinations in the median case. We further show our graph caching technique is able to reduce queries by 80%.

2   Background and Measurement

The EDNS0 `client-subnet` extension (ECS) provides a mechanism by which a host issuing DNS requests can label their requests with a subnet, indicating the origin of the request. The purpose of this extension is to aid in DNS-based replica selection and addresses challenges which arise from clients being far away from their LDNS server [12,22]. Upon receiving an ECS request, the authoritative DNS server uses the submitted subnet to perform its replica selection, according to its individual policy. When responding to the query, the answer includes a scope netmask field. If this value is less than or equal to the client-specified subnet length (*i.e.*, a larger subnet), it indicates the set of subnets which would receive the same result, for caching purposes. If the value is greater than the supplied length (*i.e.*, smaller subnet), it indicates the DNS server would like the client to resubmit with a more specific subnet.

Fury Route will take advantage of EDNS0 in two ways. First, it uses the `client-subnet` field to send requests from arbitrary locations, granting it a wide view of provider replicas from anywhere in the entire Internet. Second, it exploits the value of the scope netmask in the response in order to understand the *quality* of the set of responses. While these actual values are likely a function of each network's particular layout, policy, and current load, they still provide feedback on how well the provider was able to match a particular client subnet.

2.1 Provider Granularity

We examine the behavior of specific networks which are particularly useful in the development of Fury Route. We consider a set of CDN providers known to support EDNS [9,10,28] combined with a set of providers collected via manual inspection from a scrape of the Alexa Top500[1].

Table 1. Selected set of providers.

Provider	Hostname
Google	www.google.com
Edgecast	gp1.wac.v2cdn.net
Alibaba	img.alicdn.com
CloudFront	st.deviantart.net
CDN77	922977808.r.cdn77.net
CDNetworks	cdnw.cdnplanet.com.cdngc.net
ADNXS	ib.adnxs.com

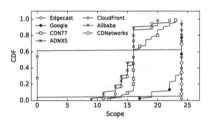

Fig. 1. CDF of observed scope netmask responses.

Table 1 shows our selection of providers and the corresponding hostname used to query each provider. Providers are "used" by issuing an A record query for a hostname belonging to that provider. We examine the response *scope netmask*, which indicates how well the subnet in the query was able to match the response. While this value is likely affected by policy, *i.e.*, both the internal mapping policy of each provider, and a DNS caching policy which attempts to take advantage of DNS caching [12], the scope netmask is undoubtedly a valid asset in Fury Route's design. Fury Route will therefore interpret the values as the quality, *i.e.*, nearness, of a given response.

We query each of the provider domain names using 25 distinct globally distributed prefixes from PlanetLab as the client subnet. Figure 1 shows a CDF of the response scopes for each provider. The providers fall into two categories: course and fine grained. CloudFront, CDNetworks, Google, return /24 subnets for nearly all requests, appearing as vertical lines at 24 in the figure. Alternatively, Alibaba, ADNXS, and Edgecast return broader scopes. While CDN77 returns many broad scopes, we also see that nearly 40% of its responses were /18s or

---

[1] Akamai, a large provider, restricts third-party ECS queries, and is not used.

smaller. We note that some providers may employ anycast, suggesting any DNS client mapping they perform is intended for coarser grained locations.

3   Fury Route

Fury Route is built on the principle that the network distance between two hosts can be estimated by constructing a path of CDN replicas between the two hosts. These CDN replicas are returned as responses to ECS queries and the paths are generated by an iterative series of ECS queries which "hop" between CDN replicas by issuing new requests on behalf of a CDN replica with the client-subnet extension. The intuition is that the replicas provide a reflection of the density of CDN deployments: crossing low density areas suggests large distances.

This entire process can be performed from any host, requires no participation on the part of the hosts being measured, and does not rely on any directly deployed infrastructure. This is possible as ECS allow single probing node to issue DNS queries as if it were any other host. While these responses may vary due to outside factors, in particular when examining the precision of an ECS response which used a CDN replica as a client subnet (a case for which they are unlikely to be optimized), they still contain information which reflects the structure of the underlying networks. Fury Route addresses this by using the subnet mask returned by the ECS query: poor matches usually come with generic answers and large subnets, which translate to large distances.

Fury Route consists of three main components: (*i*) A chain building mechanism which connects an origin host with a destination host via a sequence of CDN replicas discovered via EDNS-enabled DNS responses, (*ii*) A voting system which enables this chain-building system to make forward progress in the space of CDN hosts, (*iii*) A comparison module, which compares the lengths of the chains and estimates the relative distance between two points of interest, maximizing the information made available from the CDN-based DNS responses.

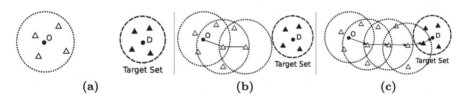

Fig. 2. A representation of the chain building procedure. The dashed circle indicates hosts in the target set. Dotted circles show hosts in a scan of all providers.

Chain Building. Fury Route is able to perform remote network distance estimations by using an approach we call *chain building*. The fundamental basis for this chain building approach is that DNS responses from CDNs which support ECS are likely to be *near* the requesting host, as indeed this is the stated purpose of ECS [12]. Fury Route builds on this notion, and constructs chains of near-by responses to estimate distance.

Fury Route begins with an origin host O and a destination host D. It further has a set of providers $P = \{p_1, \ldots, p_k\}$, where each p_i is represented by a hostname which belongs to a provider. While, as we saw in Sect. 2, a provider may span multiple hostnames, we take provider to mean an entity which can be queried by a look-up for a specific name. We therefore treat hostnames and providers as interchangeable.

To begin construction of a chain, Fury Route issues an ECS query to each provider in P, using D's address as the client subnet. It then takes the responses to each of these queries and pools them into a *target set*, which we denote $T = \{t_1, \ldots, t_n\}$, $n \geq k$.[2] These hosts represent CDN replicas which are likely close to the destination D, and therefore are indicators of its location. We use such a target set since the destination D may not be itself a CDN replica, but an arbitrary host. The target set therefore gives us a set of CDN replicas for which the algorithm is explicitly searching.

Next, Fury Route issues a set of ECS requests to the provider set P, using the origin host O's IP address as the client subnet. It then records the set of returned CDN replicas, noting their scope netmask values and the corresponding provider. It then considers each of such obtained CDN replicas, and selects one using the voting process described below. The voting procedure encourages the selection of hosts, *i.e.*, CDN replicas, which are closer to the target set T, and therefore closer to D. Fury Route then issues a new set of requests, using the previously selected CDN replica as its client subnet. This process is repeated until at least one provider returns a host which is in the target set T, or it exceeds a fixed number of scans. If it successfully encounters a replica from T, the resulting sequence of hosts is then taken as the *chain* of replicas connecting O and D.

Figure 2 shows a visual representation of these steps. Part (a) shows Fury Route's view after establishing the target set T (shown as shaded triangles within the dashed circle), and issuing the first set of ECS queries to the providers on behalf of the origin host. Non-shaded triangles show hosts returned as a result of those queries. Next, part (b) shows when it then selects one of these hosts, and issues another set of queries, offering a further set of CDN replicas. Finally, in part (c), the chain is complete, as the final round of queries to the providers returned results which land within the target set.

Voting. Fury Route employs a voting mechanism to select the next CDN replica host which is likely to provide forward-progress towards the destination host D. The mechanism is built on the heuristic that the best choice for the next hop is the one which brings the next hop closest to the target. To this end, we use the following mechanism: when considering a set of potential candidate CDN replicas, $C = \{c_1, \ldots, c_l\}$, Fury Route attempts to determine which will have the greatest overlap in ECS-enabled responses with the target set T.

---

[2] The target set can contain more CDN replicas than the number of providers, because a provider may return more than a single replica for a host.

In order to measure this overlap, Fury Route performs the following operation for each candidate CDN replica c_i. It issues an ECS query to the first provider, p_1, with c_i as the client subnet. We denote the set of responses as $R_{1,i}$. Next, it issues ECS queries to p_1 using each of the target CDN replicas in T. We combine all of the target set responses into a single collection which we denote $R_{1,T}$.

Using these sets we will determine which candidate is given the closest matching set of replicas to the target set. Formally, we measure the overlap seen by p_1 for candidate c_i, denoted $B_{1,i}$, as:

$$B_{1,i} = R_{1,i} \cap R_{1,T}.$$

If $B_{1,i}$ is non-empty, we say that this candidate has overlap with the target set as seen by provider p_1, and provider p_1 grants a single vote for c_i. If $B_{1,i}$ is empty, no vote is granted.

This process is repeated for each provider in P, and the votes are summed for the candidate. The entire process is further repeated for each potential candidate in C. It is important to note that a single provider may vote for many candidates. Fury Route then selects the candidate with the most votes, as it features the most overlap with the target set across providers, making it likely to offer the most forward progress, choosing randomly in the case of ties.

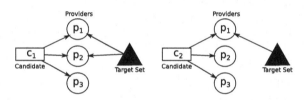

Fig. 3. An example of the voting mechanism. Providers p_1 and p_2 have overlap with the target set for c_1, but only p_1 for c_2. Therefore the system selects c_1.

Figure 3 presents an example of this process. In this example, we have 2 potential candidates, and 3 providers. We first query each of the providers and store the responses. Next, each CDN replica host is scanned for each provider, also noting the results. In the example, providers p_1 and p_2 see overlap with c_1, while only p_2 sees overlap with c_2. Therefore Fury Route selects c_1.

In the event that Fury Route finds itself with a set of candidates which have lower vote totals than the previous round, Fury Route "backtracks", abandoning the current chain branch, and returning to the candidate with the previous highest number of votes. If there is no such candidate, it then settles for the candidate with the next highest number of votes. In this way, it is able to pursue a path with the highest indication of progress, while avoiding moving further away from the target.

Chain Length. Once a chain has been constructed between the source and destination hosts as outlined above, the *length* is used as a relative comparison tool against other chains for estimating network distances. To compute the length, we use the response scope netmask field. While this is largely intended for caching purposes, Fury Route makes use of the value to estimate the *quality* of a particular response, which we take to represent the accuracy of the chosen replica. If a chain includes a link between two CDN replicas in a chain, A and B, and s is the scope netmask of the response which included B, we take the cost of traversing such a link to be cost $= \max(8, 32 - s)$. The higher the precision of the response, the smaller the cost of the corresponding link. In rare cases, we obtain a scope larger than the ECS specification's maximum length recommendation of 24. These responses are inconsistent and do not occur reliably across our providers. We "downgrade" such responses to 24, setting the minimal cost in the system to 8. Finally, responses which offer no scope information are ignored.

4 Implementation

Queries are issued to Google DNS with a modified version of the dnspython DNS library [4] to issue our queries. As in [28], we are able to achieve up to 50 queries per second, depending on the providers. All of our queries are sent with a full/32 client subnet. If a chain fails to reach the target set after a threshold of candidate selection rounds, Fury Route abandons the current chain and starts over, attempting to build the chain from the destination to the origin.

Fury Route builds a *response graph* to minimize the number of queries it performs. The response graph stores all observed replicas as nodes. Edges are used to encode the response scope from the perspective of different replicas. Nodes are further annotated with the set of providers which have been queried with that replica as a client subnet. Nodes within the same/24 subnet are combined, to avoid repeating queries with nearly identical client addresses.

4.1 Provider Selection

We divide our set of providers into two categories. The first, *voting-only* providers, are excluded from candidate selection in the chain building procedure as they lack sufficient accuracy. Nonetheless, they are very useful in voting due to their coarse-grained nature. The second, are called *candidate* providers, which participate in both voting and chain construction. Based on our findings in Sect. 2, we take Alibaba, Edgecast, and ADNXS to be voting-only providers, due to their broader scope. The remaining CDNs, are taken as candidate providers.

"Unmapped" Replica Blacklisting. In examining pathological cases, we observe that they arise from variation in CDN policy or behavior in either ECS response scope or replica selection policy. A common signature for a "poor" CDN decision is that in most cases, in absence of an informed response, CDNs practice directing such queries to "unmapped" CDN replicas. Such CDN replicas are typically recommended when a request is conducted from an address with no suitable mapping. The "unmapped" CDN replicas are easy to detect in the context of Fury Route, since the number of such CDN responses typically outweigh a regular CDN replica by up to an order of magnitude. We demonstrate that avoiding chains through such "unmapped" replicas enables our system to retain high path completion rate while avoiding extremely erronous results.

5 Evaluation

In this section we evaluate Fury Rotue with two different platforms that provide ground truth round-trip time measurements. First, we use 8,964 globally-distributed nodes from a publicly available RIPE Atlas platform [25]. Second, we consider a full mesh of chains provided by a set of 60 globally-distributed Planet Lab nodes. To establish a ground truth network distance for each pair, we perform a ping measurement (consisting of three pings) immediately prior to generating the Fury Route chain, granting an up-to-date view of the network delay between origin and destination.

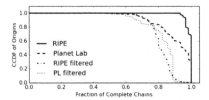

Fig. 4. The fraction of destinations for which Fury Route was able to complete a chain in different scenarios.

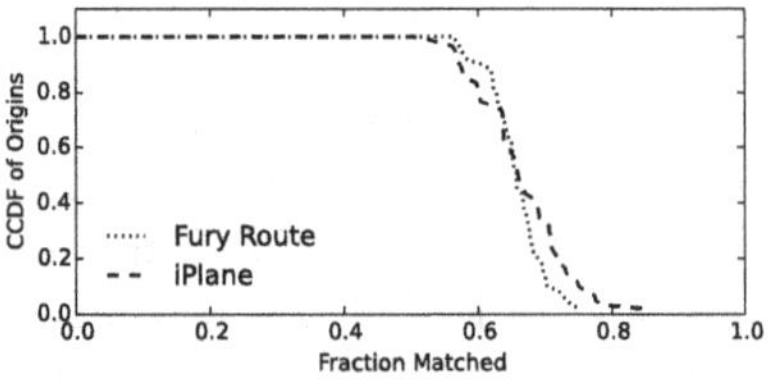

Fig. 5. The ranked ordering performance of Fury Route and iPlane on RIPE Atlas for completed chains.

5.1 Completion Rate

First, we consider the completion rate of Fury Route chains in each platform. For each pair of tested nodes, we attempt to construct a Fury Route chain. Each chain is given 25 candidate selection rounds before it is marked incomplete. Larger values provided no detectable increase in completion rate, so 25 provided a balance between exploratory freedom and run time.

Figure 4 shows the fraction of destinations for each origin server for which Fury Route was able to construct a chain as a CCDF over the set of origins. First, we focus on "raw" results, marked as "RIPE" and "Planet Lab." We see that in the median case for Planet Lab, 90% of chains are successfully completed, and in over 40% of cases, all chains were completed successfully. The results are even better for the RIPE data set, where 100% of chains are successfully completed in the median case. We found that pairs unable to complete their chains featured destinations with potentially sparse CDN deployments from our providers.

The other two curves, "RIPE filtered" and "PL filtered," show the chain completion rates for the filtered scenarios, *i.e.*, when "unmapped" replica blacklisting, explained in Sect. 4.1 above, was applied. Such filtering decreases the completion rate, such that it becomes almost identical for the two platforms. Here, most of the "bad" paths, particularly in the RIPE data set, which completed but were of poor quality, are filtered in this step. Nonetheless, Fig. 4 shows that the median Fury Route chain completion rate remains above 80%.

5.2   Comparison to iPlane

Here, we compare Fury Route's performance to the performance of an infrastructure-dependent system, iPlane [19] using RIPE Atlas. iPlane is a system for analyzing and predicting Internet path performance. It uses a distributed infrastructure to compile traceroutes from various vantage points in order to predict network paths and path attributes [19]. We show, given a fixed origin point, how well Fury Route and iPlane are able to correctly determine which of a pair of destinations is closest and which is further away. For each pair, we check if the comparison of the corresponding Fury Route chain lengths and iPlane's latency estimates matches that of the corresponding ping measurements. We then are able to count the fraction of comparisons which matched the RTT measurements.

We first compare the completion rates. For Fury Route, the curve "RIPE filtered" in Fig. 4 shows the median completion rate is approximately 80%. Our evaluation of iPlane shows a completion rate of 56% for the "RIPE filtered" set. Next, Fig. 5 shows the performance of Fury Route and iPlane ranking RIPE Atlas when completion is possible. The curves show a CDF of the fraction of matched comparisons for each of our origins for all possible pairs. The performance of Fury Route and iPlane ranking is virtually identical in the median case. Fury Route achieves comparable performance to iPlane using only DNS and CDN deployment properties instead of iPlane's necessary back-end measurement network, while significantly outperforming iPlane.

5.3   Rank Performance

Here, we analyze Fury Route's performance on a different, Planet Lab based, platform. We wish to determine how well Fury Route's chain-lengths estimate the relative ordering given by the RTT measurements in a 60-node full mesh scenario. We consider all possible pairwise comparisons between destinations for each origin, giving us up to 1770 comparisons per origin (*i.e.*, $1{,}770 = 59 + 58 + ...$), depending on completion rate.

Figure 6 shows a CDF of the fraction of matched comparisons for each of our origins. The dotted line to the left indicates all possible pairs. This result

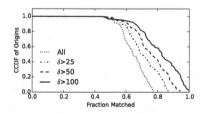   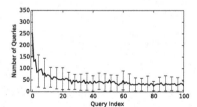

Fig. 6. A CCDF over hosts showing the fraction of comparisons the chain length matched the measured RTT ordering.

Fig. 7. The improvement of queries needed over time with the same graph.

is similar and corresponds to the one shown above in Fig. 5. Each other line indicates the performance for the subset of comparisons with a minimum distance between path RTTs of δ. For example, for an origin S, $\delta = 25$ contains all pairs of destinations, $e.g.$, A and B, for which $|\text{RTT}(S, A) - \text{RTT}(S, B)| > 25$ ms. For our set of hosts, 71% of pairs were in $\delta > 25$, 54% in $\delta > 50$, and 29% in $\delta > 100$. In nearly all cases, Fury Route is above 50% performance in terms of matches. Furthermore, we see that increasing the difference between the origin and destinations expectedly improves performance. Indeed, the best case of a difference of $\delta = 100$ gives us 83% of comparisons correct in the median case.

Many of Fury Route's misestimates stem from limits in the underlying CDN infrastructure. Targets in areas with limited deployments result in greater error in the initial hops, degrading the estimates. For example, such behavior was observed in Africa, South America, or when crossing oceans. Figure 6 shows the clearest tradeoff: when comparing similar distances, Fury Route becomes less accurate, as noise begins to dominate.

5.4 Overhead Analysis

The use of a graph to implement Fury Route provides a simple and effective caching mechanism. Fury Route can reuse the graph for multiple measurements from a single origin (the expected use case). With a sufficient cache, queries could then be executed in seconds, making Fury Route viable as a real time estimation tool. To quantify the benefits of graph caching, we conduct the following experiment. First, we randomly sample 50 Planet Lab nodes as origins. For each origin, we randomly sample 200 addresses from IPv4 space. Next, we construct chains from each origin to each of its corresponding destinations, reusing the graph for each origin.

Figure 7 presents the average number of queries for each origin: the x-axis indicates the query index, $i.e.$, how many times the graph has been reused, and the y-axis is the average number of queries, where the error bars represent a standard deviation. We see that the initial chain takes an average of 250 queries to complete, but quickly decreases, requiring only 65 queries by the 10th chain constructed with the graph. After 20 chains are constructed, the average number of queries decreases below 50.

6 Related Work

A significant body of work has been devoted to the challenge of predicting network performance. These have included large-scale measurement platforms [18,19,24–26], which attempt to measure a large number of routes and hosts from a large number of vantage points. Other systems have embedded coordinate systems, often based on measurements to a set of known landmarks or peers, to perform network distance estimations between a set of hosts without direct measurements [13–15,21,27,31]. Unlike these, Fury Route outsources the direct network measurements to a number of underlying CDNs. As a result it requires no access to the measured endpoints nor to any other third-party infrastructure.

King examines how latency can be measured indirectly by considering the latency between two nearby DNS resolvers [16]. While similar to Fury Route in that it does not require the direct participation of either host, King requires a nearby open recursive resolver, and a nearby authoritative server. However, such requirements are becoming more difficult to satisfy. A recent study has shown that the number of open recursive DNS servers is rapidly decreasing – approximately by up to 60% a year, and by around 30% on average a year [17].

The use of CDN redirections has been shown effective in terms of relative network positioning [20,29,30]. In particular, if two clients have overlapping CDN replicas, they are likely to be close to each other in the network sense. Such an approach has further been utilized by large-scale systems such as BitTorrent [11]. Contrary to such an approach, which requires a large-scale distributed system such as BitTorrent in order to be effective Fury Route has no such limitation. Indeed, it can, in principal, effectively connect any two endpoints on the Internet.

Finally, the use of ECS [12] as a measurement tool was the key principle in [10,28]. While similar in our use of ECS to obtain client-mapping information from existing infrastructure, both of these works have a different goal: exploring the deployments of specific CDNs. Fury Route, on the other hand, is attempting to use these CDNs to perform an additional task: network distance estimation.

7   Conclusions

We presented Fury Route, a system which builds on the underlying client mapping performed by CDNs and the potentials of the EDNS client subnet extension. Fury Route is the only Internet-scale system that provides an infrastructure-free mechanism to estimate distance between remote hosts, i.e., without any requirement for a measurement infrastructure nor for the manpower to administer the same. Fury Route constructs chains of responses and uses the lengths of these responses to estimate the relative network distance between remote hosts, all without any direct network measurements. We demonstrated Fury Route's ability to construct chains to over 80% of destinations in the median case. We further showed that it matches the accuracy of infrastructure-dependent systems such as iPlane. We examined the potential for caching, showing a significant capability for caching route graphs, rapidly building chains with fewer than 50 queries. Given its lack of requirement for directly controlled measurement infrastructure, low overhead, and ability to measure between arbitrary hosts, Fury Route stands to be a practical and powerful tool for estimating relative network distance.

References

1. Amazon Route 53. https://aws.amazon.com/route53/
2. Azure DNS. https://azure.microsoft.com/en-us/services/dns/
3. Dyn DNS. http://dyn.com/dns/

4. ECS dnspython. https://github.com/mutax/dnspython-clientsubnetoption
5. GoDaddy: DNS. https://www.godaddy.com/domains/dns-hosting.aspx
6. Google Cloud Platform: Cloud DNS. https://cloud.google.com/dns/
7. Neustar DNS Services. https://www.neustar.biz/services/dns-services
8. Verisign Managed DNS. http://www.verisign.com/en_US/security-services/dns-management/index.xhtml
9. Which CDNS support EDNS-client-subnet. https://www.cdnplanet.com/blog/which-cdns-support-edns-client-subnet/
10. Calder, M., Fan, X., Hu, Z., Katz-Bassett, E., Heidemann, J., Govindan, R.: Mapping the expansion of Google's serving infrastructure. In: Proceedings of IMC 2013 (2013)
11. Choffnes, D., Bustamante, F.: Taming the torrent: a practical approach to reducing cross-ISP traffic in peer-to-peer systems. In: Proceedings of SIGCOMM 2008 (2008)
12. Contavalli, C., van der Gaast, W., tale, Kumari, W.: Client subnet in DNS queries (IETF draft), December 2015. http://www.ietf.org/internet-drafts/draft-ietf-dnsop-edns-client-subnet-06.txt
13. Costa, M., Castro, M., Rowstron, A., Key, P.: PIC: Practical Internet Coordinates for distance estimation. In: Proceedings of ICDCS 2004 (2004)
14. Dabek, F., Cox, R., Kaashoek, F., Morris, R.: Vivaldi: a decentralized network coordinate system. In: Proceedings of SIGCOMM 2004 (2004)
15. Francis, P., Jamin, S., Jin, C., Jin, Y., Raz, D., Shavitt, Y., Zhang, L.: IDMaps: a global Internet host distance estimation service. IEEE/ACM ToN 9(5), 525–540 (2001)
16. Gummadi, K., Saroiu, S., Gribble, S.: King: estimating latency between arbitrary Internet end hosts. In: Proceedings of Internet Measurement Workshop (IMW) (2002)
17. Kuhrer, M., Hupperich, T., Bushart, J., Rossow, C., Holz, T.: Going wild: large-scale classification of open DNS resolvers. In: Proceedings of IMC 2015 (2015)
18. Madhyastha, H.V., Anderson, T., Krishnamurthy, A., Spring, N., Venkataramani, A.: A structural approach to latency prediction. In: Proceedings of IMC 2006 (2006)
19. Madhyastha, H.V., Isdal, T., Piatek, M., Dixon, C., Anderson, T., Krishnamurthy, A., Venkataramani, A.: iPlane: an information plane for distributed services. In: Proceedings of OSDI 2006 (2006)
20. Micka, S., Goel, U., Ye, H., Wittie, M.P., Mumey, B.: pcp: Internet latency estimation using CDN replicas. In: Proceedings of ICCCN (2015)
21. Ng, T., Zhang, H.: Predicting Internet network distance with coordinates-based approaches. In: Proceedings of IEEE Infocom 2002 (2002)
22. Otto, J.S., Sánchez, M.A., Rula, J.P., Bustamante, F.E.: Content delivery and the natural evolution of DNS: remote DNS trends, performance issues and alternative solutions. In: Proceedings of IMC 2012 (2012)
23. Padhye, J., Firoiu, V., Towsley, D., Kurose, J.: Modeling TCP throughput: a simple model and its empirical validation. In: Proceedings of SIGCOMM 1998. Vancouver, British Columbia (1998)
24. Rabinovich, M., Triukose, S., Wen, Z., Wang, L.: DipZoom: the Internet measurements marketplace. In: Proceedings of IEEE Infocom 2006 (2006)
25. RIPE Atlas. https://atlas.ripe.net/
26. Sánchez, M.A., Otto, J.S., Bischof, Z.S., Choffnes, D.R., Bustamante, F.E., Krishnamurthy, B., Willinger, W.: Dasu: Pushing experiments to the Internet's edge. In: Proceedings of USENIX NSDI (2013)
27. Shavitt, Y., Tankel, T.: On the curvature of the Internet and its usage for overlay construction and distance estimation. In: Proceedings of INFOCOM 2004 (2004)

28. Streibelt, F., Böttger, J., Chatzis, N., Smaragdakis, G., Feldmann, A.: Exploring EDNS-client-subnet adopters in your free time. In: Proceedings of IMC 2013 (2013)
29. Su, A.J., Choffnes, D., Bustamante, F., Kuzmanovic, A.: Relative network positioning via CDN redirections. In: Proceedings of ICDCS 2008 (2008)
30. Su, A.J., Choffnes, D., Kuzmanovic, A., Bustamante, F.: Drafting behind Akamai (Travelocity-based detouring). In: Proceedings of SIGCOMM 2006, Pisa, Italy, September 2006
31. Wong, B., Slivkins, A., Sirer, E.G.: Meridian: a lightweight network location service without virtual coordinates. In: Proceedings of SIGCOMM 2005 (2005)

Mobile Content Hosting Infrastructure in China: A View from a Cellular ISP

Zhenyu Li[1,2(✉)], Donghui Yang[1,2], Zhenhua Li[3], Chunjing Han[1,2], and Gaogang Xie[1,2]

[1] Institute of Computing Technology, Chinese Academy of Sciences, Beijing, China
{zyli,yangdonghui,hcj,xie}@ict.ac.cn
[2] University of Chinese Academy of Sciences, Beijing, China
[3] Tsinghua University, Beijing, China
lizhenhua1983@gmail.com

Abstract. Internet users are heavily relying on mobile terminals for content access, where the content is hosted and delivered by either third-party infrastructures (*e.g.,* CDNs and clouds) or the content providers' own delivery networks, or both. China has the largest mobile Internet population in a single country, and also has unique local regulations and network policies (e.g. heavy content censorship). The content delivery ecosystem in China, as such, may show great disparity from the western one. Yet, there is little visibility into the content hosting infrastructure in Chinese cellular networks. This paper makes the first step toward filling this gap by analyzing a passive DNS trace that consists of 55 billion DNS logs collected from a national-scale cellular ISP. Our in-depth investigation of the content-related features of major ASes reveals that content objects of popular domains are replicated deep into the examined cellular ISP. On the other hand, as much as 20% of tracking traffic, which is mainly generated by trackers owned US-based companies, goes out of China. Our findings cast useful insights for cellular ISPs, CDNs and Internet policy makers.

1 Introduction

The ever-growing popularity of smart devices greatly promotes the content demand in cellular networks. It was projected that the mobile data traffic will grow 7-fold in the upcoming years [5]. Such an enormous demand challenges not only cellular network itself, but also the content hosting infrastructure that delivers content to massive users. Typical content hosting infrastructure includes third-party infrastructures (*e.g.,* CDNs, clouds), the content providers' own delivery networks, and a mixture of the two. Content hosting infrastructures have a significant impact on ISPs' traffic engineering, and quality of experience perceived by end users. For instance, a centralized infrastructure needs to peer its data centers with ISPs for high bandwidth [12], while a distributed one needs to deploy its servers as close to users as possible for fast content access.

Content hosting infrastructures is largely shaped by the cost, network policies as well as local regulations where they are deployed. This paper examines the

© Springer International Publishing AG, part of Springer Nature 2018
R. Beverly et al. (Eds.): PAM 2018, LNCS 10771, pp. 100–113, 2018.
https://doi.org/10.1007/978-3-319-76481-8_8

mobile content hosting infrastructures in China. China has the largest mobile Internet population in a single country, and, perhaps more interestingly, has unique local regulations and network policies. For instance, Internet Content Provider (ICP) licenses are mandatory for the sites that aim at delivering content within mainland China. This regulation prevents popular CDNs (like Akamai) from deploying their replica servers in China [17].

The above factors may lead to great disparity of the content hosting infrastructures in China than the western countries. Unfortunately, we have very limited knowledge of the infrastructures in China, despite some recent studies on that in western countries. Triukose et al. [16] measured Akamai, and examined the performance benefit of using distributed deployment. Pujol et al. [15] on the other hand studied the hosting infrastructure for advertisement trackers of DSL web users. Since DNS maps end users to specific servers [10], using DNS replies can infer what content is hosted in which locations. The web content cartography introduced in [7] was the first step to use DNS replies for this purpose. However, they focused only on a small amount of domains in wireline networks. Xue et al. [17] also use active DNS measurements of a few top domains to study the server selection policies used by CDNs in China.

This paper considers all domains requested by mobile users through cellular networks. We analyzed 55 billion DNS replies collected from all recursive resolvers of a cellular ISP. The large user coverage of the data enables us to have a comprehensive view of the content hosting infrastructure. We borrow the content-related metrics in [7] to characterize the features of the ASes that accounts for majority of the DNS queries. We further propose a clustering algorithm to identify content hosting providers, and examined the features of the major providers. Finally, this paper examines the hosting infrastructure of tracking domains, which are present in mobile webs and more prominently in mobile apps [13]. We have also discussed the implications of our major findings from different aspects. To sum up, we make the following main contributions.

- *Hosting Infrastructure Concentration:* We find that cellular content infrastructure is concentrated in a few ISP ASes, rather than CDN ASes. This stems from the fact that content objects of popular domains have been deeply replicated into ISPs. On the contrary, there is a trend that non-popular domains outsource the hosting services to third-party clouds that currently rarely deploy caches into ISP networks.
- *Hosting Provider Identification:* We propose a clustering algorithm for identifying hosting providers from passive DNS replies of massive domains. Specifically, we apply spectral clustering on the bipartite graph formed by domains and IP /24 subnets. We show the evidence that major providers slice up their infrastructures to host different kinds of services.
- *Tracker Hosting Infrastructure:* We reveal that while the examined ISP account for the largest amount of tracking queries, over 20% of the tracking queries are still mapped to foreign ASes. Besides, we surprisingly observe that as many as 60% of the tracking servers (i.e., servers used to deliver tracking content) and 52 ASes are exclusively used for tracking service.

2   Data and Metrics

2.1   Data: Passive DNS Replies

We collected our DNS data from the recursive resolvers of a cellular ISP in China. Once connected to the cellular network, mobile terminals will be automatically assigned a recursive resolver that the ISP operates. A recursive resolver receives hostname resolution requests from client hosts, and iteratively interacts with the hierarchical naming system to translate the names to IP addresses. The last step of this iterating process involves contacting the authoritative servers that maintain the mapping of the queried names to addresses. The authoritative servers often map the names to the domain hosting servers that are as proximate as possible to the recursive resolvers, in the hope that the hosting servers are also close to client hosts [10].

The examined ISP keeps a record for each DNS query at its recursive resolvers. A record consists of the recursive resolver's identifier, the timestamp, the requested domain name, the IP lists in the response, and finally the return code in the response. The records contain no specific information of client hosts for privacy concerns.

In total, we obtained 55,412,725,137 records from *all* the recursive resolvers of the examined cellular ISP for a duration of 2 days in 2015. The records are of A (IPv4) queries, *i.e.*, no AAAA (IPv6) queries were seen. By looking at the return (error) code, we observe a resolution successful ratio (*i.e.*, the ratio of records with "NOERROR") of 96.76%. Besides, over half of the hostnames map to more than one IP address. Our analysis, however, takes the first IP address as the one that the hostname is mapped to. This is reasonable because, in most cases, the first IP address is used for the following connection [9].

Data pre-processing: To simplify the analysis of such a huge dataset, we map the DNS FQDNs (Fully Qualified Domain Names) to their second level domains (SLDs) using the public suffix library [2]. The simplification yields 1,410,727 SLDs. The popularity of SLDs follows a power-law distribution, where less than 1% of the domains account for 80% of the queries. We further map IP addresses to their AS number (ASN) by querying Team Cymru [3]. We further aggregate the IP addresses in DNS responses into /24 subnetworks for the examination of the network footprints of domains. This aggregation granularity takes the fact that server clusters are often deployed for content hosting to achieve resilience and load balancing [7].

Ethical issue: The DNS dataset contains no information of individual users, and we were unable to link queries to users. It is also noteworthy that such datasets are routinely gathered by DNS servers in form of logs for security and operational purposes.

2.2   Content-Related Metrics

We use two metrics to characterize the content-related features of ASes. The first one is *content delivery potential* (CDP) [7], which gauges the amount of content that can be potentially served by an AS. Given a set of SLDs R (*e.g.*, tracking domains), the AS i's CDP is $CDP_i = \frac{|S_i|}{|R|}$, where $S_i \subseteq R$ is the set of domains that the AS can serve.

The second metric is *content monopoly index* (CMI) [7], which measures the extent to which an AS hosts content that others do not have. Let R denote the set of SLDs under consideration, $S_i \subseteq R$ the set of SLDs hosted by AS i, and m_j the number of ASes that host the SLD $j \in S_i$. The CMI of AS i is $CMI_i = \frac{1}{|S_i|} \sum_{j \in S_i} \frac{1}{m_j}$. A high CMI means some content is exclusively available in the AS.

3   On Hosting Infrastructure

3.1   Content Potential of ASes

Table 1 lists the top 20 ASes in terms of the volume of DNS queries that are resolved successfully. These ASes account for over 90% of the DNS queries.

Table 1. Top 20 ASes ranked by the volume of queries.

Rank	AS name[a]	vol. (%)	CMI_{top}	CMI_{all}
1	ISP-AS1	40.99	0.18	0.63
2	ISP-AS2	24.59	0.12	0.37
3	Alibaba	6.32	0.19	0.91
4	Apple	4.88	0.05	0.12
5	Chinanet-BJ	3.91	0.13	0.57
6	ISP-AS3	2.19	0.09	0.23
7	China169-back	1.38	0.11	0.65
8	ISP-AS4	1.33	0.26	0.52
9	ISP-AS5	1.05	0.10	0.26
10	ISP-AS6	0.94	0.07	0.22
11	Chinanet-back	0.81	0.13	0.75
12	Akamai-ASN1	0.79	0.06	0.35
13	Akamai-AS	0.76	0.05	0.34
14	Chinacache	0.67	0.06	0.23
15	CNIX	0.56	0.09	0.73
16	Chinanet-SN	0.54	0.06	0.56
17	China169-BJ	0.54	0.09	0.65
18	Yahoo-SG	0.52	0.03	0.09
19	Tencent	0.50	0.11	0.83
20	Google	0.40	0.05	0.53

[a] Due to business considerations, we cannot reveal the name of the examined ISP. Rather, we use ISP to denote it.

Besides, most of the queries are resolved to ISPs, rather than third-party content hosting providers, like Akamai. An AS appearing in the top list is because of either hosting either very popular domains, or hosting a large quantity of domains. The content delivery potential (CDP) of ASes in Fig. 1 exactly answers this question, where in Fig. 1a only the top 10,000 popular domains are considered when computing CDP, while Fig. 1b considers all domains.

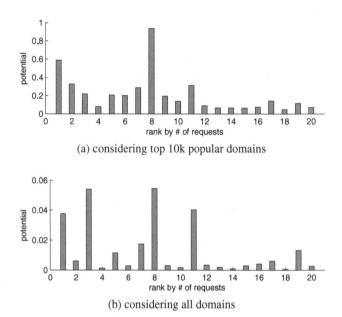

(a) considering top 10k popular domains

(b) considering all domains

Fig. 1. Content delivery potential of the top 20 ASes.

Figure 1a shows that the ASes of the examined ISP indeed hosts most of the popular domains. For instance, 95% of the popular domains can be served by ISP-AS4, and the top ranked one hosts about 60%. This observation implies that popular domains are well replicated in the examined ISP. The Apple's AS has a lower CDP, indicating that it appears in the list because of the frequent access of its domains from smartdevices, rather than hosting lots of domains.

When considering all domains in Fig. 1b, no AS hosts over 6% of the domains. This is within our expectation because most of the domains are only available in one single AS. It is also interesting to see that Alibaba cloud hosts the largest number of domains; Tencent cloud also hosts a significant fraction. The reason should be that some content owners, especially those of non-popular domains, outsource their domains to the clouds for easy maintenance and low access delay.

We further examine whether the listed ASes serve different or similar content in Fig. 2. An AS is associated with a content serving vector, and the i-th element is $< h_i, c_i >$, where h_i is a SLD and c_i is the number of queries on h_i that are mapped to the AS. We compute the similarity between two ASes using

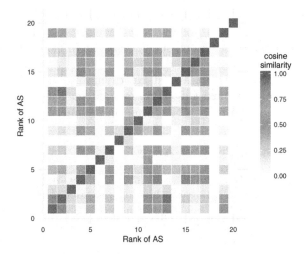

Fig. 2. Cosine similarity between each pair of ASes

the cosine similarity between their content serving vectors. Several observations are notable. First, the similarity values between the examined ISP's ASes are relative low, despite of the high content availability in the ASes. It seems that the ISP hosts different content in different ASes. Second, the relatively high similarity between Akamai's ASes and ISPs' ASes is an evidence that Akamai has already replicated content into ISPs, including the examined one and those that own China169 and Chinanet. Third, Alibaba and Tencent clouds host content that other ASes do not have, evidenced by the low similarity with other ASes. This is also confirmed by the high CMI values of these two ASes (see the last column of Table 1). Fourth, the high similarity between Apple and the ASes of Chinanet implies that Apple's content is available in Chinanet's ISP, but not the examined one. This is a potential performance bottleneck for the ISP's users to access Apple's content. Last but not least, Yahoo and Google's ASes host totally different content from others. This is because domains like google.com, flickr.com are blocked for access in China, so their content is not replicated to the ASes under consideration [8].

The above analysis, however, does not reveal the reasons of the presence of ISPs' ASes in Table 1. In fact, there are two possibilities. First, ISPs host content of popular domains that other ASes do not have, so that the queries of these domains can only be mapped to the ISPs' ASes. Second, content hosting providers deploy their content servers into the ISPs to boost the content delivery performance. Both cases may lead to a high CDP of an AS.

The content monopoly index (CMI, see Sect. 2) is used to investigate the first possibility. We observe low CMI values when considering only the top 10,000 domains (see the 4th column of Table 1), indicating that these ASes do not exclusively host content of *popular* domains that others do not have. When considering all domains, we observe high CMI values for some ASes, because they host lots of *non-popular* domains that are only available in the ASes. Moreover, the extremely high CMI values of the Alibaba cloud and Tencent cloud are further evidence of the trend of outsourcing content to clouds for non-popular domains that are less replicated.

For the second possibility, we aim at identifying the major content hosting providers. We do so in the next subsection by applying spectrum clustering on the bipartite graph formed by IP /24 subnets and domains.

3.2   Content Hosting Provider Analysis

We identify major hosting providers by clustering servers (identified by IP addresses) that are run by the same hosting provider. For this purpose, we form a bipartite graph, where one type of nodes is SLD, and the other is IP /24 subnet. An edge is present between a SLD node and a subnet node if the domain is mapped to the subnet in our dataset. Each edge is associated with a weight, which is defined later in this section. The key idea of clustering is that the /24 subnets used by a hosting provider serve the similar domains, and thus are densely connected through domains. Graph partitioning algorithms can thus be used for the clustering purpose.

Let $M \in \mathbb{R}^{m \times n}$ be the matrix representation of the bipartite graph. M would be a sparse matrix, where rows are domains (*i.e.*, SLDs), and columns represent /24 subnets. M_{ij} is the weight of the edge between the i-th domain and the j-th subnet. We set $M_{ij} = 1.0 + log(q_{ij})$, where q_{ij} is the number of queries of the i-th domain that are mapped to the j-th subnet. The intuition of weight setting is that the higher q_{ij} is, the more likely that the j-th subnet belongs to the hosting providers that deliver the i-th domain's content. We discard domains that are mapped to only one subnet to reduce the dimensionality. We finally apply a graph partitioning algorithm based on spectral clustering [14], as summarized in Algorithm 1, on M.

Algorithm 1. Spectral clustering of /24 subnets for the identification of content hosting providers

---

Input: $M \in \mathbb{R}^{m \times n}$
Output: Clusters of /24 subnets
1 $S \leftarrow M^{T} \cdot M$;
2 compute the first k eigenvectors from S;
3 k eigenvectors form $Q \in \mathbb{R}^{n \times k}$;
4 $v_i \leftarrow$ the i-th column of Q^{T} $(1 \leq i \leq n)$, *i.e.*, the dimension-reduced representation of the i-th /24 subnet;
5 Cluster the vectors (*i.e.*, /24 subnets) $\{v_i\}_{i=1,...,n}$ using the X-means clustering alg.

Each cluster yielded from the above algorithm represents a content hosting provider. To label the owners of clusters, we resort to the IP usage information from the examined ISP as well as third parties. The examined ISP maintains a table recording who uses which IP addresses (often represented in IP ranges). If there is one /24 subnet in a cluster belonging to the examined ISP, we looked up the table using the /24 subnet as key and get the entity name of the /24 subnet, which is further used as the owner of the clusters. Otherwise, we looked up third-party databases (*e.g.,* whois utility, MaxMind[1]) to infer cluster owners.

We find two exceptions during the labeling process. First, some clusters are labeled multiple owners. This happens because some domains, may leverage several CDNs for content distribution. For instance, Both Netflix and Hulu use three CDNs: Akamai, LimeLight and Level-3 [6]. The /24 subnets of these CDNs may be clustered into one cluster as they are connected by the same domains. We label them as mixed. Second, some owners have multiple clusters. This happens because an owner may provide multiple types of services, and it slices up its hosting infrastructure to host different services. For instance, Tencent uses one cluster of subnets for multimedia objects delivery and one for social network service hosting. In this case, we further infer the major services that a cluster provides by examining the domains in the cluster.

In total, we get 922 clusters. Table 2 lists the top 15 clusters, along with their network footprints and owners[2] These clusters account for over 50% of the queries. We can see the owners indeed are the major providers that provide a large amount of mobile content in China. As expected, the mixed ones contain more /24 subnets and have footprints in much more ASes than other clusters, because they contain several CDNs. The major CDN players in China, like ChinaCache and ChinaNetCenter, are included in the mixed clusters, because they are used by several popular Internet video providers (*e.g.,* PPTV, iQiyi).

The four clusters owned by Tencent distinguish from each other in the services that they provide. For instance, the first-ranked cluster hosts Tencent multimedia objects, while the second hosts Tencent social networks. We make similar observations for the Baidu's clusters. Xiaomi (a smartphone maker) appears in the list, because of the huge number of users using its smartphones, which frequently contact its cloud center for storage/retrieval of personal data, software download etc. Alibaba, on the other hand, hosts its own services (like alipay), as well as the outsourced content to it.

Akamai's clusters were identified by the prevalence of akacdn.com and akamaiedge.net in the clusters. Nevertheless, the /24 subnets do not necessarily belong to Akamai's AS, but the partners that Akamai collaborate with in China. Finally, we see Apple and Google in the list because of their prevalence in

---

[1] MaxMind: www.maxmind.com.

[2] We manually cross-checked the CNAMEs of the popular domains (FQDNs) in non-mixed clusters to validate the clustering approach. For example, the popular domains in both Baidu clusters use the CNAMEs with the same suffix shifen.com, which is run by Baidu.

Table 2. Top 15 clusters in terms of query volume

Rank	volume (%)	# /24 subs	# ASes	Owner
1	8.5	11	2	Tencent
2	7.0	4	1	Tencent
3	6.7	37	16	`mixed`
4	4.2	5	3	Xiaomi
5	3.9	3	1	Akamai[a]
6	3.6	3	1	Tencent
7	3.2	2	2	Baidu
8	2.9	6	1	Alibaba
9	2.6	4	2	Baidu
10	2.4	2	2	Akamai[a]
11	2.4	3	1	Tencent
12	2.3	81	30	`mixed`
13	2.3	47	24	`mixed`
14	2.1	8	3	Google
15	1.8	5	1	Apple

[a] The /24 subnets belong to a Chinese CDN provider, with which Akamai collaborates for content delivery.

mobile phone market. The Apple cluster mainly provides service for apple.com, and thus the volume share is less than the Apple AS showed in Table 1.

3.3   Summary and Discussion

Our analysis in this section has revealed that the cellular content infrastructure is mostly concentrated in the examined ISP's ASes. This implies a significant locality of cellular traffic. Besides, it means cellular users can get their content mostly within only one AS hop, since the ASes of the examined ISP are often peered with each other.

Our analysis also shows the trend of outsourcing non-popular domains to clouds. This implies cloud providers have already taken the niche market of content hosting. As this trend continues, cloud providers will become *de-facto* content providers that deliver a large amount of content that other ASes do not have (see Table 1). In fact, Tencent has already offered CDN service based on its cloud platform [4]. This may change the ecosystem of content hosting.

The proposed clustering algorithm provides a tool for content hosting provider identification from large-scale passive DNS datasets. The above analysis provides evidence of slicing-up infrastructure by hosting providers to deliver different kinds of content.

4   Tracker Hosting Infrastructure

This section examines the hosting infrastructure of tracking domains (*a.k.a.* trackers), because tracking is prevalent in mobile web service and mobile apps. Mobile users are getting concerned about the possible privacy leakage. Besides, it would be interesting to see the impact of content censorship on tracking behavior.

To identify the tracking domains, we used lists of trackers proposed by Ad blockers. More precisely, we merged two lists: *EasyList* (combined with the EasyList China supplementary list)[3] and *Simple Malvertising*[4]. Each queried hostname is labeled as tracker or normal depending on the suffix match with a hostname in the lists. In total, we find 124,235 tracking domains, which are further aggregated to 1,456 second-level domains.

4.1   Top Trackers

We first examine the top 10 tracking domains in terms of DNS query volume and their network features in Table 3. These domains account for 90% of total tracking queries, showing a very biased distribution of tracking traffic. It is surprising to see only 2 tracking domains are based in China, and most in US. We conjecture the prevalence of Android phones and the availability of mobile third-party analytics libraries are the main reasons for this observation [11].

Table 3. Top 10 tracking (second-level) domains

Domain	Vol.%	Type*	#ASes	Owner
flurry.com	35.07	an	11	Yahoo
crashlytics.com	25.25	an	18	Google
scorecardresearch.com	18.53	an	21	comScore
doubleclick.net	3.38	ad	24	Google
adsmogo.com	1.77	ad	9	Alibaba
tapjoy.com	1.71	ad	11	Tapjoy
inmobi.com	1.61	ad	14	InMobi
tapjoyads.com	1.56	ad	4	Tapjoy
51yes.com	1.31	an	20	51yes
vungle.com	0.84	ad	9	Vungle

* **an**: analytics, **ad**: advertiser

---

[3] https://easylist.to.
[4] https://disconnect.me/lists/malvertising.

4.2 Tracker Hosting Infrastructure

We then focus on the tracking servers (identified by IPs) that host the trackers. We say a server is a tracking server if more than 10 tracking queries are resolved to the server's IP address[5]. In total, 7,404 tracking servers are identified.

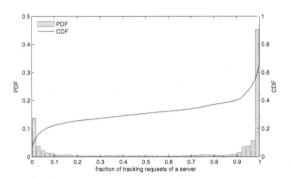

Fig. 3. Distr. of the ratio of tracking queries of servers. The left y-axis is for probability distr. function, while the right one is for cumulative distr. function.

A tracking server may host both tracking domains and non-tracking ones. For each tracking server, we compute the ratio of tracking queries (*i.e.*, queries to tracking domains) to all queries resolved to it, and plot the distribution in Fig. 3. We observe a bimodal distribution, where most of tracking servers either deliver a very small ratio of tracking queries (*i.e.*, < 0.1), or dedicate most of its capacity for tracker hosting. As in [15], we consider a server dedicated exclusively for hosting tracking service if the ratio of tracking queries exceeds 0.9. This is reasonable given that the two lists used for tracker identification may not cover all tracking domains in our trace. We surprisingly find as many as 4,427 (59.8%) tracking servers are exclusively used for hosting trackers, and these servers account for half of the tracking queries in our dataset.

Next, we study the ASes that host most of the trackers in Table 4. The tracking traffic is also mostly concentrated in the examined ISP's ASes. It means the hosting service of trackers has also been deployed into cellular networks. Besides ISPs, we also see cloud providers (Amazon and Internap), CDNs (Akamai) and search engines (Google), implying diverse infrastructures being used for tracking services. Despite of the traffic concentration in the examined ISP, a considerable fraction (> 20%) still goes to the ASes that have rare footprints in China.

We then report the ratio of tracking queries to all queries of ASes (see the 3rd column in Table 4). It is surprising to see some ASes (*e.g.*, Internap) being exclusively used for tracker content delivery. We then compute the ratio of tracking queries for the ASes that have at least 1,000 tracking queries resolved to them.

---

[5] Due to DNS caching, we may underestimate the queries mapped to individual IP addresses.

Table 4. Top 10 ASes by tracking requests

AS name	% tracking in trace	% tracking in AS	CDP	CMI
ISP-AS1	35.27	1.89	0.03	0.12
ISP-AS2	24.10	0.77	0.12	0.42
Amazon-AES	7.96	54.79	0.09	0.30
Internap-B.4	7.01	100.00	< 0.01	0.11
ISP-AS3	5.64	25.29	< 0.01	0.05
ISP-AS4	3.89	3.84	0.34	0.35
Amazon-02	2.96	14.77	0.11	0.36
GoogleCN	2.32	27.28	< 0.01	0.17
NTT	1.43	34.33	0.06	0.16
Akamai-ASN	1.04	1.74	0.09	0.20

Again, we use the threshold 0.9 to determine whether an AS exclusively hosts trackers or not. As many as 52 ASes are identified as exclusive tracking ones. They are either cloud providers (*e.g.*, Internap, Carpathia), or owners of trackers that run their own ASes (*e.g.*, Crashlytics).

We finally report the content delivery potential (CDP) and content monopoly index (CMI) of the ASes when considering only tracking domains in the last two columns of Table 4. We see low CDP (< 0.1) for most of ASes because they host only several popular tracking domains. The CMI is also relatively low, meaning that the tracking domains hosted by these ASes are also available in other ASes.

4.3 Summary and Discussion

We observe that the tracking queries are concentrated in a small number of trackers, of which most are US based. Moreover, over 20% of the tracking traffic goes out of China. These observations raise privacy and cybersecurity concerns. The analysis also reveals that multiple types of infrastructures are used for tracker service hosting.

The bimodal distribution of the tracking query ratio shows that 60% of the tracking servers exclusively provide tracking services. Monitoring the traffic going to these servers may help us find new trackers that also rely on these servers for content delivery. ISPs and mobile apps can also use this observation to block tracking activities for privacy and security concerns.

5 Conclusion

This paper uses passive DNS traces from a Chinese cellular ISP to investigate the mobile content hosting infrastructure in China. To this end, we proposed a clustering algorithm to identify hosting providers and used content-related metrics to characterize hosting infrastructure. Our key observation is that ISPs and hosting providers have collaborated to extensively replicate popular content into cellular networks. On the contrary, content of many non-popular domains and tracking domains tends to be available only in particular networks, resulting content monopoly by these networks.

Our findings provide evidences that the ISPs and CDNs in China follow the global trends of close collaboration [1,12]. However, care should be given when generalizing our findings to other countries. In addition, our dataset was collected from only one cellular ISP and the observation period is only two days. We are collecting DNS data from multiple ISPs with longer observation period, in the hope of providing an up-to-date picture of the content hosting infrastructure in China.

Acknowledgments. The authors would like to thank Rocky Chang for shepherding our paper and PAM reviewers for their feedback. This work is supported in part by National Key R&D Program of China (Grant No. 2016YFE0133000): EU-China study on IoT and 5G(EXCITING), National Natural Science Foundation of China (Grant No. 61572475 and 61502460).

References

1. Akamai and AT&T renew global alliance (2017). https://goo.gl/b2uHMT
2. Public suffix list (2017). https://publicsuffix.org
3. Team Cymru (2017). http://www.team-cymru.org/
4. Tencent Cloud CDN (2017). https://www.qcloud.com/en/product/cdn.html
5. VNI mobile forecast highlights (2017). http://www.cisco.com/assets/sol/sp/vni/forecast_highlights_mobile
6. Adhikari, V.K., Guo, Y., Hao, F., Hilt, V., Zhang, Z.L., Varvello, M., Steiner, M.: Measurement study of Netflix, Hulu, and a tale of three CDNs. IEEE/ACM Trans. Networking **23**(6), 1984–1997 (2015)
7. Ager, B., Mühlbauer, W., Smaragdakis, G., Uhlig, S.: Web content cartography. In: Proceedings of the ACM IMC (2011)
8. Calder, M., Fan, X., Hu, Z., Katz-Bassett, E., Heidemann, J., Govindan, R.: Mapping the expansion of Google's serving infrastructure. In: Proceedings of the ACM IMC (2013)
9. Callahan, T., Allman, M., Rabinovich, M.: On modern DNS behavior and properties. SIGCOMM Comput. Commun. Rev. **43**(3), 7–15 (2013)
10. Chen, F., Sitaraman, R.K., Torres, M.: End-user mapping: Next generation request routing for content delivery. In: Proceedings of the ACM SIGCOMM (2015)
11. Chen, T., Ullah, I., Kaafar, M.A., Boreli, R.: Information leakage through mobile analytics services. In: Proceedings of the ACM HotMobile (2014)
12. Frank, B., Poese, I., Lin, Y., Smaragdakis, G., Feldmann, A., Maggs, B., Rake, J., Uhlig, S., Weber, R.: Pushing CDN-ISP collaboration to the limit. SIGCOMM Comput. Commun. Rev. **43**(3), 34–44 (2013)
13. Han, S., Jung, J., Wetherall, D.: A study of third-party tracking by mobile apps in the wild. Technical report, UW-CSE-12-03-01, March 2012
14. Ng, A.Y., Jordan, M.I., Weiss, Y.: On spectral clustering: analysis and an algorithm. In: Proceedings of the NIPS (2001)

15. Pujol, E., Hohlfeld, O., Feldmann, A.: Annoyed users: ads and ad-block usage in the wild. In: Proceedings of the ACM IMC (2015)
16. Triukose, S., Wen, Z., Rabinovich, M.: Measuring a commercial content delivery network. In: Proceedings of the WWW (2011)
17. Xue, J., Choffnes, D., Wang, J.: CDNs meet CN: An empirical study of CDN deployments in China. In: IEEE Access (2017)

Characterizing a Meta-CDN

Oliver Hohlfeld[(⊠)], Jan Rüth, Konrad Wolsing, and Torsten Zimmermann

Communication and Distributed Systems, RWTH Aachen University,
Aachen, Germany
{hohlfeld,rueth,wolsing,tzimmermann}@comsys.rwth-aachen.de

Abstract. CDNs have reshaped the Internet architecture at large. They operate (globally) distributed networks of servers to reduce latencies as well as to increase availability for content and to handle large traffic bursts. Traditionally, content providers were mostly limited to a single CDN operator. However, in recent years, more and more content providers employ multiple CDNs to serve the same content and provide the same services. Thus, switching between CDNs, which can be beneficial to reduce costs or to select CDNs by optimal performance in different geographic regions or to overcome CDN-specific outages, becomes an important task. Services that tackle this task emerged, also known as CDN broker, Multi-CDN selectors, or Meta-CDNs. Despite their existence, little is known about Meta-CDN operation in the wild. In this paper, we thus shed light on this topic by dissecting a major Meta-CDN. Our analysis provides insights into its infrastructure, its operation in practice, and its usage by Internet sites. We leverage PlanetLab and Ripe Atlas as distributed infrastructures to study how a Meta-CDN impacts the web latency.

1 Introduction

Content Delivery Networks (CDNs) have become a key component of the web [7,8]. Their ongoing quest to serve web content from nearby servers has flattened the hierarchical structure of the Internet [14] and promises lower latencies, while their distributed nature promises high availability. These benefits led to a wide adoption of CDNs for web content delivery that is manifested in high traffic shares: for example, more than half of the traffic of as North American [13] or a European [20] Internet Service Provider (ISP) can be attributed to few CDNs only. Despite these benefits, customers of a single CDN are bound to its cost model and performance figures—a limitation that is solved by multihoming content on different CDNs and subsequently serving it from the CDN that currently offers better performance and/or lower costs.

To better utilize content-multihoming, *Meta-CDNs* [12] enable content providers to realize custom and dynamic routing policies to direct traffic to the different CDNs hosting their content; A concept also known as CDN-Selector [23]

Authors in alphabetical order.

© Springer International Publishing AG, part of Springer Nature 2018
R. Beverly et al. (Eds.): PAM 2018, LNCS 10771, pp. 114–128, 2018.
https://doi.org/10.1007/978-3-319-76481-8_9

and that is related to auction-based CDN brokers [16,17]. Request routing is performed by the Meta-CDN according to *custom routing logic* defined by content-providers (i.e., the customers of a Meta-CDN and CDNs). This routing logic can be informed by a broad range of factors, including CDN cost models or measured CDN performance. Content providers can thus utilize a Meta-CDN to reduce costs or to optimize performance, e.g., by implementing custom logic to direct traffic to a CDN that currently offers better performance and/or lower cost (e.g., at certain geographic regions or times). Since the routing approach employed by the Meta-CDN customers is unknown to the involved CDNs, directed traffic and thus generated revenue gets harder to predict. In particular, since decisions can be based on active performance measurements by the Meta-CDN, a (single) delivery of bad performance by the probed CDN can result in rerouting traffic to a competing CDN and thus losing revenue. Thus, while Meta-CDNs can offer cost and performance benefits to content providers, they also challenge CDN business models. Concerning Internet-users, performance-based routing decisions can yield better Internet performance and benefit end-users while cost-based decisions can have other effects (as for any server selection approach run by CDNs). While the concept is known and related work covering service specific implementations, i.e., Conviva's streaming platform [4,10,16], exists, the empirical understanding of a generic Meta-CDN and its operation in practice is still limited. We posit that this understanding is necessary.

In this paper, we thus shed light on the Meta-CDN operation by dissecting the Cedexis Meta-CDN as a prominent example that is used by major Internet companies such as Microsoft (Windows Update and parts of the XBox Live Network), Air France, and LinkedIn [1]. Given its current adoption, understanding its functionality and its usage by customers provides a first step towards understanding currently unknown implications of Meta-CDNs on Internet operation. We thus investigate the infrastructure and services powering this Meta-CDN and provide insights about its operation in practice. We analyze for *what* kind of services, e.g., media, API backends, or bulk data transfers, customers utilize Cedexis and *how* different CDNs are employed. We further investigate how the infrastructure deployed by Cedexis impacts the overall request latency performance in a PlanetLab and Ripe Atlas measurement. Specifically, our contributions are as follows:

(i) We characterize Cedexis, as a representative generic Meta-CDN, present its operation principles, and further analyze and classify its customer base. Moreover, we illustrate which CDNs are used by the customers.

(ii) We utilize globally distributed vantage points, i.e., Ripe Atlas, PlanetLab, Open DNS Resolvers and a small deployment of probes behind home user DSL connections, to obtain a *global* view on Cedexis. Based on these measurements, we analyze the deployed infrastructure of Cedexis, and are further able to investigate if the selection process varies based on the location. In addition, we find cases of suboptimal routing in terms of latency.

2   Background and Related Work

To achieve high availability, content and service providers typically employ CDN operators and utilize their already deployed and geographically distributed infrastructures [7,8]. In addition to increased availability, end-users profit from the distributed nature of these CDNs when retrieving content from close-by servers, reducing the overall latency.

Multiple works from academia and industry have investigated these infrastructures, the operation principles as well as the performance of deployed CDNs [7,8,18,19]. Besides understanding and measuring CDN infrastructures, researchers have utilized CDN routing techniques to derive network conditions [21]. In addition, approaches that optimize the routing of user requests to the respective servers within a CDN, as well as, optimized anycast load balancing have been proposed [9,11]. Poese et al. [20] present and analyze the impact of an ISP recommendation service providing insights about the current network state, e.g., topology, load, or delay, to the CDN, which in turn bases its server selection on the returned information. The idea and concept of the presented approach is revisited by Frank et al. [12] and, among other features, enables a CDN to allocate server resources within the ISP on-demand when necessary.

To further ensure the availability of content, customers may use multiple CDN deployments. Other reasons to utilize more than one CDN provider may be cost efficiency, e.g., different prices to serve content at different times or due to traffic volume contracts. However, with multiple locations at different CDNs serving the same service or content, either the customer or an additional service has to choose between the actual CDN when a user requests a service or content [12,15,23]. With respect to *multi-homed* content, i.e., content that is distributed by multiple CDNs, Lui et al. [15] present one of the first frameworks optimizing performance and cost of the resulting CDN assignment. In the case of video streaming, Conviva [4] uses a recommendation system that is utilized by the video player software [10] for the CDN selection. Besides Conviva, commercial solutions that offer to act as the CDN selector in more generic settings, e.g., websites or services, exist [1,5,6], however, there is currently little to no understanding of their infrastructures, customers, and the effects on the global CDN landscape. With respect to Meta-CDNs and especially Cedexis, Xue et al. [23] are the first to provide brief performance figures about the selected CDNs, focusing on deployments in China. We aim at more broadly characterizing Cedexis as a whole while looking at their infrastructure and performance on a global scale. Nevertheless, we find, similar to Xue, partly suboptimal performance in terms of latency, yet, we acknowledge that routing decisions may have other goals than latency. This argument is reinforced by Mukerjee et al. [16], which is closest to our work. They analyze the effect of brokers, i.e., CDN selectors, on CDNs, characterize potential problems and propose a new interface between these brokers and CDNs. While a closer interaction may improve certain aspects, it remains open whether a Meta-CDN such as Cedexis does, in fact, harm a CDN's profitability. We cannot confirm a raised concern that a broker *might* prefer certain CDNs in certain regions, as we find similar CDN choices worldwide.

The goal of this paper is to extend the currently limited understanding of Meta-CDN operation by characterizing Cedexis as a prominent example of a generic Meta-CDN. Exemplified by understanding its overall deployment, customers, and the effects Cedexis, we aim to provide a first step towards a better understanding of Meta-CDNs in general.

3 Characterizing a Meta-CDN

The general motivation behind a Meta-CDN is to enable custom and dynamic routing of requests to content that is multi-homed in different Content Distribution Infrastructures (CDIs). A CDI can involve any infrastructure ranging from simple (cloud-hosted) servers to complex CDNs [20]. Multihoming content on different CDIs enables content providers to optimize for availability, performance, or operational costs. By utilizing a Meta-CDN, content providers can realize *custom* routing logic to direct traffic to the available CDIs. Such custom routing logic can be motivated by CDIs that offer better performance and/or lower costs in certain geographic regions, at certain times of the day, or request volumes. We refer to an infrastructure that enables routing between CDIs with customer-provided routing logic as a *Meta-CDN*, a concept that is also referred to as Multi-CDN selector [23] and has similarities to auction-based CDN brokers [16]. Since the individual routing approaches employed by content providers at the Meta-CDN are unknown to the involved CDIs, directed traffic and thus generated revenue gets harder to predict. In particular, since decisions can be based on active performance measurements by the Meta-CDN, a (single) delivery of bad performance by the probed CDI can result in rerouting traffic to a competing CDI and thus losing revenue. While the effects of Meta-CDN operation are relevant to Internet operation, little is known about Meta-CDNs.

To elucidate Meta-CDN operation, we start by characterizing Cedexis as a prominent example. We base this characterization on showing *(i)* its operational principles to select and routing between CDIs based on the Cedexis site (Sect. 3.1) and *(ii)* its current use in the Internet by analyzing its customer base in Sect. 3.2 based on our measurements. Both perspectives provide a first understanding of the principle mechanisms with which Meta-CDNs can influence content distribution and their current deployment in the wild.

3.1 Operation Principles

Like most CDNs, Cedexis employs a DNS-based redirection scheme, similar to Akamai [18], to redirect the requesting user to the CDI selected for content delivery. This redirection scheme is based on Canonical Name (CNAME) records which transfer the requesting user between the different authoritative name servers (NS). We exemplify this scheme in Fig. 1. Starting at the original domain (❶), the user gets transferred to the Cedexis NS, which then selects a final CDI. The configured static Cedexis CNAME includes a Cedexis customer ID (C_{ID}) (❷) and configuration specific (App_{ID}) ❸. Both identifiers enable

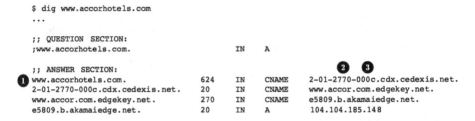

Fig. 1. Exemplary output of `dig` resolving a customer domain managed by Cedexis. The requesting user is redirected by the Cedexis authoritative DNS with a CNAME to the CDN selected to handle the request. The Cedexis CNAME contains the customer ID ❷ (C_{ID}) and a per-customer application ID ❸ (App$_{ID}$).

the Cedexis NS to perform customer-specific request routing, once the NS is contacted by the client's DNS resolver for name resolution. Similar to classic CDNs, routing can be subject to a user's location, e.g., identified by DNS resolver IP or EDNS0 client subnet extension. The Cedexis NS then points to the selected CDI, which can be an IP address in an A resource record or another CNAME, e.g., pointing to CDN (Akamai in this particular example). The selected CDI can then repeat this process to select the final server handling the request or point to another CDI. By realizing routing in the DNS, Cedexis redirects requesting users to a CDI *before* a connection to the CDI is established. This way, it is not involved in the actual content delivery itself and thus does not alter the performance or security properties provided by the selected CDI.

CDI Selection Options. The above-stated request routing approach can be arbitrarily dynamic, i.e., the user to CDI mapping in the DNS can change at any time, only limited by the cacheability of their DNS records. This aspect is utilized to enable content providers to realize custom routing logic within Cedexis using three components: *(i) Openmix* enables Cedexis customers to configure individual routing logic. Customers can choose between `optimal RTT` to select the CDI with the lowest RTT to the requesting user, `round-robin` balancing between all CDIs configured by a customer, `throughput` to select the CDI with the highest throughput, a `static routing` or by executing `customer provided code`. This routing logic can be informed by *(ii) Radar*, a large database for decision making based on active browser-based CDN measurements performed by website visitors, and *(iii) Fusion*, to retrieve data from CDNs. Every customer has the ability to configure site-specific behavior (i.e., *Apps*) which results in different App$_{IDs}$ in the DNS. This way, a customer can configure different routing profiles for *downloads.domain.tld* and for *images.domain.tld*. We next describe the two data sources and the Openmix platform to realize custom routing decisions.

Radar. Cedexis provides a community-driven CDN performance measurement platform called Radar. Radar employs active measurements performed within the web browser of visitors of Cedexis-managed websites. The in-browser measurements require the Cedexis customers to embed a Javascript in their website.

Once visited, the web browser triggers the website's onLoad event, the embedded Javascript waits for a user configurable timeout (default 2 s) and starts requesting probe instructions from Cedexis. Users can configure private probes (i.e., to estimate their own performance) and can choose to activate community probes (i.e., enabling Cedexis to measure other infrastructures). Probes can serve different purposes, latency or throughput measurements, which are expressed through a small 43 Byte file (latency) or 100 kB file (throughput) that is fetched via HTTP. After having performed the measurements, the Javascript reports the obtained values back to Cedexis such that they can later be used to guide performance decisions in the CDN selection process and to inform site operators about their site's performance.

Fusion. While Radar enables to realize performance-based routing decisions, Fusion enables realize decisions on statistics directly from a user's CDNs. CDNs typically offer statistics about traffic shares, quotas, budgets, performance and other KPIs in their web interfaces. By accessing these, Cedexis enables their customers to not only draw performance decisions but also business decisions (e.g., *will I hit my quota soon?*).

Openmix. Both Radar and Fusion data are available to customers in the Openmix platform. Openmix enables customers to customize the DNS resolution process by providing custom Javascript code that is executed in the DNS resolution step. Within this code, customers can define their subsequent candidate CDI choices and request measurement data (e.g., availability, latency, throughput) for these. While the system is powered by many probes, only singles values are returned suggesting that Cedexis preprocesses the measurement data, yet we were unable to find more information on this process. Thus, Openmix is used to realize customer-specific routing decision performed within the DNS resolution, i.e., directing traffic to a target CDI via a DNS CNAME.

Takeaway. *Cedexis offers its customers to realize site-specific, fine-granular, and dynamic traffic routing to CDIs, e.g., based on customer-provided code and informed by rich measurement data. The performed traffic routing is hard to predict (e.g., for CDIs).*

3.2   Customers

Before we analyze the infrastructure and configuration of Cedexis, we want to shed light on their customer base (in anonymous form). We are interested in which companies and businesses leverage this additional service on top of classical CDN infrastructures.

DNS Measurement Methodology. Our approach is twofold. First, we leverage the encoded customer and application IDs in the CNAME structure (see step ❷ & ❸ in Fig. 1) to **enumerate customers**. Applications are used by customers to define different routing profiles that later on map on the available CDIs and defined single redirection strategy, so e.g., a customer may have one profile that is optimized for latency, and another for throughput. Conveniently, App

Table 1. Cedexis customer information obtained from manual inspection of websites served for different customer IDs. Please note that customers may operate multiple services, e.g., multiple brands of one holding company.

Type	Share	Type	Share	Type	Share	Service	Share
Business	17.7%	Unknown	8.1%	Social	1.6%	Web	62.7%
IT	12.1%	Goods	5.6%	CDN	1.6%	Unknown	15.6%
News	11.3%	Automotive	5.6%	Patents	0.8%	Assets	12.9%
Gambling	11.3%	Advertising	3.2%	Banking	0.8%	Media	5.4%
Shopping	8.1%	Streaming	2.4%			API	2.3%
Gaming	8.1%	Television	1.6%			Bulkdata	1.1%

(a) Classification

(b) Services

IDs start at 1. Thus our approach is to simply enumerate customers by resolving all `2-01-(C_ID)-(App_ID).cdx.cedexis.net` domains. As customer and application ID each have 4 hex characters, we would need to probe $> 2.5B$ (16^8) domains. To scale-down our DNS resolution, we only enumerate the first 256 application IDs for each customer, resulting in resolving roughly 16M domains.

Domain Lists. Second, we probe domain lists to study the usage of the enumerated CNAMES in the wild and to discover application IDs beyond the enumerated 256 IDs. We thus resolve the A of `domain.tld` and the A `www.domain.tld` records for all domains in the *(i)* .com/.net (obtained by Verisign), *(ii)* .org (obtained from PIR), *(iii)* .fi (obtained from Ficora), *(iv)* .se/.nu (obtained from IIS), *(v)* .new gTLD zones (obtained from ICANN's Centralized Zone Data Service), *(vi)* obtained from our passive DNS probe, and *(vii)* the Alexa Top 1M list. We additionally include the Cisco Umbrella Top 1M list [3], which is based on the most frequent queries to OpenDNS resolvers and additionally contains subdomains, e.g., `images.domain.tld`. Depending on the size of the list, we perform daily or weekly resolutions for four weeks in August 2017 and extract all domains which have a CNAME pointer containing `*.cedexis.net`.

Customer List. We combine both data sets to a customer list that will form the basis for probing Cedexis globally in Sect. 4. The list contains all customer application tuples, of which 84% were discovered in the enumeration step, 11.2% were discovered in both the enumeration and in the domain lists, and 4.8% solely in domain lists. The reasons for the latter are application IDs larger than 256, which were not part of our enumeration. Out of all customers, 55 (20) have only 1 (2) application(s) configured. We also observe 1 customer having 84 configured. By resolving the domain lists, we find 4609 (sub-)domains pointing to 16% of all discovered (customer, application) tuples. The remaining 84% were not hit when resolving our domain lists. For 62.7% of all customer application IDs, we only find a single domain pointing to it. We find 31 (6) application IDs managing more than 10 (100) domains, respectively.

We show the popularity of Cedexis over time among Alexa-listed domains in Fig. 2. We set up our own regular DNS resolutions in December 2016 and

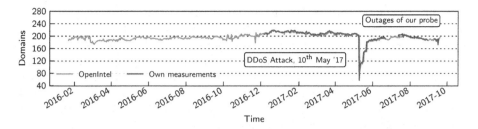

Fig. 2. Domains utilizing Cedexis in the Alexa 1M over time. The drop in May '17 was caused by a DDoS Attack on Cedexis [2]. Unfortunately, the measurement probe located at our chair experienced two outages. However, the overlap of both scans motivates the further use of the OpenIntel data set.

further show regular Alexa resolutions performed by OpenINTEL [22] in the Netherlands for the same resource records. First, we observe that both data sets overlap, suggesting that both are suitable for monitoring. Minor fluctuations in the number of domains per day can mainly be attributed to fluctuations in the Alexa listed domains. Second, we observe an outage of Cedexis in May 2017 which was caused by a DDoS attack on their infrastructure [2]. The outage motivated some customers to remove CNAME pointers to Cedexis in favor of pointing to operational CDNs instead, causing a drop of >120 domains in Fig. 2.

Customer Classification. We next classify the discovered customers by manually inspecting a randomly chosen domain for each customer and application ID. We instructed a single human classifier to visit each web site and categorize it according to an evolving set of categories. We show the resulting categorized web site content in Table 1(a). The table shows that Cedexis is used by a broad range of customers. We further classify the used service in Table 1(b). The table shows that most customers use Cedexis for general web content delivery. This includes few but large bulk download services, e.g., www.download.windowsupdate.com. This is in contrast to, e.g., Conviva which is dedicated to video delivery.

Takeaway. *Cedexis is utilized by a number of (large) web services. Decisions taken by Cedexis have the potential to impact larger bulks of Internet traffic.*

4   A Global View on Cedexis

As Cedexis customers can realize routing decisions based on (network) location, we next take a global view on its customers by using globally distributed active measurements.

Measurement Setup. We base our measurements on 35 PlanetLab nodes located in 8 countries, 6 custom Raspberry Pi (RPi) probes in 6 distinct German ISPs, and RIPE Atlas probes. We chose PlanetLab and custom RPis in addition to RIPE Atlas since they enable us to deploy custom software to perform frequent DNS resolutions. As we do not include PlanetLab nodes located in

Germany in our set, we refer to our deployed RPis when mentioning *DE* in figures or plots. We selected only few PlanetLab nodes with high availability to repeatedly measure always from the same vantage points. For our measurement, we instruct the Planet Lab and our RPi nodes to resolve each domain every 15 min and subsequently measure the latency to the resulting IPs. Moreover, we keep track of all CNAME redirections to CDNs that we observe over the course of the measurement and also resolve these. This way, we learn the set of configured CDNs for every probed domain.

4.1 Infrastructure

Authoritative DNS Deployment. Cedexis core functionality is based on a distributed infrastructure of authoritative name servers managing `*.cedexis.net`. We find four servers configured in the DNS in our measurements and in the `.net` zone file. We remark that a larger number exists which we found by enumerating their naming pattern. However, they currently appear to be unused, i.e., not included in the *.net* zone and are not discovered by our active DNS measurements.

To obtain a better understanding of its DNS infrastructure, we measure the ICMP echo (ping) latency to their authoritative name servers from ≈870 responsive (out of 1000 selected) RIPE Atlas probes. We repeated this measurement 30 times using the same set of probes and show the minimum RTT in Fig. 3(a). Based on these latency figures, we infer that Cedexis operates DNS servers located in North-America, Europe, and (probably) Asia and South America. By analyzing individual latencies and manual traceroutes per server-IP (not shown), we observe latencies of <10 ms from multiple regions (e.g., US-East, US-West, Europe, Hongkong) to the *same* DNS server IP. Since these low latencies are lower than required by the speed of light between the respective regions, it suggests that the probed server-IPs are served using *anycast* routing.

Since the additional indirection step through Cedexis contributes latency, we next measure the DNS resolution time of only their authoritative name servers.

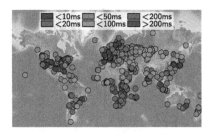

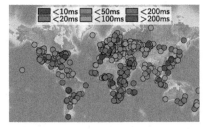

(a) Minimum `ping` RTTs to the four Cedexis authoritative nameservers.

(b) Median DNS query times to resolve an A record via Cedexis

Fig. 3. RTTs and DNS Query times obtained from ≈870 responsive RIPE Atlas Probes performing pings and DNS A Record requests.

In this step, we resolve the domain of a Cedexis customer from all authoritative name servers from the same RIPE Atlas probes, again repeated 30 times. To limit the resolution to only involve the Cedexis DNS, we chose a customer domain which directly returns an A record instead of redirecting to another CDN. This is especially important if the lifetime of the DNS records is short (which we analyze in Sect. 4.2) and clients need to frequently contact the Cedexis DNS over and over again. We show the median DNS query time in Fig. 3(b) and observe that the DNS query times follow the previously measured ping latencies. Nevertheless, we observe few regions in which Cedexis appears to be uncovered as they involve high DNS resolution latencies, e.g., Latin America or Africa.

Radar Community Probes. Cedexis customers can realize routing decisions that are based on active measurements of current service performance probed by visitors of Cedexis managed websites (Radar platform, see Sect. 3.1). Understanding this data is interesting since it can influence routing decisions. As the Radar data is not publicly available, we instead analyze live feeds of network events detected by Radar and published at https://live.cedexis.com. The events report three classes of metrics: *latency*, *throughput*, and *availability* for *ISP*, *CDN*, and *cloud* infrastructures. An event can be a latency in- or decrease, an outage, or a change in throughput. A CDN/cloud event is detected if it was reported by visitors from 5 different ASes. Likewise, an AS event is detected if it concerns 5 CDNs or clouds (see live.cedexis.com). Each event can be classified by severity into *minor*, *medium*, and *major*. Apart from being used in their decision-making process, this data allows monitoring the reported infrastructures. We thus monitored the data feed from October 9, 2017, to January 8, 2018.

Reported events further provide information *where* visitors of Cedexis-managed sites are located. This is based on fact that Cedexis customers embed Javascript measurement code into their sites that reports performance figures to the Radar platform. While the number of events is likely uncorrelated with the number of website visitors, it at least indicates the presence of a visitor in the reported AS or country. Therefore, we show the distribution of the number of events per-country in Fig. 4(a). We observe almost no events in Africa, suggesting that Cedexis customers do not have a large user base in Africa, which also coincides with the suboptimal DNS deployment there. While we see events in almost every country, most events are reported in Central Europe, North America, Brazil, and Russia.

We next analyze the reported events by their type, shown in Fig. 4(b). The figure shows the number of events per event type categorized to availability (avail), latency (rtt), and throughput (tput) for CDNs, AS, and cloud providers. Every bar is divided in the amount of confirmed and unconfirmed events. We observed that an event is marked as *confirmed* when it was reported for at least 9 min and the rolling variance of measurements from the last 5 h exceeds an event and severity level specific threshold: e.g., a latency increase of 100% – 200% for a CDN is considered as minor, while an increase between 200% and 500% is considered as medium severity. We find most of the reported events to concern

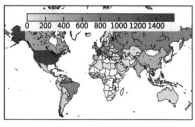 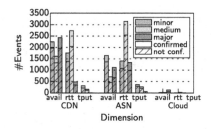

(a) Locations of confirmed events.   (b) Event types, status, and severity.

Fig. 4. Cedexis events reported from 9th October 2017 to 8th January 2018.

CDN, followed by ASes. The high amount of major availability events concern CacheFly CDN outages during our measurement period.

Takeaway. *We observe visitors of Cedexis-managed sited from almost every country. Yet, its anycast DNS platform is suggested to be based in the US, Europe, and Asia. Users in other countries can be subject to higher DNS query latencies.*

4.2 How Customers Utilize Cedexis

DNS TTL. The DNS Time To Live (TTL) defines the time a record can be cached by DNS resolver and thus the timespan between Cedexis balancing decisions. A small TTL allows more frequent switches at the cost of more frequent DNS queries to the Cedexis DNS infrastructure. This query latency can be significant, depending on the DNS resolver location.

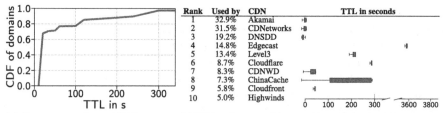

(a) Customer configured TTL from Cedexis to the next CDN.

(b) TTLs of A-record for top 10 used CDNs. (Note the gap in the time scale to display Edgecast using anycast.)

Fig. 5. DNS TTLs experienced among Cedexis-enabled domains. For (a) mappings from Cedexis to the subsequent entry and (b) the CDNs used for the final delivery.

Figure 5(a) depicts the CDF of the TTLs for the validity of the CNAME-mappings from Cedexis to the subsequent entity (see 2nd CNAME in Fig. 1) for all customer domains. We did not observe country-specific settings. Around 67% of all domains have configured a TTL of at most 20 s, indicating a rather short time scale enabling rapid reactions to changes. The next 30% are within 300 s, denoting an already moderate reaction time while around 3% have configured higher TTLs. Higher TTLs *can* hint to non-latency-based, but rather throughput or cost-based optimizations.

To compare these configurations to TTLs deployed by CDNs, we show the A-record TTLs for the top 10 CDNs in Fig. 5(b). To the right of every CDN, the figure shows the boxplot of TTLs observed for the A-records of all resolutions we performed. We see that the top 3 CDNs use a short TTL in the range of most Cedexis CNAMEs, whereas Edgecast has a lifetime of one hour (probably due to their use of anycast).

DNS Resolution Time. When employing Cedexis, an additional step in DNS resolution is required to enable CDN balancing. Figure 6(a) compares the latency for resolving (from our Planet Lab sites) a mapping at Cedexis, in case of multi-staged CDNs a further CNAME redirect (CDN) and the final resolution of the A-record. We observe that Cedexis performs similarly to the other CDNs. However, while this hints at a good DNS deployment for our vantage points, it also means that using Cedexis inflates the latency of a DNS lookup. Given the on average short TTLs, users will often incur an additional added latency when using Cedexis-enabled websites.

CDN usage of Customers. We next check how many CDNs are being used by Cedexis customers. Figure 6(b) illustrates the overall CDN selection frequency for every PlanetLab and RPi node location over the period of one month for all discovered Cedexis domains. We find that domains are usually only using one or two CDNs while there are few that use more. This finding is consistent between geolocations. Only when looking at the how often which CDN is actually selected (note: Fig. 5(b) did only show the share of domains using the CDN) we see a small geographic difference in China (CHN). Here ChinaCache is selected more often than in other geolocations, nevertheless, apart from this, all geolocations behave similarly. This finding contrasts a finding on the Conviva network [16] showing a bias in which some CDNs are selected more often than others in specific countries. In summary, we do not observe that Cedexis customer set country-specific routing decisions.

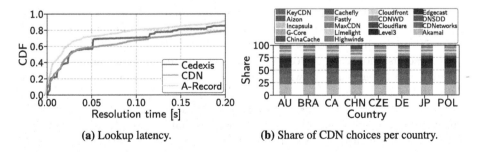

(a) Lookup latency.   (b) Share of CDN choices per country.

Fig. 6. Lookup latency in DNS resolution and final CDN choices of Cedexis customers.

To extend our global view beyond the PlanetLab nodes, we next resolve the discovered Cedexis domains from open DNS resolvers obtained from public-dns.info. To avoid overloading (low-power) devices on user-premises (e.g., home routers), we exclude all resolvers whose DNS names indicate access lines (e.g., "pppoe", "dial-up", or "dsl"). We further only select resolvers with an availability > 89%. In total, this leaves us with 1998 resolvers in 161 countries, out of which 67 *never* successfully responded. We resolve all Cedexis customer domains using all resolvers every two hours for four days. Subsequently, we group the reported results by continent and compare the top selected CDN. We observe that 66.9% always chose the same CDN in every continent. For the remaining, we observe disagreement, i.e., different CDN are chosen on each continent: 30.4% have two and 2.7% three CDNs present. We compare the complete CDN choices in countries of our PlanetLab nodes to their mapping results and observe similar distributions as in Fig. 6(b) (not shown).

Takeaway. *Most Cedexis domains configure short TTLs to enable frequent switches. We observe that most domains indeed balance between few CDNs. Switches pose a challenge to each CDN since traffic gets harder to predict.*

4.3   Latency Perspective

We next take a latency perspective on Cedexis choices, i.e., comparing the latency of the chosen CDN to all configured CDNs for every customer domain. Thus, we measure the latency to every CDN IP by performing ICMP pings. We chose ICMP pings over more realistic HTTP requests since the pings do not generate accountable costs for the probed customers but remark that the ping latency can differ from actual HTTP response latencies. Yet, the ping latency can be a reasonable performance and distance indicator for the different CDN caches.

Figure 7(a) shows the relative latency inflation for cases where Cedexis did not choose the latency-optimal CDN. We observe that around 50% of all resolutions are only marginally worse than the optimal choice regardless of the geographic location (selection shown). The curves than start to flatten indicating increased latency inflation. We observe two groups, where around 10% (20%) of the choices exhibit a latency increase of over 250%. The observed increase can be in the range of few ms for nearby servers that would still deliver good performance. Therefore, we show the absolute difference of all sub-optimal decisions in Fig. 7(b). We observe that ≈50% of all decisions indeed only differ in a couple of milliseconds, indicating almost no noticeable difference. Apart from the nodes in Brazil and Japan (not shown), around 90% of all choices are even within a 20 ms difference.

We remark that it is difficult to assess the quality and correctness of CDN choices as we do not know the routing metrics that are employed by Cedexis customers. Our measurements are motivated from the perspective of an end-user, who is interested in performance, not in potentially monetary business decisions.

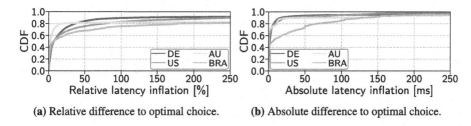

(a) Relative difference to optimal choice.   **(b)** Absolute difference to optimal choice.

Fig. 7. Ping difference to the *fastest* CDN (RTT) when the choice was not optimal.

Takeaway. *All available CDNs would deliver good latency figures in most tested cases, suggesting that the choice of CDN performed by Cedexis would not largely impact end-user experience.*

5   Conclusion

This paper presents a broad assessment of a Meta-CDN deployment, exemplified by dissecting Cedexis as a representative generic platform. By this, we enrich the existing literature describing the Meta-CDN concept with an empirical assessment of a large operator. We shed light on Cedexis customers, technology, and performance. Cedexis DNS deployment, even though using anycast, appears to be focussing on Europe, North America and parts of Asia indicated by high latencies in other regions. We find customers to mostly configure short TTL values enabling fast reactions and we indeed observe that most domains balance between few CDNs. By assessing ping latencies to all available CDNs, we observe that most available CDNs offer good performance from our distributed probe platform. However, we also find a range of sub-optimal latency choices which can indicate routing metrics other than latency.

These unpredictable routing decisions implemented by customers using a Meta-CDN pose a challenge to CDN operators since inbound traffic gets much harder to predict. In particular routing decisions can be based on active measurements by the Meta-CDN—thus, a (single) bad performance can result in rerouting traffic and thus losing revenue. Studying Meta-CDNs and their consequences thus pose an interesting angle for future work.

Acknowledgments. This work has been funded by the DFG as part of the CRC 1053 MAKI. We would like to thank Dean Robinson (Univ. Michigan) for his early contributions to the Alexa analysis, our shepherd Ignacio Castro and the anonymous reviewers.

References

1. Cedexis. https://www.cedexis.com/
2. Cedexis Blog: DDoS attack. https://www.cedexis.com/blog/ddos-attack-details/
3. Cisco umbrella list of top 1M domains. http://s3-us-west-1.amazonaws.com/umbrella-static/index.html
4. Conviva. https://www.conviva.com/
5. Dyn DNS Traffic Steering. http://dyn.com
6. FORTINET FortiDirector. http://xdn.com/fd
7. Adhikari, V.K., Guo, Y., Hao, F., Hilt, V., Zhang, Z.L.: A tale of three CDNs: an active measurement study of Hulu and its CDNs. In: IEEE INFOCOM Workshops (2012)
8. Calder, M., Flavel, A., Katz-Bassett, E., Mahajan, R., Padhye, J.: Analyzing the performance of an Anycast CDN. In: ACM IMC (2015)
9. Chen, F., Sitaraman, R.K., Torres, M.: End-user mapping: next generation request routing for content delivery. In: ACM SIGCOMM (2015)
10. Dobrian, F., Sekar, V., Awan, A., Stoica, I., Joseph, D., Ganjam, A., Zhan, J., Zhang, H.: Understanding the impact of video quality on user engagement. In: ACM SIGCOMM (2011)
11. Flavel, A., Mani, P., Maltz, D., Holt, N., Liu, J., Chen, Y., Surmachev, O.: FastRoute: a scalable load-aware anycast routing architecture for modern CDNs. In: USENIX NSDI (2015)
12. Frank, B., Poese, I., Lin, Y., Smaragdakis, G., Feldmann, A., Maggs, B., Rake, J., Uhlig, S., Weber, R.: Pushing CDN-ISP collaboration to the limit. ACM SIGCOMM CCR **43**(3) (2013)
13. Gerber, A., Doverspike, R.: Traffic types and growth in backbone networks. In: IEEE OFC/NFOEC (2011)
14. Labovitz, C., Iekel-Johnson, S., McPherson, D., Oberheide, J., Jahanian, F.: Internet inter-domain traffic. In: ACM SIGCOMM (2010)
15. Liu, H.H., Wang, Y., Yang, Y.R., Wang, H., Tian, C.: Optimizing cost and performance for content multihoming. In: ACM SIGCOMM (2012)
16. Mukerjee, M.K., Bozkurt, I.N., Maggs, B., Seshan, S., Zhang, H.: The impact of brokers on the future of content delivery. In: ACM HotNets (2016)
17. Mukerjee, M.K., Bozkurt, I.N., Ray, D., Maggs, B.M., Seshan, S., Zhang, H.: Redesigning CDN-broker interactions for improved content delivery. In: ACM CoNEXT (2017)
18. Nygren, E., Sitaraman, R.K., Sun, J.: The Akamai network: a platform for high-performance internet applications. SIGOPS OS Rev. **44**(3), 2–19 (2010)
19. Otto, J.S., Sánchez, M.A., Rula, J.P., Bustamante, F.E.: Content delivery and the natural evolution of DNS: remote DNS trends, Performance issues and alternative solutions. In: ACM IMC (2012)
20. Poese, I., Frank, B., Ager, B., Smaragdakis, G., Feldmann, A.: Improving content delivery using provider-aided distance information. In: ACM IMC (2010)
21. Su, A.-J., Choffnes, D.R., Kuzmanovic, A., Bustamante, F.E.: Drafting behind Akamai: inferring network conditions based on CDN redirections. IEEE/ACM ToN **17**(6), 1752–1765 (2009)
22. van Rijswijk-Deij, R., Jonker, M., Sperotto, A., Pras, A.: A high-performance, scalable infrastructure for large-scale active DNS measurements. IEEE JSAC **34**(6), 1877–1888 (2016)
23. Xue, J., Choffnes, D., Wang, J.: CDNs meet CN an empirical study of CDN deployments in China. IEEE Access **5**, 5292–5305 (2017)

DNS

In rDNS We Trust: Revisiting a Common Data-Source's Reliability

Tobias Fiebig[1,2,3]([✉]), Kevin Borgolte[2], Shuang Hao[4], Christopher Kruegel[2], Giovanni Vigna[2], and Anja Feldmann[3,5]

[1] TU Delft, Delft, Netherlands
t.fiebig@tudelft.nl
[2] UC Santa Barbara, Santa Barbara, CA, USA
[3] TU Berlin, Berlin, Germany
[4] University of Texas at Dallas, Richardson, TX, USA
[5] Max Planck Institute for Informatics, Saarbrücken, Germany

Abstract. Reverse DNS (rDNS) is regularly used as a data source in Internet measurement research. However, existing work is polarized on its reliability, and new techniques to collect active IPv6 datasets have not yet been sufficiently evaluated. In this paper, we investigate active and passive data collection and practical use aspects of rDNS datasets. We observe that the share of non-authoritatively answerable IPv4 rDNS queries reduced since earlier studies and IPv6 rDNS has less non-authoritatively answerable queries than IPv4 rDNS. Furthermore, we compare passively collected datasets with actively collected ones, and we show that they enable observing the same effects in rDNS data. While highlighting opportunities for future research, we find no immediate challenges to the use of rDNS as active and passive data-source for Internet measurement research.

1 Introduction

The Domain Name System (DNS) is an integral part of the Internet. Forward DNS, i.e., resolving names like www.google.com to an IP address makes the Internet usable for end-users. Its counterpart is reverse DNS (rDNS), which allows resolving the name behind an IPv4 or IPv6 address. To resolve an IP address to a name, IANA designated two second level zones below .arpa, in-addr.arpa (IPv4) and ip6.arpa (IPv6). Below them, operators receive zones corresponding to their IP network prefixes. In the assigned zones, operators can serve pointer (PTR) resource records to point to the fully qualified domain name (FQDN) for an IP address. Example use cases of rDNS are the forward confirmation of mail servers to fight spam [1], and enriching logs for improved readability and debugging [2]. Furthermore, researchers regularly leverage rDNS to gather valuable information on networks, e.g., topologies [3,4], the deployment state of IPv6 [5], etc.

The original version of this chapter was revised: The authors made corrections on page 139 and 141. For detailed information please see the erratum to this chapter, available at https://doi.org/10.1007/978-3-319-76481-8_21

© Springer International Publishing AG, part of Springer Nature 2018
R. Beverly et al. (Eds.): PAM 2018, LNCS 10771, pp. 131–145, 2018.
https://doi.org/10.1007/978-3-319-76481-8_10

Even though rDNS is a valuable data-source for researchers, it is not clear how rDNS is used, and whether its DNS zones are well maintained. Gao et al. report that 25.1% of all rDNS queries cannot be authoritatively answered [6], while Phokeer et al. report an increasing number of broken rDNS delegations for the APNIC region [7]. Furthermore, the reliability of new active collection techniques for IPv6 rDNS as used by Fiebig et al. [5] has not yet been investigated. Therefore, in this paper, we revisit prior research on the use of rDNS by operators and investigate the validity of active rDNS collection techniques. We make the following contributions:

- We re-visit the use of rDNS by clients and operators beyond the scope of earlier studies, e.g., Gao et al. [6], and observe that queries for IPv6 rDNS lack an authoritative answer less frequently than for IPv4 rDNS queries.
- We compare the technique by Fiebig et al. to actively obtain rDNS datasets with our passive trace datasets. We find that they are complementary and provide appropriate and meaningful datasets for future research relying on active rDNS traces.

2   Related Work

rDNS use by clients: Prior work on the use of rDNS itself is commonly part of more general approaches to understand DNS lookup patterns. The most notable are Hao et al. in 2010 [8], as well as Gao et al. in 2013 [6] and 2016 [9]. In their 2013 work, Gao et al. note that 25.1% of all PTR queries in their dataset do not receive an authoritative answer, which might be an indication of poorly maintained rDNS zones. We use the same data-provider as Gao et al. for the passive traces in our study.

Active rDNS traces use: Especially in the domain of topology discovery researchers heavily rely on DNS measurements. For example, Spring et al. [10], as well as Oliveira et al. [4] supplement network topology discovery with rDNS data. Similarly, rDNS information has seen use by security studies, such as Czyz et al., who leverage rDNS to identify dual-stack (IPv4 and IPv6) hosts, for which they then evaluate the host's security posture [11]. Note, that these studies use IPv4 rDNS, as it can be brute-force enumerated. Actively collecting global IPv6 rDNS traces is however possible by exploiting semantics of the DNS protocol to prune the search-tree of the rDNS zone when enumerating it, as demonstrated by Fiebig et al. [5], or by zone-walking via DNSSEC extensions [12]. In this paper, we use the technique by Fiebig et al. to collect active datasets for our study.

3   Passive Traces on rDNS: What Can We See?

We leverage Farsight's passive DNS dataset for data on real-world use of rDNS by clients. The dataset contains traces from DNS resolvers around the globe, providing a global overview of DNS lookup behavior [6,9]. A full description of the collection infrastructure is out of scope for this work. The interested reader can find a comprehensive analysis in earlier publications using the dataset [6,9]. For our study we use DNS traffic (query response pairs) observed between March 23rd, 2017 and April 17th, 2017 from midnight to midnight (UTC).

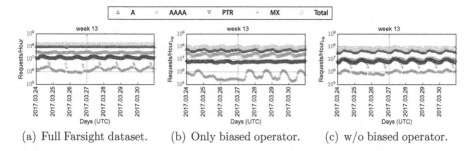

(a) Full Farsight dataset.   (b) Only biased operator.   (c) w/o biased operator.

Fig. 1. The first week of the passive trace for the three dataset splits. We visualize only the first week to enhance the readability of the figures. The outliers for MX requests (the DNS Resource Record (RR) type to denote the mailserver(s) handling mail for a domain) in Fig. 1(c) stem from a Russian ISP running a daily mass-email campaign.

3.1 Biases in the Passive Traces

In a first examination of the data, we find irregular requests from a single ISP's recursive DNS resolvers (see Fig. 1): There is no diurnal pattern for the total *No.* of requests/A requests, and the patterns for AAAA and PTR queries are disjoint. PTR queries are dominated by requests for names in ip6.int., the discontinued rDNS zone for IPv6 [13], belonging to addresses in an unused IPv6 range(7000::/8). Similarly, we observe DNS Service Discovery [14] PTR requests for icloud.com, dell.com, etc., in large (cumulative) volume but in the same order of magnitude of requests per second level zone. These offending requests stem from recursors belonging to a single operator.

Therefore, we split the dataset in two subsets: The ISP showing the unexpected requests pattern, and the remaining operators. Interestingly, the single operator contributes close to half of all queries in the original dataset (see Fig. 1(b)). Note, that the most likely source of the irregular requests is misconfigured Customer-Premises Equipment or an internal service. By excluding the operator, the remaining dataset appears more regular (see Fig. 1(c)) and conforms to the overall volumes found in earlier studies [6,9]. Hence, we acknowledge that there are biases in our dataset, and that there may be further biases we were unable to detect. Investigating these should be part of further work. Nevertheless, as we can control for the biases we do find, we consider our dataset admissible for the work at hand.

3.2 Dataset Overview

Next, we look at second level domains for which PTR queries are issued to distinguish between rDNS queries for IPv4 and IPv6 addresses and other use cases of PTR records. Comparatively, requests to in-addr.arpa (the IPv4 reverse zone), are two orders of magnitude more frequent than requests for ip6.arpa (the IPv6 reverse zone).

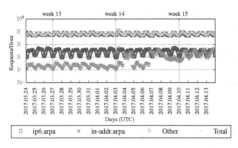

Fig. 2. Requests to ip6.arpa, in-addr.arpa and other second-level domains.

Beyond the IPv4 and IPv6 rDNS zones, we observe PTR requests to other top and second level domains. These are mostly related to DNS based service discovery (DNS-SD) by clients, which account for 77.04% of observed queries outside of .arpa (see Fig. 2). Outliers in the "Other" category starting April 4th, 2017 correspond to DNS-SD queries for services in the domain of a major news network, which leaked into the Farsight dataset through a single operator. A newly deployed model of Customer-Premises Equipment (CPE), such as a set-top box, or such a device receiving an update on or shortly before April 4th, 2017 is the most likely source for the observed behavior. For the remainder of the paper, we focus on queries to in-addr.arpa and ip6.arpa, i.e., queries that can be clearly and safely attributed to rDNS. Next, we investigate the DNS response codes of in-addr.arpa and ip6.arpa to determine if we still encounter the high number of queries that do not receive an authoritative answer in our data than it was observed by prior work.

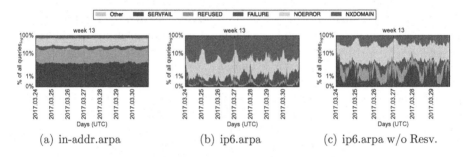

(a) in-addr.arpa   (b) ip6.arpa   (c) ip6.arpa w/o Resv.

Fig. 3. Share of response codes during the first week of our measurements. Note, that queries for reserved IPv6 addresses' rDNS accounts for over 95% of all IPv6 rDNS queries.

3.3 DNS Response Codes in in-addr.arpa

For in-addr.arpa, 47.21% of all queries are successful, while 25.36% return NXDOMAIN, and 15.47% return REFUSED, possibly because the operators want to hide internal information which could become public from host names returned for the RRs (see Fig. 3(a)). The brief increase of "Other" replies on March 29th, 2017 is due to DNS servers of a Singaporean ISP returning FORMERR for all requests. Furthermore, we find on average 3.17% of queries returning SERVFAIL, indicating that some zone delegations in in-addr.arpa are broken, or that the authoritative DNS server does not respond correctly, e.g., because the zone files/databases are inaccessible by the DNS server daemon. Another 8.77% queries result in other failures, e.g., packet loss etc., denoted as FAILURE and less than 0.02% result in FORMERR, NOTAUTH, and NOTIMP. Overall, only 12.06% of PTR requests to in-addr.arpa cannot be authoritatively answered, which stands in significant contrast to the 25.1% reported earlier by Gao et al. [6]. More important, only 3.17% of queries cannot be authoritatively answered due to broken delegations, i.e., due to a lack of care and maintenance.

3.4 DNS Response Codes in ip6.arpa

Table 1. Distribution of rcodes for ip6.arpa and in-addr.arpa during the full measurement period.

rcode	in-addr.-arpa	ip6.arpa	ip6.arpa w/o Resv.
NOERROR	47.21%	4.00%	32.30%
NXDOMAIN	25.36%	94.87%	63.87%
REFUSED	15.47%	0.14%	1.11%
FAILURE	8.77%	0.81%	1.34%
SERVFAIL	3.17%	0.18%	1.38%
FORMERR	0.01%	≤0.01%	≤0.01%
NOTAUTH	≤0.01%	-	-
NOTIMP	≤0.01%	-	-

Contrary to in-addr.arpa, for ip6.arpa, only 0.99% of all requests cannot be authoritatively answered. However, we also find that just 4.00% of queries result in a NOERROR response. Instead, ip6.arpa is dominated by NXDOMAIN replies, which account for 94.87% of all responses (see Fig. 3(b)). The large share of NXDOMAIN responses is caused by a small number of heavy hitter prefixes. Interestingly, these networks are exclusively local and reserved-use prefixes. This may be related to an, by now non-existent, effect observed by Wessels and Fomenkov for IPv4 in 2003 [15]. Excluding these hosts yields a more coherent picture, which we refer to as "ip6.arpa w/o Resv." (see Table 1 and Fig. 3(c)). After filtering out reserved addresses, the overall response rate increases and NXDOMAIN responses account for 63.87%, and NOERROR responses correspond to 32.30%. The number of FAILURE and SERVFAIL responses does not significantly change: They remain relatively low compared to in-addr.arpa. We conjecture that SERVFAIL is less frequent for ip6.arpa than it is for in-addr.arpa because in-addr.arpa has been in use much longer. As such, it provides more time for things to go wrong, i.e., delegations and systems to become stale and to break [16]. The lower REFUSED rate for ip6.arpa may be due to less security measures being in place for IPv6 systems and infrastructure [11].

4   Passive Traces: What are rDNS Use-Cases?

We make additional observations on how operators use rDNS as landmarks to cross-compare findings from our active rDNS traces later on.

4.1   RRtypes in Successful Answers

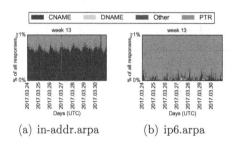

(a) in-addr.arpa   (b) ip6.arpa

Fig. 4. Share of response types.

Naturally, the RRtypes of responses to rDNS queries are dominated by PTR RRs. Given that in-addr.arpa is split at octet boundaries, while IPv4 networks are not anymore, we expect a notable number of CNAME responses for in-addr.arpa, but not for ip6.arpa. Specifically, the share of CNAMEs should be higher for in-addr.arpa as they are used to delegate rDNS authority for networks that are smaller than a /24 [17]. Indeed, we find that CNAMEs account for 0.71% of all query responses in in-addr.arpa. While the share is comparatively low, it constitutes a steady baseline compared to ip6.arpa (see Fig. 4). Similarly, we observe a small layer of DNAMEs—similar to CNAMEs, but for a full zone—for in-addr.arpa, but not for ip6.arpa. Other record types (A, SOA, etc., labeled "Other" in the graph) relate to additional information sent by authoritative nameservers, e.g., sending along the A record for the returned FQDN in a PTR request.

4.2   rDNS SMTP Forward Confirmation

Table 2. Scanned ports and protocols.

Port	Protocol	Port	Protocol
25	SMTP	587	SMTP Submission
110	pop3	993	IMAPs
143	IMAPv4	995	pop3s
465	SMTPs	-	ICMP

Following, we revisit the share of mail servers for which we see rDNS queries, most likely for forward confirmation, i.e., as a tool to mitigate email spam [1], where it was extremely successful. For the purpose of our study, mail servers are all systems with services listening to send and receive email. We performed simple active measurements for email servers on April 19th, 2017. We scan all hosts for which we see rDNS queries as soon as they appear in the dataset and we ensure that every host is only scanned once. For each host, we check if it replies to ICMP echo requests and if it at least one email related TCP port (see Table 2) is open.

Specifically, 19.98% of all addresses for which we see in-addr.arpa requests respond to ICMP echo requests, while 15.28% of all hosts for which we see ip6.arpa requests reply to ICMPv6. Hosts running email services contribute 10.05% of responding hosts in in-addr.arpa, amounting to 2.01% of all hosts for which we saw IPv4 rDNS queries. However, for ip6.arpa, 31.53% of reachable hosts, or 4.82% of all hosts, exhibit open email related ports.

Forward confirmation is commonly not performed for MUA (Mail User Agent) connections that try to relay an email. Here, the user trying to send an email is required to authenticate herself. Hence, forward confirmation should be performed mostly for: (i) spam senders, and (ii) other email servers. However,

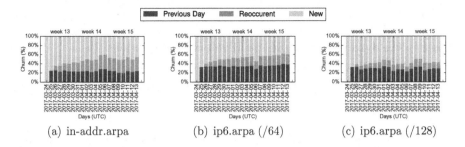

Fig. 5. Churn for requested names in in-addr.arpa and ip6.arpa.

with the increased use of blacklists, and adoption of Sender Policy Framework (SPF) and DomainKeys Identified Mail (DKIM) over the past years, spam distribution moved to using (compromised) email servers, or sending spam emails via compromised email accounts of legitimate users [18]. Although our results are a lower bound, they indicate that there are relatively more server systems among the IPv6 hosts for which we see rDNS requests than there are for IPv4 hosts for which we see rDNS requests.

4.3 Churn in Queried Reverse Names

Continuing on the notion of (more dynamic) clients and servers, we investigate the churn of queried rDNS names in our dataset, for each day, which we define as the individual shares of: (i) Names queried on the previous day as well, (ii) Names queried on any other prior, but not the previous, day, and, (iii) Names never queried before. We focus on the churn in requested names, as a heavy-hitter analysis for requesting end-hosts is not possible as this information is not included in the dataset [9] due to privacy concerns. However, if our assumption is correct, we should observe a comparatively small foundation of stable addresses, accompanied by a large amount of reoccurring and newly queried names.

Figure 5(b) and (c) show the churn for ip6.arpa aggregated to /64s and for full addresses, Fig. 5(a) shows the churn for in-addr.arpa. In both cases, we excluded queries for private and reserved addresses. Hence, we can reason about how many reverse queries are issued for server systems (i.e., systems that commonly reoccur), and how many are issued for clients with changing addresses. We include the aggregation to /64s for IPv6 to account for IPv6 privacy extensions. During our three week measurement period, in-addr.arpa and per-/64 aggregated requests to ip6.arpa exhibit around 50% of reoccurring records after three weeks (49.74% for in-addr.arpa and 54.12% for ip6.arpa), while for full IPv6 addresses, 43.35% of records reoccur. Over time, the share of seen names being queried for changes: On average, 24.29% of all records in in-addr.arpa reoccur on subsequent days, while in ip6.arpa 30.52% of names reoccur, rising to 35.46% when aggregating to /64s.

These results indicate that, especially for IPv6 a far higher number of IPv6 hosts for which we see rDNS queries are, indeed, not clients, or long-lived clients not using privacy extensions. Furthermore, we find that the small number of reoccurring hosts for full IPv6 addresses aligns with findings of prior work in respect to the dynamic use of /64s for IPv6 privacy extensions [19].

5   Active rDNS Measurements: What Can We Really See?

To continue our investigation of rDNS, we actively collected in-addr.arpa and ip6.arpa datasets employing and extending a rDNS collection technique we have previously published [5]. The resulting datasets allow us to estimate how many IPv6 addresses have a corresponding rDNS entry set, what portion of the rDNS space we can enumerate, and how the active dataset relates to the passive datasets.

5.1   Data Collection Infrastructure

We use a cluster of 16 machines to collect the dataset, each machine is comprised of an Intel Xeon X3450 CPU, 8 GB of main memory, 300 GB of hard disk storage. Each system also runs a local recursive DNS resolver (Unbound 1.4.22), against which we perform all DNS queries to benefit from caching. The cluster is orchestrated by an additional workstation that distributes jobs using GNU parallel. Lastly, there were no middle-boxes or connection-tracking routers on the path up to the default-free zone (DFZ).

5.2   Dataset and Toolchain Availability

Our toolchain is open-source, and it is documented and available at: https:// gitlab.inet.tu-berlin.de/ptr6scan/toolchain. We provide the actively collected data to other researchers on request only, due to privacy and security concerns: The collected datasets include a significant number of server-side IPv6 addresses that are not covered by prior research, likely containing vulnerable hosts [11].

5.3   IPv6 rDNS Dataset Collection

We use our previously published enumeration technique [5] to collect our dataset. Our technique utilizes that DNS servers should respond with NXDOMAIN (DNS status code 3) only if they are queried for a non-existent name in the DNS tree which has *no* children in comparison to a name for which they know that it has children, where they should reply with NOERROR (DNS status code 0) [20]. We exploit this to prune the ip6.arpa. tree while enumerating it, thereby making an enumeration of the tree feasible, despite its size [5]. In essence, our algorithm works as follows:

– We collect seeds of IPv6 prefixes by aggregating a global routing table.
– In parallel, for each seed, starting with a target length of four nibbles:

- If the seed is longer than the target length, we crop it accordingly and add both, the seed and the cropped seed back to the seed-set.
- If the seed is shorter, we request all possible children (0-f). Based on the authoritative servers response we only descent subtrees with existing children up until we reached the target length, then add these items back to the seed set.
- When we went through the whole seed-set, we increase the target length by four nibbles, up until a length of 32 nibbles (128bit, a full IPv6 record) and re-do the parallel block of the algorithm.

Our technique also accounts for dynamically generated zones, slow authoritative servers, and systems that are not vulnerable to enumeration using RFC8020 [5].

We collect data from April 22nd, 2017 04:07 UTC to April 25th, 2017 10:15 UTC, which contains more than 10.2 million reverse records. Our dataset includes intermediate information for non-terminal records, to understand how IPv6 reverse zones are delegated and to compare that to the IPv4 datasets. Furthermore, in addition to PTR records, we also collect CNAME records.

5.4 IPv4 rDNS Dataset Collection

We extended and improved our RFC8020 based technique from prior work to support the IPv4 rDNS zone. In contrast to a brute-force approach, it allows us to investigate delegation in IPv4 rDNS:

1. We collect a view on the global routing table from RIPE RIS and Routeviews and add in-addr.arpa to the seed set.
2. We use RFC8020 based enumeration to perform a breadth-first search in the tree (instead of 16, every node now has 256 possible children).
3. When the algorithm finds a terminal node, we terminate for that branch.

Leveraging our extended technique, we collect an in-addr.arpa NXDOMAIN dataset between March 31st, 2017 16:28 UTC and April 6th, 2017 05:46 UTC, which spans 1.21 billion terminal records and CNAMEs.

5.5 Visible IPv4 Space: The Size of the Internet

By comparing the in-addr.arpa dataset with the global IPv4 space, we can approach the question of how well rDNS is maintained and populated by network operators. In an ideal world, we would see rDNS names, i.e., either CNAMEs or PTRs, for all allocated IPv4 addresses. Hence, the number of all active IPv4 addresses should closely model the number of IPv4 rDNS names we find. We note, that this is merely a rough indication, and a careful evaluation would first compile a dataset of all active addresses, similar to Richter et al. [21], and then look up the rDNS names for each of the IPv4 addresses in that dataset. However, within the scope of this study, we focus on an indicative numerical comparison.

With 1.21 billion PTR records in the in-addr.arpa dataset, we observe rDNS names for 28.17% of the total IPv4 address space, which numerically corresponds to the 1.2 billion active IPv4 addresses observed by Richter et al. [21]

using active *and* passive measurements. Note, that our approach may overestimate the number of hosts in this mapping (rDNS being set for whole networks, e.g., in access networks, despite not all addresses being in use), as well as underestimate it (hosts lacking rDNS entries despite being active). Nevertheless, based on our observation we at least conjecture that rDNS zones are not only regularly delegated (see Sect. 3), but also that network operators do indeed populate and maintain their rDNS zones. Based on our prior observation that ip6.arpa zones are less frequently involved in broken delegations or have unresponsive servers than in-addr.arpa zones, we expect to see a similar overlap of active IPv6 addresses and the ip6.arpa zone.

Visible IPv6 Space: ip6.arpa vs. CDN Dataset. For evaluating the active IPv6 space, prior work leveraging the CDN dataset forms the current state of the art base-line for investigating IPv6 adoption [19]. The CDN dataset is a dataset consisting of IP addresses that were collected from a major CDN's access logs. Researchers with access to the dataset kindly provided us with comparative aggregated values on our dataset. They reported a plain overlap between our ip6.arpa dataset with 10.2 M records and their CDN dataset, with over 300M IPv6 addresses per day, of 81 K hosts, out of which they identify 70 K as stable, i.e., reoccurring on three subsequent days. Therefore, we conclude that our ip6.arpa dataset covers other parts of the IPv6 address space than the CDN dataset.

We assume that the root cause for this mismatch can be found in ISPs' handling of IPv6 access networks: ISPs commonly hand out /64s or /48s networks to their customers [19]. Therefore, they dynamically generate zones starting at the covering standard prefix size, i.e., /32s or /48s. This corresponds to the most commonly dynamically generated zones in the ip6.arpa dataset being /32s and /48s (see Fig. 6(b)). Hence, the most likely reason for the low overlap with the CDN dataset is that the CDN dataset is client-centric, while we hardly see clients as we exclude dynamically generated zones, which are common for client networks.

Visible IPv6 Space: RFC8020 Compliance. The enumeration technique we used heavily depends on authoritative servers correctly implementing RFC8020 [20]. If a major portion of the authoritative DNS servers handling IPv6 rDNS zones does not conform to RFC8020, visibility may be limited. Therefore, we investigate how frequently rDNS servers adhere to the RFC. From the Farsight dataset, we collected all successful queries for entries in ip6.arpa, a total of 361 K unique names. For each record, we determine all zone delegations up to the root (ip6.arpa) via which the leaf record can be reached, and we then query for the NS records of all intermediate zones.

Utilizing the initial leaf records, we test each of the authoritative name servers for all identified domains if they: (i) follow RFC8020; (ii) always return NXDOMAIN, even though an element in the zone tree below them exists; (iii) always return NOERROR, even though nothing exists below the queried records; (iv) do return an error (SERVFAIL, REFUSED, timeouts); and, (v) if there are any differences for this between the different authoritative servers of a domain.

We discover that 39.58% of all rDNS zones in the dataset only use authoritative servers in compliance with RFC8020, while 46.42% always return NXDO-

MAIN, and 11.61% always return NOERROR. In turn, we will detect 46.42% of zones as having no entries at all, while 11.61% of zones will be flagged as dynamically generated due to the behavior of their authoritative servers. The remaining 2.38% are split among 0.59% of zones that return errors, and 1.79% of zones exhibiting a mix of the above conditions. Interestingly, in case of the latter, at least one nameserver is compliant with RFC8020 and can be used for enumeration, while the others always return NXDOMAIN or NOERROR.

Therefore, the likelihood that the NXDOMAIN technique is effective ranges around 40% for each *individual* zone/server. Nevertheless, upon comparing our IPv6 seed set with the delegation pattern for IPv6 rDNS, we find that the majority of top-level delegations up to /48s is covered by seeds (see Fig. 6(b)). It means that we do not lose a significant number of (large) sub-trees within the rDNS tree, and instead only lose around 40% of all /64s and below, which leaves us with an estimated coverage between 16% and 40%. Furthermore, our results indicate that querying all authoritative servers of a zone during enumeration is not strictly necessary. Although it can increase the result set for some zones, the additional overhead can not be justified by the 1.79% of zones that could be enumerated additionally.

6   Comparing Active and Passive Results

6.1   CNAMEs and Delegations

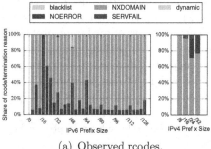

(a) Observed rcodes.

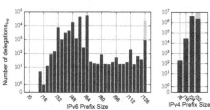

(b) Delegations (CNAMEs in yellow).

Fig. 6. rcodes and delegation for rDNS. (Color figure online)

In our passive dataset, we observed that CNAMEs are used to delegate rDNS authority for networks smaller than the minimum rDNS zone size. That is, smaller than a /24 network for in-addr.arpa (see Sect. 3). Furthermore, we find that requests to in-addr.arpa show a higher rate of SERV-FAILs than requests to ip6.arpa. Correspondingly, we should find evidence of these effects in our active traces as well. Next, we look into how delegations and CNAMES occur in our active rDNS traces.

rDNS Zone Delegation. To investigate delegation in rDNS, we build a trie from the gathered reverse zones. Specifically, we first sort the zones by corresponding prefix size, and then add them to the trie. Sorting them before adding them to the trie ensure that we do not add a longer prefix before we add the covering shorter prefix. For each input zone, we check if a less specific prefix exists in the trie. If it exists, then we check if the authority section for the associated domain is the same. If the zone in the authority section differs, then we encountered a delegation for the current prefix length. For terminal records, we also check if the zone reported in the authority section is a well-formed PTR zone, either under ip6.arpa or in-addr.arpa (depending on the zone we evaluate). If not, then it is a CNAME for a terminal record instead of a delegation.

Delegations within in-addr.arpa happen consistently (see Fig. 6(b)): /8s are delegated to RIRs (and some Internet early-adopters who received large prefixes [21]) that are then split by the RIRs and delegated to LIRs in smaller blocks, which are further delegated to end-users and small network operators. This pattern extends down to the terminal records, where we find a high number of delegation attempts, as well as 6.2 million CNAME records. Indeed, this number corresponds to 0.51% of all 1.21 billion in-addr.arpa records are CNAMEs, close to the expected 0.71% of CNAME responses (see Sect. 3). Moreover, a majority of the target-zones (92.85%) that CNAMEs point to have more than one CNAME pointing to them, conforming to the designated purpose of CNAMEs in in-addr.arpa: Delegating rDNS for networks smaller than a /24, as suggested by RFC2317 [17].

For ip6.arpa, delegations mostly occur for the most commonly assigned prefix lengths, i.e., /32s, /48s, /56s, and /64s. As expected, this relates closely to the more structured addressing policies that became possible with the significantly larger address space of IPv6. In case of IPv4, a large operator may use several smaller prefixes collected from various RIRs [21], however, with IPv6, a single prefix is enough. Hence, ip6.arpa delegation happens mostly for larger prefixes.

Following IPv6 addressing best practices, we expected that most delegations occur for /48s and /56s, because /64s are the suggested maximum prefix length for a subnet and the prefix-length that should be assigned to an interface [22,23]. We did not expect /64s to be individually delegated, as a customer with multiple subnets should receive a /48 or /56 instead. However, we find that the total number of delegations actually increases from /48s to /64s, where it peaks. We even encounter delegations for prefixes more specific than /64s, each peaking at the corresponding 4-nibble-block boundaries. Surprisingly, a high number of CNAMEs for terminal records exist, which were unexpected due to the better delegation option in ip6.arpa, with per-nibble zone boundaries.

In our dataset, 87.81% of observed IPv6 rDNS CNAMEs belong to the DHCPv6 range of a single operator, which uses them to point PTR records from a full /96 representation in the ip6.arpa zone to another zone of the form ip6.arpa-suffix.ip6.dhcp6.operator.tld. Fiebig et al. already briefly mentioned such setups [5]. Most (80.77%) of the remaining 12.19% records point to names in in-addr.arpa, to ensure coherent addressing in dual-stack scenarios. Consequently, this indicates an "IPv4 first" policy employed by operators: Operators first deploy IPv4, and then roll out IPv6 on top, leveraging CNAMEs to ensure consistency through-out the network. Yet, IPv4 remains the leading technology, even though the setup is dual-stack. Relating these numbers back to Sect. 3, we find that CNAMEs are slightly more common than expected, constituting 0.22% of the dataset. However, if we consider the single DHCPv6 operator as an artifact and exclude it, then we arrive at the expected low CNAME density of 0.02%, which matches the share of records of the passive trace.

SERVFAIL in the Active Traces. Finally, we observed that SERVFAILs are much more frequent for in-addr.arpa than for ip6.arpa (see Sect. 3). We find corroborating evidence for this in the active datasets: For in-addr.arpa, 3.40% of zones at the /16 level, and 4.87% of zones at the /24 level result in SERVFAIL (see Fig. 6(a)). In contrast, for ip6.arpa, we only find a small amount of SERVFAIL for /32s and /48s, totaling 2.14% of all /32s, and 1.02% of all /48s. We attribute this to the fact that ip6.arpa has not been in use for as long as in-addr.arpa, and, in turn, had far less time to become stale and to accumulate broken delegations.

7 Conclusion

In this paper, we revisited prior results on the use of rDNS and find that rDNS zones are by now less frequently non-authoritatively answerable than observed in earlier studies [6]. We have also revisited previously presented techniques to obtain active rDNS datasets. Network behavior that we observe in the Farsight passive trace dataset are also present in the actively collected datasets, supporting the assertion that active rDNS measurement techniques produce meaningful datasets without requiring access to expensive datasets or global network vantage points. Beyond confirming prior assumptions, we find first indications for an "IPv4-first" approach by operators, i.e., operators plan and build IPv4 infrastructures first, and then deploy IPv6 later on, in their use of zone-delegations and CNAMEs for rDNS zones. These observations should be further investigated in the future. Ultimately, we find no challenges to the use of rDNS as a data-source for Internet measurement research, even though this should be closely monitored in the future. Hence, we argue that rDNS can be relied on for Internet-wide studies.

Acknowledgements. We thank the anonymous reviewers and John Heidemann for their helpful feedback. We also thank David Plonka for his valuable feedback and the comparison with the CDN dataset. This material is based on research sponsored by the Defense Advanced Research Projects Agency (DARPA) under agreement number FA8750-15-2-0084, the Office of Naval Research (ONR) under grant N00014-17-1-2011 and N00014-15-1-2948, the National Science Foundation (NSF) under grant DGE- 1623246 and CNS-1704253, a Google Security, Privacy and Anti-Abuse Award to Giovanni Vigna, the Bundesministerium für Bildung und Forschung (BMBF) under Award No. KIS1DSD032 (Project Enzevalos), and a Leibniz Price project by the German Research Foundation (DFG) under Award No. FKZ FE 570/4-1.The U.S. Government is authorized to reproduce and distribute reprints for Governmental purposes notwithstanding any copyright notation thereon. Any views, opinions, findings, recommendations, or conclusions contained or expressed herein are those of the authors, and do not necessarily reflect the position, official policies, or endorsements, either expressed or implied, the U.S. Government, DARPA, ONR, NSF, Google, BMBF, or DFG.

References

1. Cormack, G.V.: Email spam filtering: a systematic review. Found. Trends Inf. Retrieval **1**(4), 335–455 (2007)
2. Nicholas, D., Huntington, P.: Micro-mining and segmented log file analysis: a method for enriching the data yield from internet log files. SAGE J. Inf. Sci. **29**(5), 391–404 (2003)
3. Zhang, M., Ruan, Y., Pai, V.S., Rexford, J.: How DNS misnaming distorts internet topology mapping. In: Usenix Annual Technical Conference (ATC) (2006)
4. Oliveira, R.V., Pei, D., Willinger, W., Zhang, B., Zhang, L.: In search of the elusive ground truth: Yhe Internet's AS-level connectivity structure. In: Proceedings of ACM SIGMETRICS, vol. 36 (2008)
5. Fiebig, T., Borgolte, K., Hao, S., Kruegel, C., Vigna, G.: Something from nothing (There): collecting global IPv6 datasets from DNS. In: Proceedings of Passive and Active Measurement (PAM) (2017)
6. Gao, H., Yegneswaran, V., Chen, Y., Porras, P., Ghosh, S., Jiang, J., Duan, H.: An empirical reexamination of global DNS behavior. Proc. ACM SIGCOMM **43**(4), 267–278 (2013)
7. Phokeer, A., Aina, A., Johnson, D.: DNS Lame delegations: a case-study of public reverse DNS records in the African region. In: Bissyande, T.F., Sie, O. (eds.) AFRICOMM 2016. LNICST, vol. 208, pp. 232–242. Springer, Cham (2018). https://doi.org/10.1007/978-3-319-66742-3_22
8. Hao, S., Feamster, N., Pandrangi, R.: An internet-wide view into DNS lookup patterns. Technical report, School of Computer Science, Georgia Technology (2010)
9. Gao, H., Yegneswaran, V., Jiang, J., Chen, Y., Porras, P., Ghosh, S., Duan, H.: Reexamining DNS from a global recursive resolver perspective. IEEE/ACM Trans. Networking (TON) **24**(1), 43–57 (2016)
10. Spring, N., Mahajan, R., Wetherall, D., Anderson, T.: Measuring ISP topologies with rocketfuel. IEEE/ACM Trans. Networking (TON) **12**(1), 2–16 (2004)
11. Czyz, J., Luckie, M., Allman, M., Bailey, M.: Don't forget to lock the back door! A characterization of IPv6 network security policy. In: Proceedings of Internet Society Symposium on Network and Distributed System Security (NDSS) (2016)
12. Borgolte, K., Hao, S., Fiebig, T., Kruegel, C., Vigna, G.: Enumerating active IPv6 hosts for large-scale security scans via DNSSEC-signed reverse zones. In: Proceedings of IEEE Security & Privacy (S&P) (2018)
13. Huston, G.: Deprecation of "ip6.int". RFC 4159 (Best Current Practice), August 2005
14. Cheshire, S., Krochmal, M.: DNS-based service discovery. RFC 6763 (Proposed Standard), February 2013
15. Wessels, D., Fomenkov, M.: Wow, that's a lot of packets. In: Proceedings of Passive and Active Measurement Workshop (PAM) (2003)
16. Borgolte, K., Fiebig, T., Hao, S., Kruegel, C., Vigna, G.: Cloud strife: mitigating the security risks of domain-validated certificates. In: Proceedings of Internet Society Symposium on Network and Distributed System Security (NDSS) (2018)
17. Eidnes, H., de Groot, G., Vixie, P.: Classless IN-ADDR.ARPA delegation. RFC 2317 (Best Current Practice), March 1998

18. Hu, X., Li, B., Zhang, Y., Zhou, C., Ma, H.: Detecting compromised email accounts from the perspective of graph topology. In: Proceedings of ACM Conference on Future Internet Technologies (2016)
19. Plonka, D., Berger, A.: Temporal and spatial classification of active IPv6 addresses. In: Proceedings of ACM Internet Measurement Conference (2015)
20. Bortzmeyer, S., Huque, S.: NXDOMAIN: there really is nothing underneath. RFC 8020 (Proposed Standard), November 2016
21. Richter, P., Smaragdakis, G., Plonka, D., Berger, A.: Beyond counting: new perspectives on the active IPv4 address space. In: Proceedings of ACM Internet Measurement Conference (2016)
22. IAB, IESG: IAB/IESG recommendations on IPv6 address allocations to sites. RFC 3177 (Informational), September 2001. Obsoleted by RFC 6177
23. de Velde, G.V., Popoviciu, C., Chown, T., Bonness, O., Hahn, C.: IPv6 unicast address assignment considerations. RFC 5375 (Informational), December 2008

Characterization of Collaborative Resolution in Recursive DNS Resolvers

Rami Al-Dalky[1] and Kyle Schomp[2(✉)]

[1] Case Western Reserve University, Cleveland, USA
rami.al-dalky@case.edu
[2] Akamai Technologies, Cambridge, USA
kschomp@akamai.com

Abstract. Recursive resolvers in the Domain Name System play a critical role in not only DNS' primary function of mapping hostnames to IP addresses but also in the load balancing and performance of many Internet systems. Prior art has observed the existence of complex recursive resolver structures where multiple recursive resolvers collaborate in a "pool". Yet, we know little about the structure and behavior of pools. In this paper, we present a characterization and classification of resolver pools. We observe that pools are frequently disperse in IP space, and some are even disperse geographically. Many pools include dual-stack resolvers and we identify methods for associating the IPv4 and IPv6 addresses. Further, the pools exhibit a wide range of behaviors from uniformly balancing load among the resolvers within the pool to proportional distributions per resolver.

Keywords: DNS · Resolver pools · Dual-stack

1 Introduction

The Domain Name System (DNS) [15] is the component of the Internet that maps human readable names to IP addresses. Traditionally, the DNS is considered to contain three components: (*i*) stub resolvers running on end-user devices that receive resolution requests from apps and forward DNS queries to (*ii*) recursive resolvers that perform the resolution process by iteratively querying (*iii*) authoritative nameservers that are each responsible for zones (or domains) within the DNS hierarchical namespace.

Because of the DNS' vital role in Internet transactions, it is also a convenient choice for implementing traffic management strategies, i.e., load balancing and replica selection can be implemented by authoritative nameservers handing out different hostname to IP address mappings as a function of recursive resolver source IP address and time. Several major content delivery networks (CDNs) [3–5] operate using DNS as the method to assign clients to edge servers. Because there is no direct communication between the end-user devices and the authoritative nameservers in DNS, the location and network connectivity of the

© Springer International Publishing AG, part of Springer Nature 2018
R. Beverly et al. (Eds.): PAM 2018, LNCS 10771, pp. 146–157, 2018.
https://doi.org/10.1007/978-3-319-76481-8_11

end-user device must be inferred from that of the recursive resolver. There is a mechanism for recursive resolvers to attach end-user information to DNS queries [13], but the adoption of the mechanism is still low [16,19] so recursive resolvers remain a frequently used surrogate for end-users. As such, understanding their behavior is of critical importance.

Prior art [10,18] notes that the DNS ecosystem has grown more complex than the early three component model: now recursive resolvers often act in "pools" [10]. Indeed, prior art observe that multiple resolvers may participate in a *single* resolution. The proliferation of public resolution services [6,7] are major use cases for more complex resolver architectures, as the scaling requirements of such systems are substantial.

The proliferation of recursive resolver pools has implications to the efficient functioning of CDNs as pools further obfuscate the association of end-user device to recursive resolver. Unfortunately, little is known about the structure and behavior of pools. In this work, we present what is to the best of our knowledge the first attempt to characterize recursive DNS resolver pools as observed by authoritative nameservers. Our key contributions are:

- **Determine the frequency of pooling behavior and the size of existing pools.** We find use of pools is common, with 71.4% of DNS queries in our dataset originating from pools. Further, pool sizes vary widely with some operators using pools of 2 resolvers and others using pools of hundreds[1].
- **Identify key characteristics of pools including IP, AS, and geographic diversity.** Pools often cover large portions of IP-space with 40% of IPv4 pools distributed within a /16 CIDR block or larger. At the same time, however, pools rarely cross network operator boundaries. We also observe that 10% of pools have large distances between the resolvers in the pool, potentially confusing or misleading efforts to geolocate end-user devices behind the pool.
- **Tangentially, discover dual-stacked resolvers and novel ways to associate IPv4 to IPv6 addresses.** We find many pools of 2 IP addresses are actually dual-stack resolvers and observe that patterns in IPv4/IPv6 address assignment can aid in identifying dual-stack configurations.
- **Classify pools according to several observed behaviors.** We find that pools utilize a wide range of behaviors to distribute DNS queries within the pool. We identify several behaviors including uniform load balancing, offloading, and various other uneven distributions.

The rest of this paper is organized as follows. In Sect. 2, we provide a brief summary of related work. In Sect. 3, we describe our methodology and present the experimental apparatus, dataset, and post-processing steps. Section 4 contains a characterization of pools by network properties. Section 5 classifies the pools by behavior and we draw our conclusions in Sect. 6.

---

[1] We identify resolvers by IP address and there may not be a one-to-one relationship between hardware and IP address. Regardless, our study reflects what authoritative nameservers observe.

2   Related Work

To the best of our knowledge, we contribute the first assessment of the characteristics of recursive resolver pools. However, several works [10,18] have observed the presence of resolver pools through active probing with CNAME redirections. Alzoubi et al. [10] called the collaborative pools behavior a multiport behavior and interpreted it as either a single multiport machine or load balancing across a resolver farm. Moreover, Schomp et al. [18] looked at the resolver pools from the resolver client perspective by studying the number of recursive resolvers used per client and the geographical distance between clients and recursive resolvers.

While examining DNS pools, we find many dual-stack recursive resolvers. Berger et al. [11] associate IPv4 and IPv6 addresses in DNS queries to find dual-stack machines. In the presence of pools, the authors associate sets of IPv4 and IPv6 addresses rather than identify individual dual-stack resolvers. Other research [12,17] focuses on identifying IPv4 and IPv6 dual-stack machines using TCP options and timestamps, but both methods have limitations when applied to DNS recursive resolvers. First, many resolvers are not open to answer queries from arbitrary sources on the Internet meaning active scanning techniques will miss many recursive resolvers. Second, the techniques require TCP which is a backup transport protocol for DNS and not all TCP implementations support TCP timestamp option. Our technique for discovering pools and dual-stack resolvers does not require any special support from the target resolvers.

3   Dataset & Methodology

We discover pools of recursive resolvers by first discovering pairs of collaborating resolvers and then grouping the pairs together. To find pairs of collaborating resolvers, we use DNS queries for instrumented hostnames. Resolving one of the hostnames induces a resolver to send *two* DNS queries to our authoritative nameservers, as described below. If the resolver is part of a pool, the DNS queries may arrive at the authoritative nameservers from different source IP addresses, offering an opportunity to capture a pair of collaborating recursive resolvers. Below, we describe our dataset, how we extract pairs from the dataset, and then how to form pools from the pairs.

Our dataset consists of DNS query logs from the authoritative nameservers of a major CDN. For a small fraction of Web requests, the CDN platform injects a javascript library [2] that initiates a DNS resolution for an instrumented hostname under the CDN's control. The hostname encodes the end-user device's public IP subnet, and resolves to a CNAME record—a DNS record that indicates a hostname is an alias of another hostname—for a second hostname (also under the CDN's control) that also encodes the end-user's public IP subnet. Thus, the resolution looks like:

$$n1.encoded(x.x.x.x/y).example.com \rightarrow n2.encoded(x.x.x.x/y).example.com$$

The DNS queries for both hostnames are recorded in the logs including the source IP address and a timestamp of when the query was received truncated to the

Table 1. Description of the dataset.

Description	Number
DNS queries	820M
Unique resolvers	429K
Resolver pairs	109M
Unique pairs	1.16M
Singletons	398K
Non-singletons	762K
Groups of resolver pairs	421K
Singletons	360K
Initiator pools	61.5K

Table 2. Top 10 countries with largest number of observed resolvers

Rank	Country	Resolvers
1	US	153K
2	DE	27K
3	BR	24K
4	GB	16K
5	RU	16K
6	CA	15.6K
7	JP	14K
8	AU	10.8K
9	IN	10K
10	IT	8.7K

second. We collect 1 week of logs, July 12–19 2017, containing 820M queries from 429K unique recursive resolver IP addresses. Table 1 follows the breakdown of our dataset in the remainder of this section. Using the EdgeScape [1] geolocation database, we find the recursive resolvers span 27294 ASNs and 234 countries[2]. Table 2 lists the top 10 countries by number of observed resolvers. The top 10 ASNs by number of observed resolvers account for 82.6K (19%) of the total.

Next, we group the queries that are part of the same resolution into pairs (Q_1, Q_2) to extract pairs of collaborating resolvers. Queries that are part of the same resolution are identified by the tuple: encoded end-user subnet, query type (A for IPv4 address or AAAA for IPv6 address) and timestamp. This, however, may not be a unique key because (i) multiple end-users in the same subnet may resolve the same hostname at roughly the same time, (ii) multiple recursive resolvers may "race" to return an answer fastest to the same end-user, or (iii) recursive resolvers may re-resolve the hostname, possibly due to prefetching. The third category can be particularly troublesome due to DNS TTL violations [18] where recursive resolvers may re-resolve only one of the two hostnames in the series, even though both hostnames have the same authoritative DNS TTL. To eliminate noise from these sources, we employ a sliding window of 11 s: $[i-5, i+5]$. If in second i, there is a matching pair of queries, Q_1 and Q_2, we check in the window $[i-5, i]$ for any other queries like Q_1. Similarly, we check the window $[i, i+5]$ for any other queries like Q_2. If we find either, then the pair is discarded because we cannot identify which queries should be paired. The window of 11 s was chosen to allow for up to a 5 s resolver timeout and retry, which is the default DNS timeout value in Linux [14].

The source IP addresses of each pair of queries (Q_1, Q_2) produce an ordered pair of related recursive resolver IP addresses (R_1, R_2). In total, we find 109M

---

[2] We report the results from EdgeScape, but note that the ASNs matched exactly with what is reported by Team Cymru [8] and countries disagreed for only 166 IP addresses.

sample ordered pairs consisting of 1.16M unique pairs (R_1, R_2), 66% of which were sampled more than once. We exclude 7.3K samples from 5.6K unique pairs where one of the resolver IP addresses belongs to the ASNs of Google Public DNS [6] or OpenDNS [7] and the other does not. All but 853 of the unique pairs are cases of an ISP's resolvers off-loading queries to Google or OpenDNS. We exclude these pairs as they contaminate our pool size measurements (see Sect. 4.1). The remaining 853 pairs exhibit Google Public DNS or OpenDNS off-loading queries to a third party. We suspect that these may be error introduced by query pairs outside our 11 second window. The pairs account for less than 0.1% of all our samples, so we exclude them as well. Of the unique pairs, 762K are non-singletons—$R_1 \neq R_2$—which we use as the basic unit for constructing pools. Note that singleton pairs may still be part of a pool since resolvers may collaborate in only a portion of resolutions.

Next, we merge samples together to form pools. Care must be taken in constructing the pools, because the relationships may not be symmetric. Consider the case of three recursive resolvers: x, y, and z. With observed pairs (x, y) and (x, z), we cannot conclude a direct relationship between y and z. Similarly, if we also observe pair (y, z), we still cannot conclude that all three are members of the same pool, as z may have no affiliation with x and y. Therefore, we opt to take a conservative approach and preserve directional relationships. We group all samples with the same initiator R_1. Continuing the above example, we generate the grouping $(x{:}y, z)$ where the resolver on the left-hand side *uses* all of the resolvers on the right-hand side. From our dataset, we find 421K groups of which 360K represent singletons, i.e., resolvers that did not ever use another resolver R_2 in our dataset. Excluding those, we are left with 61.5K groups that generated 780K (71.6%) of unique pairs and 77.9M (71.4%) of the total samples in our dataset. From here on, we exclude singletons from our analysis and refer to the remaining 61.5K groups as "initiator pools", or just pools where contextually clear.

4   Characterizing Resolver Pools by Network Properties

In this section, we breakdown the initiator pools by network properties. We attempt to find common network structure and characterize the pools by those structures.

4.1   Initiator Pool Size

Here, we explore the size of the discovered pools based on the number of recursive resolver IP addresses in the pool. The number of samples per pool is defined as the summation of the number of samples per unique pair in the pool. Many pools (17.5%) are only sampled once. As a result, our ability to discover the actual size of the pool is limited due to low sampling and our pool size results are a lower bound. However, since our dataset is driven by end-user action, the number of samples per pool correlates with the number of end-users behind the pool. Thus, a more frequently used pool is likely higher sampled and our measurement of size more accurate.

Figure 1 shows the number of recursive resolver IP addresses per pool. As shown in the figure, most pools are small with 38.7K (63%) of pools contain 2 resolvers. We observe that 21.5K (35%) pools with 2 resolvers contain one IPv4 and one IPv6 address and we explore them in more detail in Sect. 5.1. The largest pool we discovered consists of 317 IP addresses contained within 5 IPv4 /24 CIDR blocks and 8 IPv6 /64 CIDR blocks. All blocks belong to ASN 15169, Google Inc. In all, 85% of the pools consist of less than 10 resolvers.

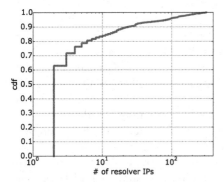 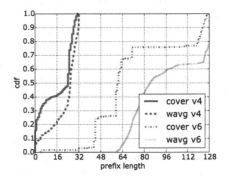

Fig. 1. Size of the initiator pools in number of resolver IP addresses

Fig. 2. Prefix length of the most specific CIDR block covering all IP addresses in the initiator pool

In comparison with previous work, Alzoubi et al. [10] observed that 90% of the discovered pools have at most 3 resolvers while a single pool consists of over 22K resolvers. We attempt to replicate their findings using their methodology for constructing pools with our dataset, but do not find a single "megapool". The largest pool we discover is caused by offloading by many third parties to Google and OpenDNS (Sect. 3), and we therefore suspect that the difference between our dataset and the dataset of Alzoubi et al. is reduced observations of offloading to Google and OpenDNS.

4.2   IP-Space Distribution

Next, we investigate how concentrated initiator pools are in IP-space. Intuitively, we expect collaborating resolvers to be closely concentrated, e.g., Google Public DNS publishes a list of whole /24 CIDR blocks that are used in recursive resolution [6]. In this section, we measure how similar the IP addresses of resolvers within a pool are to one another.

First, we calculate the length of the prefix for the most specific CIDR block that covers all IP addresses in the pool. Consider a pool with two IP addresses: 1.2.3.0 and 1.2.3.128. The longest common prefix of the two IP addresses is 24-bits, thus, the covering prefix length is 24-bits. For IPv4, the prefix length varies from 32-bits (indicating a single IP address in the pool) to 0-bits (indicating that even the leading bit does not match). The values have a similar meaning for IPv6, but extend to a maximum value of 128-bits due to the larger address size. For this analysis, we discard unique pairs where the IP versions do not match and don't plot pools without any unique pairs remaining. The filtering leaves 39.3K initiator pools, 37.7K are IPv4 and 1.6K are IPv6 pools.

The covering prefix lengths for IPv4 and IPv6 are shown in Fig. 2 in lines "cover v4" and "cover v6", respectively. In IPv4, we find that 48% of pools are covered by a prefix shorter than 24-bits and further 38% are covered by a prefix shorter than 8-bits. This indicates that a large fraction of initiator pools are greatly distributed in IP-space. There is also a large amount of variability in the prefix length as demonstrated by the relatively smooth curve. In IPv6 on the other hand, there are 4 clear typical prefix lengths: 44, 60, 70, and 120-bits. The pools with prefix lengths of 44 and 60-bits are operated by Google, while the pools with prefix lengths of 70-bits are operated by AT&T. The prefix lengths greater than 120-bits come from a variety of operators. This result highlights the differing policies network operators apply when assigning IP addresses.

The covering prefix length is susceptible to outliers, however. For example, in a pool of 10 resolvers where 9 match to 24-bits but 1 resolver only matches to 8-bits, the covering prefix length is still 8-bits. Therefore, we next compute the weighted average prefix length between the initiator and each of the other resolvers in the pool using the relative number of samples per unique pair as the weights. The result of this computation is plotted in lines "wavg v4" and "wavg v6" and show a frequently more specific prefix length than the covering prefix length. This indicates that (i) resolver usage within a pool is frequently not uniform (see Sect. 5.2), and (ii) resolvers closer in IP-space are used more frequently than resolvers further apart. This could be a preference choice, e.g., resolver operators prefer to off-load to nearby capacity, but will off-load to equipment further away if necessary (see Sect. 4.4).

4.3 Autonomous System Distribution

The previous section noted that initiator pools can be dispersed in IP-space. In this section, we endeavor to determine if the pools encompass multiple operators. First, we look at the number of autonomous systems (ASs) per initiator pool and observe that 15.2% of pools are in more than one AS and 0.7% are in more than two ASs. In the most extreme case, one initiator pool consists of 10 recursive resolvers each in a different AS. All of the ASs are Russian and each uniquely identifies a distinct Russian city.

We focus on the 8.9K (14.5%) pools in 2 ASs here and manually compare the WHOIS entries of the most commonly occurring AS pairs. The most frequently occurring pair of ASs is 7018 and 7132 which occur together in 553 pools, and both are operated by AT&T. The second most frequently occurring pair of ASs are operated by Sprint Corporation: 10507 and 3651 occur together in 201 pools. Noting the exception of Google and OpenDNS usage by third parties which we filter (see Sect. 3), we conclude that other collaboration between recursive resolvers from unrelated ASs is rare.

4.4   Geographic Distance Within Pools

In this section, we investigate the geographic distribution of recursive resolvers within a pool. Large distances between recursive resolvers can have ramifications for any system attempting to geolocate end-users by the recursive resolver that they use, e.g., CDNs that attempt to map end-users to nearby replicas for performance reasons. We attempt to determine whether recursive resolvers in an initiator pool are all in the same location, and, if not, how far the recursive resolvers are from the initiator. We calculate the Great Circle distance between the initiator and the resolvers in the pool using the geolocation information provided by EdgeScape [1]. We consider three methods for calculating the distance within a pool:

1. Minimum distance between the initiator and any resolver in the pool (the lower bound).
2. Maximum distance between the initiator and any resolvers in the pool (the upper bound).
3. Weighted average distance between the initiator and the resolvers in the pool using the number of samples per unique pair as the weights.

Figure 3 provides the distributions of those distances. We notice that 6.2K (10%) of the pools have a weighted average distance more than 160 km (100 miles) and those pools represent 3.6M (3.3%) of our total samples. This means that the majority of pools—producing 96.4% of the samples in our dataset—consist of resolvers that are close to each other geographically. We examine the pools in the tail with weighted average distance more than 160 Km and observe 319 pools where all IP addresses are within 66.102.0.0/20 and geolocate across the US[3]. The IP addresses reverse resolve to *google-proxy-${IP}.google.com*, indicating that they are Google proxies [9]. This suggest that Google proxies (*i*) perform recursive resolution themselves rather than rely upon Google's DNS infrastructure, and (*ii*) collaborate amongst themselves.

The geographically distributed pools add extra time to the resolution process as off-loading a follow-up query necessitates further network delay. Moreover, distance within the pool complicates end-user mapping in CDNs as discussed before. We observe that pool intra-distance is small for the majority of pools, a positive result for CDNs.

5   Classifying Resolver Pools by Behavior

In this section, we provide a classification of the pools by how DNS queries are distributed among the resolvers within the pool. Unfortunately, low sampling makes identifying behavior in many pools difficult. Consequently, we limit this section to the study of highly sampled pools, reducing our dataset to the 18.7K (30%) pools with at least 100 samples. The threshold was chosen because the

---

[3] We manually verified that our example cases are approximately located where EdgeScape reports by using ping measurements from nearby landmark locations.

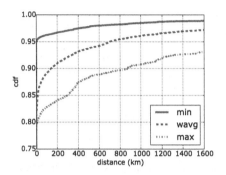

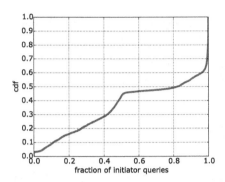

Fig. 3. Tail of the distribution of distances within pools

Fig. 4. The number of samples in an initiator pool that are initiator to initiator

distribution of samples per pool surrounding the threshold is smooth. We classify the pools into 4 categories described below: (*i*) dual-stack resolvers, (*ii*) uniform load balancing, (*iii*) off-loading and (*iv*) others. Table 3 contains a breakdown of the categories.

5.1 Dual-Stack Resolvers

We observe that 6.8K (36%) of the pools contain exactly 2 recursive resolver IP addresses where one address is IPv4 and the other is IPv6, and hypothesize that these are actually dual-stack recursive resolvers that switch between interfaces during resolution. To test this theory, we attempt to match the IPv4 and IPv6 addresses by patterns in the IP assignments: (*i*) the IPv4 octets embedded as the final 4 hextets (e.g., *1.2.3.4* and *89ab::1:2:3:4*), or (*ii*) the final IPv4 octet equal to the final IPv6 hextet (e.g., *1.2.3.4* and *89ab::4*). Of the 6.8K potential dual-stack resolvers, 696 match (*i*) and another 1.3K match (*ii*). Interestingly, We also observe 4 cases where the full IPv4 address is embedded within the IPv6 address, but not in the final 4 hextets (e.g., *1.2.3.4* and *89ab::1:2:3:4:5678*). From manual inspection of the remaining 4.8K potential dual-stack resolvers, we observe incremental IP assignment patterns among the pools within the same AS that also aid in positively identifying dual-stack resolvers. For example, in AS 46690, Southern New England Telephone Company, IP assignment appears incremental in both IPv4 and IPv6, but shifted: $w.x.y.z$ forms a pool with $a{:}b{:}c{::}\${z+C}$ where C is a constant. Anecdotally, we observe similar patterns in several ASs.

Next, we note that the IPv4 interface is heavily favored for transport in the pools that are potentially dual-stack resolvers. For each pool, we calculate the ratio of DNS queries using the IPv4 interface versus the IPv6 interface, and find the median ratio is 11:1. Only 718 (10.6%) of the pools favor the IPv6 interface over the IPv4 interface. Our findings here may be impacted by our measurement apparatus, as the DNS zone we use to collect the dataset has more IPv4 delegation records than IPv6 records: 11 and 2, respectively. Depending upon

Table 3. Breakdown of pools by classification

Description	Number of pools	Percentage of pools
Total discovered Pools	61.5K	-
with ≥100 samples	18.7K	30%
Dual-stack resolvers	6.8K	36%
Uniform load-balance pools	2.5K	14%
Off-loading pools (rare)	4.9K	26%
Off-loading pools (frequent)	300	<1%
Other	4.3K	23%

recursive resolver policy, the imbalance may cause resolvers to prefer reaching our authoritative servers over IPv4 (e.g., if the resolver selects a delegation via round robin), thus impacting the number of samples per network protocol.

Finally, we find that in 506 (7.4%) of the pools, the IPv4 and IPv6 addresses are in different ASs operated by the same company. For instance, we find pools belonging to Frontier Communications that exhibit an incremental IP assignment pattern where the IPv6 address is in AS 5650 and the IPv4 addresses is in AS 3593. Thus, having IPv4 and IPv6 addresses in different ASs does not infer that they do not both belong to a dual-stack machine. As future work, we plan to apply the patterns above to identifying dual-stack resolvers within pools of more than 2 resolver IP addresses.

5.2   Load Balancing, Off-Loading and Other Pools

Turning to the 11.9K pools that are not dual-stack resolvers, we classify them into three categories based on the scheme used by the initiator to distribute queries among the resolvers in its pool. Recall that each unique pair has an associated number of samples. Therefore, we can compute the fraction of observations for each resolver within the pool. First, we check for uniform load across the resolvers using the chi-squared test (χ^2) for uniformity. Using a standard 5% significance level, we reject the null hypothesis—that the distribution is uniform—if the p-value is less than 0.05. Otherwise, we conclude the pool is a uniform load balancing pool. Approximately 2.5K (14%) of the pools are balancing the load evenly among the resolvers within the pool.

Next, we explore the 9.5K pools where the null hypothesis is rejected. We observe that in many pools the initiator uses itself much more frequently than other resolvers in the pool. We compare the number of samples in the pool that are initiator to initiator, (x, x), with the number of samples for any other unique pair in the pool, (x, y). The line in Fig. 4 shows the ratio initiator to initiator samples over the maximum samples of any other unique pair. An x-axis value of 0.5 indicates that the initiator uses itself at least as often as any other resolver in the pool. There is a clear behavioral shift at greater than 0.5. We choose the threshold $x = 0.8$ to separate the pools into classes. The 4.9K (26%) pools where $x \geq 0.8$ we term off-loading, as the initiator prefers to use itself, but will off-load queries to other resolvers less frequently. The frequency of off-loading differs widely across pools. In the extreme, we observe 2 recursive resolvers in AS 1221—Telstra Corporation—that use each other in only 8 out of 340K samples. We postulate that resolvers like Telstra's are using a failover behavior when a DNS query is unsuccessful, possibly due to packet loss. Unfortunately, we are not able to identify the reason why queries are off-loaded from our dataset, but note that it is not a function of domain name, as all queries in our dataset are for a single domain.

At the far left of Fig. 4, there is another behavioral shift where the initiator never uses itself in 300 (<1%) of pools. In 219 of the pools, the initiator is an IPv6 resolver, and we therefore conclude that IPv4 transport preference is a main cause of the behavior.

The remaining 4.3K (23%) pools that lie in the middle, we classify as other because they exhibit a variety of behaviors. One behavior is a load distribution which is uneven, e.g., AS 20057—AT&T Mobility—uses a peer structure of IPv4 resolvers where each initiator has a peer and distributes queries roughly 52% to 48% to itself and the peer, respectively. We note our p-values for the AS 20057 pools is roughly 0.002, well below the significance level. In a slightly more dramatic example, AS 4780—Digital United—uses a distribution of 58% to 42% between their resolver peers. Larger pools of greater than 2 resolvers also use complex policies where the fraction of use varies per resolver in the pool, e.g. in a pool of 3 resolvers, they are each used in 50%, 30%, and 20% of samples. Another behavior is a combination of off-loading with uniform load balancing. We observe multiple pools in Level3's AS where all resolvers within the same /24 CIDR block are uniformly load balanced, and resolvers within a second /24 CIDR block are used roughly once out of 500 samples. The range of behaviors within the other classification comes near to the range of operators, thus we do not attempt to further refine this classification.

6 Conclusion

This paper examines the characteristics of recursive resolver pools. We find the resolver pools are not trivial and a large fraction of DNS queries originate from pools of resolvers. First, we examine the characteristics of the pools based on general network properties. We find that the pools are varied in size and confined within an operator's network. Further, we find that a large portion of pools are distributed in IP space and 10% of the discovered pools are geographically distributed. Next, we classify the resolver pools based on their operational behavior. We identify dual-stack resolvers by looking into pools of 2 resolvers which have both IPv4 and IPv6 addresses and find that 36% of the pools are dual-stack resolvers. We observe that there are different assignment patterns—varying from operator to operator—that can be used to associate IPv4 and IPv6 addresses. Further, we classify the pools into 3 major categories based on the distribution of DNS queries among the resolvers within the pool. We find that 14% of the pools uniformly distribute the load among the resolvers within the pools. Moreover, in 26% of the pools, we observe that the initiator resolver prefers to handle the resolution by itself but in some cases it decides to off-load queries to other resolvers in its pool. Finally, 23% of the pools tend to have a wide range of behaviors which varies depending on the operator.

References

1. Akamai EdgeScape (2017). https://www.akamai.com/us/en/products/web-performance/

2. Akamai Real User Monitoring (2017). https://www.akamai.com/us/en/resources/real-user-monitoring.jsp

3. Akamai Technologies, Inc. (2017). https://www.akamai.com/

4. Cloudflare, Inc. (2017). https://www.cloudflare.com/

5. Fastly, Inc. (2017). https://www.fastly.com/

6. Google Public DNS (2017). https://developers.google.com/speed/public-dns/

7. OpenDNS (2017). https://www.opendns.com/

8. Team Cymru IP To ASN Mapping (2017). http://www.team-cymru.org/IP-ASN-mapping.html

9. Agababov, V., Buettner, M., Chudnovsky, V., Cogan, M., Greenstein, B., McDaniel, S., Piatek, M., Scott, C., Welsh, M., Yin, B.: Flywheel: Google's data compression proxy for the mobile web. In: NSDI, vol. 15, pp. 367–380 (2015)

10. Alzoubi, H.A., Rabinovich, M., Spatscheck, O.: The anatomy of LDNS clusters: findings and implications for web content delivery. In: Proceedings of the 22nd International Conference on World Wide Web, pp. 83–94. ACM (2013)

11. Berger, A., Weaver, N., Beverly, R., Campbell, L.: Internet nameserver IPv4 and IPv6 address relationships. In: Proceedings of the 2013 Conference on Internet Measurement Conference, IMC 2013, pp. 91–104. ACM, New York (2013)

12. Beverly, R., Berger, A.: Server siblings: identifying shared IPv4/IPv6 infrastructure via active fingerprinting. In: Mirkovic, J., Liu, Y. (eds.) PAM 2015. LNCS, vol. 8995, pp. 149–161. Springer, Cham (2015). https://doi.org/10.1007/978-3-319-15509-8_12

13. Contavalli, C., van der Gaast, W., Lawrence, D., Kumari, W.: Client Subnet in DNS Queries. RFC 7871, RFC Editor, May 2016. https://tools.ietf.org/html/rfc7871

14. Cui, H., Biersack, E.: Trouble shooting interactive web sessions in a home environment. In: Proceedings of the 2nd ACM SIGCOMM workshop on Home networks, pp. 25–30. ACM (2011)

15. Mockapetris, P.: Domain names - implementation and specification. STD 13, RFC Editor, November 1987. http://www.rfc-editor.org/rfc/rfc1035.txt

16. Otto, J.S., Sánchez, M.A., Rula, J.P., Bustamante, F.E.: Content delivery and the natural evolution of DNS: remote DNS trends, performance issues and alternative solutions. In: Proceedings of the 2012 ACM Conference on Internet measurement conference, pp. 523–536. ACM (2012)

17. Scheitle, Q., Gasser, O., Rouhi, M., Carle, G.: Large-scale classification of IPv6-IPv4 siblings with variable clock skew. In: 2017 Network Traffic Measurement and Analysis Conference (TMA), pp. 1–9. IEEE (2017)

18. Schomp, K., Callahan, T., Rabinovich, M., Allman, M.: On Measuring the client-side DNS infrastructure. In: Proceedings of the 2013 Conference on Internet Measurement Conference, IMC 2013, pp. 77–90. ACM, New York (2013)

19. Sudrajat, F.U.: The State of Adoption of DNS ECS Extension on the Internet. Master's thesis, Case Western Reserve University (2017)

The Unintended Consequences of Email Spam Prevention

Sarah Scheffler[1(✉)], Sean Smith[1,3], Yossi Gilad[1,2], and Sharon Goldberg[1]

[1] Boston University, Boston, USA
sscheff@bu.edu
[2] Massachusetts Institute of Technology, Cambridge, USA
[3] Amazon Technologies, Inc., Chicago, USA

Abstract. To combat Domain Name System (DNS) cache poisoning attacks and exploitation of the DNS as amplifier in denial of service (DoS) attacks, many recursive DNS resolvers are configured as "closed" and refuse to answer queries made by hosts outside of their organization. In this work, we present a technique to induce DNS queries within an organization, using the organization's email service and the Sender Policy Framework (SPF) spam-checking mechanism. We use our technique to study closed resolvers. Our study reveals that most closed DNS resolvers have deployed common DNS poisoning defense techniques such as source port and transaction ID randomization. However, we also find that SPF is often deployed in a way that allows an external attacker to cause the organization's resolver to issue numerous DNS queries to a victim IP address by sending a single email to any address within the organization's domain, thereby providing a potential DoS vector.

1 Introduction

The Domain Name System (DNS) is one of the most fundamental Internet services. Most clients are serviced by a recursive resolver, which queries authoritative name servers until finding the IP address mapped to a domain name. The ubiquitous deployment of DNS servers, their critical nature, combined with rather limited security mechanisms embedded into the DNS protocol caused DNS to be exploited in many malicious activities on the Internet over the years, from denial of service (DoS) attacks [1, 21, 26] to cache poisoning [14]. A common best practice for recursive DNS resolvers to protect themselves from being exploited in such attacks is to be "closed", meaning that the resolver will not respond to requests for queries made by IP addresses located outside their organizations. A closed resolver forces the attacker to operate from inside the organization's network, e.g., by compromising an internal machine, and therefore provides a useful mitigation against attacks that do not target a specific organization. Since closed resolvers are widely deployed and provide a fundamental service, studying their operation is important to understanding how networks operate. Yet, closed

---

S. Smith and Y. Gilad—Work conducted while at Boston University.

© Springer International Publishing AG, part of Springer Nature 2018
R. Beverly et al. (Eds.): PAM 2018, LNCS 10771, pp. 158–169, 2018.
https://doi.org/10.1007/978-3-319-76481-8_12

resolvers make it difficult for researchers to measure the DNS landscape, because recursive resolvers would no longer answer remote queries. Thus performing an Internet-wide scan of DNS services becomes a challenge.

In this study, we use a method of querying closed recursive DNS resolvers by using email, taking advantage of the Sender Policy Framework [15,25], a common anti-spam defense for email. By sending an email to a mail server within the organization, we trigger an SPF check for the sender's address, triggering an intra-organization query for a domain controlled by our own authoritative nameserver, and thus bypass the "closed" defense of the resolver. This email should be caught by the spam filter aided by the receiver's SPF system, and thus is typically not noticeable by mail server administrators.

We conducted a partial Internet scan, covering 15% of the IPv4 address space, searching for mail servers, and then sent emails to each of the mail servers we found. We then studied the induced DNS queries that our email triggered using a nameserver under our control. Our results show that many mail servers use an unsafe SPF configuration that will cause more than the maximum-recommended 10 DNS queries. We ran a test on the scanned mail servers that would induce a maximum of 10 DNS queries in the recommended SPF configuration, and would induce up to 42 DNS queries in a configuration vulnerable to abuse. We received on average 34.3 induced queries, indicating that many mail servers in the wild use this potentially-vulnerable configuration. We also used the DNS queries we received to measure the deployment of various anti-cache poisoning mechanisms across closed DNS resolvers.

We provide required background on SPF in Sect. 2. We discuss measurement methodology in Sect. 3 and analyze our results in Sect. 4. Section 5 discusses related work, and we conclude with recommendations in Sect. 6.

2   SMTP and Sender Policy Framework (SPF)

Emails are sent and received by Mail Transfer Agents (MTAs). In "vanilla" SMTP, any MTA is allowed to send email from any sending address. Much like there is no mechanism to stop somebody from writing a fraudulent return address on an envelope, there is no mechanism in SMTP to stop somebody from sending from an email address with a domain they are not part of. As an anti-spam defense, the Sender Policy Framework (SPF) was introduced in 2006 [25] as means of verifying email-sender identity. It was later updated in 2014 [15].

In SPF, a TXT record is set in the sender's domain to specify which IP addresses are approved to serve as the domain's MTAs (i.e., send emails on behalf of senders in that domain). When an email is sent, the receiving MTA retrieves this record using a DNS query to determine whether the sending MTA's IP address was valid.

SPF allows for more complicated validation procedure than just querying for whitelisted MTA addresses. The TXT record contains a list of terms, which the recipient's MTA uses to check for matches with the sender's IP address. If the IP address matches a term, then the qualifier on that term determines whether the email should be delivered or rejected. It is common practice to end an SPF record with a "`-all`" term, which rejects any email address that did not match any other term. Some SPF terms can cause additional DNS queries, such as for the IP address matching a given `A` or `MX` record. One important feature of SPF we use in future sections is support for `include` terms, which allow an SPF record to tell an MTA to recursively evaluate another SPF record and use the result in the evaluation of the "top-level" record.

Limiting SPF's overhead. In order to avoid unreasonable load on the DNS, the SPF standard [15] requires limiting the number of DNS query-causing terms to 10, and if any more are found, an error must be returned. However, as we see in the next section, the `include` term allows a malicious email sender to circumvent this limit.

3   Measurement Methodology

In our experiment, we registered the domain name `emaildns.net`. We control its authoritative nameserver. The `emaildns.net` domain contains several SPF TXT records for subdomains that correspond to three different SPF configurations, which we explain in Sect. 3.3. We send emails from these subdomains to MTAs that we find by using `zmap` [5]. These emails trigger an SPF check that causes the MTA's DNS resolver to query our authoritative nameserver. We can observe the queries made to our nameserver, and therefore study the behavior of both the DNS resolvers and the MTAs they are querying for, even if those resolvers are closed.

3.1   Ethical Considerations

This study used a remote port scan, which relied on information publicly available by trying to communicate with MTAs legitimately. We sent at most three emails to each MTA we found, which would cause a maximum of 60 DNS queries per email (5 for `goodspf`, 10 for `badspf`, and 42 for `treespf` configuration, plus 1 query for the original SPF record for each configuration). We believe that this should not cause considerable load on any MTA or recursive resolver.

We did our best to ensure that as few humans as possible would receive email, by attempting to find email addresses that would not be delivered to a human. We also wrote the SPF record in the `emaildns.net` zone to deliberately fail after checking all our recursive statements, so that any correctly-configured SPF system would ultimately reject our email.

Our measurement emails referred readers to our project website https://emaildns.net which has information about our study, and contains a form that allows adding email addresses to a blacklist, if anyone wanted to opt-out of the remaining part of the study. We attempted to contact 190597 MTAs found by our `zmap` scan, and in total we sent 38720 emails successfully. During this process, 23 email addresses were added to our blacklist via our web form. We also received three emailed requests to opt-out of the study and one emailed request to send the owner of the MTA the results of our study when we completed it.

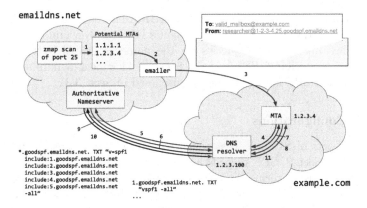

Fig. 1. Measurement technique. The example emails an MTA at IP address 1.2.3.4 using the "goodspf" configuration. The steps are detailed in the text.

We also contacted the authors of a paper that used a similar IPv4 scan [10] and used their blacklist of CIDR ranges, under the logic that anyone that opted out of that study probably would not want to be part of this one either. We noted on our website that we would add CIDR ranges to the blacklist if we received an email request to do so. We received no such requests during the scan.

3.2   Operation

Our measurement has several steps, which we summarize in Fig. 1 and describe in more detail in Sect. 3.4. First, we test whether an IP address is a potential MTA, by using zmap [5] to check if that IP address hosts a server listening on port 25, the default SMTP port. Second, because SPF is only used when an email is sent to a valid address, for each MTA IP address we attempt to find a valid email address served by that MTA, following a procedure discussed in Sect. 3.4. Third, we send emails to addresses served by the MTA to invoke the SPF check. The sending address of this email is within emaildns.net, so our authoritative nameserver for emaildns.net will be queried during the SPF check of this email. To allow measuring different MTAs/DNS resolvers in parallel, we encode information about the recipient MTA in the subdomain of the sender's address in our email. The sending address is in the form <dashed-ip4-mta-address>.<portnum>.spf-config.emaildns.net. For example, if sending to an MTA at 1.2.3.4 using the "treespf" config, the domain of the sending email address, which will be checked via the receiver's SPF, is 1-2-3-4.25.treespf.emaildns.net.

Steps 4–11 in Fig. 1 illustrate what happens after an email was sent and SPF checks begin. In step 4 the recipient's MTA issues a DNS query for the sending domain name's SPF record. In step 5 the DNS resolver at the recipient MTA side (possibly a closed resolver) sends this TXT query for the sender's domain name to the authoritative nameserver at emaildns.net, where it is logged. In steps

6–7 the response, which contains a number of `include` statements depending on the SPF configuration, is sent to the recipient's DNS resolver and then its MTA. Steps 8–11 are *induced* DNS queries for the names specified by the `include` statements in the original SPF record. Steps 8–11 repeat a number of times dependant on the SPF configuration, as discussed in Sect. 3.3.

3.3 SPF Configurations

We use three sets of SPF records, which we call goodspf, badspf, and treespf. As discussed in Sect. 2, SPF records are restricted to containing no more than 10 DNS query-causing terms. Our three SPF implementations are designed to study how this restriction works in practice. goodspf contains 5 DNS query-causing terms and is a valid SPF record. badspf contains 20 DNS query-causing terms, and is therefore invalid. treespf contains 6 DNS query-causing terms, each of which causes an *additional* 6 DNS queries, for a total of 42 induced queries, but only 6 DNS query-causing terms. We describe each of these configurations in more detail below. All three SPF configurations ultimately evaluate to `fail` so that our email will not be delivered, but only after the entire SPF check finishes.

goodspf. This record, shown in the lower left of Fig. 1, contains five `include` statements, that redirect to `i.goodspf.emaildns.net` for i from 1 through 5. The SPF for record for all `i.goodspf.emaildns.net` is "v=spf1 -all". An `include` does not result in an immediate `fail` for the main query if the included SPF check fails [15, Sect. 5.2]. These `include` terms can be thought of as SPF "dead ends". Each included check fails, but the main SPF check continues, checking all `include` terms before making its final decision.

The goodspf configuration is meant to establish a baseline for SPF behavior, ensuring that the record containing fewer than 10 DNS query-causing terms is processed as we expect it to be: one DNS query for the main SPF record, and one induced query for each of the five included SPF records.

badspf. This record has 20 include statements that each cause a single DNS query (to `i.badspf.emaildns.net` for i from 1 through 20). Each of these "sub-records" is "v=spf1 -all". It is therefore non-compliant with the SPF specification, which restricts the number of DNS query-causing terms to 10. We use the badspf record to check whether this limit of 10 queries is enforced at all — if it is, we would expect to get 10 induced queries per badspf email sent, and if it is not, then we would expect to get 20.

treespf. This record, shown graphically in Fig. 2, allows us to gain insights on how the 10 DNS-query-causing statements is enforced. While the standard limits the number of *query-causing terms* in an SPF record to 10, it does not limit the *total number* of SPF DNS queries made, and therefore treespf is RFC-compliant. The treespf configuration is compliant the standard's limitation of 10 query-causing terms, but causes many more than 10 queries, by using recursively-called nested includes. This record, shown graphically in Fig. 2, allows us to gain insight on how the limit of 10 DNS query-causing statements is enforced. While the standard limits the number of *query-causing terms* in an SPF record to 10, it

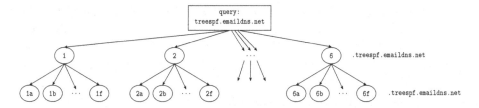

Fig. 2. In treespf, one main query directly induces 6 subqueries, each of which induces 6 more subqueries, for a total of 42 induced subqueries.

does not limit the *total number* of DNS queries made. The treespf configuration is RFC-compliant, as it contains fewer than 10 DNS query-causing terms. However, each of these terms causes more than one DNS query, by using an "include" statement to cause a recursive evaluation of an entirely new SPF query. The top level *.treespf.emaildns.net record contains includes to six other SPF records: i.treespf.emaildns.net for i from 1 through 6. Then each of those records contains includes to six additional records: 1a.treespf.emaildns.net through 1f.treespf.emaildns.net, for example. A total of 42 DNS queries are made within the SPF record, however, each individual record contains exactly six (fewer than 10) query-causing statements.

3.4 Experimental Procedure

We next describe how we performed our measurement.

Scanning for MTAs. We used zmap [5] to perform a TCP SYN scan to find services listening on port 25 over IPv4. For each shard of 2^{24} IP addresses, we first scanned the entire shard, collecting all IP addresses that responded to our TCP SYN on port 25 and saving them to a file. This process took roughly five minutes per shard. Note that we did not complete our entire IPv4 scan. Our results are an initial finding that indicate how recursive SPF check works. (We discuss our results and their limitations in Sect. 4.)

Finding valid recipient email addresses. This step uses a heuristic to get email addresses that are likely serviced by the MTA. We used usernames such as "noreply" or "postmaster", and we learned potential domains through a whois lookup and using a reverse DNS lookup. We also removed subdomains from each of these domain guesses as additional possible options. We attempt to begin delivery to each combination of these usernames and domains until we get one that the MTA recognizes.

Sending emails and logging induced DNS queries. We encode the information about the recipient MTA in our sender email address. For instance, if sending to an MTA at IP address 1.2.3.4 and using the goodspf configuration, we would send our email from researcher@1-2-3-4.25.goodspf.emaildns.net. (The "25" in the address represents the port number, and was included to allow expanding our study to more ports). We then send an email to addresses we guessed in that domain. If we do not receive a 250 OK SMTP status response, then we try the next email address that our heuristic provides. Our email sender handles in parallel addresses for 300 MTAs.

Once we found a working email address for the MTA, we sent two additional emails, so that in total an MTA receives three emails, one for each SPF configuration. Throughout this whole process, we log all DNS queries received on `emaildns.net`'s authoritative name, and we retained all of our SMTP logs.

4   Analysis of Induced DNS Queries

We broke our scan into 256 shards, based on the 8 most significant bits of the IP address. The scan ran from September 11th, 2017 through September 22, 2017 and covered IP addresses from 0.0.0.0 through 34.255.255.255. Although our results are partial, we believe that there are valuable insights to be gained from the portion of the scanned address space.

4.1   SPF Deployment

We categorize the queries that our authoritative name server receives into three bins: (1) "main queries", which are `TXT` queries for a domain that we sent an email from, for example, `1-2-3-4.25.badspf.emaildns.net`; (2) "induced queries", which are queries induced by `include` statements within our main SPF record, such as `16.badspf.emaildns.net`; and (3) other, miscellaneous queries.

SPF as DoS vector. Checking an SPF record with many nested includes could cause undue load on the SPF-validating MTA, causing it to make far more DNS queries per email than it should. This could result in degraded performance or complete denial of service. Since SPF places a limit on the number of *query-causing terms* in an SPF record, rather than the total number of queries made, an SPF record with many `include` statements can recursively cause queries to any `include` statements in *those* records, and so on. treespf is a proof of concept of this: it induces 42 queries even though it contains only 10 query-causing terms.

A more dangerous version of this would involve mutually recursive SPF records, shown in Fig. 3. Attackers could "bounce between" recursive calls to look up each SPF record, and each call would cause 9 additional `include` queries to an unrelated victim nameserver. However, this was not tested as part of this work.

SPF Configuration Results. Our results are summarized in Table 1.

As our baseline measurement to ensure the SPF check does what we expect when it sees a well-formed, typical SPF record, our goodspf record should induce 5 queries. We received 4.87 induced queries per main goodspf query (39583/8125), which is about what we expected.

To ensure that the SPF check correctly halts at 10 DNS-query causing terms in a single record, our badspf record attempted to induce 20 queries, only 10 of which should actually occur. Our badspf record on average induced 7.79 queries per main query (136881/17562). We received approximately the same number of goodspf and treespf queries, but double that number of badspf queries. We believe that the error caused by querying badspf causes some MTA software to

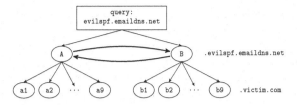

Fig. 3. A mutually recursive chain of SPF `include` statements could cause an infinite number of queries to `victim.com`.

Table 1. Expected and actual ratios for the three different SPF configurations used.

SPF configuration	Query response ratio	Expected response ratio
goodspf	4.87 (39583/8125)	5.0
badspf	7.79 (136881/17562)	10.0
treespf	34.3 (280734/8192)	either 42.0 or 10.0

query the record again after a few minutes, indicating that an SPF `permerror` may be incorrectly treated as a `temperror` by some implementations.

Our main result is the ratio of induced treespf queries. As described in Sect. 3.3, the treespf configuration contains only 6 DNS query-causing terms (below the RFC-mandated limit of 10), but each of those terms is an include statement that causes 6 additional DNS queries. If SPF performed a once-per-email-address check that halted DNS queries after 10 total queries, then we would expect to receive the same number of induced queries as in badspf. However, if the check is performed separately on all recursively-checked include statements rather than once per email address, we would expect to get 42 induced queries per main query. This conforms to the SPF RFC, but goes against the RFC's stated goal of avoiding unreasonable load on the DNS. We received 34.3 induced queries per main treespf query (280734/8192), clearly indicating that many SPF configurations perform the check per-include rather than once per email address.

It was very common for the different induced queries caused by the same main query to come from different resolvers. Because of this, it was infeasible to tie induced queries (e.g., `3b.treespf.emaildns.net`) with the exact main query that caused it (e.g. `1-2-3-4.25.treespf.emaildns.net`). Attempts at approximating the relationship between induced queries and main queries based on the timestamp and querying DNS server were very imprecise. We limit our analysis here to an aggregate: the ratio of all induced queries to all main queries.

These results show that although the SPF's standard intends to "avoid unreasonable load on the DNS" by limiting the number of DNS-querying terms in an SPF record, a malicious SPF record can use nested include statements to circumvent this limitation using recursion.

4.2   Security of DNS Resolvers

Having received DNS queries from domain names within organizations, we can study the deployment of suggested DNS security mechanisms on DNS resolvers.

Closed vs open. A fundamental defense against DNS-based attacks is to deploy recursive DNS resolvers as closed. And even among open DNS infrastructures, DNS queries are often passed from an open to a closed resolver before recursion occurs [23]. Our measurement technique gives us the IP address of the recursive resolver that queries the authoritative nameserver, regardless of whether it is open or closed, which is the one that matters for determining how SPF checks are handled. To check whether the resolver is closed, we send it a DNS query from our machine using `dig`. If it responds to our query, then we assume it is open. If it does not, we assume it is closed.

Port Randomization and TXID Randomization. It is widely accepted that DNS resolvers should randomize the source port and transaction ID in their queries, and then validate these fields as echoed in the DNS responses in order to defend against DNS poisoning [11].

To check whether or not port randomization and TXID randomization were enabled, we looked at the queries we received from each DNS server in chronological order. We used two thresholds to test whether the query transaction IDs were feasibly close to nonrandom order: first, we checked whether 70% of query TXID numbers (resp. port numbers) we received from each DNS server were within 500 of the previous one. The second check is for whether 50% of query TXID numbers (resp. port numbers) were with 1000 of the previous one.

0x20 Randomization. Dagon et al. proposed that resolvers would randomize the latter-cases in domain names queries as a cache poisoning defense [4]. Since the queried domain name is echoed in the response, this provides additional entropy to DNS queries that the resolver could validate.

The capitalization patterns of the queries we receive inform us whether or not the querying server utilizes 0x20 randomization. If the server is using 0x20 randomization, we would expect there to be roughly 50% uppercase and lowercase letters in the queries across all queries received from this nameserver. We check whether the ratio of uppercase letters is between 30% and 70%, and if it does, we determine that this querier has 0x20 randomization.

DNS Configuration Results. We received queries for our SPF records from 8889 total nameserver IP addresses. For each of these, we measured whether the server is open or closed. We required at least 4 queries received from a nameserver in order to determine whether it used randomization. 5718 nameservers sent us at least 4 queries; for these servers we measured whether source port randomization, transaction ID randomization, and 0x20 randomization were used.

Of 1160 open nameservers that sent us at least 4 queries, 1153 (99%) used both transaction ID randomization and port randomization, and the remaining 7 (1%) used only transaction ID randomization. No open nameservers used 0x20 randomization. Of 4558 closed nameservers that sent us at least 4 queries, 4547 (99%) of them used both transaction ID randomization and port randomization. 10 closed nameservers used only transaction ID randomization, and 1 used only port randomization. Only one closed nameserver used 0x20 randomization; it was among the 4547 that also used both other defenses.

We find that DNS defenses are nearly ubiquitous - 99% of all nameservers used both transaction ID randomization and port randomization, and the defenses of closed resolvers only barely differ from the defensees of open resolvers. Furthermore, most nameservers have taken the extra precaution of being closed. Of 8889 nameservers that queried us, 7303 (82%) did not respond to DNS query from outside the organization. One implication of this is that open resolvers are only a small part of the DNS ecosystem, and so DNS measurements conducted only on open resolvers may not be representative.

5 Related Work

The Domain Name System has been the main focus of many denial of service attacks for many years [21], and many methods for detection and mitigation have been proposed [1,13,17,19,26]. Prior surveys of the Domain Name System that measure both DoS mitigation and defenses against cache poisoning [2,23,24] have focused on open resolvers.

Recent work by Klein et. al. [16] also measures the responses of closed DNS servers by probing them using email. If an MTA receives an email sent to a nonexistent user, it will query the MX record of the sender's domain name in order to determine where to send a bounceback email. Sending emails to nonexistant users does not allow studying the deployment of SPF since the recipient MTA would discard the email before checking the sender's validity. Huston [12] measures the behavior of closed DNS resolvers in IPv6. The method works similarly to our own, by causing a remote server to query its own closed DNS server, but it uses targeted advertisements rather than email spam prevention.

Several works have evaluated the deployment of Sender Policy Framework in the context of email security [6–8,10,18], and several mention the risk of utilizing SPF in DoS attacks [9,20]. The updated SPF standard [15] took this into account in the new version, and made a recommendation to limit the number of DNS query-causing terms checked. However, we have shown that this defense can be circumvented using `include` statements.

6 Recommendations

Standard update. The most recent version of the SPF standard (2014)[15, Sect. 11.1] discusses the possibility of malicious SPF terms and proposes to limit the number of "void lookups" (lookups that result in a response with 0 answers, or that cause a name error) to 2 per SPF record, after which an error is returned. This is in addition to the maximum of 10 DNS query-causing terms limit. We recommend that both of these limits be global, rather than "resetting" when recursion occurs in `include` statements.

Implementations. We recommend that new versions of the SPF library [3,22] follow our previous suggestion to using global counts of DNS queries and void lookups per email, rather than resetting these to 0 when recursion occurs and a new SPF record is fetched. We envision this being the default option.

Acknowledgements. We thank Jared Mauch for contributing the machines we used to scan the Internet address space for MTAs and store our results. Sharon Goldberg thanks Haya Shulman for useful discussions about DNS resolvers and email. This research was supported, in part, by NSF grants 414119 and 1350733.

References

1. Ballani, H., Francis, P.: Mitigating DNS DoS attacks. In: Proceedings of Computer and Communications Security, pp. 189–198. ACM (2008)
2. Borgwart, A., Shulman, H., Waidner, M.: Towards automated measurements of internet's naming infrastructure. In: Software Science, Technology and Engineering (SWSTE), pp. 117–124. IEEE (2016)
3. The SPF Council. Sender Policy Framework, April 2014. http://www.openspf.org/
4. Dagon, D., Antonakakis, M., Vixie, P., Jinmei, T., Lee, W.: Increased DNS forgery resistance through 0x20-bit encoding: security via leet queries. In: Proceedings of Computer and Communications Security, pp. 211–222. ACM (2008)
5. Durumeric, Z., Wustrow, E., Halderman, J.A.: ZMap: fast internet-wide scanning and its security applications. In: King, S.T. (ed.) USENIX Security Symposium, pp. 605–620. USENIX Association (2013). ISBN:978-1-931971-03-4
6. Durumeric, Z., Adrian, D., Mirian, A., Kasten, J., Bursztein, E., Lidzborski, N., Thomas, K., Eranti, V., Bailey, M., Halderman, J.A.: Neither snow nor rain nor MITM: an empirical analysis of email delivery security. In: Internet Measurement Conference, pp. 27–39. ACM (2015). http://dl.acm.org/citation.cfm?id=2815675. ISBN:978-1-4503-3848-6
7. Foster, I.D., Larson, J., Masich, M., Snoeren, A.C., Savage, S., Levchenko, K.: Security by any other name: on the effectiveness of provider based email security. In: Proceedings of Computer and Communications Security, pp. 450–464. ACM (2015)
8. Gojmerac, I., Zwickl, P., Kovacs, G., Steindl, C.: Large-scale active measurements of DNS entries related to e-mail system security. In: International Conference on Communications, pp. 7426–7432, June 2015. https://doi.org/10.1109/ICC.2015.7249513
9. Herzberg, A.: DNS-based email sender authentication mechanisms: a critical review. Comput. Secur. **28**(8), 731–742 (2009)
10. Holz, R., Amann, J., Mehani, O., Wachs, M., Kâafar, M.A.: TLS in the Wild: An Internet-wide Analysis of TLS-based Protocols for Electronic Communication. CoRR, abs/1511.00341 (2015). http://arxiv.org/abs/1511.00341
11. Hubert, A., van Mook, R.: Measures for Making DNS More Resilient against Forged Answers. RFC 5452 (Proposed Standard), January 2009. http://www.ietf.org/rfc/rfc5452.txt
12. Huston, G.: IPv6 and the DNS, October 2016. https://blog.apnic.net/2016/10/20/ipv6-and-the-dns/
13. Kambourakis, G., Moschos, T., Geneiatakis, D., Gritzalis, S.: Detecting DNS amplification attacks. In: Lopez, J., Hämmerli, B.M. (eds.) CRITIS 2007. LNCS, vol. 5141, pp. 185–196. Springer, Heidelberg (2008). https://doi.org/10.1007/978-3-540-89173-4_16
14. Kaminsky, D.: Its the End of the Cache as we Know It. Black-Hat USA (2008)
15. Kitterman, S.: Sender Policy Framework (SPF) for Authorizing Use of Domains in Email, Version 1. RFC 7208 (Proposed Standard), April 2014. http://www.ietf.org/rfc/rfc7208.txt. Updated by RFC 7372

16. Klein, A., Shulman, H., Waidner, M.: Internet-wide study of DNS cache injections. In: INFOCOM, pp. 1–9. IEEE (2017)
17. Kührer, M., Hupperich, T., Rossow, C., Holz, T.: Exit from hell? Reducing the impact of amplification DDoS attacks. In: USENIX Security Symposium, pp. 111–125 (2014)
18. Malatras, A., Coisel, I., Sanchez, I.: Technical recommendations for improving security of email communications. In: Information and Communication Technology, Electronics and Microelectronics, pp. 1381–1386. IEEE (2016)
19. Moore, D., Shannon, C., Brown, D.J., Voelker, G.M., Savage, S.: Inferring internet denial-of-service activity. ACM Trans. Comput. Syst. **24**(2), 115–139 (2006)
20. Mori, T., Sato, K., Takahashi, Y., Ishibashi, K.: How is e-mail sender authentication used and misused? In: Proceedings of the 8th Annual Collaboration, Electronic Messaging, Anti-Abuse and Spam Conference, CEAS 2011, pp. 31–37. ACM, New York (2011). http://doi.acm.org/10.1145/2030376.2030380. ISBN:978-1-4503-0788-8
21. Paxson, V.: An analysis of using reflectors for distributed denial-of-service attacks. ACM SIGCOMM Comput. Commun. Rev. **31**(3), 38–47 (2001)
22. Schlitt, W.: libspf2 - SPF Library. https://www.libspf2.org/
23. Schomp, K., Callahan, T., Rabinovich, M., Allman, M.: On measuring the client-side DNS infrastructure. In: Proceedings of Internet Measurement Conference, pp. 77–90. ACM, New York (2013). http://doi.acm.org/10.1145/2504730.2504734. ISBN:978-1-4503-1953-9
24. Sisson, G.: DNS Survey, The Measurement Factory, November 2010. http://dns.measurement-factory.com/surveys/201010/dns_survey_2010.pdf
25. Wong, M., Schlitt, W.: Sender Policy Framework (SPF) for Authorizing Use of Domains in E-Mail, Version 1. RFC 4408 (Experimental), April 2006. Obsoleted by RFC 7208, updated by RFC 6652. http://www.ietf.org/rfc/rfc4408.txt
26. Zargar, S.T., Joshi, J., Tipper, D.: A survey of defense mechanisms against distributed denial of service (DDoS) flooding attacks. IEEE Commun. Surv. Tutor. **15**(4), 2046–2069 (2013)

Certificates

In Log We Trust: Revealing Poor Security Practices with Certificate Transparency Logs and Internet Measurements

Oliver Gasser[1]([envelope]), Benjamin Hof[1], Max Helm[1], Maciej Korczynski[2,3],
Ralph Holz[4], and Georg Carle[1]

[1] Technical University of Munich, Munich, Germany
gasser@net.in.tum.de
[2] Grenoble Alps University, Grenoble, France
[3] Delft University of Technology, Delft, Netherlands
[4] The University of Sydney, Sydney, Australia

Abstract. In recent years, multiple security incidents involving Certificate Authority (CA) misconduct demonstrated the need for strengthened certificate issuance processes. Certificate Transparency (CT) logs make the issuance publicly traceable and auditable.

In this paper, we leverage the information in CT logs to analyze if certificates adhere to the industry's Baseline Requirements. We find 907 k certificates in violation of Baseline Requirements, which we pinpoint to issuing CAs. Using data from active measurements we compare certificate deployment to logged certificates, identify non-HTTPS certificates in logs, evaluate CT-specific HTTP headers, and augment IP address hitlists using data from CT logs. Moreover, we conduct passive and active measurements to carry out a first analysis of CT's gossiping and pollination approaches, finding low deployment. We encourage the reproducibility of network measurement research by publishing data from active scans, measurement programs, and analysis tools.

Keywords: TLS · Certificate Transparency · Baseline Requirements

1 Introduction

One of the Internet's most important protocols, Transport Layer Security (TLS), relies critically on server certificates being issued with diligence by the Web's trust anchors, the Certificate Authorities. It had long been suspected that this degree of trust may be misplaced [13], but from late 2008 on a string of security incidents relating to poor certification practices [31] culminated in the compromise of the DigiNotar Certificate Authority [16]. Being one of the affected parties and a major player on the WWW, Google began work in the IETF on Certificate Transparency (CT) as a response. While this technology is not designed to prevent actual attacks from happening, it can reduce the time to detection drastically. CT essentially turns the Web PKI inside out: a number of independent

© Springer International Publishing AG, part of Springer Nature 2018
R. Beverly et al. (Eds.): PAM 2018, LNCS 10771, pp. 173–185, 2018.
https://doi.org/10.1007/978-3-319-76481-8_13

and neutral logs keep track of issued certificates. This enabled an unprecedented degree of transparency: both certificate misissuance and CA malpractice can now be detected by site operators and third parties. In the years since DigiNotar, Certificate Transparency has won widespread support. Browser vendors take incidents and malpractice seriously: a number of CAs have been called out for poor practices [27,37], and the CA PROCERT has been removed from Mozilla's products due to violations of the industry's Baseline Requirements [24]. In this paper, we carry out a thorough analysis of certificates stored in CT and assess CA compliance with the Baseline Requirements.

Main contributions: We perform Internet-wide scans to 196 M hosts, download more than 600 M entries from CT logs, and conduct passive measurements at two different vantage points. Analyzing these data sources, we find 907 k non-expired certificates in violation of Baseline Requirements, and show the proportion of offending certificates is decreasing over time. We quantify the number of domains affected by the impending Symantec distrust. To the best of our knowledge, we conduct the first analysis of non-HTTPS certificates in CT logs and find low rates of log inclusion. We make analysis data, source code, and IP addresses generated from CT log data publicly available to encourage reproducibility in research.

Outline: In Sect. 2 we give technical background on TLS and CT. Section 3 lays out related work in the Certificate Transparency and certificate analysis fields. In Sect. 4 we describe our methodology. In the following two sections we analyze the acquired data: Sect. 5 highlights adherence of CT log certificates to the CA/Brower Forum Baseline Requirements. In Sect. 6 we compare certificates from CT logs to those from active scans. Section 7 lays out results from investigating CT gossip approaches. We conclude our paper in Sect. 8.

2   Background

In this section we provide information on protocols relevant for this study.

In order to provide an industry standard for the behavior of CAs in the context of HTTPS, the CA/Browser Forum continuously negotiates technical policies for CA operations. Supplementing specifications such as RFC 5280, it publishes the Baseline Requirements (BRs) [5]. The Baseline Requirements specify important properties for Internet security, for example which algorithms used in certificates are considered secure or what the maximum life time of a certificate may be.

Certificate Revocation Lists (CRLs, see RFC 5280) provide a mechanism to withdraw trust from misissued certificates, e.g., in case of a key compromise.

Repeated misissuances of certificates have led to substantial scrutiny of CAs [9]. Certificate Transparency (CT, see RFC 6962) is a measure to monitor CA behavior. In CT, certificates are submitted into untrusted, public, append-only logs. The primary goal of CT is to allow site operators to observe which certificates were issued for their DNS names. To do this, they inspect the logs, retrieving and examining all certificates included in them. A secondary goal is improving compliance of CAs by easing discovery of misissuances.

On submission of a certificate, the log returns a signed inclusion promise called Signed Certificate Timestamp (SCT). Sites attach the SCT when presenting their certificate, notifying the browser of their participation in CT. Logs regularly produce signed commitments to a fixed entry list (Signed Tree Heads, STHs). A certificate is considered included in a log when it is covered by an STH.

Today, the Chrome browser requires CT for "Extended Validation" certificates. Starting April 2018, CT will be required by Chrome for all newly issued certificates [34]. Public logs for this purpose are operated by Google and some certificate authorities.

A possible attack by a CT log server is presenting different views to different parties, also called equivocation. This can be addressed with gossip protocols, where participants inform others about the log view presented to them. One such proposal for CT exchanges SCTs and STHs via defined API endpoints on HTTPS servers [29]. The Chrome browser implements an alternative model, where STHs are transferred to the browser via the internal component updater [35]. Inclusion proofs are requested via a custom DNS-based protocol [22].

3   Related Work

The analysis of TLS certificates has become increasingly important, in particular with HTTPS becoming a *de facto* protocol for the Web and many of its APIs [15]. A number of analyses have been carried out, most commonly based on active scans and sometimes passive traffic observation. Our methodology relies to a large degree on a new, different data source, namely CT logs.

Several published works also exploit CT logs, albeit with different research questions. *Amann et al.* [4] examine the use of Certificate Transparency in the context of general improvements to the TLS ecosystems since 2011, a year with a number of major CA incidents. The authors' focus is on the deployment and practical use of these improvements; they do not investigate the properties of logged certificates. *Aertsen et al.* [3] use CT logs to analyze the rise of the Let's Encrypt CA and the resulting more wide-spread use of encryption that enables smaller websites and hosting providers to acquire free certificates. *Gustafsson et al.* [19] use CT logs in combination with passive traffic monitoring to analyze the basic properties of logs and certificates, such as signature algorithm and key lengths of certificates. They do not investigate violations of issuance standards. *VanderSloot et al.* [42] combine CT logs with seven other certificate collection techniques to obtain a picture of the overall HTTPS ecosystem and how different data sources help to make it accurate. They conclude that no collection method covers all certificates. However, they observe that CT logs in combination with active scans cover 98.5 % of their certificates. In our work we make use of this finding to also leverage CT logs and active scans.

A number of earlier publications investigates properties of certificates and TLS deployment. *Holz et al.* [20] provides the first large-scale, long-term analysis

Table 1. Overview of conducted measurements and used data sources.

Data source	Time period	# Entries	Size
CT log downloads	until Oct. 9, 2017	600 M entries	732 GB
Active HTTPS scans			
IPv4	Oct. 3–8, 2017	196.3 M hosts[1]	259.1 GB
IPv6	Oct. 1, 2017	8.8 M hosts[1]	73.0 GB
CRL downloads	Oct. 11, 2017	25.3 M entries	1.9 TB
Passive CT over DNS			
MWN UDP/53	Sep. 20–27, 2017	2.3 G pkts	10.5 TB
DNSDB TXT #1	Jul. 2016	36.4 M RRs	6.0 MB
DNSDB TXT #2	Sep. 20, 2017	2.4 M RRs	429.8 MB

1: unique IP–domain tuples, e.g., (216.58.207.142, google.com).

of this kind; *Durumeric et al.* [11] later extends this approach to the entire IPv4 space. The publications focus on basic properties of TLS certificates such as weak encryption keys, invalid path length constraints, invalid validity periods, and revoked certificates and sibling CA certificates. *Chung et al.* [8] use TLS scans to analyze certificates without a valid root. They show that invalid certificates make up the majority of collected certificates. A large-scale study of HTTPS-induced browser errors was carried out by *Acer et al.* [1].

4   Methodology

In this section we present our methodology for conducting active and passive measurements. We use various different sources to get a large view of the certificate universe: We download certificates from CT logs, obtain certificates from active scans, retrieve CRLs, and conduct active and passive measurements to analyze CT gossiping deployment. Table 1 gives an overview of these sources, detailing the time of data collection, the number of entries, and the size of the acquired data. We also detail ethical and reproducibility considerations.

CT Log downloads. We extend Google's CT tool to incrementally download certificates and their certificate chains from 30 CT logs. We publish our extended CT tool on GitHub [39]. In total we download 600 M log entries, resulting in 216.8 M unique certificates and 7.8 M unique certificates in chains.

Active HTTPS measurements. To compare the certificates seen in CT logs to the actual HTTPS deployment we conduct active measurements over IPv4 and IPv6. First, we collect a total of 1.2 G domains from three different sources: TUM's hitlist [18], domains contained in CN and SAN of downloaded CT log certificates, and Farsight's DNSDB [14]. Second, we filter auto-generated disposable domains [6] from the DNSDB data by removing subdomains such as netflixdnstest1.com and domains with less than 100 queries within a month as

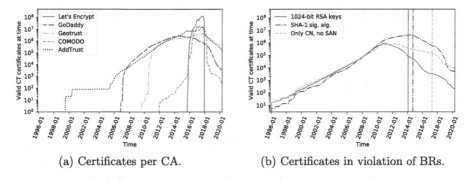

(a) Certificates per CA.   (b) Certificates in violation of BRs.

Fig. 1. Non-expired certificates in CT logs, by issuing CA and conformance with three BRs (vertical line is Chrome enforcement date). Y-axis is log-scaled.

indicated by DNSDB. Third, we resolve the remaining domains to A and AAAA records. Fourth, we conduct port scans on TCP/443 using ZMap [12] for IPv4, and our IPv6-enabled version [41] for IPv6. Fifth, we use our highly parallelized Goscanner [40] to establish TLS connections to 191.4 M and 8.8 M IP address–domain name tuples for IPv4 and IPv6, respectively. To obtain the correct certificate we send the domain name in the SNI extension. Upon successful connection establishment we send HTTP requests to retrieve the server's HTTP headers and check for the presence of gossiping and pollination endpoints [29].

CRL downloads. In order to determine the revocation status of certificates, we extract CRL URLs from certificates of active scans and CT logs. We then download these CRL files as well as Mozilla's OneCRL [28]. In total we extract 25.3 M entries from CRLs. We do not check OCSP as it is disabled in Chrome and previous work shows limited support [23].

Passive DNS measurements. To analyze the use of Google's CT over DNS approach [22], we conduct passive measurements. We evaluate one week of DNS traffic at the Internet uplink of the Munich Scientific Network. Additionally, we use Farsight's DNSDB data [14] to further improve our client coverage.

Ethical considerations. We follow an internal multi-party approval process before any measurement activities are carried out. This process incorporates the proposals of Partridge and Allman [30] as well as Dittrich et al. [10]. We assess whether our measurements can induce harm on individuals in different stakeholder groups. As we limit our query rate and use conforming HTTP requests, it is unlikely for our measurements to cause problems on scanned systems. Using the REST API provided by CT logs, we perform incremental downloads to reduce the impact on target systems. We follow best scanning practices such as maintaining a blacklist and using dedicated servers with informing rDNS names, web sites, and abuse contacts. We limit our passive measurements to DNS TXT records. The conclusion of this process is that it is ethical to conduct the measurements, but that we will only share data from our active measurements and not release passive data to protect the privacy of involved parties.

Reproducible research. To encourage reproducible research in network measurements [2,33], we publish source code and data in the long-term availability archive of the TUM University Library: https://mediatum.ub.tum.de/1422427.

5   Baseline Requirements

In this section we analyze the certificates found in CT logs, with a particular focus on their compliance with the Baseline Requirements. Figure 1a shows the result of a quantitative analysis of non-expired certificates of the top 5 CAs over time. As is to be expected, the number of current, non-expired certificates peaks for most CAs around our cut-off date of October 9, 2017. One exception is GoDaddy, whose number of issued, non-expired certificates has been decreasing since 2014. We see that the vast majority of certificates in logs are issued by Let's Encrypt (LE), which saw exponential growth after the service became publicly available in 2016. Furthermore, due to the 3 month validity period of LE certificates, a sharp decline of certificates can be seen at the beginning of 2018. Due to longer validity periods, this decline is less pronounced for other CAs.

To evaluate the conformance of certificates to BRs, we run the cablint tool [38] on all non-expired certificates found in CT logs. We find 907 k certificates (1.3 %) in violation of BRs. Three major security relevant changes in the last years are shown in Fig. 1b, with vertical bars denoting deprecation steps by the Chrome browser. We observe that the prohibition of practices such as short keys is followed by a substantial reduction in the number of affected certificates. It takes years, however, until all old non-compliant certificates are expired.

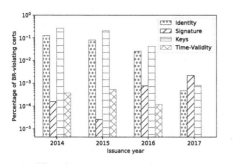
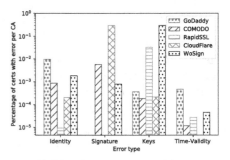

(a) Violation category over issuance.   (b) Violation category per CA.

Fig. 2. Proportion of certificates in violation of BR. Y-axis is log-scaled.

Next, we look at violations of requirements or recommendations in the current BRs. We categorize these violations as pertaining to the *identity* (e.g., SAN or CN), *signature* (e.g., hash algorithm), *key* (e.g., key usage or size), or *validity time*. Grouping certificates by year of issuance, Fig. 2a shows the proportion of certificates exhibiting errors in these categories. This allows us to see the proportion of problematic certificates independent of the issuance rate. Generally,

Table 2. Comparison of certificates found in CT logs and active scans.

Cert source	Total	Not revoked	Not expired	Not self-signed	Browser-valid	BR-valid
CT logs	216.8 M	216.6 M	70.2 M	216.8 M	70.2 M	206.3 M
Active scans	128.1 M	127.5 M	118.8 M	109.4 M	74.8 M	115.4 M

the proportion of certificates with errors is declining over time, with identity and key issues being predominant. In 2017, signature related issues become the prevalent cause of errors.

Attributing these violations to specific CAs, we select the 5 CAs with the highest number of infringing certificates. We show the number of violating certificates in the different categories per CA relative to their total issued certificates in Fig. 2b. The most significant infractions are SHA1 signatures by CloudFlare and use of non-critical key usage extensions by WoSign. Upon closer investigation we find that most certificates with BR violations are signed by revoked intermediate certificates. We use our measurement results to improve issuance practices by notifying affected CAs. Furthermore, we note that Let's Encrypt has never committed any BR violations, while issuing the most certificates. Their service therefore improves Internet security not only by democratizing encryption [3], but by doing so in exemplary accordance with best practices.

6   Comparing CT Log Data to Active Scans

In this section we evaluate the differences between certificates in CT logs and those obtained from active scans dating back until 2009. Additionally, we take a first look at the deployment of CT-specific HTTP headers and determine the value of CT logs to create IP address hitlists.

6.1   Certificate Deployment and Validity

In our active scans we collect 316.3 M certificates (32.8 M unique) from 128.3 M successful handshakes with IPv4 hosts and 4.2 M IPv6 hosts. When the same certificate is presented for a name under all its IP addresses, within and across IP versions, we call the domain *consistent*. The vast majority of domains (e.g., 99 % for IPv6) delivers consistent certificate chains. We investigate inconsistent domains and find that these are mostly due to TLS services offered by Content Distribution Networks (CDNs): 86.9 % of IPv6 inconsistencies can be attributed to CloudFlare, 5.4 % to Akamai. Inconsistent chains use the same certificate key and *Common Name* in about 80 % of the cases. *Subject Alternative Name* entries, however, are deviating to a large extent. We conclude that inconsistent certificate chains are mostly due to CDNs dynamically adding client domains to certificates. In the following we limit our analysis to the 128.1 M consistent domains in order to make quantitative statements more intuitively understandable.

We analyze the overlap of certificates in CT logs and certificates obtained from active scans and find that 109.8 M (85.7 %) certificates from active scans are logged in CT. This high percentage is an encouraging milestone towards the goal of logging all deployed certificates. Starting April 2018, the Chrome browser will only accept newly issued certificates which are logged [34].

In Table 2 we distinguish certificates by revocation, expiration, self-signed, browser-valid status, as well as conformance with the Baseline Requirements.

For CT log and active scan certificates, we find low numbers of certificates revoked through embedded CRLs or OneCRL [28].

More than 92 % of certificates found in active scans are not expired. In CT logs, however, more than two thirds of certificates are expired. This is to be expected, since CT logs explicitly keep expired certificates. This feature allows to easily evaluate trends in the certificate ecosystem over time.

The picture changes when evaluating self-signed certificates: CT logs only accept certificates valid under root stores and therefore do not contain self-signed server certificates. In active scans we find 14.6 % self-signed certificates, which is a decrease compared to previous studies [8,11]. This could be an indicator of Let's Encrypt's democratizing impact [3], where the lower end of the market moves from self-signed to free CA-signed certificates.

Next, we analyze whether certificates are accepted by web browsers. These are a subset of certificates which are neither revoked nor expired nor self-signed. Additional conditions (e.g., matching domain, correct chain to root cert) must be met as well. Since CT logs only accept root store-anchored certificates, all valid CT log certificates are accepted by browsers. However, only 63 % of not expired certificates from active scans are browser-valid. Therefore a non-negligible number of certificates found in the wild is resulting in security warnings to users.

Moreover, we compare BR violations of certificates found in CT logs and found using active scans. 95.2 % of logged certificates are valid according to the BRs, compared to 90.1 % of deployed certificates. This finding underlines the importance of logging all certificates in order to make violations more easily traceable and CAs more accountable.

Furthermore, we assess the impact of the impending distrust of Symantec root certificates [26]. We find 4.2 M domains where one of the Symantec root certificates is used. Limiting our analysis to specific certificate validity periods allows us to quantify the impact more precisely: 1.9 M domains will not be trusted anymore in May 2018, whereas 777.7 k domains will be affected by the complete removal of Symantec root certificates in October 2018. These findings show that many domains have not yet switched to other CAs and stress the importance of a smooth transition to the new Symantec CA owner DigiCert.

6.2   Legacy and Non-HTTPS Certificates in CT Logs

We use our data sets from previous work [20,21] to check how many certificates from scans dating back as far as November 2009 have been included in CT logs. Table 3 summarizes the results. A surprising number of older certificates are indeed contained in CT logs. More than 21 % of certificates used on HTTPS-secured domains on the Alexa Top 1M list from 2009 are in CT logs.

Table 3. Presence of certificates from previous work in CT logs. For the IPv4-wide scans, we group protocol-wise, combining scans via STARTTLS and direct TLS into one group. The table is to be read from left to right, i.e., 'Logged' means 'not already in HTTP scan and logged in CT'. Median expiry then refers to the latter group.

Scan	# Certs	Not in HTTP	Logged	Median expiry
Alexa, HTTPS, 2009	248.3 k	n/a	53.3 k (21.5 %)	2011-05-05
Alexa, HTTPS, 2011	222.1 k	n/a	126.9 k (57.1 %)	2012-02-29
IPv4, 2015	11.3 M	n/a	3.2 M (27.9 %)	2016-03-18
HTTPS	8.8 M	n/a	3.1 M (35.1 %)	2016-03-18
SMTPS	1.7 M	1.2 M (69.4 %)	57.8 k (3.5 %)	2016-04-25
IMAPS	1.3 M	893.3 k (71.2 %)	41.2 k (3.3 %)	2016-04-27
POP3S	1.1 M	814.5 k (72.3 %)	32.1 k (2.8 %)	2016-04-09
FTPS	753.2 k	597.0 k (79.3 %)	21.3 k (2.8 %)	2016-02-01
XMPPS	67.2 k	51.6 k (76.8 %)	1.3 k (2.0 %)	2016-05-14
IRCS	7.4 k	6.0 k (81.2 %)	181 (2.5 %)	2016-01-06

Their median expiry time is May 2011; this is well before CT was even deployed. It is known that Google scanned the Internet relatively regularly to bootstrap and fill CT logs. Of certificates retrieved in 2011, more than half are in CT logs, even though their median expiry time is the first half of 2012—CT was not even standardized then. This shows that CT logs were filled early with certificates that would already be of little use once actual CT deployment would start.

The scans conducted in 2015 [21] also considered email, messaging, and file transfer protocols. These scans provide us with insights about the logging of non-HTTPS certificates. We find a clear trend: certificates found solely in a non-HTTPS scan are generally not included in CT logs, only 3.5 % or less. Certificates that we found to be used for both HTTPS and non-HTTPS services are logged a bit more often: between 9.1 % (SMTPS) and 8.5 % (XMPPS and IRCS) fall into this category.

6.3   CT-Specific HTTP Headers

Similarly to enforcing HTTPS-only connections using the HTTP Strict Transport Security (HSTS) header (see RFC 6797), web servers can require the presence of certificates in CT logs. Requiring the presence in logs allows to detect man-in-the-middle attacks where the original server certificate is replaced by an attacker. We analyze the deployment of the unofficial RequireCT [32] and the draft RFC Expect-CT [36] headers.

We find eight domains sending HSTS headers with a RequireCT directive and 7.3 k domains with Expect-CT headers. In the following, we investigate the Expect-CT deployment. This header consists of a mandatory *max-age* field and optional *enforce* and *report-uri* fields. We find 12.1 % of domains to omit the mandatory *max-age* directive. The majority of domains sets the *max-age* to zero, effectively disabling the Expect-CT mechanism. Only 29.9 % of domains *enforce* Expect-CT, the majority makes only use of the reporting feature. With 608 domains, less than 10 % enforce Expect-CT with a duration of one day or more.

We check whether domains which send an Expect-CT header have in fact logged their certificate in CT. The majority of certificates can be found in CT logs. However, 83 Expect-CT domains (1.2 %) do not send certificates which are logged. 48 of these enforce Expect-CT with a *max-age* greater than zero. These domains do not comply with the Expect-CT specification. We find a lower misconfiguration percentage in Expect-CT compared to the more established yet complex public key pinning via HPKP headers [4].

6.4 CT Logs as a Source for IP Address Hitlists

CT logs contain not only valuable information about certificates, but are also an additional source of domain names. We analyze the value of domain names extracted from CN and SAN of logged certificates by comparing them to our publicly available hitlist [18]. TUM's hitlist provides IP addresses based on domains from zonefiles, Alexa Top 1M, Cisco Umbrella, CAIDA, and Rapid7.

The CT log data adds 82.2 M domains, 5.4 M IPv4, and 489 k IPv6 addresses to the hitlist. This corresponds to respective increases of 50.5 %, 56.2 %, and 69.6 %. Especially the large increase of IPv6 addresses can aid future measurement studies. We make the hitlist enhanced with CT domain data freely available [17].

7   Gossiping and Inclusion Proofs

CT offers gossiping protocols to detect equivocation attacks, where a log presents different views to different parties. Gossiping allows clients to exchange their log view with each other. Clients can also request inclusion proofs from the log, demonstrating that a specific certificate was indeed incorporated by the log. We conduct active and passive measurements to evaluate if these techniques are used.

As part of our active scans, we send HTTP requests to responding domains in order to evaluate the deployment of CT gossiping endpoints among HTTPS websites. These requests are targeted at specific URL paths used in CT gossiping [29]. Additionally, we send one request to a non-existent path that serves as the baseline of how web servers answer requests for non-existent paths.

In the course of these measurements, we receive answers from 109.2 M domains and inspect the HTTP return codes. We remove hosts that answer with 2xx or 3xx to the non-existent baseline path, send the same answer for CT paths as the baseline request, or answer with 4xx to the CT paths. After this filtering 16.8 k (0.015 %) domains remain. This is an upper bound of domains supporting HTTP-based CT gossiping, as web servers might be configured in a way which triggers different behavior for CT and the baseline path. To lower this upper bound, more complex measurements would need to be performed. These low numbers, however, suggest that HTTP-based gossiping is not widespread.

The gossip requests generated a magnitude more abuse notifications compared to other scans. This should be considered in the protocol specification, e.g., by using an HTTP header as a discovery mechanism less prone to undue excitement. Alternatively, browsers could gradually acclimate operators to this new reality.

In addition to active HTTPS scans, we conduct passive DNS measurements as described in Sect. 4. Since HTTPS URL paths are encrypted in TLS and therefore not visible, we instead evaluate the deployment of Google's proposal to fetch inclusion proofs over DNS [22]. Even though the CT over DNS proposal is implemented in Google's Chrome browser [7], we could not find any TXT record matching the document specification in our passive data. This was confirmed by Google, who said they never activated the protocol due to privacy concerns [25].

We conclude that protection against split-view attacks by logs which is an architectural necessity in CT has next to no deployment in the wild.

8 Conclusion

In this study we investigated the Baseline Requirements adherence of certificates found in CT logs and through active scans. We mapped these violations to issuing CAs and inform them of our findings. Furthermore, we compared the results from CT logs and active scans, finding that logged certificates exhibit less violations. We note that the log inclusion rate of non-HTTPS certificates is significantly lower. Additionally, we observed that CT gossiping, although required in the security model of CT, does currently not have any substantial deployment.

Acknowledgments. We thank Emily Stark from Google for the valuable insights into Chrome's current state of CT over DNS. The authors thank the contributors of data to Farsight Security's DNSDB. We thank the anonymous reviewers and our shepherd Steve Uhlig for their valuable feedback. This work was partially funded by the German Federal Ministry of Education and Research under project X-Check, grant 16KIS0530, and project DecADe, grant 16KIS0538.

References

1. Acer, M.E. et al.: Where the wild warnings are: root causes of Chrome HTTPS certificate errors. In: CCS 2017
2. ACM: Artifact Review and Badging (2016). https://www.acm.org/publications/policies/artifact-review-badging
3. Aertsen, M. et al.: No domain left behind: is Let's Encrypt democratizing encryption? In: ANRW 2017
4. Amann, J. et al.: Mission accomplished? HTTPS security after DigiNotar. In: IMC 2017

5. CA/Browser Forum: Baseline requirements for the issuance and management of publicly-trusted certificates. Version 1.5.0., 1 September 2017
6. Chen, Y. et al.: DNS noise: measuring the pervasiveness of disposable domains in modern DNS traffic. In: DSN 2014
7. Chromium authors: CT over DNS implementation in Chromium. https:// cs.chromium.org/chromium/src/components/certificate_transparency/log_dns_ client.cc?type=cs&sq=package:chromium
8. Chung, T. et al.: Measuring and applying invalid SSL certificates: the silent majority. In: IMC 2016
9. Clark, J., van Oorschot, P.: SoK: SSL and HTTPS: revisiting past challenges and evaluating certificate trust model enhancements. In: IEEE S&P 2013
10. Dittrich, D. et al.: The Menlo report: ethical principles guiding information and communication technology research. US DHS (2012)
11. Durumeric, Z. et al.: Analysis of the HTTPS certificate ecosystem. In: IMC 2013
12. Durumeric, Z. et al.: ZMap: fast Internet-wide scanning and its security applications. In: USENIX Security 2013
13. Ellison, C., Schneier, B.: Ten risks of PKI: what you're not being told about Public Key Infrastructure. Comput. Secur. J. **16**(1), 1–7 (2000)
14. Farsight Security: DNSDB. https://www.dnsdb.info/
15. Felt, A.P. et al.: Measuring HTTPS adoption on the web. In: USENIX Security 2017
16. Fox-IT: Black Tulip. Report of the investigation into the DigiNotar Certificate Authority breach, 8 (2012)
17. Gasser, O. et al.: IPv6 Hitlist collection. https://www.net.in.tum.de/projects/ gino/ipv6-hitlist.html
18. Gasser, O. et al.: Scanning the IPv6 Internet: towards a comprehensive Hitlist. In: TMA 2016
19. Gustafsson, J. et al.: A first look at the CT landscape: Certificate Transparency logs in practice. In: PAM 2017
20. Holz, R. et al.: The SSL landscape–a thorough analysis of the X.509 PKI using active and passive measurements. In: IMC 2011
21. Holz, R. et al.: TLS in the wild - an Internet-wide analysis of TLS-based protocols for electronic communication. In: NDSS 2016
22. Laurie, B. et al.: Certificate Transparency RFCs on GitHub (2017). https://github. com/google/certificate-transparency-rfcs
23. Liu, Y. et al.: An end-to-end measurement of certificate revocation in the web PKI. In: IMC 2015
24. Markham, G.: Mailing list: Mozilla dev.sec.policy: PROCERT decision
25. Messeri, E.: Mailing list: IETF trans: privacy analysis of the DNS-based protocol for obtaining inclusion proof
26. Mozilla: Mailing List: Mozilla dev.sec.policy: Mozilla's Plan for Symantec Roots
27. Mozilla: Revoking Trust in Two TurkTrust Certificates. https://blog.mozilla.org/ security/2013/01/03/revoking-trust-in-two-turktrust-certficates/
28. Mozilla OneCRL, October 2017
29. Nordberg, L. et al.: Gossiping in CT. Internet-Draft draft-ietf-trans-gossip-04
30. Partridge, C., Allman, M.: Ethical considerations in network measurement papers. Commun. ACM **15**(10), 58–64 (2016)
31. Ristić, I.: SSL/TLS and PKI History. https://www.feistyduck.com/ssl-tls-and-pki-history/
32. Ritter, T.: An experimental "RequireCT" directive for HSTS, February 2015. https://ritter.vg/blog-require_certificate_transparency.html

33. Scheitle, Q. et al.: Towards an ecosystem for reproducible research in computer networking. In: SIGCOMM Reproducibility 2017
34. Sleevi, R.: Certificate Transparency in Chrome - change to enforcement date Google groups, 21 April 2017. https://groups.google.com/a/chromium.org/forum/#!msg/ct-policy/sz_3W_xKBNY/6jq2ghJXBAAJ
35. Sleevi, R., Messeri, E.: Certificate Transparency in Chrome: monitoring CT logs consistency, 1 May 2015. https://docs.google.com/document/d/1FP5J5Sfsg0OR9P4YT0q1dM02iavhi8ix1mZlZe_z-ls
36. Stark, E.: Expect-CT extension for HTTP. https://tools.ietf.org/html/draft-ietf-httpbis-expect-ct-02
37. Symantec: Update on test certificate incident (2016). https://www.symantec.com/page.jsp?id=test-certs-update
38. TUM: cablint on GitHub. https://github.com/tumi8/certlint
39. TUM: CT go tool on GitHub. https://github.com/google/certificate-transparency-go
40. TUM: goscanner on GitHub. https://github.com/tumi8/goscanner
41. TUM: ZMapv6 on GitHub. https://github.com/tumi8/zmap
42. VanderSloot, B. et al.: Towards a complete view of the certificate ecosystem. In: IMC 2016

Server-Side Adoption of Certificate Transparency

Carl Nykvist, Linus Sjöström, Josef Gustafsson, and Niklas Carlsson[✉]

Linköping University, Linköping, Sweden
niklas.carlsson@liu.se

Abstract. Certificate Transparency (CT) was developed to mitigate shortcomings in the TLS/SSL landscape and to assess the trustworthiness of Certificate Authorities (CAs) and the certificates they create. With CT, certificates should be logged in public, audible, append-only CT logs and servers should provide clients (browsers) evidence, in the form of Signed Certificate Timestamps (SCTs), that the certificates that they present have been logged in credible CT logs. These SCTs can be delivered using three different methods: (i) X.509v3 extension, (ii) TLS extension, and (iii) OSCP stapling. In this paper, we develop a client-side measurement tool that implements all three methods and use the tool to analyze the SCT adoption among the one-million most popular web domains. Using two snapshots (from May and Oct. 2017), we answer a wide range of questions related to the delivery choices made by different domains, identify differences in the certificates used by these domains, the CT logs they use, and characterize the overheads and potential performance impact of the SCT delivery methods. By highlighting some of the tradeoffs between the methods and differences in the websites selecting them, we provide insights into the current SCT adoption status and differences in how domains have gone upon adopting this new technology.

1 Introduction

The majority of the internet traffic is delivered using HTTPS and encrypted using Transport Layer Security (TLS). While most of these connections use relatively strong security algorithms [20], one of the major weaknesses in securing the end-to-end communication is instead the amount of trust that is placed in the Certificate Authorities (CAs) that generate the X.509 certificates (connecting public keys to servers/domains) needed for us (and our browsers) to trust that the servers/domains that we communicate with are who they claim to be [8,15].

Browsers typically trust that the private key associated with the public key inside a certificate belongs to a given server/domain as long as (i) the certificate is signed by a CA (or an organization that a CA has delegated trust to, using chained certificates), and (ii) the CA's corresponding root certificate, or a root certificate that the certificate chains back to, is stored in the browser's root store. Unfortunately, not all CAs are equally trustworthy, CAs sometimes make

© Springer International Publishing AG, part of Springer Nature 2018
R. Beverly et al. (Eds.): PAM 2018, LNCS 10771, pp. 186–199, 2018.
https://doi.org/10.1007/978-3-319-76481-8_14

mistakes (e.g., due to human errors, intentional fraud, etc. [16]), and there is no current PKI mechanism informing domain owners of issued certificates.

The high reliance on CAs combined with some high-profile (but hard-to-detect) incidents have prompted various efforts to address the shortcomings of the TLS/SSL landscape [6,13,14,17,18,23]. One of the most successfully deployed such systems is Certification Transparency (CT) [12,18,19]. To address some of the flaws with the current TLS landscape, CT requires that certificates are published in public append-only logs and that servers provide clients (browsers) proof, in the form of Signed Certificate Timestamps (SCTs), that the certificates have been logged in credible CT logs.

CT is already used by Google's Chrome browser for certificate validation and Mozilla is drafting their own CT policies for Firefox. Existing public well-maintained logs have also proven valuable in identifying rogue certificates. Prior work have analyzed the content [12] and certificate coverage [22] of CT logs. Here, we instead, similar to parallel work by Amann et al. [2] (differences discussed in Sect. 7), study the server-side adoption. In particular, we characterize the SCT usage among the one million most popular domains according to alexa.com, which due to popularity skew are responsible for most of the web traffic [11].

SCTs can be delivered to a client in three different ways [18]: (i) using the X.509v3 extension, (ii) using the TLS extension, and (iii) using Online Certificate Status Protocol (OSCP) stapling. Each of these methods comes with their own advantages and disadvantages. In this paper, we first highlight some of these tradeoffs (Sect. 2) and then analyze the delivery choices made by different domains, including what domains select which delivery method and whether there are differences in the certificates associated with the different methods, the logs used to store the corresponding certificates, and other factors. We also use our measurements to look closer at overheads and the potential performance impact that SCT delivery may have when using the different methods.

For this work, we developed a measurement tool (Sect. 3) that extracts rich meta information about the handshake process, the SCTs, the SCT delivery, and the associated certificates. Using the tool, we collect and analyze two snapshots of the server-side SCT adoption as seen on May 30, 2017 and Oct. 6, 2017. These datasets allow us to capture the current status and comment on the impact that potential trends may have on the results. For our analysis, we first characterize the SCT usage (Sect. 4) as seen across popularities and how the number of SCTs and the log selection differ between domains that use different SCT methods. We then present a certificate-based analysis (Sect. 5) that looks closer at biases between the SCT delivery methods used and the type of certificates, signatures, and public keys, for example, providing us with some initial insight into the characteristics of the domains that use each delivery method. Finally, we present a performance and overhead analysis (Sect. 6) in which we analyze the handshake times, time until the clients obtain the SCTs, and quantify the potential delay and byte overheads associated with delivering the SCTs.

Our observations has implications on organizations running web services and our basic quantifications highlight SCTs minimal overheads. While most domains using SCTs opt to use the simplest delivery method (X.509v3 extension), which does not require any server-side changes, the fastest delivery method (TLS extension), which delivers the SCTs earlier within the handshake and only to clients requesting SCTs, is most frequently used by organizations (e.g., Google) that we (based on our measurement observations) conjecture are more performance oriented. It is also very encouraging that certificates that are accompanied with SCTs are much less likely to use weak signatures or public keys. Overall, the CT adoption, and use of the TLS extension in particular, is highest among the top domains, hopefully pushing others to follow.

2   Background

Browsers are increasingly requiring certificates to be included in CT logs. For example, since 2015, Google's Chrome browser has required that all Extended Validation (EV) certificates are accompanied by multiple SCTs before displaying visual cues to the user that normally come with these certificates. Today, they also require all certificates created by some (less trusted) CAs that have been caught misbehaving (e.g., Symantec) to be logged, and during the 39th CA/Browser Forum (Nov. 2016), the Chrome team announced plans that all certificates issued in Oct. 2017 or later will be expected to comply with Chrome's CT policy. Recently, Mozilla has also announced that CT is coming to Firefox.[1]

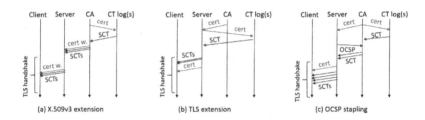

Fig. 1. High-level overview of the three SCT delivery methods.

There are three methods for a server/domain to obtain and deliver SCTs to the clients. These methods use (i) the X.509v3 extension, (ii) the TLS extension, and (iii) OCSP stapling. The methods differ *both* by how the server obtains the SCTs and how the SCTs are delivered to the client. Figure 1 summarizes the main differences. From a service provider's perspective, the X.509v3 extension is by far the simplest method and does not require any server changes. Instead, the CA submits the certificate to the logs, obtains the corresponding SCTs, and bundles them together with the certificate (as part of the X.509v3 extension), allowing the server to deliver the STCs as a bundle together with the certificate (during a regular handshake). In contrast, with the TLS extension, the server submits

---

[1] https://www.thesslstore.com/blog/firefox-certificate-transparency/.

the certificate (obtained from the CA) directly to the desired logs, obtains the corresponding SCTs, and then delivers the STCs to the client using the TLS extension option. While this method requires some changes to the server, we note that the TLS extension option comes earlier in the handshake and therefore typically allows faster delivery of SCTs. (This observation is analyzed further in Sect. 6.) Also OCSP stapling requires additional modifications on the server side; in this case to obtain an OCSP stapled SCT bundle that the CA creates after obtaining the SCTs. Compared with the other two methods, OCSP stapling results in later SCT delivery, since it takes place at the end of the handshake.

3   Methodology

Using a collection of Java APIs available via Bouncy Castle[2], we implemented a special purpose program that we use as a tool for data collection and management of measurement campaigns.[3] Given a list of domains (in our case the top one million websites according to alexa.com), our program tries to establish a TLS/SSL connection with servers representing each domain. Using the SSLSocket in the Bouncy Castle library, during the TLS handshake, the program extracts and records detailed statistics about byte overheads, the SCT bundles, the certificates, the algorithms used during the handshake, timing information (e.g., time of handshakes, and time to obtain SCT bundles), and general information regarding the handshake process (e.g., why some connections fail).

The program implements all three SCT delivery methods and records information up-to the time of the first HTTP request, when connections are fully established and all potential SCTs have been obtained. After download of SCTs, the program decodes the SCTs and collects information about the logs used and the SCTs themselves. Public lists of known object identifiers (OIDs) and issuer information are used to determine the validation method of certificates.

To allow efficient processing even when a significant number of domains timeout and reduce time-of-day effects, the program runs 600 parallel client threads. At each point in time a thread is responsible for collecting statistics for one domain. To avoid startup and end artifacts (e.g., unfair CPU availability for the first opened threads), at the start and end of an experimental run, a set of additional HTTPS "dummy" websites are processed but not included in the results. We have run experiments with other number of parallel client threads, but have found that 600 provides a nice tradeoff between the speed of the measurement campaign and representative (and stable) performance values when a client visits these domains. A measurement campaign takes on average four hours.

Limitations: Perhaps the largest limitations of our setup is that we only run experiments from a single machine, and that we thus needed to run parallel threads to obtain timely results. Naturally, the network connectivity and location of the measurement device impacts the absolute handshake and SCT delivery

---

[2] Bouncy Castle, https://www.bouncycastle.org.

[3] Code+datasets available: http://www.ida.liu.se/~nikca89/papers/pam18.html.

times reported. However, we believe that the relative timing values still provide nice insights into differences observed between SCT delivery methods and that byte overheads will likely be much less impacted by location. We therefore focus on relative differences observed between the SCT delivery methods, not absolute delivery times. Focusing on these aspects also minimizes the impact that the use of parallel threads may have on conclusions and insights.

4   Dataset and SCT Usage

Due to the current changes in the CT landscape, we present results based on two datasets collected roughly four months apart: May 30, 2017, and Oct. 6, 2017. Throughout this paper we use $x_1 \to x_2$ to indicate the values x_1 and x_2, for the same metric x, observed on these dates, respectively. The relative change provides an estimate of current change in the metric x.

Overview: For these two datasets, out of the top one million domains (according to alexa.com), 8.70→8.68% did not respond, 10.88→8.72% did not provide a certificate (and was deemed not to use HTTPS), and 23.52→26.20% resulted in the tool flagging a TLS error (typically indicating that the certificate is not valid). This left us with 557,485→563,866 sites that delivered valid X.509 certificates. While this suggests a small relative increase in the number of domains that uses HTTPS over this period, we were encouraged to see that the subset of domains that deliver SCTs with their certificates have increased more; from 130,768 (23.46%) to 148,468 (26.33%).

Figure 2 provides a breakdown of the delivery methods used by the servers to deliver these SCT bundles and how the use of the methods have changed. We note that the majority (103,482→120,002) of the SCT bundles are delivered using the X.509v3 extension. This is perhaps not surprising since this method does not require any changes to the servers. However, we also observe many SCT bundles (27,279→28,451) that are delivered using the TLS extension and a few (16→25) that are delivered using OCSP stapling. Again, both these later methods require server-side modifications. This may also explain why the X.509v3 extension is responsible for most of the increase in SCT usage.

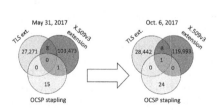

Fig. 2. Overview of dataset.

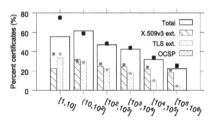

Fig. 3. Usage across domain popularities.

Popularity-based usage breakdown: Figure 3 shows the SCT usage for domains with different popularity rank. Here, and throughout all other bar graphs in the paper (except Fig. 5), we use bars to show the May 2017 values and large dots (with same colors) to indicate the corresponding Oct. 2017 values. The SCT usage is highest among the most popular domains (e.g., above 60% in among the top-100 domains and 49% among the top-1000 domains across both datasets). The top domains are also relatively equally likely to use the TLS extension and the X.509v3 extension for the delivery of the SCTs, whereas the (simpler) X.509v3 extension by far is the most popular choice among the less popular domains (e.g., X.509v3 is used to deliver 69.0→70.5% of the SCT bundles in the range $(10^4, 10^5]$ and 81.1→82.7% of the bundles in the range $(10^5, 10^6]$). The reason that OCSP stapling is not visible in the figure is that all 16→25 cases are for less popular domains, in the $(10^4, 10^6]$ range.

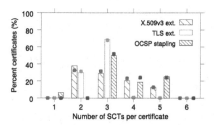

Fig. 4. Number of SCTs per certificate for each type of SCT distribution mechanism.

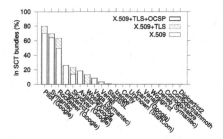

Fig. 5. Percentage of the SCT bundles that the observed CT logs covers. (Color figure online)

Bundle sizes: Certificates are expected to be accompanied by multiple SCTs. For example, with Chrome's EV policy a certificate should be logged in at least one Google operated log and one other (typically CA operated) log. The mean and median number of SCTs per bundle are relatively similar across the methods and we have not seen any major changes in the numbers. For example, in May the averages were 3.08 (X.509v3), 2.71 (TLS), and 3.56 (OCSP), respectively, and in Oct. the averages were 3.16, 2.70, and 3.72. Similarly, the median has remained equal to 3 for all three classes. However, there are substantial distribution differences between the methods. This is illustrated in Fig. 4. With the TLS extension, almost all bundles include two (30.1→31.2%) or three (69.0→68.0%) SCTs. In contrast, the size of the bundles delivered using the X.509v3 extension are much more diverse. Although, the most common cases again is that two (38.0→32.6%) or three (29.0→31.7%) SCTs are included, with the X.509v3 extension, there is also a substantial number of bundles with four (20.3→23.2%) and five (12.7→12.6%) SCTs per bundle. Also with OCSP stapling we see relatively more SCTs per bundle. For example, 44→48% of these bundles have four or five SCTs. The smaller and more homogeneous bundle sizes observed with the

TLS extensions are likely due to these sites being more performance conscious. We discuss this further in Sect. 6, when looking at the overheads and delivery times of the SCT bundles.

Logs used: Figure 5 shows the percentage of times each log is observed in an SCT bundle observed in the Oct. 2017 dataset. In general, the log usage is heavily skewed towards a small subset of logs, dominated by Google logs and logs operated by three major CAs (Digicert, Symantec, and Wosign). The main differences between the two datasets (May 2017 omitted this time) are that the Oct. 2017 dataset contains four extra logs (16 vs. 20) and that Aviator (operated by Google) has seen a drop in rank (from 4 to 6) and number (percent) of SCT bundles; from 39,889 (30.5%) to 27,336 (18.4%). This drop is explained by Aviator being frozen on Nov 29, 2016.[4]

Referring to the Chrome policy, we only found 21 SCT bundles in the Oct. dataset that did not have at least one SCT from a Google operated log. All these contained a single SCT; 4 were logged in Deneb (by Symantec) and 17 came from an "unknown" log for which we could not find a public log with the listed logID.[5] However, since all certificates with SCTs from this log (the same set of 17 single-log bundles) were issued by StartCom, we conjecture that it is operated by StartCom. Another interesting observation is that the main Digicert log (rank 4) and Aviator (old Google log with rank 6) almost entirely contains certificates for which the SCTs are delivered with the X.509v3 extension (12 of 38,964 and 6 of 27,336 non-X.509v3 extension SCTs, respectively) and that the Wosign log (rank 7) contains almost only certificates for which the SCTs are delivered using the TLS extension (only 198 of the 19,691 domains logging their certificates in this log do not use the TLS extension). This suggests that some CAs may have strong biases in how they help their customers deliver SCTs.

5   Certificate-Based Analysis

Certificate type: We have found very large differences in how different types of certificates are delivered. This is highlighted in Fig. 6, which breaks down the SCT delivery methods used for each type of certificate. We note that the SCT usage is by far the highest among domains that use EV certificates and the lowest among domains that use DV certificates. For example, 98.6→99.0% of the domains that use EV certificates use SCTs, but only 15.3→15.1% of the DV domains uses SCTs. The large SCT adoption for domains using EV certificates is expected since SCT compliance has long been required for Chrome (and soon other browsers). Perhaps more surprising is that we still observed 289→203 domains in the top-million websites that did not yet appear to deliver SCTs with their EV certificates. Despite being a decreasing fraction (1.4→1.0%), this is still a non-negligible number of domains. For OV certificates the absolute number of SCT domains is larger and increasing, although unfortunately the ratio of OV domains that use SCTs is decreasing (47.0→44.0%).

---

[4] Chrome bug report: https://crbug.com/389514.

[5] https://www.certificate-transparency.org/known-logs.

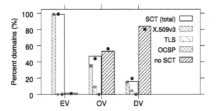

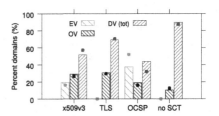

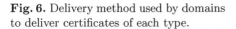

Fig. 6. Delivery method used by domains to deliver certificates of each type.

Fig. 7. Certificate types used by the domains using each delivery methods.

The X.509v3 extension is by far the dominating (98.5→98.9%) delivery method for EV domains. This may be an effect of many domains having had to scramble to deliver SCTs for their EV certificates and therefore opted to use the simplest-to-deploy method, not requiring any changes to their servers. However, it may also be due to rumors that Chrome would stop supporting the TLS extension and OCSP stapling (rumors that Google have strongly dismissed![6]), domains using the least resistance path (not requiring any server changes), and biases in the methods promoted by some CAs (e.g., Fig. 5). For domains using OV certificates, 36.8→34.8% of the domains use X.509v3 and 10.2→9.1% use the TLS extension. Figure 7 breaks down the same data on a per-delivery method basis. Again, differences between the methods are visible. For example, the domains using the X.509v3 extension typically deliver a much larger fraction of EV certificates than those that use the TLS extension.

Top issuers: Table 1 summarizes the top issuers in each category. Except Let's Encrypt, which targets the low-budget market, most top CAs appear to have increased their SCT usage. RapidSSL has seen the largest increase in SCTs delivered with the X.509v3 extension (25,130→34,006), simultaneously as dropping of the top-five list for non-SCT certificates (25,087→8,766). The other main exception is DigiCert, who now delivers less certificates with the X.509v3 extension (10,576→9,403) and slightly more non-SCT certificates (21,053→21,378).

For certificates delivered with the TLS extension, we found that 7,888→7,858 of the 8,314→8,374 OV domains used certificates from Google (typically clear Google owned domains such as google.com, google.se, or some-name.blogspot.com, for example) and Comodo was responsible for 18,335→19,458 of the 18,960→20,074 DV domains (and 57→67 OV domains). In the complete dataset, we only observed 149→193 other domains using Google issued certificates. Also these where OV certificates, but no corresponding SCTs where delivered during the handshake. These domains typically were associated with companies that have Google as parent company (e.g., nest.com). Clearly, Google has decided to use the TLS extension to deliver SCTs for their domains. One reason for this is perhaps that SCTs delivered using the TLS extension are delivered earlier in the handshake than when using the X.509v3 extension;

---

[6] CT FAQ: https://www.certificate-transparency.org/faq.

Table 1. Top-five issuers for domains using each SCT delivery method (Oct. 2017) and the number of domains using their certificates with that delivery method (in brackets).

Rank	X.509v3 ext.	TLS ext.	OCSP stapling	No SCT used
1	RapidSSL (25,130→34,006)	Comodo (18,392→19,525)	SwissSign (11→20)	Comodo (95,940→95,956)
2	GeoTrust (16,434→17,464)	Google (7,888→7,858)	DigiCert (5→5)	Let's Encrypt (52,891→65,635)
3	Thawte (12,349→13,545)	Go Daddy (358→366)	-	Go Daddy (33,000→32,474)
4	Symantec (12,649→13,260)	DigiCert (158→219)	-	cPanel (31,629→32,118)
5	AlphaSSL (8,676→10,880)	CloudFlare (121→122)	-	DigiCert (21,053→21,378)

therefore, allowing more time to process the SCTs. In Sect. 6 we look closer at this and other performance aspect.

In contrast to Google, Comodo also had issued many certificates for domains that used the X.509v3 extension (5,374→5,355) and domains that did not use SCTs (102,092→96,629), including 21→20 EV certificates without SCTs. Overall, Google and Comodo appears to be early adopters of the TLS extension. For domains using OCSP stapling, eleven used SwissSign and five used DigiCert. The set of top issuers using the X.509v3 extension was much more diverse.

Signatures: Figure 8 shows the fraction of domains that use different signature algorithms together with each type of SCT delivery method. We note that 99.9→99.8% of the certificates associated with X509.v3 SCTs are signed with RSA. This is very similar to what we observe for the certificates delivered using OCSP stapling and those that we did not associate with any SCTs. In sharp contrast, 65.0% of the certificates associated with SCTs delivered using the TLS extension are signed with ECDSA (all using SHA256).

We have also found that domains using SCTs are less likely to use weak signature algorithms than the non-SCT domains. For example, among the SCT domains, we only found 318 (0.24%)→1,017 (0.68%) domains that used SHA1 (with RSA). The corresponding numbers for non-SCT domains are 49,607 (11.6%)→44,398 (10.7%). There were even 2,048 (0.48%)→1,813 (0.44%) non-SCT domains that used MD5. The significant use of SHA1 and MD5 are concerning since they long have been known to be susceptible to attacks. While the SCT domains clearly use weak signatures algorithms much more seldom, we were surprised by the relative raise in use SHA1 among these domains. A closer look revealed that except one GeoTrust certificate, all the other 1,016 SHA1 certificates were DV certificates issued by Comodo (DV legacy server).

Public keys: Also when looking at the public keys included in the certificates, the certificates with SCTs delivered using the TLS extensions sticks out. In particular, among these 27,279→28,451 certificates, a total of 17,724 (65.0%)→18,071 (63.5%) are using Elliptic Curve (EC) keys. In contrast, among the 103,482→120.002 domains associated with SCT bundles delivered with the X.509v3 extension only 164 (0.16%)→230 (0.19%) and none of the 16→25 OCSP stapled certificates use EC. For SCT related certificates, all remaining public keys use RSA. When interpreting these results, it should be noted that RSA

(99.5→99.6%) also is dominating among the public keys seen among non-SCT domains. Again, a significant reason for the above differences are due to Comodo, who is responsible for 17,940 of the 18,071 domains using EC with the TLS extension. The other EC users in the TLS category (although using EC less frequently) are CloudFare (122), Let's Encrypt (5), DigiCert (2), and AlphaSSL (2). While omitted, we have also found that public keys not associated with SCTs are more likely to use shorter RSA key lengths.

6 Performance and Overhead Analysis

Handshake and SCT delivery times: We have not observed any significant differences in the handshake times when using our SCT enabled client with the SCT capability turned on or off, regardless if it communicates with domains that use SCTs or not. Instead, the handshake time distributions for these client variations are almost identical, regardless of the subset of domains considered. In the following, we therefore only show results for a client using all three methods.

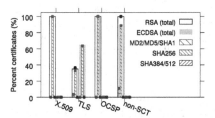

Fig. 8. Signatures used for certificates.

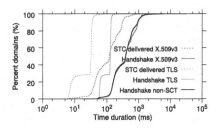

Fig. 9. Handshake and SCT delivery times of domains using different methods.

When comparing the delivery methods, on the other hand, there are significant differences in the handshake times, and (perhaps most importantly) in the times until the SCTs are delivered to the clients. Figure 9 highlights these differences. Here, we have plotted the total handshake times (solid lines) and the SCT delivery times (dotted lines) for the different delivery methods.

First, note that the handshake time distribution for domains using the X.509v3 extension is almost identical to that of non-SCT domains. In contrast, the handshake times with domains using the TLS extension are much shorter. This suggests that the domains using the TLS extension may leverage service replication (e.g., using third-party CDNs or their own distributed data centers) to a larger extent. This observation also matches our prior observation (e.g., Fig. 3) that these domains are more likely to be popular domains that perhaps are more likely to be both performance aware and early adopters. As interesting and supportive evidence for the conjecture that these domains are more performance aware, we note that the bump with low-delay handshakes is almost entirely due to Google domains. This is highlighted in Fig. 10. Here, we also separate Comodo and the "other" domains using the TLS extension; both of which have roughly the same handshake time distribution. Similar short-tailed, low-delay distributions as we observe for Google here, have also been observed when analyzing the RTTs (from many different locations) to Google infrastructure in the past [3]. It is also interesting that the other domains using the TLS extensions provide lower handshake times than both the non-SCT domains and X.509v3 domains and that those domains are responsible for the majority of the distribution. In addition, performance aware websites may select the TLS method since this method allows the SCTs to be delivered only to clients requesting SCTs.

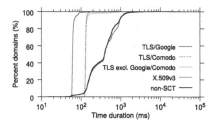 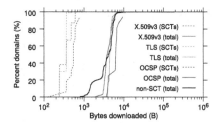

Fig. 10. Handshake times when breaking down domains using the TLS extension.

Fig. 11. Bytes delivered as part of the SCT bundles and total bytes received.

Figure 9 highlights that the SCTs often are delivered much sooner (within the handshake) when using TLS than when using the X.509v3 extension. The reason for this was highlighted in Sect. 2 and is due to the TLS extension happening earlier in the handshake. Clearly, this would give a client (browser) more time to decode the SCTs and process the information associated with them. As a reference point, the simple/naive decoder that we used was able to decode 99% of the individual SCT bundles within 0.161 ms (during the data collection). Since this delay is small compared to the handshake itself, we can approximate also the distribution of the time until the clients have the decoded SCTs with the dotted lines, again highlighting that the TLS extension would be preferred from a performance standpoint.

Finally, Fig. 11 summarizes the byte overheads associated with the SCTs. Here, we plot both the size of the SCT bundles and the total bytes received during the handshake. Overall, the byte overheads of the SCTs are very small (x-axis on log scale) and there are only small differences between the delivery methods (due to differences in the number of SCTs per bundle; see Fig. 4).

7   Related Work

Being relatively new, there is limited research characterizing the CT landscape. In parallel work to ours, Amann et al. [2] use active and passive measurements to evaluate the adoption of various improvements and additions proposed to strengthen the X.509 PKI, including CT, but do not consider overheads and client performance. Compared to that work, we use only active measurements, but place particular focus on the comparison of the relative differences in the server-side use and client-side performance of the three alternative SCT delivery methods. Gustafsson et al. [12] have characterized the usage of public CT logs and the certificates observed in these, but do not consider the use of different SCT methods. VanderSloot have evaluated the certification coverage of the CT logs [22]. Others have proposed optimizations or enhancements to CT [7,21].

There are also a lot of measurement-based research that have characterized the TLS/SSL landscape [1,4,10,15,16]. This includes many works that have tried to capture the trust landscape [16,20], identified weaknesses in the TLS/SSL connection establishment [5,9], or identified SSL error codes and their reasons [1]. These works typically excluding CT from the analysis, although a few have commented that CT may significantly change the landscape. We should also note that there have been various other attempts to address the limitations in the current TLS/SSL landscape [6,13,14,17,18,23], but thus far most other have seen limited adoption [2].

8   Conclusions

Our analysis of two snapshots (May and Oct. 2017) of the SCT usage among the one million most popular web domains provides insights into the current status of the SCT adoption and highlights key tradeoffs between the three different SCT delivery methods and the choices made by different domains. Whereas the majority of domains have opted for the simplest solution (using the X.509v3 extension) that does not require any server side changes, it is interesting to see that the method that provides the fastest delivery of SCTs (the TLS extension) is used by organizations (e.g., Google) that appear to provide much faster connection establishment, handshake times, and smaller SCT bundle sizes. We have also seen that SCT delivery has low overhead and that SCT usage is highest among the very top domains, hopefully pushing others to follow. By comparing the two snapshots we also observe some positive and encouraging trends in the adoption, including an overall increase in use of SCTs, how the use of SCTs goes hand-in-hand with a reduced use of weak signatures and public keys, and that big players such as Google is pushing the adoption. On the slightly negative side, it appears that some CAs may have a bias towards the (simpler) X.509v3 extension, although (performance-wise) many of their customers may benefit from implementing the TLS extension method (e.g., as used by Google).

Acknowledgements. The authors are thankful to our shepherd Niky Riga and the anonymous reviewers for their feedback. This work was funded in part by the Swedish Research Council (VR).

References

1. Akhawe, D., Amann, B., Vallentin, M., Sommer, R.: Here's my cert, so trust me, maybe? understanding TLS errors on the web. In: Proceedings of the WWW (2013)
2. Amann, J., Gasser, O., Scheitle, Q., Brent, L., Carle, G., Holz, R.: Mission accomplished? HTTPS security after diginotar. In: Proceedings of the IMC (2017)
3. Arlitt, M., Carlsson, N., Williamson, C., Rolia, J.: Passive crowd-based monitoring of world wide Web infrastructure and its performance. In: Proceedings of the ICC (2012)
4. Asghari, H., van Eeten, M.J.G., Arnbak, A.M., van Eijk, N.A.N.M.: Security economics in the HTTPS value chain. In: Proceedings of the WEIS (2013)
5. Beurdouche, B., et al.: A messy state of the union: taming the composite state machines of TLS. In: Proceedings of the IEEE S&P (2015)
6. Basin, D., Cremers, C., Kim, T.H.-J., Perrig, A., Sasse, R., Szalachowski, P.: Arpki: attack resilient public-key infrastructure. In: Proceedings of the ACM CCS (2014)
7. Chuat, L., Szalachowski, P., Perrig, A., Laurie, B., Messeri, E.: Efficient gossip protocols for verifying the consistency of certificate logs. In: Proceedings of the IEEE CNS (2015)
8. Clark, J., van Oorschot, P.C.: SoK: SSL and HTTPS: revisiting past challenges and evaluating certificate trust model enhancements. In: Proceedings of the IEEE S&P (2013)
9. Adrian, D., et al.: Imperfect forward secrecy: how Diffie-Hellman fails in practice. In: Proceedings of the ACM CCS (2015)
10. Fadai, T., Schrittwieser, S., Kieseberg, P., Mulazzani, M.: Trust me, I'm a root CA! analyzing SSL root CAs in modern browsers and operating systems. In: Proceedings of the ARES (2015)
11. Gill, P., Arlitt, M., Carlsson, N., Mahanti, A., Williamson, C.: Characterizing organizational use of Web-based services: methodology, challenges, observations, and insights. ACM Trans. Web **5**, 1–9 (2011)
12. Gustafsson, J., Overier, G., Arlitt, M., Carlsson, N.: A first look at the ct landscape: certificate transparency logs in practice. In: Proceedings of the PAM (2017)
13. Hallam-Baker, P., Stradling, R.: RFC6844: DNS Certification Authority Authorization (CAA) Resource Record. IETF (2013)
14. Hoffman, P., Schlyter, J.: RFC6698: The DNS-Based Authentication of Named Entities (DANE) Transport Layer Security (TLS) Protocol: TLSA. IETF (2012)
15. Holz, R., Braun, L., Kammenhuber, N., Carle, G.: The SSL landscape: a thorough analysis of the X.509 PKI using active and passive measurements. In: Proceedings of the IMC (2011)
16. Huang, L., Rice, A., Ellingsen, E., Jackson, C.: Analyzing forged SSL certificates in the wild. In: Proceedings of the IEEE S&P (2014)
17. Kim, T.H.-J., et al.: Accountable key infrastructure (AKI): a proposal for a public-key validation infrastructure. In: Proceedings of the WWW (2013)
18. Laurie, B., Langley, A., Käsper, E.: RFC6962: Certificate Transparency. IETF (2013)
19. Laurie, B., Langley, A., Käsper, E., Messeri, E., Stradling, R.: RFC6962-bis: Certificate Transparency draft-ietf-trans-rfc6962-bis-10. IETF (2015)
20. Ouvrier, G., Laterman, M., Arlitt, M., Carlsson, N.: Characterizing the HTTPS trust landscape: a passive view from the edge. IEEE Com. Mag. July 2017
21. Ryan, M.D.: Enhanced certificate transparency and end-to-end encrypted mail. In: Proceedings of the NDSS (2014)

22. VanderSloot, B., Amann, J., Bernhard, M., Durumeric, Z., Bailey, M., Halderman, J.: Towards a complete view of the certificate ecosystem. In: Proceedings of the IMC (2016)
23. Wendlandt, D., Andersen, D.G., Perrig, A.: Perspectives: improving SSH-style host authentication with multi-path probing. In: Proceedings of the USENIX ATC (2008)

Interdomain Routing

Leveraging Inter-domain Stability
for BGP Dynamics Analysis

Thomas Green[1,2](✉) (ID), Anthony Lambert[1](✉) (ID), Cristel Pelsser[3](✉) (ID),
and Dario Rossi[2](✉) (ID)

[1] Orange Labs, Paris, France
{thomas.green,anthony.lambert}@orange.com
[2] Telecom ParisTech, Paris, France
dario.rossi@telecom-paristech.fr
[3] University of Strasbourg, CNRS, Strasbourg, France
pelsser@unistra.fr

Abstract. In the Internet, Autonomous Systems continuously exchange routing information via the BGP protocol: the large number of networks involved and the verbosity of BGP result in a huge stream of updates. Making sense of all those messages remains a challenge today. In this paper, we leverage the notion of "primary path" (i.e., the most used inter-domain path of a BGP router toward a destination prefix for a given time period), reinterpreting updates by grouping them in terms of primary paths unavailability periods, and illustrate how BGP dynamics analysis would benefit from working with primary paths.

Our contributions are as follows. First, through measurements, we validate the existence of primary paths: by analyzing BGP updates announced at the LINX RIS route collector spanning a three months period, we show that primary paths are consistently in use during the observation period. Second, we quantify the benefits of primary paths for BGP dynamics analysis on two use cases: Internet tomography and anomaly detection. For the latter, using three months of anomalous BGP events documented by BGPmon as reference, we show that primary paths could be used for detecting such events (hijacks and outages), testifying of the increased semantic they provide.

1 Introduction

The Internet, from an inter-domain perspective, is a collection of routers scattered in about 60,000 Autonomous Systems (ASes) [3]. To ensure the full connectivity over the Internet, routers use the Border Gateway Protocol (BGP) [29] to announce reachability information concerning IP prefixes. More precisely, upon reception of routing updates from a neighbor, a BGP router first applies import policies, which might filter or modify the route. In case this information triggers some change of its routing table, the router may announce an update to its neighbors. Thus, each router announces *at most one best path* (except with BGP multi-path extension [35]) for each destination to its neighbors and sends an update whenever this best path changes. Best path selection is non-trivial due to complex and opaque BGP policies on the one hand, and to the fact that updates propagate hop-by-hop across the network on the other hand: particularly, this results in a limited visibility of the whole topology for any router, and can also lead to slow convergence because of the *path exploration* phenomenon [23].

Path exploration can happen whenever a BGP router has several neighbors announcing a path to a given prefix. Depending on the arrival order of announcements, a router might explore transient paths before converging to its best path. Note that path exploration may cascade: a router exploring paths may trigger the exploration of paths by its neighbors. In short, while BGP routers seek best paths, opacity and verbosity of BGP along with limited visibility make it hard to analyze BGP dynamics. It is still challenging to determine the causes of BGP updates [6,14,16,17] – which is crucial to detect and mitigate prefix hijacking, as well as for detecting misconfigurations and leakages, or troubleshooting network operations.

The new proposal of this paper is to systematically leverage inter-domain stability to preprocess BGP updates, with the goal of augmenting the data source (Sect. 2). More precisely, we first discuss and validate the notion of primary path, i.e., the most used inter-domain path for a router to a prefix in a given time period. Using primary paths as reference, updates can therefore be interpreted in terms of deviations from a nominal behavior, and grouped accordingly for further analysis (Sect. 3). By leveraging three months worth of BGP updates and publicly available data from a well-known alert service, we demonstrate interest of primary paths on two use cases: inter-domain tomography and anomaly detection (Sect. 4).

2   Related Work

BGP dynamics has been widely studied in the past, both for tomography and anomaly detection purposes. A thorough overview is out of the scope of this paper, but we briefly contextualize where our contributions take place.

Past works on tomography have mainly leveraged temporal and topological properties of updates to characterize BGP dynamics. Labovitz et al. [10,19] analyzed various temporal properties of updates from inter-arrival time to convergence time. Li et al. [20] extended these works and analyzed the evolution of these properties over a decade. Elmokashfi et al. [13] studied updates churn, pointing out recurrent events on BGP dynamics. Instead, in this article we propose to leverage inter-domain stability to characterize BGP dynamics.

Past significant works on anomaly detection have been broadly reviewed in [2]. Techniques used to analyze updates include time series analysis [22,27], statistical pattern recognition [12,32], machine learning [1,33], and historical data [15,18]. Other techniques exist, such as visualization approaches [8,9,21,25]. Historical data techniques consist in keeping track of all previously used paths to analyze new announcements. Instead, our proposal is to identify and only use stable paths to interpret updates.

It must also be noted that path stability in the Internet has already been pointed out. In 1996, Paxson [26] sampled routes in use between 37 hosts through periodic *traceroutes* and showed that they were mostly stable. Moreover, by analyzing their prevalence (probability to observe a particular route) and persistence (probability for a route to be used for a long period of time), they exhibited the existence of dominant routes. Rexford et al. [30] defined events as group of updates arriving close in time and pointed out that inter-domain paths related to popular destinations were undergoing few events. Chang et al. [7] grouped updates into bursts based on temporal thresholds and showed that many path advertisements were resulting from transient path changes. Some works also leveraged the notion of path stability for specific purposes. Butler et al. [5] showed that ASes have few distinct paths for a prefix over time and proposed to use this observation to reduce the cost of cryptographic BGP path authentication. Qiu et al. [28], assuming inter-domain stability, proposed to leverage it through machine learning to detect bogus routes. In this paper, we extend these works by showing that stability holds across the whole inter-domain and that it can be systematically leveraged for different use cases of BGP dynamics analysis.

3 Inter-domain Stability

3.1 Primary Paths

Our approach builds on the assumption that the BGP inter-domain structure is highly stable over relatively long periods of time [5, 26, 30]. We show that this is a reasonable assumption in Sect. 4.1. Intuitively, we expect this stability to follow from the timescale of changes among AS agreements that are negotiated few times a year. Consider indeed that BGP best path selection starts by assessing the *local preference* attribute, which encodes business agreements between ASes: it follows that every router r should have a set of preferred paths (with the same highest local preference) toward any prefix p over relatively long periods of time, and deviate from those only during relatively short transient periods (e.g., due to path exploration).

In this article, we additionally argue that, among those preferred paths, there is one dominant path that is consistently chosen as best path during an observation window W: we refer to this path as the **primary path** of r to p. In a more formal way, considering for the time being an offline case for the sake of simplicity, let us define as $T_x(r, p)$ the sum of the cumulative time during W that router r uses path x to reach prefix p. Then the primary path is selected as the one satisfying $argmax_x T_x(r, p)$.

Following from the given definition above, we compute primary paths in an offline fashion from updates collected at the LINX RIPE RIS route collector [31] on a three month time window (from January 1st to March 31st 2017). The dataset consists of $487,104,558$ IPv4 updates ($157,249,182$ IPv6 updates) and $5,482,564$ IPv4 $<router, prefix>$ pairs ($412,350$ IPv6 pairs). It includes 38 IPv4 vantage points (14 IPv6 vantage points) among which 7 announce a "full"

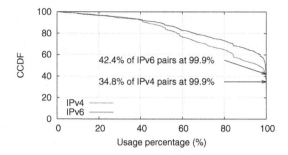

Fig. 1. Complementary CDF of the percentage of time a primary path for prefix p was used by router r over the whole observation period (January 1st to March 31st 2017).

routing table in IPv4 (10 for IPv6). To bootstrap the primary path repository, we use the last routing table dump (`bview.20161231.2359`) before the beginning of our observation window. We use BGPstream [24] to decode MRT files. Results are shown in Fig. 1. We start by confirming that in most cases primary paths dominate other paths over relatively long periods of time. Specifically, the figure shows the percentage of time that the primary path was used during the observation period $W = 3$ months for all $<router, prefix>$ pairs. Formally, denoting as before with x_1 the primary path and with $T_{x_1}(r,p)$ the sum of the cumulative time during W where router r uses path x_1 to reach prefix p, the figure shows the complementary cumulative distribution function (CCDF) of the primary path usage during the whole observation period, i.e., $T_{x_1}(r,p)/W$. The data shows that about 85% of the primary paths in IPv4 (90% for IPv6) are in use at least about half of the observation period W, and even more interesting, about 35% IPv4 (42% IPv6) primary paths are in use for over 99.9% of W.

3.2   Pseudo-events

Under the assumption of primary paths stability over long timescales, we argue that BGP dynamics can be described in terms of:

- **Transient events,** where some routers explore paths before reconverging to their primary paths (e.g., possibly due to failure, misconfiguration, attack, etc.).
- **Structural events,** where some routers explore paths before switching consistently to a new primary path (e.g., as a result of routing policy or agreement changes).

A given event can impact many primary paths from many routers to many prefixes. Therefore, to keep working at the $<router, prefix>$ pair granularity we define the notion of **pseudo-event** as the impact of an event for a given primary path x_1 used by a router r to a prefix p. Thus it is possible to further distinguish between:

- **Transient pseudo-events,** making r explore path(s) to p and reconverge to x_1.
- **Structural pseudo-events,** making r explore path(s) to p and converge to a new primary path x_1'.

Moreover, pseudo-events can be characterized by:

- **a duration:** period of time where the primary path x_1 from r to p is not used, identified by a start time t_s and an end time t_e;
- **a path exploration sequence:** sequence of $N-1$ transient paths $\underline{x} = (x_2, \ldots, x_N)$ to reach prefix p.

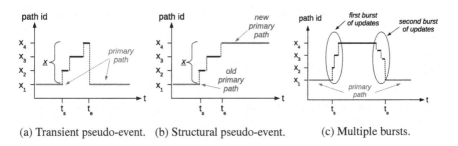

(a) Transient pseudo-event.   (b) Structural pseudo-event.   (c) Multiple bursts.

Fig. 2. Illustration of types of pseudo-events, and multiple bursts of updates scenario for a single event.

Figure 2a and b portray the above cases. Therefore, pseudo-events enable to group updates following a primary path unavailability, instead of relying on some temporal threshold [7,23,30] (which result in grouping updates into bursts). An interesting follow-up characteristic from this paradigm is that pseudo-events are resilient to long-lasting events. Indeed, the longer an event lasts (a failure for instance) the more likely it is to lead to several bursts of updates as illustrated in Fig. 2c. In such situation grouping updates based on primary paths unavailabilities will group all the bursts into a single pseudo-event. For these reasons, whereas BGP dynamics analysis typically work on the stream of BGP updates, our proposal is to work on the stream of pseudo-events instead.

3.3   Practical Primary Path Computation

In this section we study the feasibility of relying solely on routing table (i.e., RIB, for Routing Information Base) dumps to compute primary paths. Recall that in Sect. 3.1 we computed the primary path repository with BGP updates in an offline fashion. However, to be of any practical interest, primary paths should be easily computable at any time in a simple, efficient and online manner. To do this, we propose to use RIBs. As an alternate form of BGP data, we consider RIBs to be easier to work with than updates because they provide snapshots

Table 1. IPv4 primary path bootstrap accuracy: percentage of primary paths matching those of the 10-snapshots reference when using $d \leq 9$ snapshots.

Snapshots	1	2	3	4	5	6	7	8	9
Accuracy	97.4%	97.9%	98.5%	98.8%	99.0%	99.1%	99.2%	99.4%	99.7%

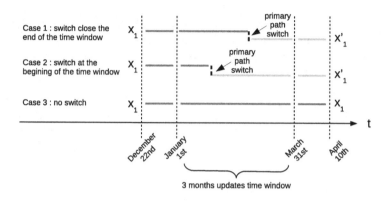

Fig. 3. Cases of primary paths switches during the observation window.

of paths for all *<router, prefix>* pairs. Besides, to bootstrap the primary path repository in Sect. 3.1 we already had to rely on a RIB dump.

First question arising is how many consecutive RIBs are required to capture stability. Indeed, there is no guarantee that a single RIB contains the primary paths. However, as primary paths are computed as the most used path over time, they should be easily identifiable from the observation of multiple consecutive dumps. The question is then *how many* consecutive RIB dumps are needed in practice for an accurate selection. To answer this question, we operate as follows. For the 10 days preceding our observation window (i.e., December 22nd to 31st 2016), we select one RIB dump per day during d consecutive days ($\forall d \in [1, 10]$). For a router r and a prefix p, we extract as its primary path the most present path in the d consecutive dumps. We then compare, for all *<router, prefix>* pairs, what fraction of primary paths obtained with different number $\forall d \in [1, 9]$ of RIB dumps match those obtained with the $d = 10$ full interval (used as reference). Results are shown in Table 1 for IPv4. It can be seen that computing primary path with RIB dumps has over 97% chances of success even from a single snapshot, and rapidly exceeds 99% accuracy by adding a few snapshots. Additionally, the results also suggest primary paths to be stable with high probability on at least a weekly timescale. Now that we know that a few RIB dumps give us the same primary paths than a large number of dumps, we aim to determine if RIB dumps are a suitable mean to compute primary paths. For this purpose, we compare the primary paths obtained with RIBs with the ones previously computed from updates in Sect. 3.1. We obtain a matching of 76.48%. The non-matching fraction could result from inefficiency of the method or from primary paths switching during the time window. In fact, if such switches occur at the beginning of the time window, then for a given $<router, prefix>$ pair the primary path x_1 computed with RIBs will differ from the one (x_1') computed with updates, as illustrated by case 2 in Fig. 3. To investigate whether the non-matching fraction is due to primary path switches, we compute primary paths using RIBs from April 1st to April 10th (i.e., the 10 days following the end of the observation window). This time, we obtain a matching of 85.95% when comparing primary paths from the RIBs in April with those computed with updates. Once again the non-matching fraction could result from method inefficiency or from switches (this time, at the end of the time window, as illustrated by case 1 in Fig. 3). Finally, it appears that 95.5% of primary paths computed on updates are either matching those computed from the RIBs of December or those of April. This confirms that most of the non-matching fraction is due to primary paths switches (i.e., structural pseudo-events) during the time window. It also highlights the need to periodically update the primary paths repository. We leave the study of the characterization of primary path turnover as part of our future work. We will show in the next section that even without updating the primary path repository periodically during the time window, we still get valuable results. In this section we have shown that the paths most present in a few RIB dumps are a good indicator of the primary paths used for the next days. In fact, these paths highly overlap with primary paths obtained from the stream of updates, meaning that RIBs are thus a viable approach to compute primary paths in practice.

4   BGP Dynamics

In this section, we apply our methodology on two classic use cases of BGP dynamics analysis: inter-domain tomography and anomaly detection.

4.1   First Use Case: Inter-domain Tomography

The Internet as a set of interacting ASes is a complex environment. Tomography intends to infer the internal characteristics of a system from external observations. Pseudo-events are groups of updates based on primary paths unavailability periods which exhibit two interesting properties: a duration and the sequence of paths explored.

We analyze updates from January 1st 2017 to March 31st 2017 ($W = 3$ months) collected at the RIPE RIS LINX, in the order of arrival. Each update is processed against the primary path repository built upon the last 10 days of December's RIBs. Upon detection of an update for a $<router, prefix>$ pair announcing the start at t_s of a primary path x_1 unavailability (i.e., the path announced is not the primary path), a pseudo-event object is created. The subsequent updates observed for the same $<router, prefix>$ pair, which relate to the ordered set $\underline{x} = (x_2, \ldots, x_N)$ of paths explored, are indexed into this object

Table 2. Volume gain in the pseudo-events domain

	IPv4	IPv6
Updates	487,104,558	157,249,182
Pseudo-events	57,066,053	17,687,525
Structural pseudo-events	1,406,392	78,995
Transient pseudo-events	55,659,661	17,608,530
Reduction factor	8.5	8.9

and can be processed further, for example to characterize anomalies (e.g., outages, hijack, etc. as explored in Sect. 4.2). If an update announcing x_1 is observed at time $t_e > t_s$, then this pseudo-event is classified as transient, and its duration is $t_e - t_s$. If at the end of the time window W the pseudo-event has not reconverged to x_1 then this pseudo-event is classified as structural, and its duration is set to $W - t_s$. Results are presented in Table 2. First of all, it can be noticed that the systematic indexing of updates into pseudo-events result in a reduction of the number of objects that will have to be further processed for analysis: i.e., rather than analyzing a stream of updates we analyze a stream of pseudo-events. The reduction factor is *almost one order of magnitude* when transforming the stream of updates into a stream of pseudo-events: more precisely, it is a sizable factor of 8.5 (8.9) volume reduction for IPv4 (IPv6). There is therefore a practical volume gain when working with pseudo-events. Moreover, as it could be expected, it appears that transient pseudo-events largely dominate structural ones: less than 2.5% of pseudo-events are structural. We now further investigate pseudo-event properties and the light they shed on BGP dynamics.

Pseudo-events duration. We first turn our attention to temporal properties of pseudo-events. Comparison of Fig. 4a and b confirms our expectations: transient pseudo-events (i.e., those which reconverge to the primary path after a path exploration) have indeed small duration (Fig. 4a), while structural pseudo-events (i.e., those which did not reconverge to the primary path) have long durations (Fig. 4b). Particularly, about 50% of IPv4 (60% IPv6) transient pseudo-events last *less than a minute*, whereas only about 11% of IPv4 (18% IPv6) structural pseudo-events last *less than a week*.

Pseudo-events path exploration. The distribution of the path exploration length card($\underline{x}$) is reported in Fig. 5a. It clearly appears that transient pseudo-events explore relatively few paths, just 1 in 60% of cases and rarely more than 10 (3% of cases) before reconverging on the primary paths. In other words, transient pseudo-events index 2 updates in 60% of cases and rarely more than 11 (3% of cases). More interestingly, if we characterize a pseudo-event by its sequence of paths explored then we can detect when a pseudo-event occurs multiple time, as illustrated on Fig. 5b. If most transient pseudo-events occurred only once

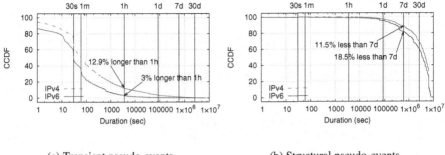

(a) Transient pseudo-events.   (b) Structural pseudo-events.

Fig. 4. Complementary CDF of pseudo-events duration $t_e - t_s$, in semi-log-x scale (bottom x-axis reports duration in seconds, top x-axis uses more human-friendly units).

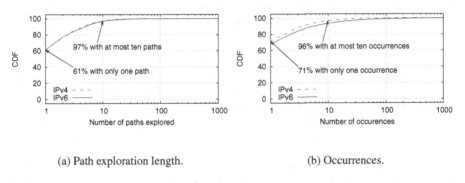

(a) Path exploration length.   (b) Occurrences.

Fig. 5. CDF of transient pseudo-events path exploration length and occurrences.

during the time window (about 70%), it also appears that a few occurred a lot (sometimes hundreds of times).

Global picture. Analysis of pseudo-events properties provide us with the following global picture. BGP dynamics are mostly made of short termed instabilities producing limited path exploration. This would suggest that classic solutions for BGP dynamics regulation such as MRAI timers [29] or route flap damping [34] are efficient (see gaps on Fig. 4a at 30 s and 60 s, most likely due to MRAI effects, pointing out its ability to limit path exploration). However, results also point out that instabilities are recurrent. In such situations, classical mechanisms are ineffective by design. To be tackled, recurrent instabilities would require advanced contention mechanisms, able to learn and recognize them, which we intend to investigate as part of our future work.

4.2   Second Use Case: Anomaly Detection

We now show how information provided by primary paths can be leveraged for anomaly detection. Specifically, we use as reference the list of noteworthy BGP events published by a well-known alert service, BGPmon [4], which classifies events as either (i) AS or country-level outages, (ii) hijacks and (iii) leaks, and for each event reports the inferred starting time. We argue that the usefulness of pseudo-events is better assessed by focusing on AS-level *outages* (i.e., an outage on AS x is an event impacting prefixes originated by AS x) and *hijacks* (a hijack on AS x by AS y is identified whenever AS y has originated some route for a prefix p, such that p is a prefix, or a more specific prefix, legitimately originated by AS x). Notice indeed that country-level outages and leaks would require to use IP geolocation databases or AS relationships databases respectively: clearly, the use of different databases than BGPmon would be a further source of uncertainty, which would unnecessarily fuzz the comparison.

Considering the same period of our dataset (January 1st to March 31st 2017), BGPmon lists 2369 events (1716 outages and 653 hijacks). Since we are using different (and fewer) vantage points than BGPmon, we need to remove non observable events. We perform this sanitization using BGP updates. For each event starting at time t_{BGPmon} we define a time window as $|t - t_{BGPmon}| <$ 120 s. The duration of this time window is chosen wide enough to take into account updates propagation time (especially due to MRAI effects) among different vantage points. For an outage on AS x, if no update was seen during the time window for any prefix originated by AS x then we say this event was not observable. For a hijack on AS x by AS y, if no update was seen during the time window for prefix p originated by AS y, then we say this event was not observable. We gather that 441 (94 outages and 347 hijacks) events were not observable at our collector, leaving us with a total of 1928 events (1622 outages and 306 hijacks). We next investigate if we find pseudo-events related to the events inferred by BGPmon.

Outages. For an outage on AS x, we look for pseudo-events for prefixes originated by AS x. As reported in Table 3a, for 1355 (83.5%) outages, we detect such pseudo-events starting during the same time window ($|t - t_{BGPmon}| < 120$): we say that we detect them *on-time*. More interestingly, for 236 (14.6%) outages, the related primary paths unavailability periods already started well before the window: in 229 out of 236 of cases, the time difference with respect to BGPmon is larger than one hour. In this case, it is rather clear that the observed starting time difference cannot be just explained by propagation delays among multiple collectors. Under our formalism, the reported starting time could correspond to some bursts of updates (recall Fig. 2c) instead of the beginning of primary paths unavailabilities. We argue in this case that we *early* detect pseudo-events related to these outages with respect to BGPmon. Finally, only 31(1.9%) outages were not detected with pseudo-events (which requires further investigation).

Hijacks. For a hijack on AS x by AS y, we record every update originated by AS y, announced within $|t - t_{BGPmon}| < 120$ by any router r for any prefix p and analyze it against our primary paths repository. More precisely, if there exists a primary path for $<r, p>$, then we compare it to the path in the update

Table 3. Relevance of primary paths for anomaly detection

(a) Outages

Reported BGPmon events	1716
Observable BGPmon events	1622
Detected pseudo-events	1591 (98.1%)
−On-time	1355
−Early	236
Undetected pseudo-events	31 (1.9%)

(b) Hijacks

Reported BGPmon events	653
Observable BGPmon events	306
Agreements	173 (56.5%)
Disagreements	133 (43.5%)
−Explicit	37
−Implicit	96

and assess whether we agree or explicitly disagree (according to our repository, AS y is legitimate to originate p) with BGPmon. If no primary path for $<r, p>$ exists, then we search for a primary path $<r, p'>$, such that p' is less specific than p (first level less specific) and compare paths. Finally, if no such primary path exists, we implicitly disagree: according to our repository it is a harmless update for a newly originated prefix.

As reported in Table 3b, for 173 (56.5%) hijacks we agree with BGPmon. For 133 (43.5%) hijacks we disagree with BGPmon, either explicitly (37 hijacks) or implicitly (96 hijacks). Investigating the reasons for this important number of disagreements, we discover that 103 of them have occurred in March and impacted the same origin AS (AS 13489) and prefix (2800::/12)[1]. In other words, during March this very prefix and origin AS was hijacked 103 times, moreover by tens of different ASes originating prefixes all more specific than 2800::/12. Analyzing Regional Internet Registries (RIR) statistics files which summarize the current state of Internet number resource allocations and assignments, and executing *whois* requests on RIR's databases, it appears that 2800::/12 is not allocated nor assigned (at the time of writing). This prefix, which started being originated by AS13489 on March 3rd (according to our dataset) should not have therefore been routed (it was no longer routed at the time of writing). On the contrary, the RIR's databases also indicates that 11622 prefixes more specific than 2800::/12 have legitimately been allocated or assigned. This more likely illegitimate origination of 2800::/12 by AS13489 would therefore have triggered hijacks detection by BGPmon for any legitimate update related to any more specific prefix than 2800::/12. As a conclusion, we are reassured in the relevance of primary paths for hijack detection. The remaining 30 hijacks are marked as disagreement, though reasons of disagreement are still uncertain and require further investigation.

---

[1] We are aware that this prefix was used in Czyz et al. [11]. We believe that the events are unrelated because they do not match either the involved parties, the time window, or the methodology described.

5   Conclusions and Future Work

This paper discusses the concepts of *primary paths* (most used inter-domain paths in a time period) and *pseudo-events* (primary path unavailability periods). Using three months of BGP updates at a collector, we verify our assumption to hold, and show how to take advantage of the inter-domain stability by augmenting the stream of BGP updates with primary paths, thus creating a new stream of pseudo-events. This new stream exhibits interesting characteristics for BGP dynamics analysis, as shown on two use cases. First, it helps us in building tomographic views of the inter-domain structure, uncovering or confirming many temporal and topological characteristics. Second, our comparison with the BGPmon alert service indicates that the knowledge of the primary path can be used for anomaly detection. It enables to promptly detect any deviation from this nominal behavior, and is also helpful in characterizing the type of deviation.

Therefore, primary paths provide a powerful repository to interpret BGP updates, and this paper just scratches the surface of their usage. As part of our ongoing work, we are investigating their topological properties (to correlate pseudo-events), analyzing temporal properties of structural pseudo-events (to characterize primary paths turnover), with the purpose of proposing an online framework to detect and mitigate BGP events.

Acknowledgments. We thank the anonymous reviewers whose valuable comments helped us improving the quality of this paper.

References

1. Al-Rousan, N.M., Trajković, L.: Machine learning models for classification of BGP anomalies. In: Proceedings of IEEE HPSR (2012)
2. Bahaa, A.M., Philip, B., Grenville, A.: BGP anomaly detection techniques: a survey. IEEE Commun. Surv. Tutor. **19**, 377–396 (2016)
3. Bates, T., Smith, P., Huston, G.: CIDR Report. http://www.cidr-report.org/as2.0/. Accessed 2018
4. BGPmon.net: Public event reporting. https://bgpstream.com. Accessed 2018
5. Butler, K., McDaniel, P., Aiello, W.: Optimizing BGP security by exploiting path stability. In: Proceedings of ACM CCS (2006)
6. Caesar, M., Subramanian, L., Katz, R.H.: Root cause analysis of BGP dynamics. In: Proceedings of ACM IMC (2003)
7. Chang, D.F., Govindan, R., Heidemann, J.: The temporal and topological characteristics of BGP path changes. In: Proceedings of IEEE ICNP (2003)
8. Chen, M., Xu, M., Li, Q., Song, X., Yang, Y.: Detect and analyze large-scale BGP events by bi-clustering update visibility matrix. In: Proceedings of IEEE IPCCC (2015)
9. Comarela, G., Crovella, M.: Identifying and analyzing high impact routing events with PathMiner. In: Proceedings of ACM IMC (2014)
10. Craig, L., Robert, M.G., Jahanian, F.: Origins of internet routing instability. In: Proceedings of INFOCOMM (1999)
11. Czyz, J., Lady, K., Miller, S.G., Bailey, M., Kallitsis, M., Karir, M.: Understanding IPv6 internet background radiation. In: Proceedings of ACM IMC (2013)
12. Deshpande, S., Thottan, M., Ho, T.K., Sikda, B.: An online mechanism for BGP instability detection and analysis. IEEE Trans. Comput. **58**, 1470–1484 (2009)

13. Elmokashfi, A., Kvalbein, A., Dovrolis, C.: BGP churn evolution: a perspective from the core. IEEE Trans. Netw. **20**, 571–584 (2011)
14. Feldmann, A., Maennel, O., Mao, Z.M., Berger, A., Maggs, B.: Locating internet routing instabilities. ACM SIGCOMM Comput. Commun. Rev. **34**, 205–218 (2004)
15. Haeberlen, A., Avramopoulos, I., Rexford, J., Druschel, P.: NetReview: detecting when interdomain routing goes wrong. In: Proceedings of NSDI (2009)
16. Holterbach, T., Vissicchio, S., Dainotti, A., Vanbever, L.: SWIFT: predictive fast reroute. In: ACM SIGCOMM (2017)
17. Javed, U., Cunha, I., Choffnes, D., Katz-Bassett, E., Anderson, T., Krishnamurthy, A.: PoiRoot: investigating the root cause of interdomain path changes. In: ACM SIGCOMM (2013)
18. Karlin, J., Forrest, S., Rexford, J.: Pretty good BGP: improving BGP by cautiously adopting routes. In: Proceedings of IEEE ICNP (2006)
19. Labovitz, C., Malan, G.R., Jahanian, F.: Internet routing instability. In: Proceedings of ACM SIGCOMM (1997)
20. Li, J., Guidero, M., Wu, Z., Purpus, E., Ehrenkranz, T.: BGP routing dynamics revisited. ACM SIGCOMM Comput. Commun. Rev. **37**, 5–16 (2007)
21. Lutu, A., Bagnulo, M., Pelsser, C., Maennel, O., Cid-Sueiro, J.: The BGP visibility toolkit: detecting anomalous Internet routing behavior. Proc. IEEE/ACM Trans. Netw. **24**, 1237–1250 (2016)
22. Mai, J., Yuan, L., Chuah, C.N.: Detecting BGP anomalies with wavelet. In: Proceedings of IEEE NOM (2008)
23. Oliveira, R., Zhang, B., Pei, D., Izhak-Ratzin, R., Zhang, L.: Quantifying path exploration in the internet. In: Proceedings of ACM IMC (2006)
24. Orsini, C., King, A., Giordano, D., Giotsas, V., Dainotti, A.: BGPStream: A Software framework for live and historical BGP data analysis. In: Proceedings of ACM IMC (2016)
25. Papadopoulos, S., Moustakas, K., Drosou, A., Tzovaras, D.: Border gateway protocol graph: detecting and visualising Internet routing anomalies. IET Inf. Secur. **10**, 125–133 (2016)
26. Paxson, V.: End-to-end routing behavior in the Internet. ACM SIGCOMM Comput. Commun. Rev. **36**, 41–56 (1996)
27. Prakash, B.A., Valler, N., Andersen, D., Faloutsos, M., Faloutsos, C.: BGP-lens: patterns and anomalies in internet routing updates. In: Proceedings of ACM SIGKDD (2009)
28. Qiu, J., Gao, L., Ranjan, S., Nucci, A.: Detecting bogus BGP route information: going beyond prefix hijacking. In: Proceedings of EAI SecureComm (2007)
29. Rekhter, Y., Li, T.: A Border Gateway Protocol 4 (BGP-4). RFC4271 (2006)
30. Rexford, J., Wang, J., Xiao, Z., Zhang, Y.: BGP routing stability of popular destinations. In: Proceedings of ACM SIGCOMM Workshop on Internet measurement (2002)
31. RIPE-NCC: Routing information service. https://www.ripe.net/ris. Accessed 2018
32. Theodoridis, G., Tsigkas, O., Tzovaras, D.: A novel unsupervised method for securing BGP against routing hijacks. Comput. Inf. Sci. **III**, 21–29 (2013)
33. de Urbina Cazenave, I.O., Köşlük, E., Ganiz, M.C.: An anomaly detection framework for BGP. In: Proceedings of INISTA (2011)
34. Villamizar, C., Chandra, R., Govindan, R.: BGP Route Flap Damping. RFC2439 (1998)
35. Walton, D., Retana, A., Chen, E., Scudder, J.: Advertisement of multiple Paths in BGP. RFC 7911 (2016)

The (Thin) Bridges of AS Connectivity: Measuring Dependency Using AS Hegemony

Romain Fontugne[1($\boxtimes$)], Anant Shah[2], and Emile Aben[3]

[1] IIJ Research Lab, Tokyo, Japan
`romain@iij.ad.jp`
[2] Colorado State University, Fort Collins, USA
`akshah@cs.colostate.edu`
[3] RIPE NCC, Amsterdam, Netherlands
`emile.aben@ripe.net`

Abstract. Inter-domain routing is a crucial part of the Internet designed for arbitrary policies, economical models, and topologies. This versatility translates into a substantially complex system that is hard to comprehend. Monitoring the inter-domain routing infrastructure is however essential for understanding the current state of the Internet and improving it. In this paper we design a methodology to answer two simple questions: Which are the common transit networks used to reach a certain AS? How much does this AS depend on these transit networks? To answer these questions we digest AS paths advertised with the Border Gateway Protocol (BGP) into AS graphs and measure node centrality (i.e. the likelihood of an AS to lie on paths between two other ASes). Our proposal relies solely on the AS hegemony metric, a new way to quantify node centrality while taking into account the bias towards the partial view offered by BGP. Our analysis using 14 years of BGP data refines our knowledge on Internet flattening but also exhibits the consolidated position of tier-1 networks in today's IPv4 and IPv6 Internet. We also study the connectivity to two content providers (Google and Akamai) and investigate the AS dependency of networks hosting DNS root servers. These case studies emphasize the benefits of our method to assist ISPs in planning and assessing infrastructure deployment.

1 Introduction

Networks connected to the Internet are inherently relying on other Autonomous Systems (ASes) to transmit data. To determine the path of ASes to go from one place to another, the Internet relies solely on the Border Gateway Protocol (BGP). Computed AS paths are the result of an involved process that considers various peering policies set by each connected AS. BGP exposes only paths that are favored by ASes hence concealing peering policies and the exact routing process. However, as the connectivity of a network depends greatly on the connectivity of other ASes, operators need to clearly understand ASes that are

© Springer International Publishing AG, part of Springer Nature 2018
R. Beverly et al. (Eds.): PAM 2018, LNCS 10771, pp. 216–227, 2018.
https://doi.org/10.1007/978-3-319-76481-8_16

crucial to their networks. Identifying these AS interdependencies facilitates decisions for deployments, routing decisions, and connectivity troubleshooting [17].

In this paper we aim at estimating the AS interdependencies from BGP data. We devise a methodology that models AS interconnections as a graph and measure AS centrality, that is the likelihood of an AS to lie on paths between two other ASes. We identify in Sect. 2 shortcomings of a classical centrality metric, Betweenness Centrality (BC), when used with BGP data. From these observations we employ a robust metric to estimate AS centrality, called AS hegemony (Sect. 3). We demonstrate the value of the proposed method with 14 years of BGP data (Sect. 4). Overall we found that AS interdependencies in IPv4 are decreasing over time which corroborate with previous observations of the Internet flattening [3]. But we also found that the important role played by tier-1 ISP is reinforced in today's Internet. The Internet flattening for IPv6 is happening at a faster rate, but we found that Hurricane Electric network is utterly central for the last 9 years. We also investigated the AS dependency of two popular networks, Akamai and Google, showing that their dependency to other networks is minimal although their peering policies are completely different. Finally, we look at two networks hosting DNS root servers and show how recent structural changes to these root servers have affected their AS dependencies.

We make our tools and updated results publicly available [1] hence network operators can quickly understand their networks' AS dependency.

2   Background

Related Work: The essence of this work is the estimation of AS centrality in AS graphs. In the literature AS centrality is commonly measured using Betweenness Centrality (BC). This is one of the basic metric used to characterize the topology of the Internet [12,18]. It was also applied for similar motivation as ours. Karlin et al. [9] consider Internet routing at the country-level to investigate the interdependencies of countries and identify countries relying on other countries enforcing censorship or wiretapping. BC is also used to identify critical ASes for industrial and public sectors in Germany [17]. Similarly, Schuchard et al. [15] select targets for control plane attacks using a ranking based on BC. Finally, researchers have also applied BC to detect changes in the AS-topology. For example, Liu et al. [11] employ BC to monitor rerouting events caused by important disruptive events such as sea cable faults. Following past research, we initially conducted our experiments using BC but faced fundamental shortcomings due to the incomplete view provided by BGP data. To introduce these challenges let's first review BC.

Betweenness Centrality: BC is a fundamental metric that represents the fraction of paths that goes through a node. Intuitively one expects high BC scores for transit ASes as they occur on numerous AS paths, and low BC scores for stub ASes. Formally, for a graph $G = (V, E)$ composed of a set of nodes V and edges E, the betweenness centrality is defined as: $BC(v) = \frac{1}{S} \sum_{u,w \in V} \sigma_{uw}(v)$ where $\sigma_{uw}(v)$ is the number of paths from u to w passing through v, and S is

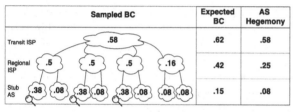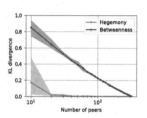

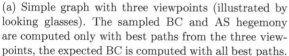

Sampled BC	Expected BC	AS Hegemony
Transit ISP	.62	.58
Regional ISP	.42	.25
Stub AS	.15	.08

(a) Simple graph with three viewpoints (illustrated by looking glasses). The sampled BC and AS hegemony are computed only with best paths from the three viewpoints, the expected BC is computed with all best paths.

(b) Sampling error forBC and AS hegemony in function of the number of viewpoints.

Fig. 1. Comparison of Betweenness Centrality (BC) and AS hegemony with a toy example and BGP data.

the total number of paths. BC ranges in $[0, 1]$, but the relative magnitudes of the scores are usually more significant than the absolute values.

Challenges: In theory, to compute BC one needs the set of all paths in the graph. With BGP data, however, we are restricted to paths bounded to a small number of viewpoints. We found that this singular type of path sampling greatly impairs BC results. To illustrate this, Fig. 1a presents a simple example with 13 ASes and three viewpoints. If we had viewpoints in all ASes, thus access to all paths in the graph, we would obtain the highest BC score for the transit ISP (.62) and lowest scores for the stub ASes (.15). But, using only paths bound to the three viewpoints, the computed BC scores are substantially different (Sampled BC in Fig. 1a). Because a third of the paths converge to each viewpoint, BC values for ASes close to the viewpoints are undesirably high. This bias is so pronounced that the BC for stub ASes accommodating viewpoints (.38) is twice higher than the BC of one of the regional ISP (.16). Theoretical studies have already reported the shortcomings of BC with sampled data [10], but this issue has been rarely acknowledged in the networking literature. Mahadevan et al. [12] reported that BC is not a measure of centrality when computed with network data, but we stress that this issue comes from the non-random and opportunistic sampling method used to collect BGP data rather than the metric itself.

In our experiments we construct a global AS graph using all data from the Route Views, RIS, and BGPmon project on June 1st 2016. This corresponds to an AS graph of more than 50k nodes with 326 viewpoints (we consider only full-feed BGP peers), and only 0.6% of all the AS paths on the Internet (16 M paths out of the 2.5B). As collected paths all converge to the 326 viewpoints, ASes accommodating viewpoints and their neighboring ASes are seemingly more central than other ASes. To measure the bias obtained with real BGP data we conduct the following experiment. First, we compute the BC for all ASes with data from all 326 viewpoints, then we compare this distribution of BC values to BC values obtained with a smaller set of randomly selected viewpoints. The distance between two distributions is measured with the Kullback-Leibler divergence. Figure 1b shows that changing the number of viewpoints invariably reshapes the BC distribution, meaning that the obtained BC values are conditioned by the number of viewpoints. From these results, we hypothesize that having more viewpoints would yield different BC values, thus the BC values obtained with the 326 viewpoints might not be representative of AS centrality.

3   Methodology

To address the above BC shortcomings, we devise a monitoring method based on a robust centrality metric called AS hegemony. The proposed method consists of two basic steps. First we generate graphs from AS paths advertised via BGP. Then, using AS hegemony, we estimate the centrality of each AS in the graphs. We consider two types of graphs, global and local graphs.

Global graph: A global graph is made from all AS paths reported by the BGP viewpoints regardless of the origin AS and announced prefix. Consequently, these graphs represent the global Internet and central nodes stand for transit networks that are commonly crossed to reach arbitrary IP addresses. In 2017, IPv4 global graphs typically contains about 58 k nodes and 188 k edges (14 k nodes and 43 k edges for IPv6). The structure of these graphs is complex, yet they are valuable to monitor the Internet altogether and reveal Internet-wide routing changes.

Local graph: A local graph is made only from AS paths with the same origin AS. Thereby, we compute a local graph for each AS announcing IP space globally. Each local graph represents the different ways to reach its origin AS and dominant nodes highlight the main transit networks towards only this AS. These graphs are particularly useful to monitor the dependence of an AS to other networks. In addition, structural changes in local graphs can expose important routing changes that may be detrimental to the origin AS reachability.

AS Hegemony: The core of the proposed method is to quantify the centrality of ASes in the generated graphs. To circumvent BC sampling problems we extend the recently proposed AS hegemony metric [5]. This metric measures the fraction of paths passing through a node while correcting for sampling bias.

Computing the hegemony of AS v from AS paths collected from several viewpoints consists of the two following steps. First, AS paths from viewpoints that are biased towards or against AS v are discarded. A viewpoint bias towards AS v means that the viewpoint is located within AS v, or topologically very close to it, and reports numerous AS paths passing through AS v. In contrast, a viewpoint bias against AS v is topologically far from v and is reporting an usually low number of AS paths containing v. Therefore, viewpoints with an abnormally high, or low, number of paths passing through v are discarded and only other viewpoints are selected to compute the hegemony score. Second, the centrality of v is computed independently for each selected viewpoint and these scores are aggregated to give the final AS hegemony value. That is, for each selected viewpoint j the BC of v (hereafter referred as $BC_{(j)}(v)$) is computed only from AS paths reported by j. And the average BC value across all selected viewpoints is the AS hegemony score of v.

These steps can be formally summarized into one equation. Let n be the total number of viewpoints, $\lfloor . \rfloor$ be the floor function and $0 \leq 2\alpha < 1$ be the ratio of disregarded viewpoints. That is, the top $\lfloor \alpha n \rfloor$ viewpoints with the highest number of paths passing through the AS and do the same for viewpoints with the lowest number of paths. Then the AS hegemony is defined as:

$$\mathcal{H}(v, \alpha) = \frac{1}{n - (2\lfloor \alpha n \rfloor)} \sum_{j=\lfloor \alpha n \rfloor + 1}^{n - \lfloor \alpha n \rfloor} BC_{(j)}(v),$$

where $BC_{(j)}$ is the BC value computed with paths from only one viewpoint j (i.e. $BC_{(j)}(v) = 1/S \sum_{w \in V} \sigma_{jw}(v)$) and these values are arranged in ascending order such that $BC_{(1)}(v) \leq BC_{(2)}(v) \leq \cdots \leq BC_{(n)}(v)$.

Figure 1a depicts the AS hegemony obtained for the simple graph with three viewpoints ($\alpha = .34$). Unlike the sampled BC, the AS hegemony is consistent for each type of node: transit ($\mathcal{H} = 0.58$), regional ISP ($\mathcal{H} = 0.25$) and stub AS ($\mathcal{H} = 0.08$). AS hegemony scores are intuitively interpreted as the average fraction of paths crossing a node. For example, on average a viewpoint has one fourth of its paths crossing a regional ISP ($\mathcal{H} = 0.25$).

In order to compare the robustness of AS hegemony and BC with real data, we reproduce the experiment of Sect. 2 with AS hegemony. Figure 1b shows that the hegemony values with 20 or more viewpoints are very similar to the ones obtained with the 326 peers. Meaning that path sampling has significantly less impact on AS hegemony than on BC. Note that we randomly select peers across different projects (e.g. Route Views, RIS) to obtain a diverse set of viewpoints. Selecting viewpoints from the same collector may yield poor results [5].

Path Weights: We extend AS hegemony to account for path disparities. In a nutshell, we weight paths according to the amount of IP space they are bound to. For example, a path to a /24 IP prefix represents a route to a smaller network than a path to a /16 IP prefix, thus we want to emphasize the path to the /16. The network prefix length alone is however not sufficient to resolve the IP space bound to a path. IP space deaggregation [2,6] should also be taken into account. For example, a viewpoint reports the path 'X Y Z' for the prefix $a.b.c.0/17$ and the path 'X W Z' for the prefix $a.b.0.0/16$. Meaning that BGP favors path 'X Y Z' for half of the advertised /16. Here there is no need to give more emphasis to the path bound to the /16 as each path represents a route to 2^{15} IP addresses.

Consequently, we modify our definition of BC to account for the size of the IP space reachable through a path. Formally, $\sigma_{uw}(v)$ is the number of IP addresses bound to the paths from u to w and passing through v. That is the number of IP addresses corresponding to the advertised IP prefixes minus the number of IP addresses from covered prefixes (i.e. deaggregated and delegated prefixes [2]) that are not passing through v. In the rest of the paper this weighted version of BC is applied for the calculation of AS hegemony in IPv4, but as the relation between number of addresses and prefix size in IPv6 is more ambiguous we keep the classical BC definition for the calculation of AS hegemony in IPv6.

4   Results

Our Python implementation of the above method fetches BGP data using the BGPStream framework from CAIDA [13] and computes AS hegemony of all ASes in the global graph as well as AS hegemony for ASes in all local graphs. Our tool and updated results are made publicly available [1].

Parameter tuning: Setting the value of α is a trade-off between sampling robustness ($\alpha \approx 0.5$) and sensitivity to local routing changes ($\alpha \approx 0$). For example, setting $\alpha \approx 0.5$ achieves the most robust results to path sampling but conceals routing events affecting less than half of the monitored BGP peers. To monitor routing changes we seek for a small value of α that is still robust to path sampling. In Fig. 2 we compare robust AS hegemony scores ($\alpha = 0.49$) to scores obtained with different values of α. For the following experiments we set the parameter $\alpha = 0.1$, as it provides results similar to those obtained with $\alpha = 0.49$ but is more sensitive to local changes.

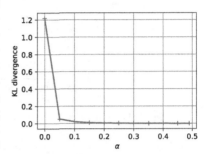

Fig. 2. KL divergence between AS hegemony scores obtained with $\alpha = 0.49$ and different values of α (global graph on 2017/12/15 with rv2, LINX, rrc00, and rrc10 collectors).

Dataset: The following results are all obtained using BGP data from four BGP collectors, two from the RouteViews project (route-views2 and LINX) and two from the RIS project (rrc00 and rrc10). These four collectors are selected from the collectors sensitivity results presented in [5]. For IPv4 they represent from 51 to 95 BGP peers respectively in 2004 and 2017. For IPv6, however, as the number of BGP peers is rather small before 2007 (i.e. less than 10 peers) and AS hegemony values might be irrelevant with such low number of peers (see Fig. 1b), we report only results obtained from 2007 onward using from 11 to 44 peers. The results presented below are obtained with RIB data of all peers for the 15th of each month from January 2004 to September 2017.

4.1   IPv4 and IPv6 Global Graphs

As the starting point of our analysis, we investigate the AS interdependency for the entire IP space. We monitor the evolution of AS hegemony scores in the global AS graph from 2004 to 2017. Here large AS hegemony scores represent transit networks that are commonly crossed to reach arbitrary IP addresses. Figure 3 depicts the distribution of the yearly average AS hegemony for all ASes in the IPv4 and IPv6 global AS graphs. In these figures each point represent an AS, and those on the right hand side of the figures stand for nodes with the highest hegemony values.

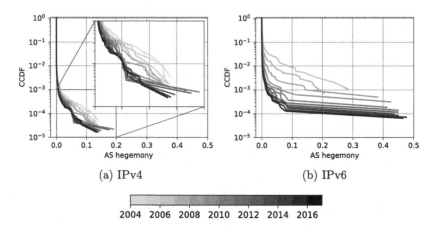

(a) IPv4   (b) IPv6

2004 2006 2008 2010 2012 2014 2016

Fig. 3. Distribution of AS hegemony for all ASes in the global graph.

As the distribution of AS hegemony values for IPv4 is overall shifting to the left over time (Fig. 3a), we observe a global and steady decrease of AS hegemony values. This is another evidence of Internet's flattening [3], as networks are peering with more networks we observe less dominant ASes. Nonetheless, Fig. 3a suggests that the AS hegemony for the most dominant networks (i.e. points on the right hand side) is quite stable.

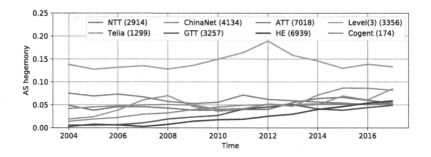

Fig. 4. AS hegemony for Tier-1 ISPs from 2004 to 2017 (global graph, IPv4).

We further investigate this by selecting the eight most dominant ASes found in our dataset and monitor their yearly AS hegemony (Fig. 4). The AS hegemony for these networks is indeed either steady, or increasing, which is contradictory with the global Internet flattening observed earlier. These two observations provide evidences of dense connectivity at the edge of the Internet but the role of large transit ISP is still very central to connect remote places in the Internet. This can be explained by the growth of public peering facilities (IXP) that allows regional networks to keep traffic locally and peer directly with content providers. Yet transiting to remote locations requires the international networks of tier-1 ISPs. In recent years this distinction between tier-1 ISP and other networks is event more visible, as we observe in Fig. 3a a clear gap between most networks ($\mathcal{H} < 0.03$) and tier-1 ISPs ($\mathcal{H} > 0.05$).

Figure 4 also depicts the dominance of Level(3) through the entire study period. After Level(3) acquisition of Global Crossing (AS3549) in 2011, it reached in 2012 the highest AS hegemony score monitored for the IPv4 global graph ($\mathcal{H} = 0.19$). We also found that from 2008 to 2010 Global Crossing was the most dominant AS in Level(3) local graph, meaning that it was the most common transit network to reach Level(3). These results thus assert that Global Crossing acquisition was the most effective way for Level(3) to attain new customers. It also illustrates the benefits of our tools for deployment and business decisions.

For IPv6 (Fig. 3b) we observe a faster Internet flattening than for IPv4. We hypothesize that this is mainly because the Internet topology for IPv6 in 2007 was quite archaic. But IPv6 has drastically gained in maturity, the AS hegemony distribution for IPv6 in 2017 is then very close to the one for IPv4 in 2009. The most striking difference with IPv4 is the central role played by Hurricane Electric (HE) in the IPv6 topology. After doubling its number of peers in 2009 [8], HE has been clearly dominating the IPv6 space from 2009 onward. It reaches an impressive AS hegemony $\mathcal{H} = 0.46$ in 2017, largely above the second and third highest scores (0.07 and 0.05), respectively, for Level(3) and Telia. Consequently, our tools confirm the dominant position of HE observed previously [4] and permit to systematically quantify the overall IPv6 dependency to HE.

4.2   Case Studies: Local Graphs

Our analysis now focuses on results obtained with local graphs. Unlike the global ones, local graphs shed light to AS dependency only for a specific origin AS. We found that the structure of local graphs is very different depending on the size and peering policies of the origin AS. On average in 2017, an IPv4 local graph contains 98 nodes but 93% of these nodes have an hegemony null ($\mathcal{H} = 0$). Typically ASes hosting BGP peers have an hegemony null and AS hegemony scores increases as the paths converge towards the origin AS. Thereby, the upstream provider of a single-homed origin AS gets the maximum hegemony score, $\mathcal{H} = 1$. By definition the origin AS of each local graph also features $\mathcal{H} = 1$, therefore, we are not reporting the AS hegemony of the origin AS in the following results.

In 2017, local graphs have on average 5 ASes with $\mathcal{H} > 0.01$, which usually corresponds to a set of upstream providers and tier-1 ASes. We also noticed interesting graphs containing no dominant AS, and other graphs containing numerous nodes with non-negligible AS hegemony scores. To illustrate this we pick a local graph from both end of the spectrum, namely, AS20940 from Akamai and AS15169 from Google.

Akamai and Google: The IPv4 graph for Akamai's main network, AS20940, is the local graph with the largest number of nodes in our results. In 2017, it contains on average 30 nodes with an AS hegemony greater than 0.01 (see Fig. 5a). Meaning that accessing Akamai IP space relies on a large set of transit networks. This is true for our entire analysis period as shown in Fig. 5a. Our manual inspection of Akamai BGP announcements reveals that Akamai is heavily fragmenting

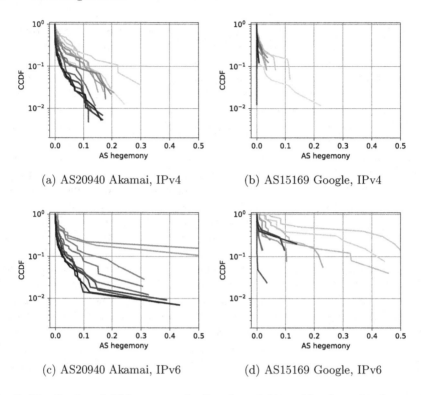

(a) AS20940 Akamai, IPv4

(b) AS15169 Google, IPv4

(c) AS20940 Akamai, IPv6

(d) AS15169 Google, IPv6

Fig. 5. Distribution of AS hegemony for Google and Akamai local graphs. Same color scale as Fig. 3.

its IP space and advertising small prefixes at various Points of Presence (PoPs). Consequently, each prefix is accessible only through a very limited number of upstream providers and all BGP peers report AS paths going through these providers. In summary, Akamai local graph contains a lot of nodes with weak but non-negligible AS hegemony scores implying that Akamai has numerous weak AS-dependencies.

On the other hand, the IPv4 graph for Google (AS15169) in 2017 contains no node with an hegemony greater than 0.01 (see Fig. 5b). Our manual inspection of Google BGP advertisements reveals that, unlike Akamai, Google announces all their prefixes at each PoP. Because Google is peering at numerous places, all BGP peers report very short and different AS paths with almost no AS in common hence no relevant hegemony score. Nonetheless, Google's local graphs before 2012 feature a different AS hegemony distribution with a few high AS hegemony scores (Fig. 5b). Level(3) is the most dominant AS observed until 2012. But then Google has clearly succeeded to bypass Level(3) and alleviate its dependency to this AS (usually $\mathcal{H} < 0.00005$ from 2014). Now Level(3) is rarely seen in paths towards Google. In summary, we observe that Google used to depend on a few ASes but it is now mostly independent from all ASes. This is not an isolated case, we measured no AS dependency for a few other ASes, notably, Microsoft (AS8075), Level(3) (AS3356), HE (AS6939), and Verisign (AS7342).

For IPv6, the situations for Akamai and Google are a bit different. The local graph for Akamai contains a lot of nodes with a high AS hegemony (Fig. 5c). But HE is quite outstanding and features an AS hegemony ($\mathcal{H} = 0.43$) very close to the one observed for HE in the IPv6 global graph (Fig. 3b). HE is also the dominant node in Google's IPv6 local graph (Fig. 5d) but at a much lower magnitude ($\mathcal{H} = 0.12$). Thereby, our results show that Google's aggressive peering policy has partially succeeded to bypass HE ubiquitous IPv6 network.

DNS root servers: Monitoring an AS with our tools provides valuable insights into its AS dependency. This is particularly useful for networks hosting critical infrastructure, as operators of these ASes try to minimize their dependencies to third-party networks. To illustrate the benefits of our tools, we present results for the local graphs of ASes hosting DNS root servers. Notice that understanding AS dependency of root servers is usually a complicated task as most root servers are using anycast and more than 500 instances are deployed worldwide. Due to space constrains, we detail only IPv4 results for networks hosting the F-root (AS3557) and B-root (AS394353) servers as they had significant structural changes in 2017.

In early 2017, we observe three dominant transit ASes for the network hosting the F-root server (Fig. 6a). AS30132 and AS1280 are direct upstream networks managed by ISC, the administrator of the F-root server. AS6939 is HE, the main provider for AS1280, and is found in about a third of the AS paths toward the F-root server. From March, Cloudflare (AS13335) starts providing connectivity to new F-root instances [7]. This new infrastructure is clearly visible in our results. Starting from March 2017, Cloudflare hegemony is fluctuating around 0.2 and seems to divert traffic from other instances as the three other transit networks have their hegemony proportionally decreased. From these results we deduce that the addition of Cloudflare has successfully reduced F-root dependencies on other ASes.

For the B-root server (Fig. 6b), we observe two dominant ASes in January and February 2017, Los Nettos (AS226) and NTT America (AS2914). Los Nettos reaches $\mathcal{H} = 1$ because at that time the B-root server was unicasted and Los Nettos was the sole provider. NTT also has a very high AS hegemony score, in fact more than 80% of analyzed AS paths also cross NTT's network. From March 2017, we observe two other transit nodes AMPATH (AS20080) and HE (AS6939). Our manual inspection of the advertised paths reveals that a single /24 prefix is advertised with AMPATH as the first hop and usually HE as the second hop. This prefix is one of the two /24 prefixes advertised by the network hosting the B-root server (AS394353) but is not the one containing the server IP address. We believe that B-root operators were testing anycast in preparation for the deployment of the second instance of B-root at Miami that happened in May [14]. In May we acknowledge the deployment of the second instance hosted at AMPATH as the hegemony of that AS is raising again and the one for Los Nettos had significantly decreased. From July onward, however, we observe a sudden decrease of AMPATH hegemony while hegemony for Los Nettos is getting back

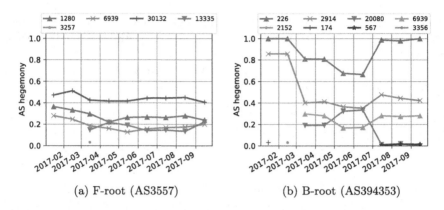

(a) F-root (AS3557)   (b) B-root (AS394353)

Fig. 6. AS hegemony for nodes in F-root (AS3557) and B-root (AS394353) local graphs from 15th January to 15th September 2017.

close to 1. A manual comparison of AS paths in June and July reveals that Los Nettos is trying to fix this by prepending its ASN to paths through HE. Despite these efforts, most of the paths that were transiting through HE and AMPATH in June are replaced by paths going through HE and Los Nettos in July. The addition of the second instance in Miami had uncertain benefits, first, it considerably mitigated the dependence on NTT and Los Nettos networks in May and June, but then, from July Los Nettos is once again totally dominating the B-root connectivity. Results for IPv6 are quite different, after the deployment in Miami we observe higher hegemony values for AMPATH. Both the IPv4 and IPv6 observations have been confirmed by the B-root operators.

Future directions: The structural changes observed for the F and B root servers illustrate the value of AS hegemony to monitor significant routing events. We are now designing an automated detection process to identify significant changes in AS hegemony scores. This detector reports sudden routing changes such as the recent BGP leak from Google [16]. During this event Google became a transit provider for NTT OCN, which exhibits a sudden and significant increase in Google's AS hegemony for NTT's local graph. Thanks to AS hegemony detecting this type of event is fairly easy, while state of the art tools employed by network operators (e.g. BGPmon provided by OpenDNS) have usually missed this significant event. As the details and evaluation of this detector go beyond the scope of this paper we leave this for future work.

In the future we are also planning to investigate different weighting schemes. For example by assigning paths' weight based on traffic volume an ISP can emphasize destinations that are favored by its customers.

5   Conclusions

We presented a methodology to quantify the AS interdependency in the Internet. It deals with the various AS paths reported via BGP and produce AS hegemony scores, that are robust estimates of the ASes centrality. Using 14 years of BGP data we proved that this method permits to monitor structural changes in the Internet and identify most important ASes to reach a certain part of the IP space. We also demonstrated with case studies the benefits of our tools to help ISPs to plan and assess infrastructure deployment. To assist network operators in these tasks we make our tools and results publicly available [1].

References

1. AS Hegemony Results (2017). http://ihr.iijlab.net/ihr/hegemony/
2. Cittadini, L., Muhlbauer, W., Uhlig, S., Bush, R., François, P., Maennel, O.: Evolution of internet address space deaggregation: myths and reality. IEEE JSAC 8(28), 1238–1249 (2010)
3. Comarela, G., Terzi, E., Crovella, M.: Detecting unusually-routed ases: methods and applications. In: IMC, pp. 445–459. ACM (2016)
4. Dhamdhere, A., Luckie, M., Huffaker, B., Elmokashfi, A., Aben, E., et al.: Measuring the deployment of ipv6: topology, routing and performance. In: IMC, pp. 537–550. ACM (2012)
5. Fontugne, R., Shah, A., Aben, E.: As hegemony: a robust metric for as centrality. In: Proceedings of the SIGCOMM Posters and Demos, pp. 48–50. ACM (2017)
6. Gamba, J., Fontugne, R., Pelsser, C., Bush, R., Aben, E.: BGP table fragmentation: what & who? In: CoRes (2017)
7. Grant, D.: Delivering Dot (2017). https://blog.cloudflare.com/f-root/
8. Pan, E.H.: Gigabit/ATM Monthly Newsletter. Information Gatekeepers Inc., November 2009
9. Karlin, J., Forrest, S., Rexford, J.: Nation-state routing: censorship, wiretapping, and BGP. CoRR, abs/0903.3218 2009
10. Lee, S.H., Kim, P.-J., Jeong, H.: Statistical properties of sampled networks. Phys. Rev. E **73**, 016102 (2006)
11. Liu, Y., Luo, X., Chang, R.K., Su, J.: Characterizing inter-domain rerouting by betweenness centrality after disruptive events. IEEE JSAC **31**(6), 1147–1157 (2013)
12. Mahadevan, P., Krioukov, D., Fomenkov, M., Dimitropoulos, X., Claffy, K.C., Vahdat, A.: The internet as-level topology: three data sources and one definitive metric. In: SIGCOMM CCR, vol. 36(1), pp. 17–26 (2006)
13. Orsini, C., King, A., Giordano, D., Giotsas, V., Dainotti, A.: BGPstream: a software framework for live and historical BGP data analysis. In: IMC, pp. 429–444. ACM (2016)
14. Root Operators. B-Root Begins Anycast in May (2017). http://root-servers.org/news/b-root-begins-anycast-in-may.txt
15. Schuchard, M., Mohaisen, A., Foo Kune, D., Hopper, N., Kim, Y., Vasserman, E.Y.: Losing control of the internet: using the data plane to attack the control plane. In: CCS, pp. 726–728. ACM (2010)
16. Toonk, A.: BGP leak causing Internet outages in Japan and beyond, August 2017. https://bgpmon.net/bgp-leak-causing-internet-outages-in-japan-and-beyond/
17. Wählisch, M., Schmidt, T.C., de Brün, M., Häberlen, T.: Exposing a nation-centric view on the german internet – a change in perspective on AS-Level. In: Taft, N., Ricciato, F. (eds.) PAM 2012. LNCS, vol. 7192, pp. 200–210. Springer, Heidelberg (2012). https://doi.org/10.1007/978-3-642-28537-0_20
18. Zhou, S., Mondragón, R.J.: Accurately modeling the internet topology. Phys. Rev. E **70**(6), 066108 (2004)

Revealing the Load-Balancing Behavior of YouTube Traffic on Interdomain Links

Ricky K. P. Mok[1]([⊠])(iD), Vaibhav Bajpai[2], Amogh Dhamdhere[1],
and K. C. Claffy[1]

[1] CAIDA, UCSD, San Diego, USA
{cskpmok,amogh,kc}@caida.org
[2] Technische Universität München, Munich, Germany
bajpaiv@in.tum.de

Abstract. For the last decade, YouTube has consistently been a dominant source of traffic on the Internet. To improve the quality of experience
(QoE) for YouTube users, broadband access providers and Google apply
techniques to load balance the extraordinary volume of web requests
and traffic. We use traceroute-based measurement methods to infer
these techniques for assigning YouTube requests to specific Google video
content caches, including the interconnection links between the access
providers and Google. We then use a year of measurements (mid-2016 to
mid-2017) collected from SamKnows probes hosted by broadband customers spanning a major ISP in the U.S. and three ISPs in Europe.
We investigate two possible causes of different interdomain link usage
behavior. We also compare the YouTube video cache hostnames and IPs
observed by the probes, and find that the selection of video cache has
little impact on BGP selection of interdomain links.

1 Introduction

Over a billion users collectively watch billions of hours of videos every day [25],
making Google's YouTube the most popular video streaming web service on
the Internet. The tremendous growth in volume of users and video content has
occurred in parallel with – and as a key driver of – the development and improvement of broadband infrastructure around the world. Indeed, many consumers
have canceled their cable television subscriptions in favor of media services such
as YouTube or Netflix available over the Internet. Accompanying this evolution
are growing performance expectations of users – that the streaming video quality
of experience should match that of cable television, a service historically provided over a dedicated private network infrastructure. In parallel, the evolution
of video technologies, such as 8K resolution, 60 frame per second (fps), and High
Dynamic Range (HDR), has increased the network bandwidth requirement and
has further challenged network provisioning economics.

ISPs can coordinate (contracts) with Google to install Google Global Caches
(GGCs) inside their networks, and can also rely on their peering relationships

© Springer International Publishing AG, part of Springer Nature 2018
R. Beverly et al. (Eds.): PAM 2018, LNCS 10771, pp. 228–240, 2018.
https://doi.org/10.1007/978-3-319-76481-8_17

with Google (AS 15169/AS 36040) to connect users to Google/YouTube front-end servers and video caches inside Google's Points of Presence (PoPs). Many of these interdomain links are of significant and growing capacity, but they can still experience congestion during peak hours [17] that may induce inflated round-trip delay and packet losses, and thus degrade user QoE.

We report the results of a study that combines interdomain topology measurement and YouTube-specific probing measurements to investigate performance-relevant traffic dynamics of ISPs that do not deploy GGCs. We inferred interdomain router-level topology by executing the bdrmap [18] tool on ∼50 of CAIDA's Archipelago (Ark) probes [7]. We used a recently developed end-to-end YouTube performance test [3] that streams a video clip similar to a normal client, and reports information including the hostname and IP address of the YouTube video cache (GGC) streaming the video. The test then immediately performs a paris-traceroute [4] toward that IP to capture the forward path information. The test ran on ∼100 SamKnows probes [6] for about a year (May 2016 to July 2017) [5]. We selected the SamKnows probes connected to ISPs that did not deploy GGCs internally, but whose interdomain topology to Google was captured by our bdrmap measurements. This constraint limited our study to 15 SamKnows probes connected to four major ISPs: 1 in the U.S., 3 in Europe.

Our study had two major goals. The first one was to investigate factors that influence ISP strategies for distributing YouTube traffic flows across different interdomain links. We studied two possible factors – geographic location and time of day. We developed a metric of *link usage probability* to characterize the link usage behavior observed by our probes. Our results revealed that geographic location appeared to influence interdomain link assignment for Comcast users, i.e., proximate users were more likely to use the same set of links to reach a cache. We also found that a German ISP (Kabel Deutschland) showed different link usage behavior during peak vs. off-peak hours; other ISPs did not show such a significant difference. By analyzing the interdomain topology, we also discovered three European ISPs that relied on the YouTube AS (AS 36040) rather than the primary Google AS (AS 15169) to reach YouTube content. Our second goal was to study whether YouTube's cache selection approach could also determine the choice of interdomain links due to the topological location of the cache. We did not observe such a correspondence; more than half of the video caches we observed used at least two interdomain links. We also discovered that the DNS namespace for YouTube video caches (*.googlevideo.com) had a more static hostname-IP mapping than front-end hostnames (e.g., youtube.com and google.com), which used DNS-based redirection [8]. 90% of video cache hostnames were reported (by the probes) to have the same IP, even if they were resolved by different probes.

Section 2 presents related work on YouTube measurement. Sections 3, 4, and 5 describes our datasets and methodology, reports our findings, and offers conclusions, respectively.

2   Related Work

Previous studies have evaluated the architecture or characteristics of YouTube by actively sending video requests. Pytomo [22] crawled YouTube video clips from residential broadband (volunteer) hosts, and collected YouTube server information including hostname and network throughput. They found that the YouTube cache selection depended on user's ISP rather than geographical proximity. Adhikari *et al.* [2] dissected the architecture of YouTube by requesting video clips from PlanetLab nodes. To increase the coverage, they exploited various geographically distributed public DNS servers to trigger DNS-based redirection in YouTube front-end servers. Recent studies [8,10] used the EDNS extension to geolocate Google's CDN infrastructure. A closely related work by Windisch [24] deployed five monitors in a German ISP and parsed YouTube responses to analyze selection of video caches. These studies did not investigate interdomain link structure, which could impact latency and streaming performance. Our study fills this gap by integrating interdomain topology and end-to-end measurement to understand the ISP's role in load balancing YouTube traffic.

Others have used passive measurement to study YouTube traffic, including analyzing traffic characteristics of video flows [12,13] and cache selection mechanisms [23]. Casas *et al.* [9] used a 90-h `Tstat` trace to contrast YouTube traffic characteristics between fixed-line and mobile users. YouLighter [14] used passive monitoring to learn the structure of YouTube's CDN and automatically detect changes. Because passive measurement relies on user traffic, it is hard to perform a longitudinal study from the same set of clients to observe changes in load balancing across interdomain links over time.

3   Methodology

We deployed the YouTube test [3] on ~100 SamKnows probes connected to dual-stacked networks representing 66 different origin ASes [5]. The probes were mostly within the RIPE (60 probes) and ARIN (29) region, and hosted in home networks (78). The YouTube test ran once per hour for IPv4 and then for IPv6. Each test streamed a popular video from YouTube, and reported the streaming information and performance, including start-up delay, YouTube cache hostname and IP. We then ran `paris-traceroute` [4] with `scamper` [16] toward the cache IP reported by the YouTube test, obtaining forward path and latency measurements. Details of the YouTube tests and SamKnows probe measurements are in [3] and [5], respectively.

To identify which interdomain links (if any) were traversed on the paths from our SamKnows probes to YouTube servers, we first compiled the set of interdomain interconnections of the access network visible from a vantage point (VP) in that network. We used `bdrmap` [18], an algorithm that infers interdomain interconnections of a VP network visible from that VP. In the collection phase, `bdrmap` issues traceroutes from the VP toward every routed BGP prefix, and performs alias resolution from the VP on IP addresses seen in these traceroutes.

In the analysis phase, **bdrmap** uses the collected topology data along with AS-relationship inferences from CAIDA's AS relationship algorithm [19], and a list of address blocks belonging to IXPs obtained from PeeringDB [21] and PCH [20] to infer interdomain links at the router level. The **bdrmap** algorithm then uses constraints from traceroute paths to infer ownership of each observed router, and identifies the routers on the *near* and *far* side (from the perspective of the VP) of every observed router-level interdomain link. We could not run **bdrmap** from the SamKnows probes, so we used the results of **bdrmap** running on Ark VPs located in the same ASes as the SamKnows probes.

3.1   Identifying Interdomain Links from YouTube Dataset

The first step of identifying interdomain links seen in our YouTube traceroutes is to extract all the interdomain links to the Google ASes (AS 15169/AS 36040) observed by Ark VPs. Each link is represented by a pair of IP addresses indicating the interfaces of the near and far side routers. We used these pairs to match consecutive hops in the traceroutes to YouTube video caches. This approach avoids false inference of links, but could miss some links with the same far side IP but a near side IP that **bdrmap** did not observe, because **bdrmap** and the YouTube traceroutes run from different VPs. Section 4.1 describes why we consider our coverage of interdomain links to be satisfactory.

The next step is to aggregate pairs with the same far side IP, because different VPs in the same network may take different paths before exiting via the same interdomain link; in such cases, they likely observe different addresses (aliases) on the near router. Even though **bdrmap** has performed some IP alias resolution, multiple links may connect the same near and far side routers. We resolve this ambiguity by conducting additional IP alias resolution with MIDAR [15] on these far side IPs. Table 1 shows the number of inferred interconnection links at each stage.

Table 1. Number of identified interdomain links at each stage.

Stages	Number of links
Interdomain links to Google inferred by **bdrmap**	1,268
Links identified in YouTube traceroutes	468
Aggregated with far side IPs	61
IP alias resolution with MIDAR	45

3.2   Descriptive Statistics

We analyzed data collected from May 17, 2016 to July 4, 2017, which included a gap in data between January 4, 2017 and February 15, 2017 for all probes due to technical problems. The data includes more than 74,000 experiment sessions/traceroute records, collected from 15 SamKnows probes connected to 4 broadband ISPs in the United States and Europe. We only used a small subset of the entire YouTube traceroute dataset in our study, constrained by our needs for: (1) co-located Ark VPs in the same ISP to obtain `bdrmap` coverage, and (2) ISPs without GGC deployment internal to their network. The YouTube test collected more than 3,000 distinct video cache hostnames and IPs. Table 2 shows the details of the combined dataset. We adopt the notation #XX to represent SamKnows probes. The number (XX) matches the probe ID in the metadata of the SamKnows probes listed in (https://goo.gl/E2m22J).

Table 2. Summary of the combined dataset.

ISP		Comcast	Kabel[a]	Italia[b]	Free
Country		US	DE	IT	FR
No. of SamKnows probes		12	1	1	1
No. of interdomain links with Google		26	5	10	4
No. of observed video caches by	Hostname	2,918	303	183	176
	IP	2,983	300	185	185

The full company name: [a]Vodafone Kabel Deutschland;
[b]Telecom Italia Sparkle S.p.A.

4 Results

We analyzed load balancing behavior on both the ISP and server side, by characterizing the use of interdomain links and the video cache assignment. These choices are interdependent, since ISPs route YouTube requests according to the IP address of the video cache assigned by YouTube. We attempted to isolate these two behaviors and investigate them separately. We investigated the impact of two factors – geographic location and time of day. We also used hostnames and IP addresses of YouTube caches to estimate the influence of YouTube's video cache selection mechanism on interdomain paths traversed by YouTube requests.

4.1 Interconnection Between ISPs and Google

Consistent with public data [21], we observed multiple interdomain links connecting ISPs to Google in various locations. Figure 1(a) and (b) are two heatmaps showing the interdomain links used by probes in Comcast and the three European ISPs, respectively. Each row represents a SamKnows probe; changing colors on a row represent changing interdomain links. The YouTube tests and traceroutes execute once per hour, so the time resolution of each cell in a row is 1 h. Gray color indicates no data available. Apart from the blackout period, some probes began probing after the measurement period starts (e.g., #89 and #96) or went offline. White color indicates the probe was online, but we could not identify an interdomain link discovered by `bdrmap` measurement from the traceroute. For Comcast, which hosts multiple Ark VPs, we identified an interdomain link in 83.4% of traceroutes. For ISP Free (#71) and Italia (#43), we identified an interdomain link in only 40.2% and 77.7% of traceroutes, respectively. The large white portion in #02 after February 2017 was caused by relocation of the probe from a Kabel user to a M-net (another German ISP) user. Ark did not have any VP in the M-net network.

We found that each probe used at least 2 interdomain links throughout the measurement period. Some probes (e.g., #78, #43) observed more than 6 links. Load balancing among links was frequent, reflected by a change in color over time. Although not clearly visible in the heatmap, we observed some monitors cease using a link that other monitors continued to use, suggesting another reason for the switch than a link outage. We observed only one link (light blue color) captured by five monitors (#27, #67, #44, #60, #32) that switched entirely to

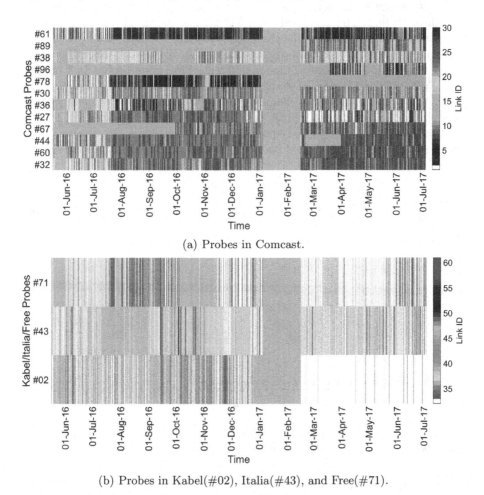

(a) Probes in Comcast.

(b) Probes in Kabel(#02), Italia(#43), and Free(#71).

Fig. 1. Observed interdomain links against time. Changing colors represents the switching of interdomain links. (Color figure online)

another link (darker blue) after mid-February 2017. The set of links used by two different monitors differed widely, even in the same ISP. For example, there was no intersection of links between #61 and #44, unlike #44 and #32.

We systematically studied the assignment of interdomain links to probes by computing the probability of observing each link by the probes. We define the *link usage probability*, P_l^b as

$$P_l^b = \frac{n_l^b}{\sum_{\forall i \in \mathbb{L}} n_i^b}, \tag{1}$$

where $\mathbb{L}$ is the set of all 45 interdomain links observed in our data, n_l^b is the number of observations of link l by probe b. Higher values indicate higher probability for the probe to use that link.

Due to space limitation we show results of only six representative probes (including 38 links and all 4 ISPs) in Fig. 2. The x-axis of the figure shows different interdomain links, while the y-axis indicates the link usage probability (log scale). Different color bars distinguish results of the six probes. The gray dotted vertical lines separate links of different ISPs. Four probes in Comcast (#61, #38, #78, #44) showed slight overlap in interdomain link use (e.g., Link ID 2 and 8). Three probes in Comcast (#38, #78, #44) showed comparable probability of using at least 2 links, indicating load balancing behavior. Probes #02, #43, and #71 distribute requests to at most 10 links. To demystify the assignment of links, we examined two possible factors: geographical location and time of day.

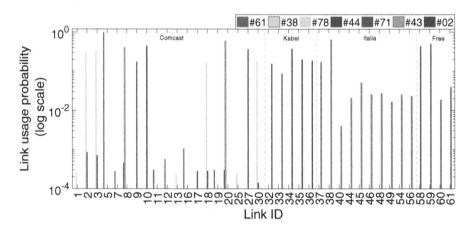

Fig. 2. Link usage probability of 6 probes. Each ISP employs at least two interdomain links to load balance the traffic to video caches. (Color figure online)

Geographic Location. The first factor to study is the relationship between geographic location of probes and the use of interdomain links. Figure 1(a) shows that different probes in Comcast showed similar/dissimilar behavior in terms of link use. We investigated this sharing of interdomain links among probes.

We characterize this behavior by computing a *link usage probability vector*, $\boldsymbol{P^b} = <P_1^b, P_2^b, ..., P_i^b>, \forall i \in \mathbb{L}$, for each probe. We then performed agglomerative hierarchical clustering in Matlab, and used squared Euclidean distance as a similarity measure between two vectors. We considered only Comcast monitors, because interdomain links will not overlap across ISPs. Figure 3 shows the dendrogram of the resulting five clusters, which reflect the locations of the probes.

The leftmost cluster (red) consists of 6 monitors in the Northeastern U.S. The second cluster (#30) is in the Southeastern U.S. The remaining three clusters are in northern central, southwest, and central areas of the U.S., respectively. This clustering is consistent with the goal of reducing latency of requests by routing them across the nearest interconnection.

Time of Day. Another important factor is time of day, because ISPs or YouTube can employ different load balancing strategies during peak hours. We adopted the "7 p.m. to 11 p.m." definition of the peak usage hour from the FCC Broadband America Report [11], and recomputed the link usage probability for peak and off-peak hours. The German ISP (Kabel) showed a significant difference in terms of link usage probability in the two time periods. Figure 4 shows the five interdomain links observed by probe #02. During the off-peak hours, the five links were somewhat evenly utilized. In the peak hours, only three of the five links were significantly used. The link usage probability of the three links increased 5% to 15% relative to off-peak hours. For the other ISPs, we did not find significant differences in link usage (not to be confused with utilization!) between peak and off peak hours.

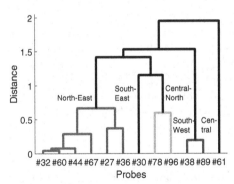

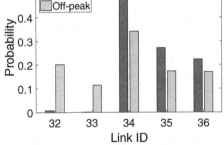

Fig. 3. Dendrogram for hierarchical clustering of Comcast probes. (Color figure online)

Fig. 4. The link usage probability of Kabel (#02) during peak/off-peak hours.

4.2   Destination Google AS

According to [1], ISPs can establish peering with Google on two ASes—AS 15169 and AS 36040. The former is the most common option and can access all Google services and content, while the latter provides only the most popular content and is not available at all IXPs [1]. Table 3 shows the link usage probability according to the destination AS of the links. Values in brackets are the number of links in the respective categories.

Table 3. Link usage probability (number of interdomain links) to Google ASes.

Google AS	Comcast	Kabel	Italia	Free
15169	0.99 (25)	0.76 (3)	0.16 (6)	0.04 (1)
36040	0.0001 (1)	0.24 (2)	0.84 (4)	0.94 (2)
43515	0	0	0	0.02 (1)

Comcast mostly connects users to Google with AS 15169. For the other three ISPs in Europe, load balancing with AS 36040 is more common. ISP Italia has more interdomain links peering with AS 15169, but accesses YouTube caches mainly using AS 36040. This arrangement could be for historical reasons, because AS 36040 was assigned to YouTube before the merger (Today, the AS name is still 'YouTube'). For the German ISP Kabel, we found that the links (Link ID 32 and 33) mostly used in the off-peak hours (see Fig. 4) were peering with AS 36040, while the remaining three links were peering with AS 15169.

Interestingly, we found that ISP Free connected users to Google with AS 43515 between Jun 1, 2016 and Aug 17, 2016. Google currently manages this AS for its core network but not for peering purposes [1]. These YouTube test sessions were assigned to video caches with IP prefix (208.117.224.0/19), announced by AS 43515. We believe that the purpose of this AS recently changed. Some video caches were still assigned to AS 43515 during that time period, but now no longer responded to ICMP ping, as other caches did. This example illustrates that ISPs may have different preferences in engineering traffic to and from Google ASes.

4.3   Video Cache Assignment

YouTube mainly employs two techniques to load balance requests, namely DNS-based redirection and HTTP-based redirection. DNS-based redirection assigns users to a front-end server according to the DNS server making the querying [8,10]. These front-end servers, apart from serving static web elements on youtube.com, are responsible for assigning users to video caches hosted under the domain *.googlevideo.com. In some cases, the video content is not available in the assigned video cache (cache miss), Google uses HTTP-based redirection to redirect users to another cache using HTTP response status code 302.

We investigated whether the video caches selected by the front-end server considered the use of interdomain links. Our YouTube measurements captured more than 3,000 hostnames and IPs of video caches. The SamKnows probes resolved these hostnames with their default list of DNS servers, during each YouTube measurement. We found that around 90% of the hostnames mapped to a single IP address, except a special hostname (`redirector.googlevideo.com`) designed for handling cache misses. This result indicated that DNS-based redirection is not common for hostnames of Google's video caches.

To study the mechanism of video cache selection method, we compared video cache hostnames and IPs between any two probes. In Sect. 4.1 we described how user geographic location appears to influence selection of interdomain link. If Google uses video cache selection to engineer the desired use of specific interdomain links, the front-end servers will likely direct nearby probes to a similar set of caches. Figure 5 depicts the overlapping in video cache hostname/IP mappings for any two monitors, with probes (rows) sorted according to the clustering results in Fig. 3. The lower/upper triangular part of the matrix compares the hostnames/IPs collected by the two probes, respectively. The triangular symmetry is a reflection of the largely one-to-one mapping between IPs and hostnames. From the similarity of the use of interdomain links, we expect nearby probes (e.g., #32, #60, and #44) should share a similar set of video caches (i.e., many over-

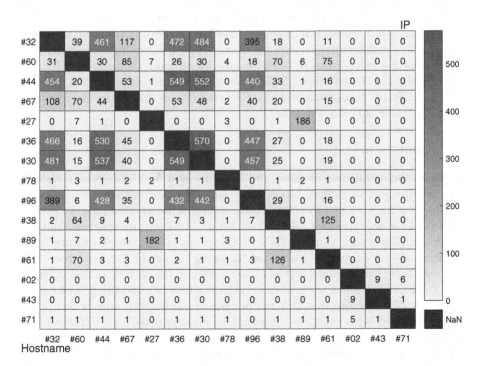

Fig. 5. Number of overlapping Hostnames and IPs across all probes. Probes showed similar interdomain link usage behavior did not show the same degree of similarity in video cache selection.

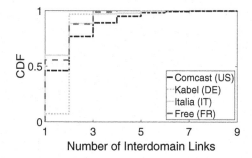

Fig. 6. The CDFs of the number of links used to reach the same video cache IP. Multiple links are used to access the same video caches.

lapping IPs or hostnames). However, the two probes with the highest similarity (#32 and #60) had fewer than 40 overlapping IP/hostname pairs. Surprisingly, probes #32 and #30 had the most such IP/hostname pairs. These two Comcast probes were around 1,500 km apart. There was no overlapping interdomain links among ISPs, but we observed 16 cross-ISP overlapping video cache IPs between Italia (#43) and Free (#71). Given these dissimilar patterns with the use of interdomain links we presented in previous sections, we believe that video cache selection did incorporate any interdomain link preference.

ISPs can also balance YouTube workload by distributing traffic to the same video cache via different interdomain links. In our measurements, around half of the YouTube video cache IPs were accessed with more than one interdomain link (Fig. 6). For Kabel, about 90% of the video caches were reached with at least two different links, suggesting that access ISPs are heavily involved in load balancing traffic to/from YouTube.

5   Conclusion

We used topological measurement and inference and YouTube-specific end-to-end measurement to explore how Google and ISPs perform load balancing of YouTube traffic. By incorporating interdomain link information, we discovered that ISPs play an important role in distributing YouTube traffic across multiple interdomain links that connect ISPs to Google infrastructure. Unsurprisingly, location and time-of-day influence load balancing behaviors. For the server side, our analysis of DNS bindings between hostnames and IPs of video caches suggests that YouTube front-end servers select video caches by controlling hostnames, rather than DNS-redirection. We further observed that the same video cache can be accessed with multiple interdomain links, and the varied patterns of such links across different access ISPs suggests that ISPs, rather than Google, play a primary role in balancing YouTube request load across their interdomain links toward Google. In the future, we plan to investigate the impact of load balancing behavior on video streaming performance and its correlation to user-reported QoE.

Acknowledgment. This work was partly funded by the European Union's Horizon 2020 research and innovation programme 2014–2018 under grant agreement No. 644866, Scalable and Secure Infrastructures for Cloud Operations (SSICLOPS), and by U.S. National Science Foundation CNS-1414177. This work represents only the position of the authors, and not of funding agencies.

References

1. Google edge network. https://peering.google.com/. Accessed 11 Oct 2017
2. Adhikari, V.K., Jain, S., Chen, Y., Zhang, Z.-L.: Vivisecting YouTube: an active measurement study. In: IEEE INFOCOM (2012)
3. Ahsan, S., Bajpai, V., Ott, J., Schönwälder, J.: Measuring YouTube from dual-stacked hosts. In: PAM (2015)
4. Augustin, B., Teixeira, R., Friedman, T.: Measuring load-balanced paths in the Internet. In: ACM IMC (2007)
5. Bajpai, V., Ahsan, S., Schönwälder, J., Ott, J.: Measuring YouTube content delivery over IPv6. In: ACM SIGCOMM CCR (2017)
6. Bajpai, V., Schönwälder, J.: A survey on internet performance measurement platforms and related standardization efforts. IEEE Commun. Surv. Tutor. **17**(3), 1313–1341 (2015)
7. CAIDA: Archipelago (Ark) measurement infrastructure. http://www.caida.org/projects/ark/
8. Calder, M., Fan, X., Hu, Z., Katz-Bassett, E., Heidemann, J., Govindan, R.: Mapping the expansion of Google's serving infrastructure. In: ACM IMC (2013)
9. Casas, P., Fiadino, P., Bar, A., D'Alconzo, A., Finamore, A., Mellia, M.: YouTube all around: characterizing YouTube from mobile and fixed-line network vantage points. In: EuCNC (2014)
10. Fan, X., Katz-Bassett, E., Heidemann, J.: Assessing affinity between users and CDN sites. In: IFIP TMA (2015)
11. FCC: Measuring broadband America fixed broadband report, December 2016. https://www.fcc.gov/reports-research/reports/measuring-broadband-america/measuring-fixed-broadband-report-2016. Accessed 15 Oct 2017
12. Finamore, A., Mellia, M., Munafò, M.M., Torres, R., Rao, S.G.: YouTube everywhere: impact of device and infrastructure synergies on user experience. In: ACM IMC (2011)
13. Gill, P., Arlitt, M., Li, Z., Mahanti, A.: Youtube traffic characterization: a view from the edge. In: ACM IMC (2007)
14. Giordano, D., Traverso, S., Grimaudo, L., Mellia, M., Baralis, E., Tongaonkar, A., Saha, S.: YouLighter: a cognitive approach to unveil YouTube CDN and changes. IEEE Trans. Cognit. Commun. Netw. **1**(2), 161–174 (2015)
15. Keys, K., Hyun, Y., Luckie, M., Claffy, K.: Internet-scale IPv4 alias resolution with MIDAR. IEEE/ACM Trans. Netw. **21**(2), 383–399 (2012)
16. Luckie, M.: Scamper: a scalable and extensible packet prober for active measurement of the Internet. In: ACM IMC (2010)
17. Luckie, M., Dhamdhere, A., Clark, D., Huffaker, B., Claffy, K.C.: Challenges in inferring Internet interdomain congestion. In: ACM IMC (2014)
18. Luckie, M., Dhamdhere, A., Huffaker, B., Clark, D., Claffy, K.C.: bdrmap: inference of borders between IP networks. In: ACM IMC (2016)
19. Luckie, M., Huffaker, B., Dhamdhere, A., Giotsas, V., Claffy, K.C.: AS relationships, customer cones, and validation. In: Proceedings of ACM IMC (2013)

20. Packet Clearing House: Full exchange point dataset (2017). https://prefix.pch.net/applications/ixpdir/menu_download.php
21. PeeringDB (2017). http://www.peeringdb.com
22. Plissonneau, L., Biersack, E., Juluri, P.: Analyzing the impact of YouTube delivery policies on user experience. In: ITC (2012)
23. Torres, R., Finamore, A., Kim, J.R., Mellia, M., Munafo, M.M., Rao, S.: Dissecting video server selection strategies in the YouTube CDN. In: IEEE ICDCS (2011)
24. Windisch, G.: Analysis of the YouTube server selection behavior observed in a large German ISP network. In: EUNICE (2014)
25. YouTube: Youtube for press. https://www.youtube.com/intl/en-GB/yt/about/press/. Accessed 10 Oct 2017

Analyzing Protocols

A Closer Look at IP-ID Behavior in the Wild

Flavia Salutari[✉], Danilo Cicalese, and Dario J. Rossi

Telecom ParisTech, Paris, France
{flavia.salutari,danilo.cicalese,dario.rossi}@telecom-paristech.fr

Abstract. Originally used to assist network-layer fragmentation and reassembly, the IP identification field (IP-ID) has been used and abused for a range of tasks, from counting hosts behind NAT, to detect router aliases and, lately, to assist detection of censorship in the Internet at large. These inferences have been possible since, in the past, the IP-ID was mostly implemented as a simple packet counter: however, this behavior has been discouraged for security reasons and other policies, such as random values, have been suggested.

In this study, we propose a framework to classify the different IP-ID behaviors using active probing from a single host. Despite being only minimally intrusive, our technique is significantly accurate (99% true positive classification) robust against packet losses (up to 20%) and lightweight (few packets suffices to discriminate all IP-ID behaviors). We then apply our technique to an Internet-wide census, where we actively probe one alive target per each routable /24 subnet: we find that the majority of hosts adopts a constant IP-IDs (39%) or local counter (34%), that the fraction of global counters (18%) significantly diminished, that a non marginal number of hosts have an odd behavior (7%) and that random IP-IDs are still an exception (2%).

1 Introduction

The IP identifier (IP-ID) is a 16 (32) bits field in the IPv4 (v6) header [24]. Originally, along with the fragment offset, IP-ID was used to assist packet segmentation and reassembly and it was unique per each combination of source, destination and protocol. Yet, with technology evolution and the adoption of the MTU path discovery [21], IP fragmentation is much less common nowadays, so that the last normative reference [27] allows IP-ID of atomic datagrams to be non-unique. As a consequence, IP-ID fields values are determined by the specific implementation of the Operating System [22]. Over time, different behaviors have been observed such as global and per-flow counters, pseudo-random sequences and constant values [2], as well as odd behaviors such as those due to load balancing [6] middleboxes, or host implementations using the wrong endianness [22]. Given that some of the above implementations maintain state at the IP level, the IP-ID has been widely studied [2,20,26], abused [6,14,15], and more recently used to assist host identification [4,19,22,23].

© Springer International Publishing AG, part of Springer Nature 2018
R. Beverly et al. (Eds.): PAM 2018, LNCS 10771, pp. 243–254, 2018.
https://doi.org/10.1007/978-3-319-76481-8_18

In particular, the majority of research work focus their attention on the *global* counter implementation, which used to be the most common implementation about a decade ago [28]. However, due to recent evolution of the standards [10,27], a wider range of behaviors can be expected nowadays. Given this context, we can summarize our main contributions in this work as:

- we design and implement a lightweight methodology to classify the full range of IP-ID behaviors, based on a handful of ICMP packets
- we carefully validate our method against a dataset comprising about 1,855 sample hosts, for which we built a ground-truth by manual inspection
- we apply the methodology to an Internet-wide campaign, where we classify one alive target per each routable /24 subnet, gathering a full blown picture of the IP-ID adoption in the wild

Specifically, whereas the global counter (18% in our measurement) implementation was the most common a decade ago [28], we find that other behaviors (constant 34% and local counter 39%) are now prevalent. We also find that security recommendations expressed in 2011 [10] are rarely followed (random, 2%). Finally, our census quantifies a non marginal number of hosts (7%) showing evidence of a range of behaviors, that can be traced to poor or non-standard implementations (e.g., bogus endianness; non-standard increments) or network-level techniques (e.g., load balancing, or exogenous traffic intermingled to our probes confusing the classifier). To make our findings useful to a larger extent, we make all our dataset and results available at [1].

2   Background and Related Work

Background. The IP-ID field identifies unique fragments of a packet and it is used to handle the re-assembling process. First documented in the early 80 s by RFC791 [24] its use has been updated in several RFCs [5,8,10,11,27,28]. Whereas [24] does not fully specify IP-ID behavior (i.e., it only states that each packet must have a unique IP-ID for the triplet of source, destination and protocol), different behaviors (namely Global, Local and Random, illustrated in Fig. 1) are detailed in 2006 by RFC4413 [28].

In 2008, RFC5225 [8] observed that some hosts set the IP-ID to *zero*: at the time of [8], this was a not legal implementation as the field was supposed to be unique. Yet, in 2012 [22] observed that the actual IP-ID implementation depends on the specific Operating System (OS) and versions[1]. In 2013, RFC6864 [27] updated the specifications by affirming that the IPv4 ID uniqueness applies to only non-atomic datagrams: in other words, if the don't fragment (DF) bit is set, reassembly is not necessary and hence devices may set the IP-ID to zero.

At the same time, concern has been raised about security problems following the predictability of IP-ID sequences [9,11,13,17]. In particular, in 2012

---

[1] In particular [22] reports Windows and FreeBSD to use a global counter, Linux and MacOS to use local counters and OpenBSD to use pseudo-random IP-IDs.

RFC6274 [10] discouraged the use of a global counter implementation for many security issues, such as stealth port scan to a third (victim) host, and in 2016 RFC7739 [11] addressed concerns concerning IPv6-specific implementations. In light of the recent evolution of the standards, a re-assessment of IP-ID usage in the wild is thus highly relevant.

Related work. Additionally, the IP-ID has been exploited for numerous purposes in the literature. Notably, IP-ID side-channel information helped to discover load balancing server [6], count hosts behind NAT [2,22], measure the traffic [6,14] and detect router alias [3,16,26]. More recently, [19] leverages IP-ID to detect router aliases, or infer router up time [4] and to reveal Internet censorship [23], refueling interest in the study of IP-ID behavior. Whereas the above work [2,6,14,23,26] mostly focus only on the global IP-ID behavior, in this work we not only consider all *expected* IP-ID behavior, but additionally quantify *non-standard* behaviors: in particular, we provide a methodology to accurately classify IP-ID behaviors, that we apply to the Internet at large, gathering a picture of the relative popularity of each IP-ID behavior.

In terms of methodologies, authors in [20] use ICMP timestamp and IP-ID to diagnose paths from the source to arbitrary destinations and find reordering, loss, and queuing delay. In [15], the authors identify out-of-sequence packets in TCP connections that can be the result of different network events such as packet loss, reordering or duplication. In [6], they use HTTP requests from two different machines toward 150 target websites, to discover the number of load-balancing server. Authors in [23] use TCP SYN-ACK from multiple vantage points to identify connectivity disruptions by means of IP-ID fields, which then they use as a building block of a censorship detection framework. In this work, we leverage ICMP traffic (spoofing IPs to craft sequences of packets that are precisely interleaved when they hit the target under observation) to build an accurate, robust and lightweight IP-ID classification technique.

3   Methodology

To provide an accurate and comprehensive account of IP-ID behavior in the wild, we need (i) a reliable classifier, able to discriminate among the different typical and anomalous IP-ID behaviors. At the same time, to enable Internet coverage, (ii) the classifier should rely on features with high discriminative power, extracted from an active probing technique that is as lightweight as possible. In this section we illustrate the practical building blocks and their theoretical foundations, that our classification framework builds upon.

IP-ID classes. From the host perspective, several IP-ID behaviors are possible as depicted in Fig. 1. It shows sequences s of 25 IP-ID samples sent from 2 different host (dark and white) where the packets are sent alternatively to the target. The different behaviors depicted are, from left to right: (i) **constant** counters are never incremented (and for the most part are equal to 0x0000); (ii) **local**

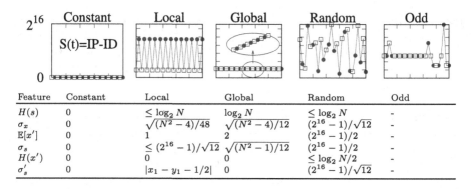

Fig. 1. Illustration of Constant, Local, Global, Random and Odd sequences (top) and tabulated expected values for selected features (bottom)

or per-host counters that are incremented at each new packet arrival for that flow (mostly by 1 unit): as a consequence, while the black or white per-host sub-sequences are monotonically increasing, the aggregate sequence alternates between the two; (iii) **global** counters are incremented by 1 unit (rarely by 2 units) at each new packet arrival for any flow: thus, the sequence s is mono-tonically increasing (by 1 unit), and the black or white per-host sub-sequences are monotonically increasing but at a faster rate (by 2 units); (iv) **random** IP-IDs are extracted according to a pseudo-random number generator. Finally, a special mention is worth for the class of (v) **odd** IP-ID behaviors, that are not systematically documented in the literature and that arise for several reasons (including bugs, misconfiguration, non-standard increments, unforeseen interaction with other network apparatuses, etc.).

Active probing. To gather the above described sequences, our measurement technique relies on active probing. We craft a tool able to send and receive ICMP packets, running at two vantage points (VP) with public IP addresses in our campus network.

Specifically, we send a stream of N ICMP echo requests packets in a *back-to-back* fashion, which forces the target machine to generate consecutive ICMP echo replies: thus, assuming for the time being that no packet were lost, we gather a stream of N IP-IDs samples for that target. Sending packets back-to-back is necessary to reduce the noise in the IP-IDs stream sequence: if probe packets were spaced over time, the sequence could be altered by exogenous traffic hitting the target (e.g., in case of global counter). As a result, the sequence would depend on the (unknown) packet arrival rate in between two consecutive probe packets, likely confusing the classifier [25].

A second observation is that, whereas a single vantage point may be sufficient to distinguish among constant, random and global counters, it would fail to discriminate between global vs local counters. However, sending packets from two different VPs is not advisable, due to the difficulty in precisely synchronizing the sending patterns so that packets from different hosts alternate in the sequence.

Therefore, a better alternative is to receive packets on two different VPs, x and y, but use only one of them, x, as sender: by letting x spoof the address IP_y of the colluding receiver y, it is possible to generate a sequence of *back-to-back packets* that are also *perfectly interleaved* as in Fig. 1. The use of back-to-back packets reduces as much as possible interference with exogenous traffic hitting the same destination, that could otherwise alter the sequences [25]. To identify reordering, packet loss and duplication, we additionally control the sequence number in the stream of generated probe packets.

Features. To build a reliable classifier we need to define features able to discriminate among IP-IDs implementations. We send N packets with the source address alternating between consecutive requests to a given target t, whose replies are sent back to our two VPs x and y: we indicate with s the aggregated sequence comprising N IP-IDs sent back by t, as we receive it at the edge of our network[2]. By abuse of language, we indicate with x and y the sub-sequences (each of length $N/2$) of IP-IDs, sent back by t and received by the homonyms host. From these sequences x, y and s we further construct derivative series x', y' and s' by computing the discrete differences between consecutive IP-IDs (i.e., $x'_i = x_i - x_{i-1}$). We summarize these series with few scalar features by computing the first $\mathbb{E}[\cdot]$ and second moments $\sigma.$ of the IP-ID series, as well as their entropy $H(\cdot)$.

Intuitively, we expect the mean of the constant sequence to be unknown, but its derivative to be null. Similarly, derivative of a global counter would have a value of $1(2)$ for the aggregate sequence s (subsequences x and y). Entropy of the sequence is expected to increase from a minimum of the constant sequence, to a global counter, to local counters, and to be maximum for random sequences. Actually, for each feature we can derive an *expected value* in the ideal[3] case (so that no expected values is reported for the odd class): for lack of space, we do not report the full mathematical details in this paper, that the reader can find in [1], but we summarize the main takeaway in the bottom part of Fig. 1. Specifically, for each of the observed classes shown on the top plots, the expected values for 6 relevant features (namely $H(s), \sigma_x, \mathbb{E}[x'], \sigma_s, H(x'), \sigma'_s$) are tabulated. The specific choice is motivated by the fact that these features happen to have the highest discriminative power, as later shown.

4   IP-ID Classification

From the values tabulated in Fig. 1, we expect classifiers that use this set of features to be able to fully discriminate the set of IP-ID well-defined behaviors under ideal conditions. However, as we shall see, unexpected behavior may arise in the Internet, due to a variety of reasons, which are hard to capture in general.

---

[2] Notice that packet losses and reordering may let us receive less than N packets, or receive packets in a slight different order than what sent by the target. We come back to this issue later on.

[3] Sequences from well behaving hosts that have no software bug or malicious behavior, and that are neither affected by losses nor reordering.

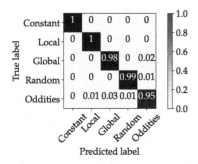 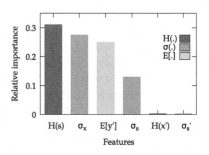

Fig. 2. Validation: (a) Confusion Matrix of 20-fold validation over $\mathcal{G}$ and (b) Relative importance for the most useful features of the classifier.

We thus opt for a *supervised classification* approach, which allows to learn a predictive model with decision trees (DTs), based on the above features. Specifically, we resort to the Classification And Regression Trees (CART) [18], that builds trees having the largest information gain at each node. DTs are part of the *supervised* machine learning algorithms, and infer a classification function from a (i) *labeled* training dataset, that we need to manually build and that is useful for training and validation purposes. Additionally, we investigate (ii) to what extent the classifier is robust against losses, and finally (iii) assess the minimum number of samples N needed to achieve a reliable classification.

Validation. We first train and validate our classifier using a real dataset $\mathcal{G}$ of IP-ID sequences for which we construct a ground truth. For this purpose, we perform a small-scale measurement campaign where we select 2,000 Internet targets and send sequences of $N = 100$ ICMP probes. We include in this dataset only the 1,855 hosts from which we receive 100% of the replies, and perform manual inspection of each of the sequences. We repeat the process twice, with two very different choices of the ground-truth datasets ($\mathcal{G}$ sampled uniformly from the hitlist and $\mathcal{G}'$ where about 75% samples belong to the same IP/8 subnet), paying attention to ensure class balance. Both datasets yield to consistent results: for reason of space, we refer the reader to an extended technical report [25] for further details on the ground truth datasets, which we make available at [1].

Interestingly, we find a small but non marginal fraction (about 7%) of sequences that are hard to classify: a deeper investigation reveals these odd behaviors to be due to a variety of reasons – including per-packet IP-level load balancing, wrong endianness, non standard increments in the global counter, etc. While we cannot completely rule out interference of exogenous traffic altering our IP-ID sequences, lab experiments suggest that the use of back-to-back packets lessen its impact [25]. However, more care is needed to further explore the odd behavior class, which remains an open point. Nevertheless, these samples provide a useful description of the odd class, that would otherwise have been difficult to define. We assess the classification accuracy over $\mathcal{G}$ with a 20-fold cross-validation, whose results are reported in Fig. 2(a) as a confusion matrix:

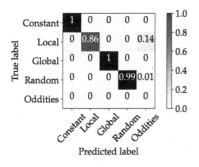
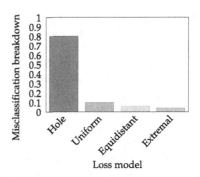

Fig. 3. Robustness: (a) Confusion Matrix of a classifier trained over a real lossless sequence $\mathcal{G}$ and tested over synthetic lossy sequences $\widetilde{S}$ and (b) Misclassification breakdown of the (local, odd) (14%) for the different loss models.

we can observe that the classifier is extremely accurate, with 100% true positive in the constant and local classes, 99% for the random and 98% for the global class. The worst case is represented by 95% true positive for the odd class (that represent only 7% of the samples): these very few misclassifications are erroneously attributed to local, global or random classes, and additional series definition (e.g., to compensate for wrong endianness) could help reducing if needed.

Additionally, Fig. 2(b) depicts the importance for the most useful features of the classifier (that were early tabulated in bottom part of Fig. 1). Four main takeaways can be gathered from the picture: first, just four features are necessary for a full discrimination, which is reasonable as the cardinality of the classes to discriminate is small; second, as expected features that measure the dispersion (entropy and standard deviation) are prevalent; third, both original and derivative sequences are useful in the detection; fourth, subsequence metrics are highly redundant (i.e., $H(x) = H(y)$, $\sigma_x = \sigma_y$, etc.).

Robustness. We next assess the robustness of our classifier against packet losses, which may introduce distortion in the features. Since the expected values in the ideal conditions are significantly apart, we expect the classifier to be resilient to a high degree of losses. For reason of space, we limitedly consider robustness to losses here and refer the reader to [25] for more details. Without loss of generality, we consider an extreme case where only 80 out of 100 samples are correctly received (i.e., a 20% loss rate). While for simple loss patterns (e.g., uniform i.i.d. losses) it is still possible to analytically derive expected values in closed form, for loss models where losses are correlated, this becomes significantly more difficult. As such, we opt for an experimental assessment of classification accuracy in presence of different synthetic loss models, that we apply to synthetic ideal sequences by purposely discarding a part of the sequences. Specifically, we consider: (i) a **uniform** i.i.d. loss model; (ii) a **hole** model where, starting from a random point in the sequence, 20% of consecutive samples are removed;

(iii) an **extreme** model where we remove 20% of the initial values (or equivalently the final 20% of the sequence); and finally (iv) an **equidistant** model where losses start at a random point and are equally spaced over the sequence.

We apply these loss models to obtain a synthetic loss dataset $\widetilde{S}$ and assess the accuracy of the previously validated model, i.e., the one trained on the real lossless dataset $\mathcal{G}$. Specifically, for each loss model we generate 5,000 loss sequence pattern, for an overall of 20,000 test cases. Results of these experiments are reported in Fig. 3. In particular, the confusion matrix reported in Fig. 3(a) shows the aggregated results over all loss models: we can observe that most of the classes have a true positive classification of 99% or 100% even in presence of 20% packet losses, and irrespectively of the actual loss pattern.

Additionally, we observe that in the case of the *local class*, only 86% of the sequences are correctly classified, whereas 14% of the local sequences in presence of heavy losses are erroneously classified as being part of the "odd" behavior class. Figure 3(b) dig further the reasons of this discrepancy, showing that the misclassification mostly happens for the *hole* loss model, while in the other cases is a very rare event. Recalling the odd behavior early shown in the top right plot of Fig. 1, we notice that this model induces a gap in the sequence, which is possibly large enough to be statistically similar to cases such as load balancing, where the sequence alternates among multiple counters.

Overall, we find the classifier to be robust to very high loss rates and, with a single exceptions, also invariant to the actual loss pattern – which is a rather desirable property to operate the classifier into a real Internet environment.

Probing Overhead. We finally assess how large the number of samples N needs to be to have accurate classification results. In principle, features tabulated in Fig. 1 are diverse enough so that we expect high accuracy even for very small values of N.

To assess this experimentally, we take the real lossless dataset $\mathcal{G}$ and only consider that we have at our disposal only $N' < N$ out of the $N = 100$ samples gathered in the experiment. For each value of N', we perform a 20-fold cross validation, training and validating with N' samples. We start from a minimum of $N' = 10$ (i.e., 5 packets per host) up to the maximum of $N = 100$ (i.e., 50 probes per host) samples. Figure 4 clearly shows that accuracy is already very high[4] at 0.95 when $N' = 4$ and exceeds 0.99 when $N = 100$.

At the same time, these results are gathered in the context of an ideal sequence, whose replies are collected in order and without losses. It is intuitive that there is a trade-off between robustness against losses and lightweight: we expect the accuracy to degrade in presence of losses and reordering for short $N < 4$ probe sequences, whose detailed analysis we leave for future work.

---

[4] Notice that even in the extreme case with as few as $N' = 2$ packets, random and constant classification are correctly labeled, whereas the remaining global vs local cannot be discriminated, yielding to 0.70 accuracy in the $\mathcal{G}$ set.

5   Internet Measurement Campaign

Measurement. Finally, we apply our classifier in the wild, and perform a large scale Internet measurement campaign. We want to avoid putting stress on the infrastructure carrying a full Internet census: as we aim at providing an accurate picture of the *relative* popularity of IP-ID implementations on the Internet, it suffices to collect measurements for a large number of targets, namely 1 alive IP/32 host per each /24 prefix. We observe that, while our classifier is able to perform a very accurate classification even with few samples, we need to deal with loss rates, which is unknown a priori. Hence, we prefer for the time being use a simple and conservative approach and select $N = 100$ samples that is very accurate also in presence of very high loss rates. We instead leave the use of an adaptive sample set size (i.e., start with $N = 10$ and re-probe the same target with a larger N only in case of losses) for future work.

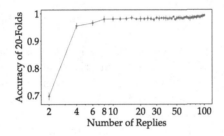

Fig. 4. Lightweight: Accuracy as a function of the sample set size

For the targets selection, we rely on the public available hitlist regularly published by [12], comprising 16 millions of targets IP/32. The hitlist contains targets for all /24, including those who have never been replied to the probing: excluding them from our target list, leaves us with approximately 6 millions of potential targets. To further reduce the amount of probe traffic, we then decide to be even more conservative: we preliminary probe the remaining targets sending two ICMP echo requests, and include in our final target list the approximately 3,2 million responsive hosts (in line with [7,29]).

We send a batch of $N = 100$ back-to-back probe packets to each target, but otherwise probe at a low average rate, so that we complete a /24 census in about 3 days. Figure 5(a) shows the empirical cumulative distribution function (ECDF) of received packets at our VPs. We observe that we receive almost all the replies from most of the targets: the 90% (80%) of the targets answer to more than 40 (all) packets per each host, corresponding to a 20% (0%) loss scenario. A large plateau in the CDF also indicates that the distribution is bi-modal, i.e., the remaining hosts generally reply with very few packets (e.g., 10 or less per each VP or over 90% loss rate). This suggests that future campaigns could be safely conducted with a smaller $N' < N$.

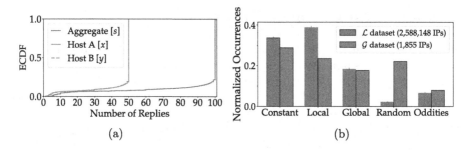

Fig. 5. Internet campaign: (a) ECDF of the number of packet replies and (b) Normalized classes occurrences for the training $\mathcal{G}$ and Internet-scale $\mathcal{L}$ dataset

To provide accurate classification results, in light of our robustness analysis, we limit our attention to the 2,588,148 hosts for which we have received at least $N = 80$ packets. We make this large-scale dataset, that we annotate with classification results and denote with $\mathcal{L}$, available for the community at [1].

Comparison with related work. We apply the classification to batches of 100,000 hosts, and for each class c, compute the relative breakdown of the class in that batch $\hat{n}_c = n_c / \sum_i n_i$, evaluating the confidence intervals of $\hat{n}_c$ over the different batches. Results are reported in Fig. 5(b), where we additionally report the breakdown in our $\mathcal{G}$ training set comprising just 1,855 population samples: it can be seen that while $\mathcal{G}$ has no statistical relevance for the census, it is not affected by class imbalance and thus proves to be a good training set.

Results are particularly interesting to put in perspective with current literature knowledge. Specifically, past work [6,9,20,28] consistently reported the global counter to be more widespread: in 2003, [20] reported that 70% (over 2000 probed targets) were using an IP-ID counter (global or local implementation); in 2005, [6] reported that 38% (over 150 hosts) used a global IP-ID; in 2006, [28] affirms the global implementation to be the most common assignment policy (among 3 behaviors); in 2013, [9] asserts 57% (over 271 DNS TLD servers) to implement global counter. On the contrary, we find that only 18% (over 2,5 million targets) are still using global counter implementation: this in line with 2017 results that reports slightly more than 16% global IP-IDs [23] (whose main aim is to detect censorship in the Internet). While this decreasing trend is possibly affected by the comparably smaller population size of early studies, however we believe this trend to be rooted into OS-level changes in IP-ID policy implementations: e.g., Linux and Solaris, which previously adopted a global counter, for security reasons later moved to a local counter implementation [10].

The sole quantitative assessment of IP-ID behavior over multiple classes dates back to 2013. This is limited to 271 Top Level Domains TLDs probed by [9] (whose main aim is to propose practical poisoning and name-server blocking attacks on standard DNS resolvers, by off-path, spoofing adversaries). In particular, the 2013 study (our census) finds 57% (18%) global, 14% (39%) local and 9% (34%) constant IP-IDs, which testify of a significant evolution. Additionally, [9] suggests that 20% of DNS TLD exhibit evidence of "two or more sequential sequences mixed up, probably due to multiple machines behind load balancer", much larger than the 7% fraction of the larger "odd" class (including but not limited to load balance) that we find in this work. Finally, despite 2012 recommendations [10], the percentage of random IP-ID sequence was (and remains) limited 1% (2%).

6 Conclusions

This work presents, to the best of our knowledge, the first systematic study of the prevalence of different IP-ID behaviors in the current IPv4 Internet (extending this work to IPv6 is a future, necessary, work). Our first contribution is to devise an accurate, lightweight and robust classifier: accuracy of the classifier follows from a principled definition of the statistical features used to succinctly describe the IP-ID sequence; robustness is a consequence of this choice, as features remains wide apart even under heavy losses.

Our second contribution is to carry on a manual investigation effort for a moderate size dataset coming from real Internet measurements: this valuable ground truth allow us to adopt a supervised classification techniques to train a model able not only to detect well-defined behaviors, but also to correctly recognize a wide range of odd behaviors.

Our final contribution is to apply this classification to an Internet-scale measurement campaign, obtaining a very accurate picture of nowadays IP-ID behavior prevalence, which we release as open dataset at [1]. This dataset is possibly instrumental to other relevant work in the measurement field [2,6,23,26], and by updating and consolidating the scattered knowledge [6,9,20,23,28] of IP-ID prevalence, contributes in refining the current global Internet map.

Acknowledgments. We thank our shepherd Robert Beverly and the anonymous reviewers whose useful comments helped us improving the quality of our paper. This work has been carried out at LINCS (http://www.lincs.fr) and benefited from support of NewNet@Paris, Cisco Chair "NETWORKS FOR THE FUTURE" at Telecom ParisTech (http://newnet.telecom-paristech.fr).

References

1. https://perso.telecom-paristech.fr/drossi/dataset/IP-ID/
2. Bellovin, S.M.: A technique for counting NATted hosts. In: Proceedings of the IMW (2002)
3. Bender, A., Sherwood, R., Spring, N.: Fixing ally's growing pains with velocity modeling. In: Proceedings of the ACM IMC (2008)
4. Beverly, R., Luckie, M., Mosley, L., Claffy, K.: Measuring and characterizing IPv6 router availability. In: Mirkovic, J., Liu, Y. (eds.) PAM 2015. LNCS, vol. 8995, pp. 123–135. Springer, Cham (2015). https://doi.org/10.1007/978-3-319-15509-8_10
5. Braden, R.: RFC 1122, Requirements for Internet Hosts - Communication Layers (1989)

6. Chen, W., Huang, Y., Ribeiro, B.F., Suh, K., Zhang, H., de Souza e Silva, E., Kurose, J., Towsley, D.: Exploiting the IPID field to infer network path and end-system characteristics. In: Dovrolis, C. (ed.) PAM 2005. LNCS, vol. 3431, pp. 108–120. Springer, Heidelberg (2005). https://doi.org/10.1007/978-3-540-31966-5_9

7. Dainotti, A., Benson, K., King, A., Huffaker, B., Glatz, E., Dimitropoulos, X., Richter, P., Finamore, A., Snoeren, A.C.: Lost in space: improving inference of IPv4 address space utilization. In: IEEE JSAC (2016)

8. Pelletier, K.S.G.: RFC 5225, RObust Header Compression Version 2 (ROHCv2): Profiles for RTP. UDP, IP, ESP and UDP-Lite (2008)

9. Gilad, Y., Herzberg, A.: Fragmentation considered vulnerable. In: ACM TISSEC (2013)

10. Gont, F.: RFC 6274, Security assessment of the internet protocol version 4 (2011)

11. Gont, F.: RFC 7739, Security implications of predictable fragment identification values (2016)

12. Heidemann, J., Pradkin, Y., Govindan, R., Papadopoulos, C., Bartlett, G., Bannister, J.: Census and survey of the visible internet. In: Proceedings of the ACM IMC (2008)

13. Herzberg, A., Shulman, H.: Fragmentation considered poisonous, or: one-domain-to-rule-them-all.org. In: IEEE CCNS (2013)

14. Idle scanning and related IPID games. https://nmap.org/book/idlescan.html

15. Jaiswal, S., Iannaccone, G., Diot, C., Kurose, J., Towsley, D.: Measurement and classification of out-of-sequence packets in a tier-1 IP backbone. In: IEEE/ACM TON (2007)

16. Keys, K., Hyun, Y., Luckie, M., Claffy, K.: Internet-scale IPv4 alias resolution with MIDAR. In: IEEE/ACM TON (2013)

17. Klein, A.: OpenBSD DNS cache poisoning and multiple O/S predictable IP ID vulnerability. Technical report (2007)

18. Loh, W.-Y.: Classification and regression trees. Wiley Interdiscipl. Rev.: Data Mining Knowl. Discov. 1, 14–23 (2011)

19. Luckie, M., Beverly, R., Brinkmeyer, W., et al.: Speedtrap: internet-scale IPv6 alias resolution. In: Proceedings of the ACM IMC (2013)

20. Mahajan, R., Spring, N., Wetherall, D., Anderson, T.: User-level internet path diagnosis. ACM SIGOPS Oper. Syst. Rev. 37(5), 106–119 (2003)

21. Mogul, J.C., Deering, S.E.: RFC 1191, Path MTU discovery (1990)

22. Mongkolluksamee, S., Fukuda, K., Pongpaibool, P.: Counting NATted hosts by observing TCP/IP field behaviors. In: Proceedings of the IEEE ICC (2012)

23. Pearce, P., Ensafi, R., Li, F., Feamster, N., Paxson, V.: Augur: Internet-wide detection of connectivity disruptions. In: IEEE SP (2017)

24. Postel, J.: RFC 791, Internet protocol (1981)

25. Salutari, F., Cicalese, D., Rossi, D.: A closer look at IP-ID behavior in the wild (extended tech. rep.). Technical report, Telecom ParisTech (2018)

26. Spring, N., Mahajan, R., Wetherall, D., Anderson, T.: Measuring ISP topologies with rocketfuel. In: IEEE/ACM TON (2004)

27. Touch, J.: RFC 6864, Updated Specification of the IPv4 ID Field (2013)

28. West, M.A., McCann, S.: RFC 4413, TCP/IP field behavior (2006)

29. Zander, S., Andrew, L.L., Armitage, G.: Capturing ghosts: predicting the used IPv4 space by inferring unobserved addresses. In: Proceedings of the ACM IMC (2014)

A First Look at QUIC in the Wild

Jan Rüth[1]([✉]), Ingmar Poese[2], Christoph Dietzel[3], and Oliver Hohlfeld[1]

[1] RWTH Aachen University, Aachen, Germany
{rueth,hohlfeld}@comsys.rwth-aachen.de
[2] Benocs GmbH, Berlin, Germany
ipoese@benocs.com
[3] TU Berlin/DE-CIX, Berlin, Germany
christoph@inet.tu-berlin.de

Abstract. For the first time since the establishment of TCP and UDP, the Internet transport layer is subject to a major change by the introduction of QUIC. Initiated by Google in 2012, QUIC provides a reliable, connection-oriented low-latency and fully encrypted transport. In this paper, we provide the first broad assessment of QUIC usage in the wild. We monitor the entire IPv4 address space since August 2016 and about 46% of the DNS namespace to detected QUIC-capable infrastructures. Our scans show that the number of QUIC-capable IPs has more than tripled since then to over 617.59 K. We find around 161 K domains hosted on QUIC-enabled infrastructure, but only 15 K of them present valid certificates over QUIC. Second, we analyze one year of traffic traces provided by MAWI, one day of a major European tier-1 ISP and from a large IXP to understand the dominance of QUIC in the Internet traffic mix. We find QUIC to account for 2.6% to 9.1% of the current Internet traffic, depending on the vantage point. This share is dominated by Google pushing up to 42.1% of its traffic via QUIC.

1 Introduction

Recent years have fostered the understanding that TCP as the de-facto default Internet transport layer protocol has become a technological bottleneck that is hard to update. This understanding is rooted in the fact that optimizing throughput is no longer a key concern in the Internet, but optimizing latency and providing encryption at the *transport* has become a concern. The focus on latency results from shifted demands (e.g., by interactive web applications) and is currently proposed to be addressed in part by TCP extensions at the protocol level, e.g., TCP Fast Open [15] or Multipath TCP [16]. While optimizing latency there is an additional demand to also provide an encrypted transport, typically realized by TLS on top of TCP. Since this additional encryption adds additional latency, further optimizations address this latency inflation, e.g., 0-RTT in the upcoming TLS 1.3 standard [17]. While these approaches present clear advantages, their deployment is currently challenged by middleboxes and legacy systems.

© Springer International Publishing AG, part of Springer Nature 2018
R. Beverly et al. (Eds.): PAM 2018, LNCS 10771, pp. 255–268, 2018.
https://doi.org/10.1007/978-3-319-76481-8_19

Google's Quick UDP Internet Connections (QUIC) protocol [10] aims to address these shortcomings in a new way. Like TCP, it provides a connection-oriented, reliable, and in-order byte stream. Yet unlike TCP, it enables stream multiplexing over a single connection while optimizing for latency. By fully encrypting already at the transport layer, QUIC provides security and excludes (interfering) middlebox optimizations; thereby paving the way for a rapidly evolving transport layer. By implementing QUIC in user space on top of UDP, its ability to rapidly update and customize a transport per application has yet unknown consequences and motivates measurements. It was first introduced to Chromium in 2012 and has undergone rapid development and high update-rate since then—as we will partly show in our measurements. Since 2016, the IETF QUIC working group [2] is working on its standardization. Google widely enabled QUIC for *all* of its users in January 2017 [10,18], motivating our study capturing its first 9 months of general deployment. Yet, in contrast to TCP and TLS, there is very limited tool support to analyze QUIC and the academic understanding is currently limited to protocol security [7,8,12] and performance [3,5,9,10].

In this paper, we complement these works by providing the first large-scale analysis of the current QUIC *deployments* and its *traffic share*. To assess the QUIC deployment, we regularly probe the entire IPv4 space for QUIC support since August 2016. In our scans, we observe a growing adoption on QUIC reaching 617.59 K IPs supporting QUIC in October 2017, of which 53.53% (40.71%) are operated by Google (Akamai). We additionally probe the complete set of .com/.net/.org domains as well as the Alexa Top 1 M list, i.e., around 46% of the domain name space [20]. To assess the traffic share that these deployments generate, we analyzed traffic traces from three vantage points: *(i)* 9 months of traffic in 2017 on a transit link to an ISP (MAWI dataset [13]), *(ii)* one day in August 2017 at a European tier-1 ISP, representing edge (DSL + cellular) and backbone traffic, and *(iii)* one day in August 2017 at a large European IXP. In these networks, QUIC accounts for 2.6%–9.1% of the monitored traffic. The observed traffic is largely contributed by Google (up to 98.1% in the ISP) and only marginally by Akamai (0.1% in the ISP and 59.9% in the IXP), despite having a large number of QUIC-capable IPs. Our contributions are as follows.

– We analyze the development and deployment of QUIC in the IPv4 Internet.
– We present the first view on QUIC deployment and traffic outside of Google's network from three different vantage points.
– We build and together with this paper publish tools to: Enumerate QUIC hosts and tools to massively grab and decode QUIC protocol parameters.
– We publish all our active measurement data and future scans on [1].

Structure. Section 2 introduces the QUIC handshake as a basis for our host enumeration. Section 3 presents our view on QUIC in IPv4 and in three large TLDs as well as the tools that drive our measurements. Section 4 shows how QUIC reshapes traffic in local and ISP/IXP networks. Section 5 discusses related works and Sect. 6 concludes the paper.

2   An Introduction to QUIC's Handshake

We first introduce the QUIC connection establishment phase that we utilize in our measurements for host enumeration and certificate grabbing. For a broader discussion of QUIC's features and design choices we refer to [10]. We focus on the QUIC early deployment draft as the IETF draft is not yet fully specified.

One of QUIC's main features is a fast connection establishment: In the ideal case, when cached information of a prior connection is available, it does not even take a single round-trip (0-RTT) to send encrypted application data. Yet, in the worst case (without prior connections as in our measurements), QUIC needs at least three round-trips as shown in Fig. 1 and explained next.

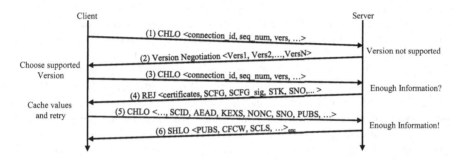

Fig. 1. A long QUIC handshake including version negotiation and caching of values.

Clients initiate a connection using a Client Hello (CHLO) (1) including the QUIC version it desires to use. In case the server does not support this version, it may send a version negotiation packet (2) enabling the client to choose from a list of supported versions for a second try. We will utilize packet (1) to quickly probe for QUIC-capable hosts with only a single packet exchange and analyze their supported versions provided in (2). Using a supported version, the client may advance in the handshake by sending another CHLO (3), without prior communication, it does not possess enough information about the server to establish a valid connection. The server supplies the necessary information (4), in one or multiple exchanges (i.e., (3) and (4) may be repeated until all required data is available). In these step(s), the client will be given a signed server config (SCFG) including supported ciphers, key exchange algorithms and their public values, and among other things the certificates authenticating the host. We will utilize these information to analyze the server-provided certificates. With this information, the client can issue another CHLO (5) including enough information to establish a connection, the client may even send encrypted data following the CHLO which depicts the optimal case for a 0-RTT connection establishment. Following the CHLO, the server acknowledges (6) the successful connection establishment with a Server Hello (SHLO), containing further key/value-pairs enabling to fully utilize the connection.

3   Availability: QUIC Server Infrastructures

We start by analyzing the availability of QUIC in the Internet, i.e., how many
IPs, domains, and infrastructures support QUIC. If not stated otherwise, the
results are based on scan data obtained in the first week of October 2017.

3.1   Enumerating QUIC IPv4 Hosts

IP Scan Methodology. To quickly probe the entire IPv4 space for QUIC
capable hosts, we extend ZMap [6], which enables to rapidly enumerate IPv4
addresses. To identify QUIC hosts, we use QUIC's version negotiation feature
(see Sect. 2). As QUIC is build to enable rapid protocol development and deployment, negotiation of a supported version (i.e., supported by client and server) is
fundamental to its design. That is, the protocol requires to announce a version
identifier in the initial packet sent from the client to the server. In case the version
announced by the client is not supported by the server, it sends a version negotiation packet. This packet lists all supported versions by the server, enabling
the client to find a common version that is used in a subsequent handshake. We
leverage this feature and sent a valid handshake message containing a version
that is likely to be *unsupported* by the other party, i.e., by including a version
that is not reserved and does not follow the current pattern. In response, the
server will not be able to continue the handshake as both versions do not match,
thus, it will send a version negotiation packet containing a list of its supported
versions. Using an invalid version has the advantage that we not only enumerate
valid QUIC hosts but also gain further insights about the server, namely the list
of its supported versions. We declare an IP as QUIC-capable, if we either receive
a valid version negotiation packet or a QUIC public reset packet (comparable
to a TCP RST). We build and publish [1] ZMap modules implementing this
behavior enabling rapid enumeration of QUIC hosts in the IPv4 space.

QUIC Hosts. Figure 2 shows that the total number of QUIC-capable IPs
(sum of stacked area) has more than tripled from 186.77 K IPs in August

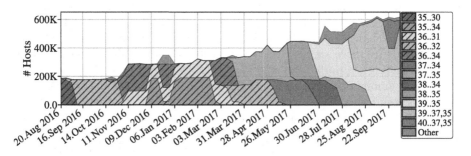

Fig. 2. Number of QUIC-capable IPs and support for sets of certain QUIC versions,
here we display versions when there was support by at least 20000 hosts once. Versions
that first appeared in 2016 are hatched.

2016 to 617.59 K IPs in October 2017. As of October, we find IPs in 3.04 K Autonomous Systems (ASs). To analyze who drives this trend, we attribute QUIC IPs to providers: we classify IPs by *(i)* AS information, *(ii)* per-IP X509 certificate data (e.g., who issued the certificate, who owns it), and *(iii)* per-IP reverse DNS data (e.g., Akamai configures rDNS entries such as *.deploy.static.akamaitechnologies.com), using data available at Routeviews and scans.io. As of August 2016, we can already attribute 169.52 K IPs to Google. They have since doubled their QUIC-capable infrastructure to 330.62 K IPs as of October 2017, accounting for 53.53% of all QUIC-capable IPs. We identify Akamai as the second largest QUIC-enabler: they started to increasingly deploy QUIC on their servers in November 2016, while we find around 983 Akamai IPs in August, the number jumps to 44.47 K IPs in November 2016. Akamai has since then continued to deploy QUIC having 251.43 K IPs as of October 2017 accounting for 40.71% of all QUIC-enabled IPs.

To classify the remaining 35.54 K hosts, we executed TCP HTTP GET/on port 80 for these IPs. However, for 23.91 K IPs we could not get any data due to i/o timeouts. Apart from this, we find 7.34 K hosts announcing a *LiteSpeed* server string, a web server that added QUIC support in mid of July 2017 [11]. We find servers announcing *gws* (1.69 K) and *AkamaiGHost* (1.44 K), hinting at even more Google and Akamai installations. The fourth largest group of servers announces *Caddy* (356) as the server string, this server uses the quic-go [4] library and can also be used as a reverse proxy for other TCP-only servers.

Takeaway. *We observe a steady growth of QUIC-capable IPs, mainly driven by Google and Akamai. Few IPs already use third-party server implementations.*

QUIC Version Support. Since QUIC is under active development, it requires clients and servers to be regularly updated to support recent versions. To understand how the server infrastructure is updated, Fig. 2 shows the number of hosts supporting a certain set of versions (recall: A host may support multiple versions!). The figure shows that many version combinations have a short lifespan in which old versions fade away and new versions appear. For example, hosts supporting version Q035 down to version Q030 switch to versions Q036, . . . , Q032, thus losing support for two versions. Yet, while some versions fade away, we also see that, e.g., version Q035 is supported by almost all hosts over the course of our dataset. Even though, to the end of our observations support for version Q036 is dropped. While this shows that some versions offer a long-term support, the figure also shows how vibrant the QUIC landscape is.

Given that some versions introduce radical protocol changes without backward compatibility, questions concerning the long-term stability of a QUIC-Internet are raised. On the one hand, the ability to easily update the protocol offers the possibility to quickly introduce new features and thereby to evolve the protocol. On the other hand, updating Internet systems is known to be notoriously hard. The vast amount of legacy systems raises the question of long-term compatibility—designing implementations to be easy to update is challenging.

Takeaway. *QUIC is currently subject to rapid development reflected in frequent version updates. Given its realization in user space at the application-layer, this property is likely to stay: future transports can be potentially updated as frequently as any other application. This motivates future measurements to assess the potentially highly dynamic future Internet transport landscape.*

3.2   Enumerating QUIC Domain Names

Methodology. We develop a second tool that finishes the handshake and enables to further classify previously identified hosts and infrastructures. To account for mandatory Server Name Indication (SNI), it can present a hostname that is necessary for the server to deliver correct certificates when hosting multiple sites on a single server. We base our tool [1] on the quic-go [4] library which we extended to enable tracing within the connection establishment to extract all handshake parameters (see Fig. 1).

IP-based Certificate Scan. In a first step, we cluster all QUIC-enabled IPs discovered in Sect. 3.1 by their X509 certificate hash. This step enables to better understand QUIC-enabled infrastructures. Since the server's hostname is unknown at the request time when enumerating the IPv4 address space, we present dummy domains (e.g., foo.com) to each IP and retrieve the X509 certificate. The retrieved certificate provides information on the domain names for which the certificate is valid, which can indicate the hosting infrastructure. We remark that this approach yields the *default* website that is configured at a server and will not identify different sites in the presence of SNI. In fact, we find that 216.64 K hosts require SNI and do not deliver a certificate (for which we account for when scanning domain zones later). Figure 3 shows that we only observe 320 different certificates for the probed 617.59 K QUIC IPs. The heavy-tailed distribution shows the top-five (ten) certificates already represent 95.41% (99.28%) of the IPs, most prominently Google and Akamai. We validated that these IPs actually belong to both companies by requesting content via TCP and HTTP on port 80 on the same hosts. We next assess QUIC support among domain names.

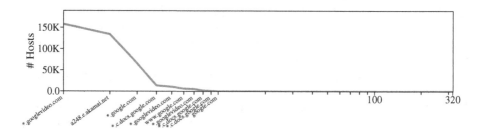

Fig. 3. Number of hosts giving out the same certificate on the y-axis. First listed common names for the 10 certificates with the highest coverage shown on the log x-axis.

Probing complete domain lists. Presenting a non-existing SNI name in our previous measurement will miss any server that enforces to present a valid hostname, thus we next assess the QUIC support by probing complete domain name lists. That is, we probe all domains in the .com/.net/.org zone files and in the Alexa Top 1 M list. These zones are available at Verisign [19] (.com/.net) and PIR [14] (.org). Together they contain more than 150 M domains, i.e., about 46 % of the domain space [20]. We use zDNS to resolve the domains and for each successful resolution, we use our tool to check for QUIC support and to grab all parameters from the connection establishment. The whole process takes roughly 15 h and is thus feasible to run on a daily basis. Yet, as QUIC CHLO packets are padded to nearly fill the MTU, the scan easily saturates a 1 Gbit link.

Table 1 shows the QUIC-support in the .com/.net/.org zones as well as in the Alexa Top 1M list. We define *QUIC-enabled* domains as being able to initiate a QUIC handshake. A domain is tagged as *Timeout* when we received no response to our initial QUIC CHLO within 12 s, e.g., in the absence of QUIC support. We furthermore show some specific errors as well as *DNS-failures*.

Table 1. QUIC support in different TLDs and in the Alexa Top 1 M list. Weekly data is available at https://quic.comsys.rwth-aachen.de.

	06. Oct 2017 .com	03. Oct 2017 .net	04. Oct 2017 .org	08. Oct 2017 Alexa 1M
#Domains	129.36 M (100.0%)	14.75 M (100.0%)	10.37 M (100.0%)	999.94 K (100.0%)
QUIC-enabled	133.63 K (0.1%)	8.73 K (0.06%)	6.51 K (0.06%)	11.97 K (1.2%)
Valid Certificate	2.14 K (0.0%)	181 (0.0%)	159 (0.0%)	342 (0.03%)
Timeout	114.63 M (88.61%)	10.80 M (73.23%)	8.09 M (78.06%)	826.67 K (82.67%)
Version-failed	29 (0.0%)	6 (0.0%)	1 (0.0%)	5 (0.0%)
Protocol-error	606 (0.0%)	222 (0.0%)	0 (0.0%)	1 (0.0%)
Invalid-IP	322.24 K (0.25%)	59.24 K (0.4%)	40.15 K (0.39%)	15.42 K (1.54%)
DNS-failure	13.76 M (10.64%)	2.40 M (16.26%)	1.18 M (11.41%)	49.34 K (4.93%)

Overall QUIC-support is very low. Depending on the zone, 0.06%–0.1% domains are hosted on QUIC-enabled hosts. Only 1.6%–2.44% of these domains present a valid X509 certificate. This questions how many domains actually deliver content via QUIC.

Landing Page Content. Websites can utilize different server configuration and even different server implementations for different protocols. The successful establishment of QUIC connections does thus not imply that meaningful content is being served. To assess how many QUIC-capable domains deliver content similar to their HTTP 1.1/2 counterparts, we instruct Google's QUIC test client (part of the Chromium source) to download their landing page via QUIC. We then compare their content to their HTTP 1.1/2 counterparts which should be similar if these QUIC-capable domains are properly set up. We disabled certificate checks to probe all capable domains. Out of the probed 161 K domains,

16 K (9.8%) return no data and 33 K (20.7%) >1 kB via QUIC. In case of the latter, 33 K domains (22 K served by Akamai) do deliver content similar to their HTTP 1.1/2 counterparts. We define similarity by structural HTML similarity (e.g., in the number of tags, links, images, scripts, ...) and require >3 metrics to agree to define a web page to be similar. Domains delivering similar content over QUIC are thus in principle ready to be served by a QUIC-capable browser. To be discovered by a Chrome browser, they, however, need to present an alternative service (alt_srv) header via TCP-based HTTP(S) pointing to their QUIC counterpart. 11 K domains present this header via HTTPS (5 K hosted by Google and 0 by Akamai) and only 7 via HTTP. Thus a large share of the domains would not be contacted by a Chrome browser even though QUIC support is in principle available. The header further specifies the QUIC versions supported by the server, of which at measurement time Chrome requires QUIC version 39. Only 5 K domains present this version in their alt_srv header, all hosted by Google. We remark that our content analysis only regards *landing* pages and does not account for additional assets (e.g., images or videos). Particularly CDNs offer dedicated products for media delivery, whose QUIC support can differ. Assessing their QUIC support in detail thus provides an interesting angle for future work.

Takeaway. *The limited number of X509 certificates retrieved in our IP-based scan hints at the small number of different providers currently using or experimenting with QUIC. Furthermore, only a small fraction of the monitored domains are hosted on QUIC-capable infrastructures–an even smaller fraction can actually deliver valid certificates for the requested domains. Regardless, of the certificate, many QUIC-enabled domains do deliver their pages via QUIC. Yet in our measurements, many would not be contacted by a Chrome browser, either because of a non-present alt_srv header or insufficient version support. There is thus a big potential to increase QUIC support. We next study how this QUIC-support is reflected in actual traffic shares.*

4   Usage: QUIC Traffic Share

We quantify the QUIC traffic share by analyzing three traces representing different vantage points: *(i)* 9 months of traffic in 2017 on a transit link to an upstream ISP (MAWI dataset [13]), *(ii)* one day in August 2017 at a European tier-1 ISP, representing edge (DSL + cellular) and backbone traffic, and *(iii)* the same day at a large European IXP.

Traffic Classification. We use protocol and port information to classify HTTPS (TCP port 443), HTTP (TCP port 80), and QUIC (UDP port 443). We chose this classification since it is applicable to all of our traces: MAWI (PCAP header traces) and ISP + IXP (Netflow traces without protocol headers). We remark that this classification can *(i)* miss protocol traffic on non-standard ports and can *(ii)* wrongly attribute other traffic on the monitored ports. However, it still enables to report an upper bound on the protocol usage on standard ports. We show the per-trace traffic shares in Table 2 which we discuss next.

Table 2. Average traffic shares (overall), among the operators, and among the protocol. Operator's share is e.g., from all of Google's traffic the share of the QUIC traffic at a vantage point. Share in Protocols denotes the traffic share of a protocol at a vantage point, e.g., the amount of Google QUIC traffic from all other QUIC traffic.

	Overall				Operator's share			Share in Protocol		
	HTTP	HTTPS	QUIC		HTTP	HTTPS	QUIC	HTTP	HTTPS	QUIC
MAWI	28.0%	44.9%	6.7%	-	-			-		
ISP	37.7%	40.1%	7.8%	Akamai	67.9%	32.1%	0.1%	27.2%	12.6%	0.1%
				Google	1.4%	59.5%	39.1%	0.7%	28.8%	98.1%
Mobile ISP	24.8%	55.4%	9.1%	Akamai	57.7%	42.3%	0.0%	28.5%	9.6%	0.1%
				Google	1.6%	64.4%	34.0%	1.8%	29.5%	96.9%
IXP	32.2%	30.9%	2.6%	Akamai	33.3%	33.3%	33.3%	5.0%	5.2%	59.9%
				Google	3.1%	70.0%	26.9%	0.3%	7.2%	33.1%

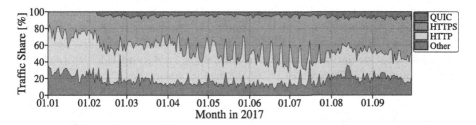

Fig. 4. Traffic share of QUIC compared to HTTP and HTTPS in the MAWI trace.

MAWI Backbone Trace. We start by analyzing traffic on a trans-Pacific WIDE backbone link provided by the MAWI working group [13]. We analyze anonymized header traces available at the MAWI repository (*samplepoint F*). The monitored link is a transit link connecting the WIDE backbone to an upstream ISP. The traces involve 15 min of traffic captured at 14 h on each day. Each packet is caped to the first 96 bytes.

We begin to analyze traffic on January 1st 2017, since Google enabled QUIC for all of its Chrome and Google-developed Android App users in January 2017 [10]. Figure 4 shows the traffic volume until end of September 2017. The trace shows that the QUIC traffic share is 0.0% in January. This is in contrast to the Google report of having widely enabled QUIC in January, suggesting that the monitored user-base is not using Google products (e.g., Chrome) at the time, QUIC has not been enabled for this network or that traffic is routed differently. We observe the first QUIC traffic in February where the QUIC traffic share is at 3.9%. It continues to increase to 5.2% in March and reaches 6.7% in September. QUIC offers an alternative to TCP+TLS, which is the foundation of legacy HTTPS, its share is at around 44.9%, even the unencrypted version HTTP is still at around 28.0%. As the provided trace anonymizes destination and source addresses, we cannot attribute this traffic to infrastructures (e.g., Google or

Akamai) or services (e.g., YouTube). We leave this analysis to the ISP trace for which we have AS-level information available.

Takeaway. *Within nine months after its general activation by Google, QUIC already accounts for a non-negligible traffic share, demonstrating its ability to evolve Internet transport.*

European Tier-1 ISP. We obtained anonymized and aggregated Netflow traces from all border routers of a large European ISP for one day in August 2017. The Netflow traces were aggregated to 5-min bins and all IP addresses were replaced by AS numbers before they were made available to us. Thus the traces do not reveal the behavior of individual users. The captured traffic contains *(i)* edge traffic by DSL, *(ii)* cellular customers, and *(iii)* transit backbone traffic.

Figure 5 shows the traffic volume (up- and downstream) over the course of 24 h by protocol and prominent infrastructures (the traffic volume (y-axis) has been removed at the request of the ISP). As our previous host-based analysis (see Sect. 3) showed that QUIC is mainly supported by Google and Akamai servers, we also show their traffic shares (according to their AS numbers). At first, we observe that QUIC traffic follows the same daily pattern as HTTP and HTTPS. On average QUIC accounts for 7.8% of the traffic with a standard deviation of σ: 1.0%. This deviation is similar to HTTP (σ: 1.2%) and HTTPS (σ: 1.4%) which account for 37.7% and 40.1% of the traffic, respectively.

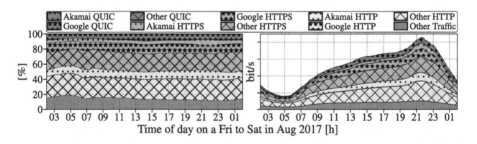

Fig. 5. QUIC traffic share in a major European ISP (up- and downstream). Left, relative share of QUIC. Right, total traffic compared to HTTP(S), y-axis has been anonymized at the request of the ISP. Nearly all QUIC traffic is served by Google.

The observed QUIC traffic is almost exclusively contributed by Google: They account for 98.1% of the overall observed QUIC traffic. Among all of Google's traffic, 39.1% is using QUIC (σ: 2.3%), peaking at 42.1%. This is a larger share than a global average of 32 % reported by Google in November 2016 [10]. Currently, QUIC is mainly supported by Google-developed applications (e.g., Chrome or the Youtube Android app). In the absence of QUIC libraries, third-party support is low (e.g., Opera has optional QUIC and Firefox no QUIC support). The availability of QUIC libraries thus has the potential to drastically improve client support and therefore increase QUIC's traffic share.

In contrast, Akamai only serves 0.1% of its traffic via QUIC—despite contributing a large portion of the overall QUIC-capable IPs (40.71%, see Sect. 3.1). This discrepancy between the number of IPs and the traffic share suggests that QUIC is not yet widely activated among all customers/products. Yet on average, Akamai accounts for 10.3% (HTTP) and 5.1% (HTTPS) of all traffic and thus, together with the fact that they already have a QUIC-capable infrastructure, has the potential to shift more traffic towards QUIC. A higher QUIC share has several implications, while QUIC and TCP are generally similar in nature, subtle differences in the protocols may influence the performance of whole networks, e.g., by default QUIC uses larger initial congestion windows than those standardized for TCP by IETF and demands pacing for smoothing the traffic.

Mobile ISP. The ISP supplied us with information which traffic is for their mobile (cellular) customers, which we show in Fig. 6. Please note that the reported mobile traffic is also contained in Fig. 5. In contrast to the entire network of the ISP, the mobile traffic shows a different traffic pattern: while its throughput also decreases over night, mobile traffic rapidly increases in the morning and stays rather constant over the course of the day. Apart from this, the average QUIC share in the mobile network of 9.1% (σ: 1.4%), the highest share among all traces (see Table 2). In contrast, among the entire mobile Google traffic, only 34.0% (σ: 2.6%) is served via QUIC, lower than overall for the ISP. Also for mobile traffic, Akamai only serves a negligible share of its traffic via QUIC and thus has the potential increase the QUIC traffic share.

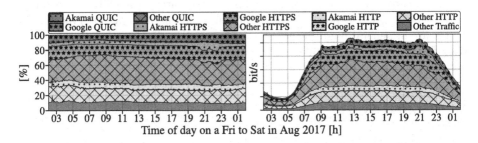

Fig. 6. Mobile network traffic share of QUIC in a major European ISP. Left, relative share of QUIC traffic. Right, absolute traffic share compared to HTTP(S), y-axis has been anonymized at the request of the ISP.

Takeaway. *QUIC traffic shares do (yet) not reflect server support. While Akamai operates a comparably large infrastructure in the number of QUIC-capable IPs, QUIC traffic is (still) almost entirely served by Google: this is likely to change.*

European IXP. We obtained sampled flow data of a large (European) IXP for the same day in August as for the ISP and show its traffic share in Fig. 7. We classify Google and Akamai traffic by customer port information—since both

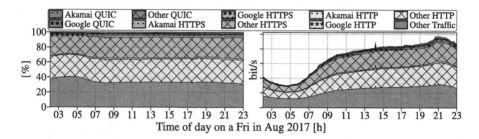

Fig. 7. QUIC traffic share at a large European IXP. Left, relative share of QUIC traffic. Right, absolute traffic share compared to HTTP(S), y-axis has been anonymized at the request of the IXP.

peer at the IXP—and plot their HTTP(S) and QUIC traffic shares similar to the ISP. On average QUIC accounts for 2.6% (σ: 1.0%) of the traffic, which is lowest share among all traces (see Table 2). Unlike the ISP, the largest portion is now contributed by Akamai (59.9%) and we observe a lower share of Google traffic (33.1%)—recall that Google contributed 98.1% of the QUIC traffic at the ISP.

Takeaway. *(Per-CDN) traffic shares largely depend on the chosen vantage point.*

Discussion. We observe different QUIC traffic shares at the ISP/IXP and particularly different shares of the QUIC traffic by Google/Akamai (relative to the overall traffic of each vantage point). These vantage point dependent differences are likely caused by different traffic engineering strategies since both providers peer at both vantage points. These differences highlight that observed traffic shares are in general highly vantage point dependent. Understanding the incentives for these different traffic engineering strategies is an interesting starting point for future research.

5   Related Work

QUIC Security. A first security analysis QUIC's key exchange is presented in [7], followed by a later analysis of the complete protocol [12]. These works on the security analysis are complemented by presenting an attack vector in which the server config can be computed offline to impersonate the server [8].

QUIC Performance. An early performance comparison of QUIC and HTTP1 [3] indicates that QUIC can provide better goodput and lower page loading times as traditional HTTP1 over TCP. A more extensive evaluation in [5] also involves the comparison to HTTP2 and shows that QUIC can outperform HTTP2 over TCP/TLS, a finding that is supported by extensive evaluations in [9]. The reported performance experience by Google [10] shows that QUIC lowers the Google search latency by 3.6–8% and reduces YouTube rebuffering by 15–18%.

We complement these works by providing the first broad assessment of QUIC usage in the wild and outside Google's network. We study both the QUIC-enabled infrastructures and its traffic shares from three vantage points.

6   Discussion and Conclusion

This paper presents the first broad assessment of QUIC, nine months after the general activation by Google for all of its users. We study both the available *infrastructure* in terms of the number of QUIC-capable IPs and domains and their *traffic share* at three vantage points. By probing the entire IPv4 address space, we find a steadily growing number of QUIC-enabled IPs which has tripled since August 2016 and reached 617.59 K in October 2017. This growth is mainly driven by Google and Akamai, which account for 53.53% and 40.71% of these IPs. When regularly probing ≈150 M domains for QUIC support, we observe 161 K capable domains of which 33 K serve content similar to their HTTP1/2 counterparts and only 15 K present valid certificates. Many (of the non-Google hosted) domains would not be contacted by a Chrome browser, either because of a non-present alternative service headers in HTTP(S) or insufficient version support. This infrastructure size does, however, not reflect their traffic share: depending on the vantage point, Google accounts for 98.1% (ISP) of the QUIC traffic and Akamai contributes 0.1% (ISP) to 59.9% (IXP), despite operating a similarly large number of QUIC-capable IPs. Given the factors that impede QUIC support, the QUIC traffic share is likely to increase in the future when being largely enabled at a wide range of infrastructures.

Realized as user space application-layer protocol, QUIC paves the way towards a rapidly evolving transport that can be updated as easily and as frequently as any application. This aspect is manifested in the short lifetime of QUIC versions observed in our measurements while the protocol is still under development. In light of these findings we expect a highly dynamic future Internet transport landscape to be studied and observed by future work.

Acknowledgments. This work has been funded by the DFG as part of the CRC 1053 MAKI and SPP 1914 REFLEXES, and by European Union's Horizon 2020 research and innovation programme under the ENDEAVOUR project (grant agreement 644960). We would like to thank the network operators at RWTH Aachen University, especially Jens Hektor and Bernd Kohler. We further thank our shepherd Tobias Flach and the anonymous reviewers. Furthermore, we would like to thank Konrad Wolsing for maintaining our changes to the quic-go implementation.

References

1. Active measurements and tools. https://quic.comsys.rwth-aachen.de
2. IETF QUIC working group. https://datatracker.ietf.org/wg/quic/about/
3. Carlucci, G., et al.: HTTP over UDP: an experimental investigation of QUIC. In: Proceedings of the 30th Annual ACM Symposium on Applied Computing (2015)

4. Clemente, L.: quic-go. https://github.com/lucas-clemente/quic-go
5. Cook, S., et al.: QUIC: better for what and for whom? In: IEEE ICC (2017)
6. Durumeric, Z., et al.: Zmap: Fast internet-wide scanning and its security applications. In: USENIX Security (2013)
7. Fischlin, M., Günther, F.: Multi-stage key exchange and the case of Google's QUIC protocol. In: ACM CCS (2014)
8. Jager, T., et al.: On the security of TLS 1.3 and QUIC against weaknesses in PKCS#1 V1.5 encryption. In: ACM CCS (2015)
9. Kakhki, A.M., et al.: Taking a long look at QUIC: an approach for rigorous evaluation of rapidly evolving transport protocols. In: ACM IMC (2017)
10. Langley, A., et al.: The QUIC transport protocol: design and internet-scale deployment. In: ACM SIGCOMM (2017)
11. LiteSpeed Technologies Inc., LiteSpeed – Release Log. https://www.litespeedtech.com/products/litespeed-web-server/release-log
12. Lychev, R., et al.: How secure and quick is QUIC? Provable security and performance analyses. In: IEEE Symposium on Security and Privacy (2015)
13. MAWI Working Group Traffic Archive. http://mawi.nezu.wide.ad.jp/mawi/
14. Public Interest Registry. Zone File Access. http://pir.org/
15. Radhakrishnan, S., et al.: TCP fast open. In: ACM CoNEXT (2011)
16. Raiciu, C., et al.: How hard can it be? designing and implementing a deployable multipath TCP. In: NSDI (2012)
17. Rescorla, E.: The Transport Layer Security (TLS) Protocol Version 1.3. Internet-Draft draft-ietf-tls-tls13-21, Internet Engineering Task Force (2017). WiP
18. Swett, I.: QUIC - Deployment Experience @Google. https://www.ietf.org/proceedings/96/slides/slides-96-quic-3.pdf
19. Verisign. Zone Files For Top-Level Domains (TLDs). verisign.com
20. Verisign. The verisign domain name industry brief, September 2017. https://www.verisign.com/assets/domain-name-report-Q22017.pdf

TCP CUBIC versus BBR on the Highway

Feng Li[1], Jae Won Chung[1], Xiaoxiao Jiang[1(✉)], and Mark Claypool[2]

[1] Verizon Labs, 60 Sylvan Road, Waltham, MA 02451, USA
xiaoxiao.jiang@verizon.com
[2] Worcester Polytechnic Institute, 100 Institute Road, Worcester, MA 01609, USA

Abstract. 4G Long Term Evolution (LTE) networks present new features of high capacities together with end-user mobility. These challenges have led to a gap in the understanding of the effectiveness of TCP congestion control algorithms in LTE networks with mobile users. To further understanding, we conduct a detailed measurement study comparing TCP CUBIC with Bottleneck Bandwidth and Round-trip propagation time (BBR) – a new congestion control alternative developed by Google – in a high-speed driving scenario over a tier-1 U.S. wireless carrier. Our results show CUBIC and BBR generally have similar throughputs, but BBR has significantly lower self-inflicted delays than CUBIC.

1 Introduction

Access between urban towers is one of the most important features of 4G LTE networks, providing mobility for end users, particularly when driving. While studies have helped to better understand LTE performance [2,5,7,10,13], unfortunately, there has been little systematic research on "in the wild" TCP performance for driving at high speeds (e.g., on the U.S. Interstate). This lack of knowledge makes modeling and simulating TCP over LTE networks difficult and slows development of TCP improvements for mobile networks. Moreover, the new Bottleneck Bandwidth and Round-trip propagation time (BBR) congestion control algorithm [3,4] has yet to be evaluated over 4G LTE.

To better understand TCP performance in highway driving conditions and provide valuable mobility performance data on U.S. LTE networks, we collect real-world network traces from a tier-1 wireless carrier while driving on a U.S. interstate highway between Worcester, MA, and Morristown, NJ, driving about 8 h and 400 miles (675 km) round-trip. Our traces include physical and medium access control layer measurements (e.g., signal strength and tower handover), correlated with higher-layer TCP performance (e.g., throughput and round-trip time).

Our results show that: (1) there is a fairly uniform distribution (0 to 30 dB) of signal to interference-plus-noise ratios (SINRs) along the route; (2) the round-trip times from the mobile device to servers in the wireless AS are modest, mostly ranging from 40–80 ms; (3) most downloads (20 MBytes) do not experience a tower handover despite the highway speeds; (4) for 20 MB downloads, BBR and CUBIC have similar throughputs, but BBR has significantly lower

© Springer International Publishing AG, part of Springer Nature 2018
R. Beverly et al. (Eds.): PAM 2018, LNCS 10771, pp. 269–280, 2018.
https://doi.org/10.1007/978-3-319-76481-8_20

round-trip times; (5) for 1 MB downloads, BBR has higher throughputs but also higher round-trip times; and (6) for 20 MB downloads, BBR experiences far fewer duplicate ACKs than does CUBIC (median less than 1% versus about 5–10%).

The rest of paper is organized as follows: Sect. 2 summarizes related research; Sect. 3 describes our methodology for measuring TCP over 4G LTE while highway driving; Sect. 4 presents the physical and medium access control layer measurement results; Sect. 5 compares the performance of TCP under the experiment conditions; and Sect. 6 concludes our work and presents possible future work.

2   Related Work

Huang et al. [5] studied the performance of TCP over LTE through packet traces collected from a carrier's network. Although their results confirm shorter round-trip times over LTE compared to 3G, they do not provide physical nor medium access control layer analysis. Xiao et al. [12] measured TCP throughput and round-trip times over stationary, driving and railway scenarios in LTE. While their results show TCP throughput degrades in high-speed conditions, their measured throughputs are lower than what is typically available with LTE. Merz et al. [7] conducted a measurement study focusing on the performance of LTE in high-speed conditions, but their measurements do not include upper layer performance (e.g., the Transport layer).

Most closely related to our study, Eneko et al. [2] and Remi et al. [10] investigated performance with wireless mobility for five different TCP congestion control algorithms (CCAs): CUBIC, New Reno, Westwood+, Illinois, and CAIA Delay Gradient (CDG). Although they used Linux kernel code [11] for the CCAs, their network was simulated via ns-3,[1] making it difficult to determine how well their results match real highway driving conditions.

Our work differs from the above by providing comparative TCP performance in a highway driving scenario, with insights into radio conditions, and a first look at the performance of the Bottleneck Bandwidth and Round-trip propagation time (BBR) algorithm [4] over 4G as it compares to CUBIC. Plus, we have an opportunity to confirm some of the simulated results by Robert et al. [10] with experimental measurements, and compare some measured results by Xiao et al. [12], Huang et al. [5] and Cardwell et al. [4] to our measurements.

3   Methodology

Figure 1 depicts details of our measurement methodology. Shown are the congestion control algorithms (CCAs) studied (Sect. 3.1), the experiment setup (Sect. 3.2) and the driving scenario (Sect. 3.3).

---

[1] https://www.nsnam.org.

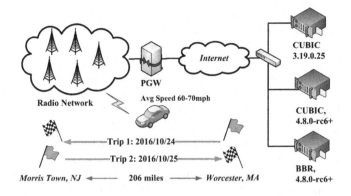

Fig. 1. Measurement setup and driving scenario

3.1 Congestion Control Algorithms

Our study focuses on three TCP CCAs:

CUBIC (k3.19) and CUBIC (k4.8) – the default CCA in most Linux servers. The CUBIC version used for production servers is generally based on the series 3 kernel, but CUBIC for the series 4 kernel is slightly different. So, one testbed server runs CUBIC on a 3.19.0-25-generic kernel and another CUBIC on a 4.8-rc6 kernel, treating each as separate CCAs for this study.

BBR [4] – a new congestion control algorithm which calculates the congestion window size by measuring the bottleneck bandwidth and round-trip propagation time and sends packets at a paced rate. One of our testbed servers runs BBR with *net-next*[2] as a patch for Linux kernel 4.8-rc6.

3.2 Experiment Setup

We perform measurements on a tier-1 wireless carrier while driving in Southern New England (U.S.) on two consecutive weekdays, October 24th and 25th, 2016. Before starting, we setup three separate servers – one for each TCP CCA studied – each a HP Proliant 460c Gen9 blade with 128 GB RAM and a dual socket 2.60 GHz ten-core Intel Xeon ES-2660v3 CPUs on the same chassis. All three servers are inside the wireless carrier AS, connected to the Internet through the same HPE 6120XG 10 Gbps switch.

The three servers are configured with the same parameters, except for the Linux kernel version and CCA (see Sect. 3.1). All kernel parameters are set to their default values, except for two Ethernet parameters tweaked to improve throughput: (i) Ethernet transmission queue size (`txqueuelen`) increased to 10 k packets for higher throughput; and (ii) MTU reduced to 1428 bytes to accommodate GTP headers, avoiding fragmentation on the LTE network. Based on recommendations by Cardwell et al. [4], we enable fair queuing and pacing using

---

[2] git://git.kernel.org/pub/scm/linux/kernel/git/davem/net-next.git.

Linux Traffic Control (`tc`) utilities on the BBR server only (such settings are not known to impact CUBIC performance and generally are not enabled).

All three servers run Apache 2.4.7 with PHP 5.5. A custom PHP script dynamically generates 20 MB files with random content (to avoid any possible caching) for the smart phone to download. `Tcpdump` captures packet traces, setup to record 300 bytes per packet to provide complete TCP headers (the servers send only TCP traffic to the smart phone). Tests show the PHP script and `tcpdump` have less than a 1% CPU load on each server. Note, the three servers are dedicated to our performance study, reachable only from a small number of smart phones from our test device pool.

The client smart phone is an LG G2 VS980 with 2 GB RAM and a 32-bit Qualcomm Snapdragon S4 Prime Quad Core CPU, running Android 4.3.2 and continually at full charge via a power brick. The phone runs Qualipoc, measuring radio characteristics each second, baseline round-trip times via ping (ICMP), and throughput via HTTP download.

The cellular network provides LTE services over two radio spectra: Band XIII and Advanced Wireless Service (AWS). AWS normally provides more link capacity in urban areas while Band XIII provides a larger coverage over rural areas. Since no U.S. carrier provides continuous AWS coverage along highways, the smart phone is locked to Band XIII for this study.

Our measurement test suite contains 40 test iterations. Each iteration pings the server (three 56-byte ICMP packets, separated by one second), pauses 3 s, and then serially downloads a 20 MB file from each of the three servers. The suite pauses about 10 s between iterations. In total, one test suite run takes about 1 h, providing an opportunity for a driver break between suite runs.

3.3 Driving Scenario

As shown in Fig. 2, our highway driving measurements are between Worcester, MA and Morristown, NJ on two consecutive days: departing Worcester on October 24, 2016 at 3:37 pm to Morristown and returning from Morristown on

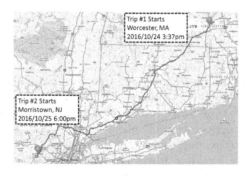

Fig. 2. Driving route

6:00 pm on October 25th to Worcester. The average driving speed is 65–70 mph (about 30 m/s). The total driving distance is about 400 miles (675 km) and takes 8 h, including traffic, breaks, and refueling. On each trip, the full test suite is run three times, with the driver stopping only in-between test suites.

4   Radio Network Characteristics

This section analyzes select radio network characteristics as one aspect of LTE performance.

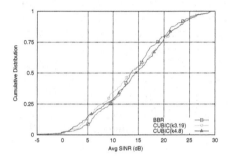   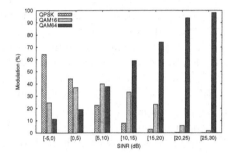

Fig. 3. SINR distribution   **Fig. 4.** Downlink modulation vs. SINR

Figure 3 shows the distribution of Signal to Interference-plus-Noise Ratios (SINRs) for the different TCP congestion control algorithms (CCAs). The x-axis is the SINR, averaged over a trial (file download), with a trendline shown for each CCA. From the figure, the trendlines overlap, suggesting that each CCA experiences similar radio conditions on aggregate, allowing for an equitable comparison of overall performance. Based on this lack of differentiation, we do not present breakdown by CCA for further physical and medium access control layer analysis. For comparison, our observed SINRs match those Merz et al. [7] measured on inter-city trains in Europe, suggesting similarity in radio coverage.

The modulation (or encoding scheme) selection in LTE depends on the SINR measured by both user equipment (UE) and radio tower computers (eNodeBs). Figure 4 shows a histogram of the downlink modulations used for different SINRs. The x-axis is the recorded SINR (in dB) clustered into 5 dB bins, and the y-axis is the percentage of transmission blocks (TBs) sent at that modulation. For the best radio conditions (SINRs greater than 20 dB), more than 90% of TBs are transmitted in 64 QAM (6 bits per symbol). For the worst (SINRs less than 5 dB), most of TBs are transmitted in QPSK (4 bits per symbol). In between (SINRs between 5 dB and 15 dB), the eNodeBs adapt transmissions among all three modulations.

5   CCA Performance

5.1   Single Trial

For illustration, this section compares a single trial of BBR and CUBIC (k4.8)[3] over time. Both trials had an SINR greater than 20 dB with no tower handover and neither flow experienced TCP retransmissions nor packet drops. In Fig. 5, the left figure compares the bytes in flight (the as-yet unacknowledged transmitted bytes), while the right figure shows the round-trip times (RTTs) measured via TCP ACKs. The BBR flow averaged 45 Mbps and the CUBIC flow averaged 36 Mbps. For comparison, the CUBIC throughputs are about the same as the maximum simulated throughputs for stationary UEs by Robert et al. [10], confirming their simulations with our measurements.

From the figures, BBR transmits aggressively during its initial probing phase showing a packet and RTT burst, reducing the congestion window to around 500 KB after about 1 s, which also reduces the RTT. After the probing phase, BBR maintains an RTT under 80 ms and a congestion window around 500 KB. CUBIC, on the other hand, exits from slow start early in the download (around 0.5 s) with a small congestion window. Although CUBIC's congestion window is able to grow up to 1 MB by the end of the download, it is unlikely to fully utilize the radio link resources for the duration.

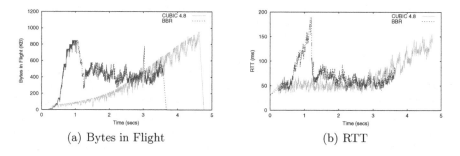

(a) Bytes in Flight   (b) RTT

Fig. 5. Single trial downlink for BBR and CUBIC (k4.8)

5.2   Throughput

For a core measure of performance, Fig. 6(a) shows the cumulative distribution of TCP throughputs over all trials, with the x-axis the throughput measured for each trial. Each CCA is shown with a different trendline. Table 1 summarizes the means, standard deviations, medians and 95% confidence intervals (CI) of the means.

From Fig. 6(a) and Table 1, the throughput ranges considerably for all three CCAs with Q1 (the first quartile) at about 7 Mbps and Q3 (the third quartile) at about 20 Mbps. All three CCAs can occasionally achieve more than 30 Mbps.

---

[3] CUBIC (k3.19) behaves similarly to CUBIC (k4.8).

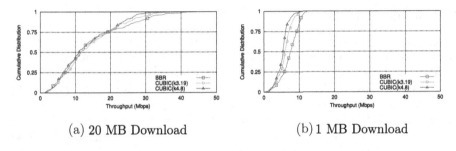

(a) 20 MB Download   (b) 1 MB Download

Fig. 6. TCP throughput distribution

At the highest, BBR achieves slightly more than 44 Mbps, close to the theoretical maximum downlink bit rate of 45 Mbps on a 10 MHz channel with 64 QAM modulation [6]. However, most of the BBR distribution is similar to that of CUBIC, with overlapping confidence intervals, suggesting comparable performance. For comparison, Nguyen et al. [8] only report a throughgput of 2–4 Mbps when simulating vehicle mobility in ns-3, showing real-world measurements can be much higher. Xiao et al. [12] report even lower LTE throughput measurements of around 1.5 Mbps on a train at about 100 kph (around our average speeds), and much lower at 300 kph. Cardwell et al. [4] measure 2x to 25x greater throughputs for BBR versus CUBIC for a high-speed (wired) WAN, suggesting BBR's throughput benefits may not carry over to LTE.

Table 1. Summary statistics of TCP throughputs

Congestion control algorithm	Mean (Mbps)	Median (Mbps)	95% CI of Mean	
			Left	Right
BBR	14.1 ± 9.5	11.6	13.1	15.2
CUBIC(k3.19)	14.0 ± 8.4	11.6	13.2	14.8
CUBIC(k4.8)	13.0 ± 7.8	11.1	12.2	13.8

Since 90% of flows from LTE networks carry less than 36 KB on their downlink payload, and only 0.6% of flows carry more than 1 MB on their downlink payload [5], to represent small downloads, we also analyze our packet traces truncated after the first ACK with a sequence number larger than 1 MB.

Figure 6(b) shows the cumulative distribution of TCP throughputs with the same axes and trendlines as for Fig. 6(a). From Fig. 6(b), BBR's probing phase results in higher throughputs than CUBIC's slow start, with a median 1 MB throughput for BBR about 50% higher than for CUBIC. In comparison to the throughputs in Fig. 6(b), the highest TCP throughputs (anything larger than 12.5 Mbps) are only achieved for flows larger 1 MB.

5.3 Round-Trip Time

Two methods to measure the round-trip time between the smart phone and our servers are used: (i) the average of 3 ICMP pings before each trial, and (ii) the TCP connection setup time measured through the three-way handshake.

Figure 7 compares the cumulative distributions of RTTs measured by ICMP pings to RTTs measured by TCP three-way handshakes for all trials. As Fig. 7 shows, the TCP handshake RTTs and the ping RTTs are generally in the same range, with the bulk of both distribution between 40 to 80 ms. This suggests that the TCP three-way handshake can be used to effectively estimate window sizes for congestion control [13]. The ping RTTs have a more fine-grained variation in time, possibly due to timers on the end systems. Some high RTTs over 100 ms in the tail of the distributions can cause CCA timeouts and also make RTT-based bandwidth estimation more difficult [4]. For comparison, our results confirm metropolitan LTE measurements by Huang et al. [5] that observe median RTTs of 70 ms, but also see RTTs over 400 ms.

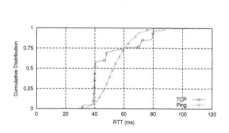

Fig. 7. TCP/Ping RTT distribution   **Fig. 8.** TCP Throughput vs. SINR

5.4 Throughput and SINR

SINR is the key performance metric for cellular networks [7], significantly affecting modulation selection (see Sect. 4) and, potentially, TCP throughput.

Figure 8 compares the TCP throughputs (the y-axis) for different SINRs (the x-axis), clustered into 5 dB bins. The measured throughputs for each CCA across all trials are shown with boxplots. From the figure, throughput correlates strongly with SINR. BBR achieves slightly higher throughput than either CUBIC CCA only at SINRs between 20–25 dB. For all other SINRs, the throughputs of the three CCAs are comparable.

5.5 Throughput and Handovers

When transferring data during mobility, a UE may be handed over from one LTE tower to another for two reasons: (i) the current serving eNodeB assumes the UE is leaving its serving zone, or (ii) the UE discovers another eNodeB with better radio conditions (i.e., stronger SINR).

While 3GPP standards [1] state packets can be forwarded to the next serving eNodeB during tower handover to avoid possible service interruptions, packets may still be lost, especially important during rapid movement (e.g., highway driving), and confusing bottleneck link capacity estimation algorithms (e.g., used in BBR [4]).

Figure 9 shows distributions of the number of serving and detected cell towers for all TCP downloads. Despite mobility at driving speeds, only 35% of the TCP downloads have 1+ handovers, and less than 4% of the downloads have 2+ handovers. Although handovers can affect TCP performance, the impact on Web traffic (usually < 1 MB) or even streaming traffic (segment size ∼ 4 MB) is likely insignificant due to the low probability of handovers during short flows. For comparison, our handover numbers are consistent with Xiao et al's. [12] report of average handovers every 25 s at top speeds (300 kph), and every 250 s at our driving speeds (100 kph). We leave more detailed analysis of the impact of handovers on TCP performance as future work.

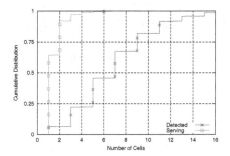

Fig. 9. Cell sector distributions

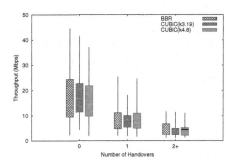

Fig. 10. TCP Tput. with handovers

Figure 10 shows distributions of throughputs (y-axis) versus number of handovers (x-axis), with each CCA distribution shown with a boxplot. From the figure, when there is a handover, all three TCP CCAs have lower throughput than with no handovers, and perform comparably with each other.

5.6 Self-Inflicted Delay

Traditionally, TCP increases data rates until it saturates the bottleneck queue. While potentially maximizing throughput, this enqueued data increases the minimum RTT (see Fig. 7) – i.e., it is a "self-inflicted" delay. We calculate self-inflicted delays as the average time between sending a data packet and receiving the response ACK (excluding duplicate ACKs) minus the initial TCP handshake.

Figures 11(a) and (b) depict CDFs of the self-inflicted delays. For the full 20 MB download, the minimum self inflicted delays are similar for all distributions, but the bulk of the BBR distribution is much lower than either CUBIC. For the 1 MB download, BBR has a slightly higher median delay (50 ms versus 25 ms), but CUBIC has a heavier tail (e.g., a much higher maximum), particularly for k3.19.

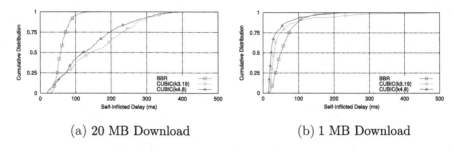

(a) 20 MB Download   (b) 1 MB Download

Fig. 11. Self-inflicted delay distribution

5.7 Retransmission

Duplicate ACKs impact RTT measurements (which are not updated for duplicate ACKs [9]) and retransmissions (which occur with 3 duplicate ACKs). Figure 12 shows the distribution of duplicate ACKs (x-axis), calculated as the number of duplicate ACKs over total ACKs, and Fig. 13 shows the distribution of retransmission percentages (x-axis). BBR has significantly fewer duplicate ACKs than either version of CUBIC, which should further aid BBR's RTT measurements, and BBR has significantly fewer retransmissions which should yield improved radio efficiency.

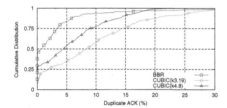

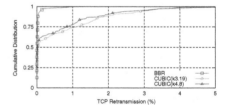

Fig. 12. Duplicate ACK dist.   **Fig. 13.** TCP retransmission dist.

5.8 Summary

Figures 14(a) and (b) summarize the results of three CCAs under highway driving conditions. For both Figures, there is one point for each CCA, corresponding to throughput (y-axis) and RTT (x-axis) averaged across all trials, with error bars (vertical and horizontal) showing 95% confidence intervals on the means.

For the full downloads, Fig. 14(a), BBR has higher average throughput than either version of CUBIC, but the overlapping confidence intervals mean the measured difference is not statistically significant. On the other hand, the lower self-inflicted delay for BBR is about one-third that of CUBIC and is statistically significant. For the first MB, Fig. 14(b), the story is reversed, with BBR having higher throughputs than CUBIC, but also higher self-inflicted delays (about 50% higher in both cases).

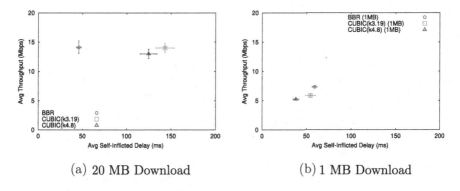

(a) 20 MB Download   (b) 1 MB Download

Fig. 14. Throughput vs. self-inflicted delay

6   Conclusions

This paper presents the first of its kind measurement study comparing TCP CUBIC (x2) and BBR under highway driving condition over LTE. While driving 800 miles (1350 km), a mobile phone downloaded $700 + 20$ MB files on a tier-1 U.S. wireless carrier's network, recording physical, IP and transport layer data. Performance metrics include throughput, round-trip time, and retransmissions, correlated with LTE SINR and modulation. To the best of our knowledge, not only is this the first study analyzing BBR "in the wild", but is also the first published analysis of LTE characteristics while driving using a U.S. wireless network.

Analysis shows the driving conditions cover a range of Signal to Interference-plus-Noise Ratios (SINRs), some of which yield throughputs near 40 Mbps, but with relatively few tower handoffs despite the speeds. For 20 MB downloads, CUBIC and BBR perform comparably for throughputs but BBR has significantly lower average self-inflicted delays and experiences significantly fewer duplicate ACKs. For 1 MB downloads, BBR has higher throughput but also higher self-inflicted delays.

Since large buffers can lead to "bufferbloat" and degrade TCP performance, algorithms that limit queue occupancy (measured by self-inflicted delays) can be effective for LTE networks. However, buffering allows flows to take advantage of small-scale variation in LTE capacity, suggesting tuning congestion control algorithms to keep buffers appropriately filled. The data from this study should be helpful for future models and simulations of LTE networks that further develop protocols, particularly for mobile environments.

Acknowledgments. We would like thank our shepherd, Moritz Steiner, and the anonymous PAM reviewers for their valuable feedback. We also thank our colleagues Eduard Rubinstein, Vijay Nanjundan, James Flynn, and Atreya Praveen for their helpful discussions and assistance.

References

1. 3GPP TS 36.423 Evolved Universal Terrestrial Radio Access Network (E-UTRAN); X2 Application Protocol (X2AP) (Release 12), September 2014
2. Atxutegi, E., Liberal, F., Grinnemo, K.J., Brunstrom, A., Arvidsson, A., Robert, R.: TCP behaviour in LTE: impact of flow start-up and mobility. In: Proceedings of WMNC, July 2016
3. Cardwell, N., Cheng, Y., Gunn, C., Yeganeh, S., Jacobson, V.: BBR: congestion-based congestion control. Commun. ACM **60**(2), 58–66 (2017)
4. Cardwell, N., Cheng, Y., Gunn, C.S., Yeganeh, S.H., Jacobson, V.: BBR: congestion-based congestion control. ACM Queue **14** (2016)
5. Huang, J., Qian, F., Guo, Y., Zhou, Y., Xu, Q., Mao, Z.M., Sen, S., Spatscheck, O.: An in-depth study of LTE: effect of network protocol and application behavior on performance. ACM SIGCOMM Comput. Commun. Rev. **43**(4), 363–374 (2013)
6. Johnson, C.: Long Term Evolution in Bullets, 2nd edn. CreateSpace Independent Publishing Platform, Northampton (2010)
7. Merz, R., Wenger, D., Scanferla, D., Mauron, S.: Performance of LTE in a high-velocity environment: a measurement study. In: Proceedings of the Workshop on All Things Cellular, Chicago, IL, August 2014
8. Nguyen, B., Banerjee, A., Gopalakrishnan, V., Kasera, S., Lee, S., Shaikh, A., Van der Merwe, J.: Towards understanding TCP performance on LTE/EPC mobile networks. In: Proceedings of the 4th Workshop on All Things Cellular: Operations, Applications, & Challenges, pp. 41–46, August 2014
9. Paxson, V., Allman, M., Chu, J., Sargent, M.: Computing TCP's Retransmission Timer. IETF Request for Comments (RFC) 6298 (2011)
10. Robert, R., Atxutegi, E., Arvidsson, A., Liberal, F., Brunstrom, A., Grinnemo, K.J.: Behaviour of common TCP variants over LTE. In: Proceedings of IEEE GLOBECOM, December 2016
11. Tazaki, H., Uarbani, F., Mancini, E., Lacage, M., Camara, D., Turletti, T., Dabbous, W.: Direct code execution: revisiting library OS architecture for reproducible network experiments. In: Proceedings of ACM CoNext, Santa Barbara, CA, December 2013
12. Xiao, Q., Xu, K., Wang, D., Li, L., Zhong, Y.: TCP performance over mobile networks in high-speed mobility scenarios. In: Proceedings of ICNP, Research Triangle Park, NC, October 2014
13. Zaki, Y., Pötsch, T., Chen, J., Subramanian, L., Görg, C.: Adaptive congestion control for unpredictable cellular networks. In: Proceedings of the ACM SIGCOMM, London, UK (2015)

Erratum to: In rDNS We Trust: Revisiting a Common Data-Source's Reliability

Tobias Fiebig, Kevin Borgolte, Shuang Hao, Christopher Kruegel,
Giovanni Vigna, and Anja Feldmann

Erratum to:
Chapter "In rDNS We Trust: Revisiting a Common
Data-Source's Reliability" in: R. Beverly et al. (Eds.):
Passive and Active Measurement, **LNCS 10771,**
https://doi.org/10.1007/978-3-319-76481-8_10

In the original version of this chapter, coloring was off in the in-addr.arpa part of Fig. 6a on page 141. IPv4 rDNS zones returning SERVFAIL were illustrated using the beige reserved for dynamic zones in the IPv6 graphs, instead of the correct wine-red used for SERVFAIL zones. In Section 5.3 on page 139, we reported that we used an ip6.arpa rDNS dataset collected between March 26th, 2017 01:04 UTC to March 30th, 2017 10:49 UTC. However, we collected the dataset we analyzed between April 22nd, 2017 04:07 UTC and April 25th, 2017 10:15 UTC. No incorrect data was reported, however, and the results remain valid. The original chapter has been corrected.

We thank our fellow researchers Robert Beverly from the Naval Postgraduate School and Oliver Gasser from TU Munich for pointing out these mistakes. They would not have been discovered without the publication of our collected dataset. Therefore, we would like to take this opportunity to plead in favor of Open Data in the field of network measurements.

The updated online version of this chapter can be found at
https://doi.org/10.1007/978-3-319-76481-8_10

© Springer International Publishing AG, part of Springer Nature 2018
R. Beverly et al. (Eds.): PAM 2018, LNCS 10771, p. E1, 2018.
https://doi.org/10.1007/978-3-319-76481-8_21

Author Index

Printed in the United States
By Bookmasters